International Law and the Global South

Perspectives from the Rest of the World

This book series aims to promote a complex vision of contemporary legal developments from the perspective of emerging or developing countries and/or authors integrating these elements into their approach. While focusing on today's law and international economic law in particular, it brings together contributions from, or influenced by, other social sciences disciplines. Written in both technical and non-technical language and addressing topics of contemporary importance to a general audience, the series will be of interest to legal researchers as well as non-lawyers. In referring to the "rest of the world", the book series puts forward new and alternative visions of today's law not only from emerging and developing countries, but also from authors who deliberately integrate this perspective into their thinking. The series approach is not only comparative, post-colonial or critical, but also truly universal in the sense that it places a plurality of well-informed visions at its center.

The Series

- Provides a truly global coverage of the world in reflecting cutting-edge developments and thinking in law and international law
- Focuses on the transformations of international and comparative law with an emphasis on international economic law (investment, trade and development)
- Welcomes contributions on comparative and/or domestic legal evolutions

Thamil Venthan Ananthavinayagan ·
Amritha Viswanath Shenoy
Editors

The Wretched of the Global South

Critical Approaches to International Human Rights Law

Springer

Editors
Thamil Venthan Ananthavinayagan
School of Law
Woxsen University
Hyderabad, Telangana, India

Amritha Viswanath Shenoy
Kathmandu School of Law
Bhaktapur, Nepal

ISSN 2510-1420 ISSN 2510-1439 (electronic)
International Law and the Global South
ISBN 978-981-99-9274-4 ISBN 978-981-99-9275-1 (eBook)
https://doi.org/10.1007/978-981-99-9275-1

This Springer imprint is published by the registered company Springer Nature Singapore Pte Ltd.
The registered company address is: 152 Beach Road, #21-01/04 Gateway East, Singapore 189721, Singapore

Paper in this product is recyclable.

For the People of the Global South

Foreword

In his foreword to *The Wretched of the Earth*, John Paul Sartre speaks of the emergence of "a new generation" that took on the inhumanity of colonialism and exposed the toxicities of European humanism. Most important, he says, in Fanon's voice, "the Third World finds itself and speaks to itself." This book pays homage to Fanon not only in its title, but also by engaging in a parallel project of exposing international law's complicity in the brutalities it claims to condemn and overcome; in this it communicates a "thirdworldist" voice in international human rights law and policy that "finds itself and speaks to itself." Thus, this intervention by a new generation of scholars—a collective voice crafted as the editors describe it in Kathmandu, Singapore and Dublin—can be situated in a tradition of anti-colonial critique that stretches from the era of colonialism to the post-colonial present. Indeed, this book is an inspiring attestation to the vitality of that tradition, and the incisive critical voice that marks its contemporary articulation in a new generation of human rights scholarship.

What then are the hallmarks of anti-colonial critique that are articulated in these pages? It is characterised by several noteworthy dimensions. Firstly, it is invested in unmasking the Eurocentricism that is threaded through the dominant human rights framework but also keen to underscore that it is a dominance that is deeply contested. Thus, the book speaks to how social movements in the global south have sought to wrest the framework from its received moorings, and steer human rights in new directions, including by anchoring human rights in the justice and self-determination struggles of subaltern communities. Secondly, it is significant that the book's investment in the decolonisation of human rights is accompanied by an investment in decolonising the nation-state form that monopolised anti-colonial movements in an earlier moment. Thus, several chapters highlight the internal critique advanced by indigenous peoples, women and minorities of the majoritarian, patriarchal and settler-colonial logics that informed so much of the first generation of anti-colonial nationalism. Finally, the book seeks to marry critique to construction and marry the deconstruction of the received edifice of the human rights framework with a reconstruction of an expanded and enriched discourse and agenda for human rights projects today.

Frantz Fanon concludes *The Wretched of the Earth* with a searing call for a new humanism. He argues that violence saturates the colonial world, not only as a strategy the coloniser uses to subdue the colonised but also as the animating ethos of colonial ontologies. Fanon describes the task of decolonisation as involving not only the overthrow of the coloniser to take the reins of self-governance but also the building of alternative epistemologies, alternative normative frameworks, and breaking through the psychological dynamics of the colonial relationship with a new humanism. There has been much debate about whether humanism offers the most promising framing of future horizons, both because of the racial capitalist signature on the figure of the human, and the ways in which climate change has pressed a recognition of the apocalyptic limits of an anthropocentric construction of world order. Despite those important challenges, however, Fanon's revolutionary humanism conveys something significant about how we must radically remake the path we must walk on—that we must invent, discover, and dream anew. It is this philosophy and practice of reinvention that he emphasises in his concluding chapter and it is the clarion call he ends on: "comrades, we must turn over a new leaf, we must work out new concepts, and try to set afoot a new man." This book is a response to that call, seeking to turn the human rights system over to work out new concepts and set forward with a Fanonian spirit of revolutionary humanism.

New York, USA Vasuki Nesiah

Contents

Editors and Contributors

About the Editors

Dr. Thamil Venthan Ananthavinayagan LL.M. (Maastricht University), Ph.D. (NUI Galway), is a former Human Rights Academic at the University of Nottingham/ UK and currently serves as Assistant Principal and Senior Legal Advisor to the Minister of Justice, Republic of Ireland. He is also an Adjunct Professor in Law at the Woxsen University, India. Prior to this position, he worked as a university teacher for public international law, international human rights law, international humanitarian law and international criminal law at various Irish universities from October 2013 to December 2020. He worked as Fellow and Research Assistant at the Irish Centre for Human Rights in Galway, Ireland. His doctoral research focused on the engagement of Sri Lanka with the United Nations human rights machinery. Before his occupation at the Irish Centre for Human Rights, he studied law at the universities of Bonn and Marburg (Germany) and Maastricht University (The Netherlands). Subsequently, he had worked at different research institutions, universities, politicians, and policymakers in Bonn, Düsseldorf and Berlin, Germany. Finally, he worked as a junior lawyer for the tenants' association in Bonn, Germany. He is an expert on human rights and decolonisation, having delivered guest lectures at think tanks, international organisations and universities around the world at, inter alia, Berlin, Bologna, Braga, Dublin, Edinburgh, Galway, Geneva, Hong Kong, London, New Delhi, Padova, Pisa, Seattle, Seoul, Singapore, Kathmandu, Warwick, and Leicester. He has written on numerous issues regarding international human rights law, decolonisation and United Nations.

Dr. Amritha Viswanath Shenoy is an Assistant Professor at Kathmandu School of Law. She pursued M.Phil., Ph.D. from Centre for International Legal Studies, School of International Studies, Jawaharlal Nehru University, New Delhi, India. She worked as a Research Associate in the project titled "History of Legal System in Pre-Colonial India" in Centre for Comparative Law, National Law University, New Delhi, India. Her area of research includes on history of international law from a Global South perspective, TWAIL, human rights among others. She teaches international law and human rights in Kathmandu School of Law.

Contributors

Hadeel S. Abu Hussein Utrecht University, Utrecht, Netherlands

Flávia do Amaral Vieira Federal University of Santa Catarina, Florianópolis, Brazil

Punsara Amarasinghe Institute of Law, Politics and Development, Scuola Superiore Sant Anna, Pisa, Italy

Thamil Venthan Ananthavinayagan School of Law, Woxsen University, Hyderabad, India;
Researcher Department of Justice, Dublin, Republic of Ireland

Moara Assis Crivelente Center for Social Studies (CES), University of Coimbra, Coimbra, Portugal;
University of Coimbra, Coimbra, Portugal

Alejandra Ramírez Bermeo Bogotá, Colombia

Selbi Durdiyeva Philipps University Marburg, Marburg, Germany

Omkar Hemanth Bangalore, India

Jeevan Justin National Law University Odisha, Cuttack, India

Yi Seul Kim The University of Hong Kong, Hong Kong, China

Kanak Mishra International Collaborations, O.P. Jindal Global School, Sonipat, India

Oreva Olakpe Toronto Metropolitan University, Toronto, Canada

Kumarjeeb Pegu National Law University Odisha, Cuttack, India

Jackeline Caixeta Santana Federal University of Uberlandia, Uberlandia, MG, Brazil

Amritha Viswanath Shenoy Kathmandu School of Law, Bhaktapur, Nepal

Tatiana Cardoso Squeff Federal University of Rio Grande do Sul, Porto Alegre, RS, Brazil

Nguyen Toan Thang Comparative Law Institute, Hanoi Law University (HLU), Hanoi, Vietnam

La Minh Trang Department of International Law, Hanoi Law University (HLU), Hanoi, Vietnam

Nguyen Thi Hong Yen Department of International Law, Hanoi Law University (HLU), Hanoi, Vietnam

Editor's Introduction

Thamil Venthan Ananthavinayagan and Amritha Viswanath Shenoy

The editors met for the first time in TWAIL Conference held in Singapore in 2018. Thereafter, we organised (along with our colleagues) the Critical Approaches to International Law Symposium in Dublin in 2019 with the focus to amplify the voices of emerging Global South scholars. Organising the workshop helped us delve into critical perspectives of international law and at the same time realise that when Global South scholars in different parts of the world work together, distance does not matter in this globalised world. Our meeting in Kathmandu in 2020 led to planning of this edited volume on critical perspectives to human rights from the viewpoint of Global South. Pandemic hit us hard, yet we conducted online meetings, invited contributors, edited, and reviewed the book with our fortified pillars of support, Jeevan Justin and Omkar Hemanth. They provided commendable research assistance for the project. The book speaks for itself for its diverse perspectives from different parts of Global South.

International Law narratives particularly on human rights are mostly from a Global North perspective. The literature traces the origin of human rights to the Western World. In this regard, Micheline R. Ishay[1] opines, "*The Enlightenment thinkers not only invented the language of human rights discourse, they discussed issues that continue to preoccupy current human rights debates. Now as then, we find ourselves pondering the role of the state as both the guardian of basic rights and as the behemoth against which one's rights need to be defended.*" Ishay traces the history of human rights to different religions and philosophies. However, her emphasis is that the origin,

[1] Micheline R. Ishay (2008), *The History of Human Rights: from Ancient Times to the Globalization Era*, London: University of California Press, p. 8.

T. V. Ananthavinayagan (✉)
School of Law, Woxsen University, Hyderabad, India
e-mail: thamil.ananthavinayagan@woxsen.edu.in

A. Viswanath Shenoy
Kathmandu School of Law, Bhaktapur, Nepal

T. Venthan Ananthavinayagan and A. Viswanath Shenoy (eds.), *The Wretched of the Global South*, International Law and the Global South,
https://doi.org/10.1007/978-981-99-9275-1_1

proliferation, and interpretations of human rights are attributed to the Global North. In recent times, due to scholarly contributions from Global South, critical perspectives to international law create a niche in the discipline. Recently, a major contribution in this field is an edited book by Prabhakar Singh and Benoit Mayer; "Critical International Law: Postrealism, Postcolonialism and Transnationalism". However, for Human Rights, literature on critical perspectives confines to few perspectives. For instance, José-Manuel Barreto's edited volume, "*Human Rights From a Third World Perspective: Critique, History and International Law*" is very significant. However, other critical perspectives are necessary to delve into the vast realm of human rights law. The present volume is a leap forward for a Global South Critical Perspective to Human Rights. The scholars from Global South should continue writing to challenge the cognitive power of mainstream international law. As the title of the book is influenced by Frantz Fanon, his advice for contributors is apt to be quoted here,

> The colonized man who writes for his people ought to use the past with the intention of opening the future, as an invitation to action and a basis for hope……..The responsibility of the native man of culture is not a responsibility vis-à-vis his national culture, but a global responsibility with regard to the totality of the nation, whose culture merely, after all, represents one aspect of that nation.[2]

The present contribution to the field covers comprehensive, but not complete aspects of human rights ranging from women, indigenous peoples, children, food security, hegemony of States and Corporations, critique of social movement among others. These issues cover various regions in the Global South. Be that as it may, many more volumes would be required to compete with the cognitive power exercised by the Global North that shows a beautiful picture of human rights.

The contributions are divided into three parts. **Part I** is on "The Global South and the Pursuit of Justice". The four articles in this part connect human rights to seek justice. The authors here seek to analyse the emancipatory nature of human rights simultaneously criticising the West-centric approach. Critical approaches here provide for 'constructive proposals'.[3]

In the first article by Alejandra Ramírez Bermeo titled "*The Discursive Dissociation of Human Rights and Justice: Experience of Afro-Columbian Displaced Women from Columbia*" challenges the Western approach to human rights. She uses Enrique Dussel's theoretical perspective on Community of Victims to analyse the lives of three displaced Afro-Columbian women living in Cali. The in-depth interviews conducted by the author for the article show how these women reject or mould the dominant human rights perspective to suit their needs.

---

[2] Frantz Fanon (1963), *The Wretched of the Earth*, Translated by Constance Farrington, New York: Grove Press, pp. 232–233.

[3] Critical approaches in international law are known to criticise the discipline without providing 'constructive proposals' as pointed out by Sebastian Jodoin and Katherine Lofts, "What's Critical about Critical International Law? Reflections on the Emancipatory Potential of International Legal Scholarship" in Prabhakar Singh and Benoit Mayer (2014), *Critical International Law: Postrealism, Postcolonialism and Transnationalism*, Oxford University Press.

Similarly, Moara Assis Crivelente's article, "*Contradictions and Opportunities for National Liberation in Human Rights Law and Practice*" explores the emancipatory role of human rights, if used conscientiously. The author links national liberation and human rights, thereby studying the ideas of nation, state, etc. With this theoretical lens, the article views the national liberation struggles of Palestinians and Western Saharawians.

Transitional justice is inextricably interlinked to human rights. An alternative perspective is imperative for both these fields. Therefore, Selbi Durdiyeva opines that decolonising the idea of transitional justice is the need of the times in the article "*Towards Decolonial Agenda for Transitional Justice: 'The Old is Dying and the New Cannot be Born*'". The author argues that post-colonial ideas in the field try to impose the Western model in the Global South. Therefore, decolonising the epistemology, ontology and teleology of Transitional Justice will bring a true transition.

The above articles call for decolonisation because colonisation has reverberations at present. Oreva Olakpe's article, "*Forced Displacement and Borderlands in International Law: Perspectives from Below*" reminds us that internal displacement is one of the causes of colonisation. Looking at the issue from the light of TWAIL, Oreva conducts a study of Mubi, Adamawa State in Northern Nigeria and analyses the impacts of colonisation and asymmetries in the division of states particularly in Africa.

Part II of this book is titled *The Global South and Forgotten Voices.* This part lends voice to four different issues that are hardly heard in human rights discourse. The issues of indigenous peoples, Ethnic Minority Women, and Caste that in the Asian context are discussed by very few scholars. TWAIL and other critical approaches raise various issues. However, these approaches fail to notice the most marginalised peoples.[4]

In "*The Children of Kuveni: A Critical Analysis of the Derogated Status of Vedda Community in Post-Independent Sri Lanka*", **Punsara Amarasinghe** urges the need to protect indigenous peoples' rights to save them hybridisation with the majority community by focusing on the plight of the Vedda community in Sri Lanka. Neither the constitution nor any legal enactment assures the rights of the Vedda Community that live on forest produce, hunting, gathering honey and other similar forms of livelihood.

Another neglected community in the Global South is the forest-dependent pastoral communities in India. Contextualising pastoral rights of indigenous peoples in India, **Kumarjeeb Pegu** points out the lacuna in defining indigenous peoples by international law in "*Nomads and Forest Rights, Is it a Myth? An Indian Perspective on the forest-dependent pastoral communities and their practices in protected areas*". Furthermore, the Indian laws are not clear about the tribes in India. This remains a primary problem to provide rights. The legislations in India on environment strengthen state control over the forests neglecting indigenous population and their

---

[4] Srinivas Burra (2016), "TWAIL's Others: A Caste Critique of TWAILERS and Their Field of Analysis", *Windsor Yearbook of Access to Justice*, 33: 111–128.

rights. The author suggests that their presence can only be dangerous if they cause irreversible damage.

The third chapter of Part II is by Toan Thang Nguyen, Thi Hong Yen Nguyen, and Trang La Minh, the contributors from Vietnam, trace the status of Ethnic Minority Women of South East Asia to the patriarchal roots of Sinosphere in the contribution, "*Impacts of Sinosphere on Ensuring Equal Rights of Ethnic Minority Women in South East Asian Countries: Barriers, Challenges and Recent Developments*". The paper describes the philosophy that influences lack of awareness and gender inequality. Furthermore, it points out the discrimination of EMW in private and public sphere.

Apart from these issues of particular communities, Thamil Venthan Ananthavinayagan alongside Jeevan Justin, Kanak Mishra and Omkar Hemanth attribute hindrance to the progress of Global South to practices of different forms of caste system. This practice was initially exploited by the colonisers and the third-world elite continues to do so. The author points out how TWAIL as a major alternative approach has failed to point out the discriminatory system in its literature.

The Global South's Vision for the Future is **Part III** of the book. It brings together four different issues. Social movements of Global South, fight for self-determination, accountability of transnational corporations and business enterprises, and right to food are a way forward for the future of Global South. A panacea for all the problems definitely does not exist for the mammoth issues faced today by the peoples. Nevertheless, few solutions that the contributors bring forward are worth applause.

Social movement is a way forward for the Global South. Tatiana Cardoso Squeff and Jackeline Caixeta Santana question whether the "*Law Found on the Street*" reaches the Inter-American Court of Human Rights or not? They analyse it in the recognition of communal property right of indigenous peoples. The title of the article is "Has 'The Law Found on the Street' reached the Inter-American Court of Human Rights? A Socio-Legal Analysis of Communal Property Right Recognition". On the theoretical part, the authors compare the concept of *O Direito Achado na Rua* (The Law Found on the Street) to the TWAIL approach to social movements as put down by Balakrishnan Rajagopal.[5]

Despite the voices of peoples on self-determination, many peoples are oppressed by military might. As suggested by the title itself, "*The U.S. Recognition of Jerusalem as a Capital of Israel and the Movement of its Embassy to Jerusalem: The Question of Jerusalem and Beyond*", **Hadeel Abu Hussein** elucidates the implications of recognition of Jerusalem as the Capital of Israel by the USA. It impacts the self-determination movement of the Palestinians, proving that the US was never a "neutral mediator" in the Israel-Palestine dispute. Many predecessors of Trump agreed that Jerusalem is the capital of Israel. According to her, Trump moved beyond to take this decision. But this article, fitting with the overall theme of the book, applies the idea of the right to self-determination as the dominating right behind which the Global South rallies to encounter Western hegemony. To this end, Palestine is the emblematic case

[5] Rajagopal, Balakrishnan (2003), *International Law From Below: Development, Social Movements and Third World Resistance*, Cambridge: Cambridge University Press.

study to underscore the urge for the realisation of human rights amid the ongoing reverberations of colonialism. Colonialism never ended, it is now.

A major part of decolonisation process is played by knowledge production. Conducting an empirical study on the negotiations for a binding treaty on Business and Human Rights by the Open-ended Intergovernmental Working group on Transnational Corporations and Other Business Enterprises with respect to Human Rights (OEIGWG), **Flavia do Amaral Vieira** emphasises on the power asymmetries in the process of treaty making in "*The Struggles for Corporate Accountability in the UN: A Global South Perspective*". She explores the participation of civil society and by using TWAIL methodology, the author points out how the Global South can play the role of knowledge production.

Finally: Some human rights are considered secondary over others. One such neglected right is right to food. **Yi Seul Kim** connects the violation of right to food in North Korea to socio-political reasons in the article "Using Law to Prevent Further Unequal Access to Food in North Korea". She criticises that policy of *juche* where politically influential people stay in the capital of Pyongyang and enjoy the rights, thereby excluding the others.

The editors believe that the readers would learn, reflect upon, think and criticise various unexplored topics discussed herein. The book is a reflection of diversity of the Global South. The diversity is with regard to issues, perspectives, and solutions. Nevertheless, the diversity does not stop us from uniting to raise voices against imposition of a single perspective of human rights.

The Global South and the Pursuit of Justice

The Discursive Dissociation of Human Rights and Justice

Experiences of Afro-Colombian Displaced Women from Colombia

Alejandra Ramírez Bermeo

Abstract Meanings of human rights are neither self-evident nor fixed. Instead, they are embedded in specific worldviews and remain contested terrains both in theory and practice. This text explores the juxtaposition of human rights discourse with how it is understood by displaced Afro-Colombian women exercising community leadership in Cali, Colombia. The first part of this chapter takes readers through some of the critical theoretical and strategic paradigms within which human rights have been debated and defined, linking it with perspectives on social movements where struggles for economic, political, and symbolic justice take place. Current community leadership in Colombia is conditioned by different contexts: urban, economic, generation, gender, and ethnic/race. In these women's case, their leadership is woven from an urban, gender, and ethnic/race approach that is interconnected with their own and learned notions of rights and justice that are not based on the dominant narrative of human rights. In the light of Enrique Dussel's *victims' community* approach, the document analyses the political activism of women community leaders in Cali Colombia as social movements intertwined with other signs and broader networks. To achieve this, the chapter relies on fieldwork and in-depth interviews, narrating both their organisational efforts and their perceptions about their political being in defence of rights for *their* people and who simultaneously subject themselves to the politicised sphere of meanings of justice in Colombia. Concerning the above, the text shows how the women leaders interpret the prevailing discourse of human rights, embedding itself in a broader campaign on the right to justice from their definitions. Each woman, depending on her biography, location, and current context in the city, is subject to policies that determine her leadership while she takes a particular position facing those policies. This situation leads to the need to take a critical distance from the hegemonic definitions of human rights and locate its *own* meanings in a politicised environment, subject to debate, recognised as a disputed terrain by the women leaders themselves. This chapter presents alternative local freedom practices that decentralise human rights as the only liberation discourse.

A. R. Bermeo (✉)
Pedagogical Advisor, Despacio Foundation, 110121 Bogotá, Colombia
e-mail: alejandra_rb@outlook.com

T. Venthan Ananthavinayagan and A. Viswanath Shenoy (eds.), *The Wretched of the Global South*, International Law and the Global South,
https://doi.org/10.1007/978-981-99-9275-1_2

1 Introduction

This chapter aims to explore the discourse of human rights in contemporary social movements, specifically, the case of Afro-Colombian displaced women leaders who watch over the rights of black communities, women, and youth at the local level.

In this way, the text shows how human rights are disarticulated from social movements. These dominant concepts of rights do not make visible the tensions related to social class and race/ethnicity. It is argued that the Afro-Colombian community women leaders' movement is relevant because, even though it is a network in the process of being woven, it manages to question the Western approach, which is the dominant vision of human rights.

The chapter is organised into five parts. First, it contextualises the movement of black communities in Colombia and presents the study methodology. Second, it analyses perspectives on human rights and social movements, especially Dussel's proposal concerning the *community of victims*. Third, it analyses Afro-Colombian women leaders' political activism in light of the *community of victims* proposed by Dussel. To achieve this, the chapter relies on fieldwork and in-depth interviews, narrating both their organisational efforts and their perceptions about their political being in defence of justice for *their* people. Fourth, the text shows how the displaced Afro-Colombian women who exercise community leadership use alternative local freedom practices that decentralise human rights as the only liberation discourse.

Finally, it is concluded that while Afro-Colombian women leaders use alternative discourses on human rights, at the same time, they are subject to other challenges, especially related to the rights of black communities.

2 Socio-Historical Context and Methodology

Historically, the largest population of black communities in Colombia has been located in the Caribbean region, San Andrés y Providencia, and in the Pacific region, specifically in four departments: Chocó, Valle del Cauca, Cauca, and Nariño. These departments are known for being territories with immense natural resources (timber, gold, coal, and fish, among others) and one of the most biodiverse places in the world. However, despite all its wealth, the Pacific coast has been geographically isolated, poor, and marginalised and the presence of state institutions has been weak.

It is in this context that, at the end of the 1980s, pro-development discourse and practices set their sights on this area to bring it out of its "backwardness" and commodify its natural resources. Being a target of economic and political measures, the Pacific coast and its black communities saw how their habitat was transformed while being part of the extractive development plan of the State leading to the devastation of sizeable tropical rainforest areas. Simultaneously, the resident communities suffered from extreme invisibility (Grueso et al. 1997), their worldviews were devalued, as was their relationship with the *territory*[1] to which they attach a symbolic and social meaning.

It was amid this political and social conjuncture that the country saw the awakening of a student movement that emerged with La Séptima Papeleta[2] concluded in the construction of the National Constituent Assembly. Its primary purpose was to reform the Constitution of 1886 and give rise to differential rights for ethnic communities. The Assembly was made up of 70 members elected by national popular vote in December 1990; however, there was no representation of black communities because "there was no consensus regarding the parameters of black rights nor any common strategy for framing black demands on the national stage. The black coalition was nascent, loose, and fragile" (Asher 2007).

Before forming the National Constituent Assembly, black organisations were local, rather than national, their "heterogeneity [meant] that there [were] multiple understandings of the genesis and history of black resistance" (Asher 2007) in connection with their political struggles and expressions. Although such expressions had meeting spaces such as the National Coordinator of Black Communities (CNCN), the profound differences made the CNCN not prosper. This scenario made it possible to reveal the different political and ideological tendencies reflected in the "interests and historical insertion modes of the country's various black sectors" (Grueso et al. 1997). The lack of representation of the black communities in the National Constituent Assembly led an indigenous constituent to take their proposals, achieving a provisional inclusion as Transitory Article 55 (AT 55).[3]

The National Constituent Assembly concludes with the issuance of the 1991 Constitution, in which Colombia is recognised as a multicultural and multiethnic country. The new constitution promoted black communities' discussion stage, giving rise to their expression and cultural, territorial, ethnic, and mobilisation demands. As a result of this dynamic, the Black Communities Process (PCN) emerged in October 1993, a national organisational expression that assumes the regulation of Transitory

[1] As stated by Grueso and Arroyo, territory "is seen as a constructed by the communities on the basis of the 'use spaces' (espacios de uso) of the ecosystems that sustain the life project of the community. The territory is the space where the social matrix is woven generation after generation, linking past, present, and future in a close relationship with the natural environment" (2005).

[2] 'La séptima papeleta' (the 'Seventh Ballot') was the name by which both the student movement and the reform itself became known, which proposed in the legislative elections of 1990 the formation of a National Constituent Assembly. This reform was voted by more than 50% of the voters in the new Constitution of 1991.

[3] Description of the article (own translation): "Within the two years following the entry into force of this Constitution, Congress will issue, after a study by a special commission that the government will create for this purpose, a law that recognises the black communities that have been occupying lands, wastelands in the rural areas bordering the rivers of the Pacific Basin, under their traditional production practices, the right to collective property over the areas to be demarcated by the same law. Representatives elected by the communities involved will participate in the special commission referred to in the preceding paragraph. The property thus recognised will only be alienable under the terms established by law. The same law will establish mechanisms for protecting the cultural identity and the rights of these communities, and the promotion of their economic and social development". Available at: https://dacn.mininterior.gov.co/la-institucion/normatividad/articulo-transitorio-55-de-la-constitucion-politica-de-1991.

Article 55 that would later become Law 70 of 1993 or the Law of Black Communities. This law's achievement is considered one of the greatest reaches of the black people in Colombian legislative matters (PCN, available at https://renacientes.net/quienes-somos/). Said Law is composed of 68 articles that are distributed in 8 chapters and stipulates that:

> The purpose of this law is to recognise the black communities that have been occupying uncultivated lands in the rural areas bordering the rivers of the Pacific basin, following their traditional production practices, the right to collective property, under the provisions of the following articles. It also aims to establish mechanisms for the protection of the cultural identity and the rights of the black communities of Colombia as an ethnic group, and the promotion of their economic and social development, to guarantee that these communities obtain real conditions of equal opportunities compared to the rest of Colombian society (Law 70 1993).

This event represents a triumph for black communities, which, despite not being homogeneous for historical, political, and cultural reasons, managed to define themselves and characterise themselves as a sector:

> That group organisation and people with different experiences and visions but unified around some principles, criteria and purposes that differentiate us from other sectors of the social movement of black communities. But we are also a proposal to the national black community, with the aspiration of building a single movement of black communities that collects their rights and aspirations (PCN cited in Grueso et al. 1997).

However, despite winning this battle in the legislative arena, it did not prepare the country to recognise and vindicate the territories-region agreements as spaces of Afro-Colombian and indigenous ethnic incidence (Grueso 2008–2010). As stated by Libia Grueso, "Law 70 in particular, accelerates this dispute. The central contradiction occurs between the Pacific, as a strategic area in the economic opening versus territory-Region of ethnic groups with their vision of the future" (2008–2010).

As a result, the State's relations with ethnic groups were a clash of worldviews, where those related to indigenous and Afro-Colombian communities in the Pacific territory-region were:

> (...) based on the conservation of natural habitats as vital spaces in cultural recreation and construction of options for the future, based on their worldview. However, this political-organisational project is going through a serious crisis due to its contradictions with the economic and political interests that have been imposed on the region, including the interests of the government and some representatives of the national State. The black community organised around this project of cultural and territorial rights constitutes the population sector with the largest number of people displaced by the armed conflict and with a significant number of murdered leaders (Grueso 2008–2010).

In 2011 under the Santos Calderón government, the Law 1448 Victims and Land Restitution Act and the Law Decree 4635 were created as tools with which the State undertook to generate a series of economic, symbolic, psychological, educational, and political strategies, seeking to re-establish the rights of people affected by violent conflict. The Peace Agreement emphasises many of the commitments from these previous laws, but on this occasion, incorporating the requests of the victims, who were part of the negotiating table, which allowed the agreements to directly address the needs of the population from a differential strategy by ethnic group adding a gender scope.

> The cultural impact [of the conflict] has been especially relevant among Afro-descendant and indigenous women. Being black or indigenous, being poor and women, have been conditions that have led to greater victimisation. Violence is transversal to the conditions of marginalisation and poverty of different ethnic groups (Ruta Pacífica de las Mujeres 2013).

As can be seen, the State has made some legislative progress. However, the prevalence of a development project that excludes the vision and socio-cultural context of black communities, which leads to the violation of their cultural, economic, and social rights, is still in force and submerging these groups in a constant struggle for their representation in decision-making scenarios.

Methodology

This text is based on in-depth interviews of three displaced Afro-Colombian women living in Cali and their relation to the dominant human rights narrative. Gillian Rose considers that "feminist, post-colonial and post-Marxist critiques argue that all knowledge is produced in specific circumstances and that those circumstances shape it in some way" (1997). The knowledge of these three women, based on personal experiences including the circumstances of forced displacement, location, activism, loss and resilience, is where the human rights discourse is shaped.

The three women interviewed have their node of work in the East of Cali. They belong to grass-roots organisations where they play an active role as leaders, and their voices represent mainly Afro-Colombian people. They are not requesting temporary solutions for the communities they represent; instead, the women are demanding minimum subsistence conditions for all the people they advocate.

The interviewed women agreed for their real names to be used in this chapter. The interviews were semi-structured and divided into two modules; the first one concentrated on their background as leaders, the second associated with their approach to human rights. The semi-structured interviews allowed the research to "unfold in a conversational manner offering the participants the chance to explore issues they [feel were] important" (Longhurst 2003).

Erlendy Cuero Bravo is a 47-year-old leader; she has national and international influence. She was born in Buenaventura and started her community leadership once she was displaced to Cali. Nowadays, she lives in Ciudad 2000 neighbourhood. She is the AFRODES Cali coordinator (Asociación Nacional de Afrocolombianos Desplazados, in English National Association of Displaced Afro-Colombians) and its vice-president at the national level. In recent years, Erlendy has been committed to empowering young Afro-Colombian from the East of Cali, specifically from the neighbourhood of Llano Verde.

Eloísa Montaño Guerrero is a 59-year-old leader and artisan from Buenaventura. She started her process working for the communities once she moved to Cali. Eloísa is currently living in the neighbourhood El Guabal, developing her clothing brand, leading the Afro Committee in her *comuna.*[4] She is a businesswoman whose primary purpose is to articulate her work in the Afro Committee to the young collectives from the comuna where she has influence.

Johana Patricia Perlaza Prado is a 40-year-old leader born and raised in Cali but an intra-urban displaced person. Her leadership vocation began when she was very young, Johana was part of the program World Vision[5] in the neighbourhood Manuela Beltrán. As an adult, her husband was murdered, leading to a series of threats that forced her to leave her area to move around other neighbourhoods and municipalities until she reached the El Valladito settlement. According to the Red de Salud de Oriente, the *comunas* 13, 14 and 15 are "neighbourhoods that were mainly formed by invasion processes and illegal urbanisations, with a population of scarce economic resources coming from other places in the city and displaced from the countryside" (Red de Salud de Oriente 2011). Now she works with PAPSIVI[6] and at the same time carries out community work with the youth of that territory.

These three women tell their stories from a current place and time, where despite the difficulties to cope with community work, they have decided to lead their lives in favour of the people they represent. The context in which these women's struggles are framed has presented them with a series of challenges and prospects, which, as Bjarnsen and Vigh put it, "may result in new opportunities for empowerment in or liberation from suppressive social hierarchies" (2016). Of course, this empowerment process that they have advanced for themselves has a generational renewal component, which explains their orientation to work with young people; they understand that these liberation processes take time and persistence.

[4] Cali's municipality has a political-administrative division made up of 22 comunas; each comuna gathers together neighbourhoods that share socio-economic and demographic particularities. According to the Encuesta de Calidad de Vida, 2012–2013 (in English, Quality of Life Survey 2012–2013), "the comunas 7, 13, 14, 15 and 21 have the largest proportion of the Afro-Colombian population with 48%, followed by the centre-east conglomerate (comunas 8, 11, 12 and 16) with 15% of the population that identifies itself as Afro-descendant" (as cited in Alcaldía de Santiago de Cali 2015). As a socio-economic demarcation, the neighbourhoods are categorised from strata 1 to 6, with strata one being the lowest in the hierarchy, characterised by socio-economic features such as deficiency in public services, security problems, and poverty (Castillo et al. 2012). Adding to this, the most common strata in the neighbourhoods gathered in the Comuna 10 and 11 is the 3; the Comunas 13, 14, 15, and 21 have the most common level 1 and 2 (Alonso et al. 2007).

[5] World Vision is a global development organisation, humanitarian aid and Advocacy (political incidence and mobilisation), created in 1950, focused on the well-being and comprehensive protection of children in vulnerable situations. The organisation has developed programs, attention to emergencies and the promotion of justice, without political, religious, race, ethnic or gender distinction. World Vision has had a presence in Colombia since 1978 and is currently in five regions of the country and 20 departments. Available at: https://www.worldvision.co/quienes-somos.

[6] PAPSIVI: Programa de atención psicosocial y salud integral a víctimas (Psychosocial care and comprehensive health care program for victims). According to the Colombian Health Ministry, "The PAPSIVI constitutes the technical line that allows the different actors to address the psychosocial impacts and damage to the physical and mental health of the victims caused by the armed conflict, at the individual, family and community levels (included in this the subjects of collective reparation), to mitigate their emotional suffering, contribute to physical and mental recovery and the reconstruction of the social fabric in their communities". Available at: https://www.minsalud.gov.co/proteccionsocial/Paginas/Victimas_PAPSIVI.aspx.

Narrative inquiry was used as "a form of case-centred research" (Mishler 1996 as cited in Riessman 2014) where "the 'personal troubles' that participants represent in their narratives (…) tell us a great deal about social and historical processes" (Riessman 2014). The women's narratives were interpreted using thematic analysis to understand how the narrators construct the meaning of human rights and how they incorporate the concept daily. This type of analysis helped theorise across the three stories, "finding common thematic elements across research participants and the events they report" (Riessman 2005).

3 Theoretical Perspectives

This research uses interdisciplinary theoretical perspectives to combine critical approaches to human rights, and post-colonial thinking. It uses the *community of victims* approach by Dussel (1998) as both a theoretical and analytical tool. This approach places at the centre of the current hegemonic system the Other who is the victim that cannot develop their life with dignity because, as oppressed, poor, or invisible has been unjustly excluded as a participant with rights in the hegemonic community (Dussel 1998). However, those interactive dimensions of inequality "can mutually strengthen or weaken each other" (Crenshaw as cited in Winker and Degele 2011), shaping women's experiences and their narratives. This chapter finds gender and race/ethnicity[7] elements of identity affiliation, cultural symbols, and social structures, tracing them in women's stories (Winker and Degele 2011) about their call for justice and human rights.

The stories of these three women narrate unique experiences of specific people who suffer the violence of the system in their physicality and project a way of being in the world, being a victim.[8] Based upon the interviews that have been conducted, the narratives are indifferent to the place or time in which it corresponds to live; they

[7] Throughout multicultural Colombia, black populations have been categorised in racial terms; however, the 1991 Constitution refers to communities as ethnic groups with rights to autonomy, self-governance and rights over their territories. This is why "in the process of making claims under these new legal regimes, Afro-Latin Americans in general have rearticulated their relationships with the rest of the nation and the state by shifting from a legal rubric of race to one of ethnicity" (Ng'weno 2007). Some authors consider that emphasising ethnicity leaves aside discussions on racism. This is the case of Wade (2002) and Hooker (2005) who believe that an analysis of cultural differences is privileged over racial discrimination. For this chapter, both terms will be used interchangeably, as this is the way in which the women interviewed make use of these concepts. Expanding on this point, Ng'weno argues that "race and ethnicity are in a co-dependent relationship that has solidified legally in new ways with the worldwide turn towards multiculturalism. In particular, there has been a solidification of ethnicity as being culturally evident and of race as referring to physical appearance" (2007).

[8] In this set of ideas, women are vulnerable not for their lack of agency, but because the educational system, the market, political entities and the state are not functioning well to address their needs. The vulnerability theory is a useful tool that guides the analysis to "recognise the ways in which power and privilege are conferred through the operation of societal institutions, relationships and the creation of social identities, sometimes inequitably" (Albertson 2017).

are human beings who have been oppressed or not recognised by the current system, so they cannot develop their life in dignified conditions. From this perspective, when the other is not recognized as equal, they are excluded from the system, leaving them without minimum guarantees of subsistence and much less without legitimising their speeches, commonly anti-hegemonic. The women stories refuse to be standardly narrated, they speak of difference broadening the conceptions of human rights.

3.1 Perspectives on Human Rights

From many perspectives, the discourse of human rights is biased due to the following reasons: because its locus of enunciation occurs in the Global North, because it is based on dominant liberal discourses, because does not take seriously epistemic interventions from the Global South (in a way that matters epistemically) and because "is no longer a discourse capable of meaningfully addressing contemporary problems" (McNeilly 2019). The reflections of some exponents are collected below.

In modern international law, what generates change is explained from two aspects, from the edge of voluntarism, which indicates that legal changes occur because the states accept them; and from functionalism, which suggests that legal changes occur because they are a reflection of social reality or because they respond to social needs (Rajagopal 2005). From that point of view, mass movements and social struggles are outside of this recognition as agents that generate change, which indicates that international law, which includes human rights discourses, have its focus on the state.

Paradoxically, social movements end up being appropriate for internationalist purposes, whose.

> Strategy implies a double movement of appropriation and invisibility: on one level, they appropriate the resistance of the mass movements as empirical evidence of the triumph of the human rights discourse (...); at another level, the praxis of these movements largely ignores the substance of democratic movements, by not taking seriously alternative conceptions of territory, autonomy, rights or identity (Rajagopal 2005).

To give an example from an economic stand: The Colombian model of development combines economic liberalism with top-down solutions that clashes with the right to the land by peasant or ethnic communities. Although there are arguments from both sides that validate the positions, the human rights discourse adopted by the state is based on notions of international law, while the communities do so based on their belonging to minority groups and ancestral ownership of the territory.

It is precisely in contrary conceptions that a dividing line is established between what human rights proposes as a narrative that claims universal validity and local contexts, where discourses are adapted, refuted, or unknown. With the above, Barreto considers that it is wrong:

> The idea of a universal human nature that is apprehended for a reason; that of human dignity that stands in a superior echelon above the dignity of animals and nature, and the need for protecting individual autonomy by a society organised as an aggregate of particular subjects (Barreto 2014).

And it is not only from the perspective of what or who are subjects of law but also from their individualistic approach to rights. Merry warns, "human rights ideas displace alternative visions of social justice that are less individualistic and more focused on communities and responsibilities, possibly contributing to the cultural homogenisation of local communities" (2006). Following the same argument, Wendy Brown considers worrisome that.

> Human rights activism is a moral–political project and if it displaces, competes with, refuses, or rejects other political projects, including those also aimed at producing justice, then it is not merely a tactic but a particular form of political power carrying a particular image of justice, and it will behoove us to inspect, evaluate and judge it as such (Brown 2004).

However, O'Connell's critical discussion of the displacement thesis points out that the theory of displacement does not hold, as many social movements use the discourse of human rights without limiting their own interpretations and quest for emancipation (2018). The author considers that although the displacement thesis raises important questions about the nature of human rights and its engagement with social movements, it oversights "the actual practices of social movements and human agency in articulating human rights claims" (O'Connell 2018). For in many cases, groups and movements use a range of languages and discourses to make claims for justice, equity and social transformation.

In this respect, applying human rights in local places becomes a dilemma. On the one hand, the discourse of human rights has birthed in the field of law science (rationalist) and is positioned as a bet on culture. Such opposition will lead to both being in permanent tension (Rajagopal 2005) by remaining in a posture that "impedes adapting those standards to the particulars of the local context" (Merry 2006). On the other hand, Merry stresses that although human rights are more readily adopted as a whole, their transformative nature makes more sense if they challenge the "existing assumptions about power and relationships" (Merry 2006). She proposes that for human rights discourse to be persuasive and effective, it is presented in local cultural terms (values and images) while challenging existing power relations (2006).

Sumi Madhok (2021) adds to this interpretation of the human rights discourse by recognising that it is an incomplete discourse that reproduces the vast epistemic power and compromises the complex differential dynamics and political struggles for rights and human rights in the world. The author insists that the discourse of human rights should move out of its hegemonic place of enunciation and become localised or vernacularised through its transfer to local contexts. In this way, the hegemonic discourse of human rights, which currently says nothing about justice and much less about inequality, would acquire a political tinge in which local social movements could see themselves reflected.

For Santos (1998), the way out is to relate global capacity with local legitimacy to advance towards a progressive policy of human rights in which social justice goes in its search for equity. In that order of ideas, "Santos approaches human rights to strengthen their emancipatory power in the world as a whole—advanced by social movements struggling for justice—by relying on the global appeal and local, culturally grounded legitimacy of human rights" (Barreto 2014). In other words, human rights must be reconceptualised as multicultural so that there is a balance between global competitiveness and local legitimacy.

Other arguments that point to human rights discourse being biased have to do with the place of enunciation from which they were created. According to Santos, there are a series of assumptions on which human rights rest, and those are:

> There is a universal human nature that can be known by rational means: human nature is essentially different from, and superior to, the rest of reality; the individual has an absolute and irreducible dignity that must defend from society or the State; the autonomy of the individual requires a society organised in a non-hierarchical way, as a sum of individuals (1998).

The previous paragraph shows how inherent is the relationship of these assumptions with the context from which they emerge, in this case, the European geographic space. Since these premises are born during European socio-historical and cultural circumstances and are based on a modernisation model (among others), they cannot claim to be universal. Their notions are historical-specific, local, like any concept that arises in some other place in the world. For this, Barreto argues, "once a connection is made between history and knowledge, it is evident that the hegemonic theory of human rights is the progeny of a perspective grounded in a particular historical and geographical context, that of Europe" (Barreto 2018).

On the other hand, the problematic interaction of the Global South countries with those of the Global North has its roots in the time of colonisation. This historical precedent has no representation in the field of human rights; therefore, this discourse is biased and incomplete, "they are not universal invalidity, neither comprehensive of the extra-European history of human rights nor the history of colonialism" (Barreto 2018).

Twining (cited in Barreto 2018) suggests a series of steps for decolonising human rights: critique, recognition, and dialogue:

> The first step puts into evidence the parochial character of Western understandings of human rights, which have been elaborated with superficial or no reference to other versions of human rights (...) The second moment acknowledges as valid interlocutors in the global debate those who have thought human rights from the Global South's perspective. Thus, the canon of legal texts is extended to include the contributions to the theory and history of human rights made by those outside the West. The third move promotes and engages in a fruitful encounter and debate between Western and Southern, or Eastern, perspectives (Barreto 2018).

To overcome this difference, Mutua's multicultural approach to the body of human rights proposes "balancing … individual and group rights, giving more substance to social and economic rights, relating rights to duties, and addressing the relationship between the corpus and economic systems" (Barreto 2014). At the same time, Barreto suggests a cultural right, that is, 'legal sensibility' that allows the legal encounter from the dialogue with 'other modes of thought and feeling' (Barreto 2014). Hence the need to locate human rights following the needs defined by local groups, as in terms of Feyter,

> For human rights to be relevant to all, they will need to be situation-specific. They will need to be localized. Localization implies taking the human rights needs as formulated by local

people (in response to the impact of economic globalization on their lives) as the starting point both for the further interpretation and elaboration of human rights norms,and for the development of human rights action, at all levels ranging from the domestic to the global (De Feyter 2006).

3.2 *Dussel's Community of Victims*

In relation to the critical perspectives on human rights, Dussel's community of victims will be used as a tool for analysis and as a source and forum of struggle.

Enrique Dussel, in the framework of his Ethics of Liberation (2011), proposes a series of stages in which a victim, for example of the colonialist hegemonic system, transcends her adverse condition of existence to position herself as a conscious subject who achieves her vindication and liberation. The author describes the victims' process of awareness in which "the beginning is always the Victim, the Other who cannot develop her life with dignity because as oppressed, poor or invisible has been unjustly excluded as a participant with rights in the hegemonic community" (Guerra 2017).

According to Dussel, "the victim is a living human being and has her unfulfilled demands in the reproduction of life in the system. The responsibility for the Other, of the victim as a victim, is also a condition of possibility, because, originally, the destitute one cannot yet stand up" (1988).

This victim is a universal representation of many others who, like her, have suffered a series of violence, limiting their way of being in the world. Once the victim knows her condition and has undergone a dialectical process where she understands that she is immersed in a system that excludes her, she begins to connect with other people like her, establishing a community to transform society.

Dussel postulates that the exercise of the transformative praxis or praxis of liberation[9] is divided into three levels: the first one called 'the naive conscience of the victim', where (1) the oppressed cannot express themselves clearly. In the *moment of denial*, they feel the effects of being oppressed or excluded; (2) at the *moment of affirmation*, the victim expresses her desire and struggles to live with dignity, to be recognised; (3) the victim awakens her *ethical-critical conscience* where she discovers her asymmetric position or exclusive in discursive non-participation; (4) to make an *ethical-critical judgement* about the system, perceived as unfair because it is the cause of her condition as a victim (1998).

In the second level, the victims come together to build a symmetrical community. As in the previous level, a series of moments occur: (5) they do an exercise of *critically-negatively questioning other victims* who have not awakened their

[9] According to Dussel, the praxis of liberation is an exercise that calls the system into question. Is also a practice performed not only on one's own behalf, but also in the service of others "it is a work done for the other with responsibility, for the other's liberation. It is an innovative activity using instruments put at the service of the poor. The praxis of liberation is the procreation of a new order, of its new structure, and at the same time of the functions and beings that compose it. It is the ultimate realization creative, inventive, innovative" (Dussel 1985).

conscience, and they also do it with (6) people who can be in solidarity or allied to their cause and who can be from other socio-economic background of the system, this is to generate co-responsibilities that allow them not only to expand their community but also develop a new *practical-critical position* in front of the system (*forming a critical community*), (7) this *progressive awareness, dialectical analysis and scientific explanation* (to which co-managers such as academics, politicians, and experts have been added) lead to an understanding of the causes of the denial of the victims, for which (8) possible *positive dialectical alternatives* are outlined from an exercise of reason (Dussel 1998).

In the third and final level, (9) the community of victims denies or deconstructs hostile systemic conditions from feasible *transformative actions* and (10) constructs previously analysed positive alternatives to opt for new norms, activities, institutions, or systems; that is, it concludes in a *constructive-liberating affirmation* (Dussel 1998).

For purposes of analysis, this proposal by Dussel will be used as a tool in understanding the leadership work of Afro-Colombian women as a social movement and analysing their discourse of human rights.

4 Under the Light of the Community of Victims: Afro-Colombian Women Experiences

Erlendy, Eloísa, and Johana are Afro-Colombian women who have lived through violence experiences as a consequence of the Colombian armed conflict. The women stories are narratives that can be close to the entire world or community (Dussel 1998) because their stories represent many people who are victims of a system that excludes them because they are women, black, and because are immersed in a system that leaves them at a disadvantage.

This section will seek to understand Afro-Colombian women community leaders' collective action, theoretically and empirically, as a social movement. For that, we will use the concept of the community of victims developed by Enrique Dussel (1998), who, through his postulate, will help us to reveal how they are constituted, but also what discourses prevail in their exercise of leadership. It will also be useful to connect to Rajagopal's theory of human rights and social movements, as the author understands that the place of enunciation of the people of the so-called *third world* is constructed from non-institutional spaces: in the family, in the informal economy and in non-partisan political spaces (Rajagopal 2005). This perspective invites an understanding of "the practices of various locally-based social movements, to assess whether they offer alternative visions and agendas for social change that do not rely on human rights discourse alone" (Rajagopal 2005).

As it has been outlined in the theoretical framework of this chapter, the Ethics of Liberation accounts for the multiple unequal daily processes where oppression is directed towards certain genders, races, ethnicities, and cultures, leaving them in a situation of no-rights, therefore, at a disadvantage in relation to those who are on the other side of the abyssal line (Santos 2007). Within the framework of this ethic, Dussel proposes a series of steps in which a community of victims is consolidated, starting from a progressive consciousness in which life's experience is assumed in a negative way (that is, everything that is denied). The causes of that original negation are discovered, which are the starting point to seek liberation.

This praxis of liberation is developed in three levels of critical consciousness that will conclude in forms of organisation that challenge what causes oppression:

Level 1

At the first level, there is a pre-original consciousness that is the starting point for the entire process of emancipation, the experience is decisive in defining the place from which the victim speaks. Dussel identifies four moments that will contain the perspectives of the three women who participated in this project:

A. Moment of denial

Let's take a closer look at this moment. According to Dussel, the victim from her corporality experiences an inevitable pain that immobilises her because of the historical domination. In rural territories, this domination came from the armed groups that controlled the area but was also experienced through the lack of access to education, health, and basic services that guarantee that a person remains excluded from the system.

According to the account made by Erlendy, Eloísa, and Johana, their first moment of denial occurs at the very moment of the victimising act: the murder of the father, constant extortion, and the murder of the husband, respectively (situations occurring in the context of the internal armed conflict). These situations generated a state of alert and shock, where the immediate impulse responded to an instinct for self-preservation. It is that pain as a turning point that invites a new beginning and that "without [that] madness in the confines of the heart, the one would be reconstituted and, in the heart of his passion, the essence would restart. Ambiguous adversity of pain!" (Lévinas cited in Dussel 1998).

However, the experiences of the pain of Erlendy, Eloísa, and Johana do not mark a starting point in zeros. They have had leadership role models since they were little. Those models came from their mothers, fathers, or uncles who guide these women to position themselves from a different starting point that of the majority of the victims:

> I believe that my solidarity today is on the way to that collective construction, to get rid of all those individual aspects, but rather to share. And that sharing I can bring up with an example from my great-uncle.
>
> My dad gave me the answers because my dad understood my thinking since I was very young. My questions have been against this system.

Based on the above, the 'recognition' of the other obeys an exercise of pre-original ethical reason, which occurs before making a criticism or outlining an argument, affirming an another-victim as a subject, "who is denied or ignored in the system as subject" (Dussel 1998). At this point, women still do not clearly recognise why they are subjected to violence or why the state is absent in the majority Afro-descendant territories. Women can only identify that the violence comes from one direct actor: the armed group.

B. Moment of affirmation

At this point, the statement about what is desired, in women's case, is a desire for justice, recognition and decent conditions to live. They have become aware of the loss of their territories (in rural or urban places) and their support networks (family, friends, neighbours) and contact with their customs. And this they want to recover it, without implying returning, but as a way of projecting it in the present or soon.

The new context into which the violence threw them makes them detect and empirically verify their 'negativities' such as poverty, hunger, trauma, pain, pathologies, and many other dimensions (Dussel 1998), which probably in the previous context, they were not obvious. Now, "that 'subject' who fights does so 'because of misfortune in the sense of suffering', that pain is produced when his life is taken from him as 'loot' by the victors" (Dussel 1998). This winner is initially identified as the perpetrator or perpetrators of the violent act because the entire apparatus of injustices behind that act is not yet in sight.

So far, Erlendy, Eloísa, and Johana wish decent living conditions for them. Johana expresses that there is "hope that in the future you will have something that helps you to support your family and that you can leave a legacy to your family, from your work" (2020). Meanwhile, Eloísa claims "nothing has been given to black people. On the contrary, we have to fight for everything. We don't want them to give us anything, what we want is to have dignity and equality" (2020).

C. Moment of ethical-critical awareness

The three women interviewed intuit their disadvantage concerning other social subjects; it is a reading that they do from their corporalities as black women. For example, Erlendy points out that "it is that my situation is not the same (as a black woman) to yours as a white woman that you will have more possibilities and even from the academy" (2021).

This asymmetric or exclusive position is also reflected in the area of economic security, which leads to possibilities to survive, which Erlendy and Eloísa point out,

> A child with a mother and father, who support him, who is there for a little breakfast or lunch, is not the same as many children do. What if there is a daily meal, but in most cases not even, but a child has to go to school hungry. The way of learning is not going to be the same when I prepare myself in a school in the city than in a school in a remote territory such as in Chocó, La Guajira or the Pacific when there are different conditions when I have some comforts to learn.
>
> [In Europe] everyone has a house or lives with dignity, they have the right to water, energy, a hospital, why not in Colombia? Because all this has to be seen as a luxury.

In these experiences, depending on the conditions, one is or is not subject to rights. That is why for Erlendy, "we are in a country that is exclusive and that according to your economic capacity, your skin colour, to your academic training they treat you likewise and likewise your rights are respected" (2021). These concerns are those that strengthen the subsequent mobilisation of women, and that comes from a process of awareness that "results from the intersection between movements and crossroads of events, related to their own experiences and transformations that push women towards the decision to convert in [community leaders]" (Laako 2016).

From the framework of rights, women identify a series of inconsistencies that become evident in a discourse that promises to guarantee equal conditions for all people. However, in reality, they are not fully executed or do not start from the premise that each social subject has particular needs, "rights have to be guaranteed for everyone, they have to be respected by being equal. Because concerning the issue of law, we are all equal, the conditions should be according to each human being, to each community".

From these points of view, it is perceived that they no longer speak from an individual, but a collective self, the reading about what they seek to improve their living conditions that seem exceptional has been extended, so they understand their needs, they are also those of their fellows.

D. Moment of ethical critical—judgement

The current ethics system has established norms, actions, and institutions that must guarantee that there are no victims from ethical principles; however, the opposite occurs (Dussel 1998). This situation forces people to emerge from their place of victims to "[confront] that structure that causes victims, and, therefore, their mere responsibility manifested in the criticism" (Dussel 1998).

In women's case, this attack can be direct when there are no guarantees of protection for their work as community leaders. It can come in two directions: from the precarious State to provide security conditions and the present criminal structures in the territories where they have their range of action:

> I left my neighbourhood Manuela Beltrán, where I grew up. I went to Brisas de Comuneros. After that, threats were coming to me in pamphlets. I moved to Comuneros 1, from there I went to Llano Verde, the same thing also happened. Outside of that, they realised that I was a leader. That's when the National Protection Unit came in, and they were going to provide me with security support, but I think that because of the pandemic, nothing has happened.
>
> Leadership for us is difficult because you have to fight against those who do not want you to change and against these people who want to change but do not dare to change. And now, with all these processes, it was time to lower the guard a little because I have only one daughter, and the moment came when she told me, "Mommy, you stay in a statistic and who's the one who needs you? Me". The moment is not very good for leaderships.

Concerning the above, Dussel indicates that it occurs because the person responsible for the victim before the system is persecuted by the power that causes it (1998). This situation suggests that by exercising his power of criticism as responsibility, she is at constant risk. That is why, Erlendy says, "for each leader who is killed today is a setback for the people, for the indigenous communities, for the peasant women, because it is not easy to form leadership in our territory, in vulnerable communities" (2021).

At this point, Dussel states that:

> Before anyone else and when she is critical, in solidarity and community, the same victim responsibly recognises the other victims as victims (...) But said responsible recognition, for

> its part, although it affirms the Other, does so from more original negativity: the fact of being a victim in the suffering of its corporality (1998).

This position is evident in Johana's speech when she says that "I am a warrior and I have to see how far I can go. Whatever God wants, I am here to serve my community, the people of the settlement, of the territory" (2020). From the victims' perspective, the future is synonymous with hope. That is why their struggles go in the direction to transform the current conditions where they cannot freely live; today, their criticism is the spear with which they will open the way for future generations.

It may be appropriate to mention here that authors such as Ernest Bloch, grant daydreaming a motivating force that can lead people to move towards a goal (as cited in Theilen 2017). This dream or hope that can push other people to reach a collective goal is what Johana sustains in her discourse. It is this same collective feeling that drives the leadership of Erlendy and Eloísa, who have been formed as critical subjects of their context and have affirmed that the personal is political, bringing their hopes and affirmations to the field of collective action. As cited by Theilen "progress towards utopia will by no means be automatic or linear, but rather dependent (at the very least) on human acts of will" (2017).

Up to the previous level, a gradual awakening leads to the construction of a symmetrical community. At the second level, after the victim is aware of his/her place in the current system, she begins an exercise of critical-discursive reason from which to question an other. This other is attached to her liberating project "discerning utopian alternatives from the creative (liberating) imagination- feasible (possible) transformation, future systems in which the victims can live" (Dussel 1998).

Level 2

In order to build a symmetrical community, victims must come together by questioning other victims, building networks, and integrating people from different fields to enlarge their critical perspective on the system and move towards dialectical alternatives, resulting from a collective exercise of reason. Dussel identifies four moments for this level:

E. Moment to question other victims

By this moment, the victims have a practical and material experience that makes them feel responsible for the other before any "decision, commitment, linguistic expression or communication regarding them" (Dussel 1998). In this regard, Schopenhauer considers that "the metaphysical basis of ethics [...] would consist in the fact that an individual would recognise in the other directly himself, his own true being" (cited in Dussel 1998), from that moment compassion, emerges understanding that the other alien is not such. As exemplified by Eloísa.

> My neighbourhood means unity and strength. I thought I was the only facing struggles, but after all these things have happened, you talk to people, and you realise that it is everyone's struggle. So the perception changes, right? Each one from their shore was trying to do things, but in the long run, after talking, almost everyone goes to the same side. Then why continue fighting each other on their side if it is better to articulate (2020).

On the other hand, something that feeds that responsibility with the other is the Will that, according to Lévinas, occurs when, from a position of asymmetry, an Other appears as a victim, for which one must be responsible:

> The Will is free to assume this responsibility in the sense it wants, but it is not open to reject this responsibility in itself; it cannot be free to ignore the meaningful world into which the face of the Other introduces it. In the hospitality of the beginning, the Will opens up to reason (Dussel citing Lévinas 1998).

When the other becomes so close, a sense of responsibility is born before any agreement or contract. Erlendy explains it "solidarity means to be able to feel empathy for my people, to accept that I don't know everything, that I need to other people. That every day I can have that strength to accept things that are also positive in my concept but above all, to follow that path of support, of helping others" (2021).

F. Moment of practical-critical position—forming a critical community

The liberation process has been an exercise that starts from the empirical and individual reflection of the victims that is later related to the experiences of an other who goes through the same journey.

In the construction of the critical community, "instrumental reason intervenes, because technical, economic, scientific, political mediations are needed" (Dussel 1998) to expand this critical perception of reality; only then will they manage to emerge as historical subjects, community members with full critical awareness, not only that of the victims' 'common sense', but, now, of the scientific and philosophical critical understanding of experts mutually articulated in the liberation process (Dussel 1998).

In this regard, Erlendy and Eloísa have gone through this liberation praxis, the first of them says:

> At this moment, we have set out to sign an agreement with UniCatólica, and we are going to have two training schools, one Political and Gender and the other focused on Ethnic Racial Rights. So one is exclusive for the youth issue and another for women and men, so these new leaderships are integral.

When the encounter between practical experience and scientific experience occurs "then, the decisive moment arrives in which the critical [subject] intervenes, who contributes to the [other] the discovery of his victim status. But the [subject] to carry out his work, 'must begin by educating himself with the content that the [other] himself gives him" (Guerra about Dussel 2017). Therefore, those who participate in this critical exercise are nurtured in two ways. In this way, not only the victims who have advanced their consciousness process are strengthened but they also encourage those people who are still in their awakening to have spaces of discernment for the construction of a non-hegemonic critical thought.

Therefore, Dussel promotes a type of alliance that has the effect of an expansive wave, in which.

> The extraordinary commitment (engagement) of the Other for the third party calls for control, the search for justice, society and the State, comparison and having, thought and science,

> commerce and philosophy, and, from there, to anarchy the search for the beginning. Philosophy is this measure that contributed to the infinity of being-for-the-Other of proximity and as the wisdom of love (Lévinas cited in Dussel 1998).

G. Moment of progressive theoretical-practical awareness

Women are aware of gaps that will only fill if they dominate the hegemonic discourse to strengthen their position, hence their claims for justice and their communities' rights. By having collaborators and co-managers, they also enrich the critical readings of their context and the oppressive situation in which they find themselves. As Dussel explains, what happens from a hegemonic shore:

> Theoretical reason captures the empirical content and makes a judgement. The reproductive drives face a contradiction: if the institutions are the repetition of successful acts to avoid pain and postpone death and thus achieve happiness, the 'victim' is their absolute contradiction -because being the result of that institution-, nevertheless suffers pain and anticipates his death (1998).

The search at this time consists of making the institution and victim dialogue expand the panorama of analysis of the first and give scenarios of discussion and visibility to the second. This relationship will lead the victim to become aware of herself but positively, positioning herself negatively in front of the system. Eloísa says,

> I want you to know me, so you know who I am. I already know who I am. Many black people don't know who they are, and we are going to tell them. But if you don't know me and don't know you, how will we have a meeting? That is what we are doing, a not very biased work (2020).

These meetings will also have an approach in which rational thought is put at the victims' service, not the other way around. In this scenario, Erlendy raises an experience,

> A cousin told me, "I want to connect with national or international organisations that allow me to lead the development of my community. But without losing our essence of what we are and why we have to support ourselves", I believe that we have to target it and move towards that (2021).

Using their racial/ethnic background to articulate it to rights hegemonic discourses is how these women begin to navigate the system. From that place, they begin to ask themselves bigger questions those of power, justice, and poverty. In this way, the claims of women in social mobilisation appropriate and translate the discourse of human rights to frame them in a deeper concern against injustices: the degradation of their community well-being with the claims of rights articulated at the intersection of race/ethnicity, gender, and socio-economic status.

H. Time for possible dialectical alternatives

For Johana, for Erlendy and Eloísa, the particularities of being displaced Afro-Colombian women constitute the reason for their empowerment. They have resignified what it means to be black women, they have done it from their individuality, and it has been strengthened in the community act.

This moment of self-worth, in which the victim affirms their identity and their culture, "then begins with the critical awareness of that oppression that will eventually drag them into a liberation struggle" (Guerra about Dussel 2017). In this regard, Rajagopal considers that committing to culture as a field of struggle and resistance "has highlighted the rights to identity, to the territory, to some form of autonomy and, even more important, alternative conceptions of modernity and development" (Rajagopal 2005). That is how Dussel (1998) maintains that asserting oneself about culture allows a process of liberation to be advanced, as long as the victim has understood that he/she is immersed in a dominator-dominated, system-exclusion relationship.

At first, women have been reflected in an equal other who suffers similar conditions of violence and from now on, they begun to compare themselves with a man that is mestizo and urban, who has not experienced the loss of family and friendly ties, nor the loss of territory due to the conflict. The women have begun to notice that the lack of state presence is evident in ethnic territories and that it is the women's bodies that are used as spoils of war by the different illegal armed groups that are present in the areas from which they were forced to leave.

Like indigenous groups, Afro-Colombian communities have burdened with centuries of oppression and exclusion. That, thanks to "the ethical-critical awareness of that oppression-exclusion, of the fact of being victims; [has] made possible [...] the affirmation of their valuable being; From that affirmation, a liberation struggle begins with an ethical conscience of being victims. This statement is the result of a dialectical process where the dominator-dominated relationship, system exclusion are the horizon of understanding" (Dussel 1998). As reinforced by Erlendy and Eloísa within their organisation,

> The subject of memory and identity is worked a lot with them. That for us, it is much stronger than they know, what has happened to the black communities. What has happened to our country, and why is it essential that they create awareness in the face of these struggles. But also with this clear identity of who they are and what they have. They do not have to continue carrying this inheritance of that self-discrimination.
>
> What happens is that the Afro Committee claims our rights, but it is something transversal; it is not because we are Afro; we have to be biased, no. You have to work hand in hand with everyone because how are you going to build.

All of the above refers to a type of resistance that "is not always and simply a reaction against hegemony but is a complex multitude of alternative views on social relations and, therefore, on the history of humanity" (Rajagopal 2005). From this place, women and their communities come together to propose alternatives that allow them to open spaces for sustained participation and representation. They are grouped at the neighbourhood, community, urban, and national level to promote actions that make their tensions visible and echo city issues.

The third and last level of this praxis of liberation is the result of a transformation of primary consciousness that is nurtured by the exchange of individual and collective experiences in settings that involve co-managers and collaborators that enrich the emancipatory experience.

For Dussel, it is from dialogue, exchange, and the encounter between the others that the possibility of transforming the world is created (1998). This possibility begins as a negative moment of enunciation in which the system that causes the oppression is criticised. In turn, it forces the others to consider alternatives guided by a utopia and constituted as a positive moment. These steps lead to a praxis of liberation that becomes possible when in the community. Therefore, the pedagogical act that occurs from the empirical and scientific exchange leads to the transformation of reality favouring the oppressed (Dussel 1998).

Level 3

At this level, the community of victims deconstructs the hostile and systemic conditions to propose transformative actions that lead to their constructive—liberating affirmation. The author breaks this level down into two moments.

I. Moment for transformative actions

There is only one way for the victims to live well and live better, a scenario where there are justice, solidarity, and goodness among the victims. However, for this to happen, it is necessary to start by criticising the order given to transform it or create a new one (Dussel 1998).

When the culture understood as 'wisdom' where the relationship between the system and the affected-excluded is questioned, it fosters a dynamic for liberation that transcends the desires for self-preservation or survival (Dussel 1998). It is not passive resistance; it is a full and positive affirmation that occurs if they have understood that.

1. Oppression and exclusion weigh on their culture.
2. From their critical and self-reflective conscience, they realise their own value (Dussel 1998).

To be understood in such terms, it makes it possible that the liberation process is no longer personal but becomes a historical commitment to rewrite the story (Freire cited in Dussel 1998). Such commitment demands from the victims a series of actions aimed at a better future, but for that, it is necessary to consolidate themselves in communities that have a clear north and are gaining territory to raise their voice, the action is the organisation, and in this regard, Johana says.

> What unites me is that we are for the same cause: my community, my rights, and my duties. I do not want boys and girls to continue to be lost; I want them to get ahead, to be someone in life (2020).

While Erlendy says that in her work with young people, her actions are aimed at three thematic axes.

> The main issue is the issue of racial discrimination. The other is self-recognition, that strengthening of our memory, of our history. One of the strong axes that I work on is cultural identity; my strength has been that. May our youth carry on, but without forgetting where they come from. That once they achieve the fortress, remember their territories. We have to work a lot in that country-village relationship, as Law 70 says. And regardless of where we are, we always have to come back. We must return for the strength it gives us, but also to see how we help there. That what is done here has an impact on our communities (2021).

From their organisations and work with young people, the actions have been aimed at their representation in cultural spaces, entrepreneurship, peaceful demonstrations as a form of political participation and social work in terms of access to food resources. The three women have community dining rooms to remedy this lack of food in the sectors where they impact. Their project is to achieve alliances to supply their dining rooms and to achieve adequate physical space to serve the population.

All these actions are based on a principle of hope, which, as Ernst Bloch says, is "situated exactly at the positive moment of projecting (as affect and reason) the possible alternatives, not yet-realised" (cited in Dussel 1998). And as Guerra says, referring to Dussel, "at this moment, hope fulfils an essential function, as it projects the life of the weak (…) towards a promising future. The hope of a life without material deficiencies springs, then, from those human beings who suffer the increasing lack of the joy of life in their corporality" (2017).

It is important to understand that "black women as political actors use their feelings, collective affections, and Afro aesthetic politics to make their exclusion, marginalization, and resistance practices visible" (Hernández Reyes 2019). For women, there is no form of resistance and reconceptualisation of rights outside of their black identities. They are women who champion their culture (in crafts, dance, music or gastronomy), their feelings, and their collective affections as places of resistance from where they produce practices and discourses of liberation.

J. Moment to build positive alternatives

The community of victims, once constituted, has the ethical obligation to amend the contextual conditions that violate them for the full realisation of their lives and their fellow men. For that, they constitute a social movement that groups together various forms of organisation where "they fight for the recognition of their new rights and the responsible realisation of new institutional structures of a cultural, economic, political, instinctual nature, etc." (Dussel on Freire 1998).

These women, who have made a process of self-criticism, who have built a network and have articulated themselves with other forms of knowledge "simultaneously face multiple oppressions [and] are in a position to reimagine emancipatory politics, produce and embody difference, and create and experiment with new subjectivities" (Seppälä as cited in Hernández Reyes 2019).

According to the theories of social movements, the community of victims is defined from collective action, with self-awareness and flexible organisation that are not necessarily grouped as formal associations or organisations (Laako 2016). The community of victims, of which Erlendy, Eloísa, and Johana are part, mobilises for issues that they consider unfair to the community they represent to make visible or resolve an existing social conflict and achieve participation spaces at the local and national level. As an example of this, Erlendy shares her experience with her youth group:

> They have learned to participate, to establish positions in meetings. They are very young, and they already know what they want. They are good interlocutors, they went to a meeting in Bogotá, and they always set a position and speak with strength (2021).

As a starting point, both Erlendy, Eloísa, and Johana and the young people with whom they work have the desire to make possible a real liberation project that allows them to develop their lives dignified. This desire is the instinctual moment of enthusiasm referred by Dussel (1998); it is characterised by waiting and hoping for the probable.

This enthusiasm and feelings of hope can be related to the creative utopia to which Freire refers (cited in Dussel 1998). Since it is the source of creative inspiration so that groups, networks or organisations that come together from below can propose alternatives and establish a project that is "compatible and worthy with the lives of the oppressed" (Guerra 2017). This hope is reflected in the current work that women do, thinking about the generations that lie ahead, Eloísa expresses it this way.

> It interests me that the new generations do not go through those we have already gone through. I believe that my work is focused on leaving a better future for girls. And that mothers begin to raise children as human beings, not machines. I am working so that when my granddaughter is an adult, she does not encounter these barriers. We are raising an entrepreneur so that if tomorrow she does not want to go to an office or they are going to close the doors, she does not have any problem that she can employ other people. If I am not there, it will be a grain of sand left from all these struggles that we are now having (2020).

This community of victims has reached its critical validity because they recognise themselves as different and excluded from the oppressive system. In response, they have articulated in fluid networks to reach agreements on what affects them. Finally, such a critical consensus "is based on rational argumentation and is motivated by co-solidarity drive" (Dussel 1998), which guarantees its sustainability over time and recognition as a social movement whose struggle persists as long as they continue to be subjects of injustices.

The collective action of Afro-Colombian women community leaders can be understood theoretically in light of the community of victims raised by Dussel (1998) and empirically from community work experiences that these women have advanced over the years. They are constituted as a social movement because they emerge as a collective action with a shared consciousness about the injustices they are subject to. The previous statement is reinforced by Laako when she affirms that "social movements are born thanks to changes in the structures of opportunity in society or because a cognitive framework of interpretation of the existing conditions emerges that allows generating awareness for collective action" (2016).

These women's organisational efforts as a community of victims pursue a dynamic, non-linear struggle, that as asserted by Kathryn McNeilly (2019) follows "alternative temporal movements [that are] engaged to conceptualize the relation between past, present and future in international human rights law". Such a way of connecting temporality with human rights far from conceptions of time that are dominant, allows the women to continually question themselves to raise awareness about other individual and collective existence dimensions, in the rights framework.

5 Decentralising Human Rights: Alternative Local Freedom Practices

In the previous section, a long path was followed to frame the Afro-Colombian women community leaders' movement as a community of victims—a stand from where they raised their concerns about race, gender and social inequalities. Those concerns are framed under three stages, one of primordial conscience, the other about questioning the established system (and constitutes a critical community) and finally, imagining and developing feasible alternatives to the human rights discourse.

On this occasion, the levels proposed by Dussel (1988) will not be detailed but rather will approach analysis from a broader framework that ties in with concepts that emerge from women's discourses and their moment of consciousness praxis for liberation.

Level 1: Ethical responsibility

The ethical-pre-original reason is a specific type of rationality that appears as a first rational moment since it is before any other exercise of reason and occurs before any decision, commitment or communication that we maintain in the community. This ethic arises as a responsibility for the other's life (Dussel 1998), being there where feelings of empathy, sympathy, and solidarity emerge and guide our actions concerning an Other victim.

As cited in Barreto, "Horkheimer understands sympathy not as mere emotion but as an emotion mediated by knowledge, not only in the process of its constitution but also in its application, and depending on an interpretation of the human condition" (Barreto 2006). Afro-Colombian women usually refer to the motives that sustain their leadership from an emotional and moral stand, as told by Jhoana and Erlendy.

> My leadership is born out of affection for myself and my people.
>
> Solidarity, in my case, is being able to do something, being able to help my community. May that footprint and path that I am leaving guide another to follow it. Solidarity is feeling empathy for my people, accepting that I do not know everything, that I need other people, but above all, following that path of support, of helping others. Support, not in the sense of getting used to giving, but of to build.

The responsibility with the Other, states Erlendy, does not occur from a welfare approach but as the transformation of the forms of support that might lead to the change of injustice structures. Quoting Dussel, "proximity is the root of praxis and the starting point of all responsibility for the Other. Only the one who has lived proximity in justice and joy takes responsibility for himself for the poor, for the victim whom he desires the proximity of his equals" (Dussel 2011). The previous invites to conclude that victims' ethical responsibility leads Afro-Colombian women community leaders to claim their historical and social place.

Barreto draws attention to Horkheimer ethics of sympathy by indicating that its centre relies on "the moral sentiment of compassion or sympathy that aims at the alleviation of suffering and turns into solidarity" (2006). The German author says that when moral sentiments guide human beings, the possibility of morality emerges in compassion and determines the psychic disposition of the moral action. As Barreto interprets him, “sympathy would be the consequence of the experience of being witness to the suffering of others and would imply recognition of oneself in the suffering of the other” (Barreto 2006). The previous is reflected in Eloísa’s experience,

> We meet when someone needs something. We make a route for that person so that he/she can be given help. Not only do we do it with people from the commune, but we also do it with people from any part of Cali who is hungry; we do the accompaniment.

According to Barreto, “a sentimental education would point to make us more able to put ourselves in the place of those strange people who are the object of cruelty or destitution, who are in need or in pain of those who have been victims of human rights violations” (2006). The former will take us to question our identity, while the later pushed us to be in solidarity, as individuals or a political community (Barreto 2006).

What motivates women’s leadership happens at first because of empathy and responsibility for others’ pain. They do not reflect on what it implies to embark on the other’s care, either from specific actions, such as planning a day to open a community dining room or from the desire for personal growth that allows them to acquire knowledge to put it at the service of others. The three leaders “promote ‘mutual aid’ as a collective system through which they share and ‘maintain a constant social interaction among the different family groups, reinforcing ties of friendship and solidarity’” (Bernasconi as cited in Hernández Reyes 2019).

To conclude with this point, Barreto’s suggestion for the adoption of ethics of emotions as ethics of human rights (2018) seems to be in line with the exercise of community leadership and the discourse of Afro-Colombian women. The author says, “the adoption of an ethics of emotions as ethics of human rights has been put forward as a path for advancing the sentimental education of the epoch, and for strengthening the human rights culture” (Barreto 2006).

Level 2: Dignity as justice

The discourse on justice that Afro-Colombian women community leaders usually allude to is none other than dignity. The previous is an approach that does not start from a theory of human rights but has its starting point in personal experiences and in the dialectical constructions that, throughout their work, they have integrated into their discourse.

On the western epistemological side, a series of discourses and theories do not account for the place of enunciation in which they are produced. Their rational approach makes them far from local communities where symbols and emotions determine the ways of relating. From this point of view, Marry reflects,

> There are fissures between the global settings where human rights ideas are codified into documents and the local communities where these rights live and work. Human rights ideas, embedded in cultural assumptions about the nature of the person, the community, and the State, do not translate easily from one setting to another. (Merry 2006).

For this reason, women who have advanced a liberation project have an empirical idea of justice and have their own human rights understanding. On the one hand, the images that women relate to the concept of justice are with the country's judicial apparatus, where they locate the Constitution, some laws and the police. On the other hand, they understand justice in terms of decent living conditions. Jhoana and Eloísa bring two examples of the first emphasis.

> Well, I am going to tell you this, I do not work with police officers. I respect their space because the one who is in danger, the one they know, is Johana. So I have never liked working with the police.
>
> I think that justice also enters into a set of rights. Justice could be what organised all this disorder. Justice is that rights are equal for all. If I commit a crime, I will be judged for my crime regardless of my social condition, race, religion, or colour. Justice should be the same for everyone, which is a utopia. I believe that justice should be equality and fairness for everything

As we have seen above, the discourses mix some issues about punitive justice and the judicial apparatus. However, they relate that justice is not applied to everyone based on equality. Some intersections determine what kind of social subject is worthy of justice. To contribute to this discussion Sadurski.

> Criticises this distinction between social and legal justice, stating that "what we usually call 'legal justice' is either an application of the more fundamental notion of 'social justice' to legal rules and decisions or is not a matter of justice at all". In other words, the law is but one institution where matters of social justice or otherwise can find their expression, and law constitutes a practical field where social and legal justice are held as interdependent (Sadurski as cited in Watts and Hodgson 2019).

This meaning of justice is limited; however, it is part of the imaginary that local communities relate to the concept.

In the second approach, dignity is at the centre of the women's enunciation of justice. As their community of victims, the women leaders are aware of their needs and their ignored claims for nourishment, economic, health, and education means. They express their desire to achieve "a set of basic human entitlements, similar to human rights, as a minimum of what justice requires for all" (Nussbaum 2004). Then, the community unit is the space where liberation processes and the co-creation of ethical liberation are gestated. A community that calls for action and asks for the minimum conditions to live:

> Justice seen from a human being would be to give each one what is due. That people avoid committing so many negative actions. Moreover, it is just one to serve. Justice is that people are recognised for their actions. It is fair that in this country, everyone can have minimal living conditions. Not everyone has wealth, but people do not have to live in miserable, deplorable ways as they continue to live together and with so much social inequality. For me, justice is having a distribution of what there is and that everyone has access to it according to their actions. Work, prepare but give people the opportunities. That there is a way that people can be educated and be trained, but that there are also possibilities for these people to generate income. The fair thing is that we have a country that does not have to be assisting, but that people can generate what they need. We have some exceptions that must be applied, a person with a disability, an older adult, a mother who has several children; from there, justice has to look different.

> The fair thing for my community is that they have the same rights and obligations as everyone else: the right to a decent job and the right to a decent home. It is no secret to anyone that the most impoverished spaces are those of black people. Furthermore, it is not because black people like to live like this or because they are lazy; that comes from something very systematic. Because the State is not interested in improving that and when it is interested, it will improve, it will stop giving alms to people and put people to live in a different concept. However, politically, when there is a very vulnerable population, you can manipulate it whenever you want.

It is important to note, in both stands that they believe their "local communities can be understood as groups that are united by common needs and interests and that are based at the level of a geographical community" (Oré Aguilar, cited in Vandenbogaerde 2015). Their community affiliation is rooted by their common experience as oppressed, poor or invisible, as people who share a similar status within society.

Only Eloísa also relates her perception of justice interconnecting issues of gender and race as systems of oppression:

> We seek the vindication of black people to be respected and have the same rights as any citizen. That, if one of us studies, he has the same opportunities as the others. And the vindication of women because it is that I, as a woman and an afro, have had the most challenging fight. The struggle is double for us black women.

As for the human rights discourse, the three women are less certain and can relate to them from a general scope. Local communities, says Marry, "often conceive of social justice in quite different terms from human rights activists. They generally lack knowledge of relevant documents and provisions of the human rights system" (Merry 2006). When a hegemonic discourse does not meet the people, it is supposed to represent, its validity tremble.

> I know from Human Rights that all people have the right to equality, that they have the right to a name, a surname. Article 51 tells us that this is the right to equality for everyone. Apart from that, the Victims Article 1448 says that we as victims have rights and duties with the State. I realise my rights, my duties and offer them to my community.
>
> I am clear that my rights end where yours begin, that the rights of men and women are equal, that children's rights should have certain concepts. Human Rights are fundamental; since you are born, you are a subject of law. Here Human Rights are in quotation marks that are violated every day. Additionally, respect. That you have the right to a decent home, to health, to education, to a decent job where you can give yourself your things where you have hope that in the future you will have what helps you to support your family and that you can leave a legacy to your family, of your work, human rights are the right to health, respect for others, respect for your condition as a woman, the right to choose in your body.

The problem that the discourse of human rights is not close to local communities represents a problem for the oppressed because they cannot claim them from their interlocutors (who oppress them). In this case, communities have to overcome another hurdle in claiming their rights.

> Our struggle or our dynamics of advocacy in the face of claiming rights is based on the fact that we (Afro-Colombian communities) are not on equal terms. Therefore, it is necessary to protect the one in the most unfavourable conditions. When a community does not know its rights, it does not argue when claiming them and allows them to be violated. But precisely,

> our work as leaders of this community is to work so that these situations do not continue to arise.

As can be seen, none of the hegemonic discourses comes close to the work done by the community leaders. On the contrary, there are multiple meanings of the concept of justice and different adoptions of the human rights discourse. It is for this reason that local Afro-Colombian perspectives have woven together ways of demanding a dignified life: ways closer to practices such as their orality, music, dance, aesthetics, or craftsmanship.

Level 3: A different discourse

Following Rajagopal, the author mentions, "most people in the Third World live and interact in non-institutional spaces: in the family, in the informal economy and in non-partisan political spaces" (2005), which explains the little relationship of women with the discourse of human rights, a circumstance that pushes them to imagine other forms of resistance that are not representable within the hegemonic logic.

In this sense, the search for an alternative model is "important to understand the practices of various local-based social movements, to assess whether they offer alternative visions and programs for social change that are not supported by the discourse of human rights only" (Rajagopal 2005). This task would merely be reducing the place of reason in the Constitution of an ethic, giving rise to emotions to make them morally relevant (Barreto 2006).

Rajagopal also proposes to change the perspective from a focus on social movements. They converge as extra-institutional resistance fields that "move away from the cognitive limits of the only discourse of resistance authorised by international law, that is, human rights" (Rajagopal 2005). Although Erlendy, from her organisation AFRODES, does not move away entirely from the human rights discourse, she approaches it from an alternative perspective,

> What I do is framing that conglomerate of fundamental rights and those of the Magna Carta. The added value that I give them is ethnic-racial rights because of the conflict's disproportionate impact, and the criminal actions are different from particular populations. It is not the same what ethnic groups are suffering today (indigenous communities, Afro-descendants) compared to their impact on other communities.

The case of the Process of Black Communities accounts for some particular dynamics that occur in Afro-Colombian communities. That can be the starting point for an alternative human rights discourse,

> A look at these scenarios and relationships reveals the symbolic dimension of a project based on joy and freedom, a pillar of thought and political proposal of important sectors of the Afro social movement, as proposed by the Process of Black Communities PCN (Grueso, 2008-2010).

Erlendy, Eloísa, and Johana do not question in detail the human rights discourse and scope simply because they do not feel a direct association with it. For Johana, the discourse of human rights is a matter outside her work, she frames it as a political matter, or that is in the hands of the country's judicial branch. For Eloísa, human rights are an incomplete tool because they are guaranteed for a few who are not the black, indigenous, or peasant communities.

When a discourse like that of human rights is associated with privileges, what remains for communities is to use a language they feel is their own. A language with which they feel comfortable and identify. That is why Erlendy talks about readjusting them from an ethnic perspective; only then will they have the impact they were created for, from hegemonic dialogue towards local dialogue.

One way that women associate themselves with their exercise of leadership is through empathy and emotionality. In this line, Barreto considers that starting from "the recognition of the suffering of the other and the expression of some form of solidarity, which is the active form of such feeling, would make one who is suffering the object of the concern and solidarity of the one who witnesses his or her suffering" (Barreto 2006). In this way, the community of victims maintains its praxis of liberation, starting from the pre-original ethical reason, which advances in a sentimental education that strengthens human rights' contemporary culture. Such sentimental education, Barreto points out, will be "as the formation or socialisation of people concerned about others, sentimental education would not pass by the process of finding a priori rational universal rules and obeying them, but it would have to do with the cultivation of some character traits, particularly the capacity for sympathy" (Barreto 2006).

Another way to reframe human rights from decolonial thought is to enable a dialogue between Western reason and emotion. The ethics of emotions is adopted as human rights ethics (Barreto 2012). However, the communities decide the best way to approach human rights discourse, whether from reform or other discursive alternatives.

6 Conclusion

It is possible that in broader participation scenarios, there are discussions and counter-discourses about human rights. The focus of this chapter is on a particular community level where, although there may be a contact with this discourse through the institutions that are in charge of their promotion; they are unable to adhere to the daily life of women, who find it easier to speak from the place of emotionality. As valid as other forms of speech.

Human rights discourse begins in the West, expanding to a Latin American neighbourhood or community setting in Cali. Nevertheless, it comes only from its most fundamental notions: housing, health, education, free expression, and decision about one's own body. It is there where it is born but here where it ends, like a broken phone whose message is lost in the distance.

With all of the above, the contingencies that a discourse such as that of human rights is irrelevant for people who are in struggles for justice reduces the possibility of financing their community projects. It is well known that as long as a speech is not part of the one sponsored by the organisation, institution, or entity, it will hardly be selected to benefit financially. That is reason enough for communities to be forced to enter into these dynamics if they want to make their community process expandable and sustainable.

The three women community leaders have a distinct approach to the discourse of human rights. Still, their struggles are aimed at reaffirmation and gendered ethnic recognition processes, which are not sensitive issues in the human rights discourse. Therefore, it makes more sense for them to reflect on a shore that vindicates their identities and allows them to build their leadership from the local, with their community, a community of victims.

Only Erlendy reframes human rights with an ethnic approach for two reasons: she is a woman who has been in the leadership process for 21 years (twice as many as the other two women) and is pursuing her career in Law. She does not resist human rights discourse, none of them does, but only Erlendy from her organisation and with her community adjusts them to her needs.

Hence, the need to promote dialogue between epistemologies leads to agreements with a global impact but with a local focus. And position emotions as valid reasons to lead the narrative of human rights, as in the actions of social movements.

References

Albertson Fineman, M. 2017. Vulnerability and Inevitable Inequality. *Oslo Law Review*, 4:133–149. https://ssrn.com/abstract=3087441

Alcaldía de Santiago de Cali. 2015. *Diagnóstico Del Municipio*, pp. 1–87

Alonso, J, M. Arcos, J, Solano and Vera, R and Gallego, A. 2007. *Una Mirada Descriptiva a Las Comunas De Cali.* Universidad Icesi

Asher, Kiran. 2007. Ser Y Tener: Black women's activism, development, and ethnicity in the pacific lowlands of Colombia. *Feminist Studies*, 33(1):11–37. http://www.jstor.org/stable/20459116

Barreto, J.M. 2006. Ethics of emotions as ethics of human rights: a jurisprudence of sympathy in Adorno, Horkheimer and Rorty. *Law and Critique* 17: 73–106. https://doi.org/10.1007/s10978-006-0003-y.

Barreto, J.M. 2012. Decolonial strategies and dialogue in the human rights field: a manifesto. *Transnational Legal Theory* 3 (1): 1–29. https://doi.org/10.5235/TLT.3.1.1.

Barreto, J.M. 2014. Epistemologies of the South and human rights: santos and the quest for global and cognitive justice. *Indiana Journal of Global Legal Studies* 21 (2): 395–422. https://doi.org/10.2979/indjglolegstu.21.2.395.

Barreto, J.M. 2018. Decolonial thinking and the quest for decolonising human rights. *Asian Journal of Social Science* 46: 484–502. https://doi.org/10.1163/15685314-04604006.

Bjarnesen, J., and H. Vigh. 2016. Introduction: the dialectics of displacement and emplacement. *Conflict and Society* 2 (1): 9–15.

Brown, Wendy. 2004. "The Most We Can Hope For": Human rights and the politics of fatalism. *The South Atlantic Quarterly,* 103(2):451–463. https://www.muse.jhu.edu/article/169139.

Castillo, M., D. Escandón, and O. Gonzales. 2012. Cali, ¿Cómo Vamos En Pobreza? Efectos De Zona, Comuna y Hogar En La Percepción De La Pobreza. *Coyuntura Económica: Investigación Económica y Social* 42 (1): 117–138.

De Feyter, K. 2006. *Localizing Human Rights.* Instituut voor Ontwikkelingsbeleid en -beheer (IOB), IOB Discussion Papers: Universiteit Antwerpen.

De Vita, A. 2014. La justicia internacional entre el humanitarismo y el igualitarismo global. *Andamios. Revista De Investigación Social* 11 (25): 13–49.
Dussel, Enrique. 1985. *Philosophy of Liberation.* Orbis Books
Dussel, Enrique. 1998. *Ética de la liberación en la Edad de la Globalización y de la Exclusión.* Editorial Trotta
Grueso, Libia, and Leyla A. Arroyo. 2005. Women and the defense of place in Colombian black movements struggles. In *Women and the Politics of Place*, ed. W. Harcourt and A. Escobar, 100–114. Kumarian Press Inc.
Grueso, L., A. Escobar, and C. Rosero. 1997. El proceso organizativo de comunidades negras en Colombia. *Ecología Política* 14: 47–64.
Guerra, I. 2017. *La validez antihegemónica de la comunidad de las víctimas* [Módulo 5]. Seminario filosofía de la liberación: perspectivas y prospectivas. Asociación de Filosofía y Liberación, México D.F., México
Hernández Reyes, C.E. 2019. Black women's struggles against extractivism, land dispossession, and marginalization in Colombia. *Latin American Perspectives* 46 (2): 217–234. https://doi.org/10.1177/0094582X19828758.
Hooker, J. 2005. Indigenous inclusion/black exclusion: race, ethnicity and multicultural citizenship in Latin America. *Journal of Latin American Studies* 37: 285–310.
Laako, H. 2016. Los derechos humanos en los movimientos sociales: El caso de las parteras autónomas en México. *Revista Mexicana De Ciencias Políticas y Sociales* 61 (227): 167–194.
Ley N. 1993. *70. Congreso de la República de Colombia*, Bogotá, Colombia. Retrieved February 24, 2021, from http://www.suin-juriscol.gov.co/viewDocument.asp?ruta=Leyes/1620332#:~:text=ARTICULO%201%C2%B0%20La%20presente,conformidad%20con%20lo%20dispuesto%20en
Longhurst, Robyn. (2003). Semi-structured interviews and focus groups. In *Key methods in geography*, 3rd ed., pp. 117–132, eds Clifford, Nicholas, Shaun French, Thomas W. Gillespie, and Meghan Cope. Sage.
Madhok, S. 2021. *Vernacular rights cultures: the politics of origins, human rights, and gendered struggles for justice.* Cambridge University Press.
McNeilly, K. 2019. Are rights out of time? international human rights law, temporality, and radical social change. *Social & Legal Studies* 28 (6): 817–838. https://doi.org/10.1177/0964663918815729.
Merry, Sally Engle. 2006. *Human rights and gender violence: translating international law into local justice.* University of Chicago Press
Ng'weno, B. 2007. Can ethnicity replace race? Afro-Colombians, indigeneity and the Colombian multicultural state. *The Journal of Latin American and Caribbean Anthropology* 12: 414–440. https://doi.org/10.1525/jlat.2007.12.2.414.
Nussbaum, M. 2004. Beyond the social contract: capabilities and global justice. *Oxford Development Studies* 32 (1): 3–18.
O'Connell, Paul. 2018. Human rights: contesting the displacement thesis. *Northern Ireland Legal Quarterly*, 69(1):19–35. https://doi.org/10.53386/nilq.v69i1.76
Rajagopal, Balakrishnan. 2005. *Derecho internacional desde abajo. El desarrollo, los movimientos sociales y la resistencia del Tercer Mundo.* Instituto Latinoamericano de Servicios Legales
Riessman, C.K. 2005. Narrative Analysis. In *Narrative, memory & everyday life*, ed. N. Kelly, C. Horrocks, K. Milnes, B. Roberts, and D. Robinson, 1–7. University of Huddersfield.
Riessman, Catherine Kohler. 2014. Analysis of personal narratives. In *The SAGE handbook of interview research: the complexity of the craft*, 2nd ed, eds Gubrium, Jaber F., James A. Holstein, Amir B. Marvasti, and Karyn D. McKinney, 367-380. SAGE Publications, Inc
Rose, G. 1997. Situating knowledges: positionality, reflexivities and other tactics. *Progress in Human Geography* 21 (3): 305–320.
Ruta Pacífica de las Mujeres. 2013. *La Verdad De Las Mujeres. Víctimas Del Conflicto Armado En Colombia*, (2). Ruta Pacífica de las Mujeres

Santos, B.S. 2007. Beyond abyssal thinking: from global lines to ecologies of knowledges. *Review (fernand Braudel Center)* 30 (1): 45–89.
Santos, Boaventura de Sousa. 1997. Toward a Multicultural Conception of Human Rights. *ZeitschriftFuer Rechtssociologie* 18(1)
Santos, Boaventura de Sousa. 1998. *De la mano de Alicia: de lo social y lo político en la posmodernidad*. Ediciones Uniandes.
Theilen, J. 2017. Of wonder and changing the world: philip allott's legal utopianism. *German Yearbook of International Law*, 60. https://ssrn.com/abstract=3061966
Vandenbogaerde, Arne. 2015. *The human rights council from below: a case study of the declaration on the rights of peasants*. University of Antwerp
Wade, P. 2002. Introduction: The Colombian Pacific in perspective. *The Journal of Latin American Anthropology* 7 (2): 2–33.
Watts, Lynelle, and David Hodgson. 2019. *Social justice theory and practice for social work: critical and philosophical perspectives*. Springer
Winker, G., and N. Degele. 2011. Intersectionality as multi-level analysis: dealing with social inequality. *European Journal of Women's Studies* 18 (1): 51–66.

Contradictions and Opportunities for National Liberation in Human Rights Law and Practice

Moara Assis Crivelente

Abstract The vital exercise of imagining "other worlds", for oppressed peoples, is done not in peaceful contemplation, but in constant resistance.

List of Acronyms

IHL	International Humanitarian Law
IHRL	International Human Rights Law
NAM	Non-Aligned Movement
NIS	Newly independent states

This Chapter is the Result of Research Done for the International Relations Doctoral Program at the Faculty of Economics of the University of Coimbra and the Center for Social Studies (CES), Portugal. I received the support of the Tokyo and Nippon Foundations, through the Sylff Fellowship Program, for field research at the UN Human Rights Council in Geneva and the Palestinian and Saharawi Refugee Camps in Lebanon and Algeria, and a visiting research stay at the School of Law at Warwick University. I Also Express My Gratitude to the Book's Editors for the Opportunity to Contribute and to Anonymous Reviewers for Pertinent Questions, Inspiring Comments, and Editing Suggestions.

M. Assis Crivelente (✉)
Center for Social Studies (CES), University of Coimbra, Coimbra, Portugal
e-mail: moaracrivelente@ces.uc.pt

Faculty of Economics, University of Coimbra, Coimbra, Portugal

T. Venthan Ananthavinayagan and A. Viswanath Shenoy (eds.), *The Wretched of the Global South*, International Law and the Global South,
https://doi.org/10.1007/978-981-99-9275-1_3

1 Introduction

> Y los derechos se toman, no se piden; se arrancan, no se mendigan. Hasta los déspotas, si son hidalgos, gustan más del sincero y enérgico lenguaje que de la tímida y vacilante tentativa. (José Martí, Discurso en honor del periodista Adolfo Márquez Sterling. La Habana, 21 April 1870)

The vital exercise of imagining "other worlds", for oppressed peoples, is done not in peaceful contemplation, but in constant resistance. Comprehending the ground of struggle is thus always an emergency, if these peoples are to become the subjects of their history. From Africa, Asia, and Latin America, emancipatory movements and newly independent states (NIS) have pushed their way into an international system and institutions where normative claims meet power. The main category mobilised for that entrance is the nation and international law is the instrument, in an operation most clearly expressed in the claim for self-determination as both a way in and a way to remain in a course of liberation.[1]

The 1950–1970s, decades of anti-colonial wars and NIS' entrance into the United Nations (UN), are usually covered as a key period of self-determination's graduation from principle to right, a period that inspired further ethical and concrete claims for recognition and distribution, as markers of what Third World peoples aspire for and of their project for a new international order (Prashad 2007; Abi-Saab 2016; Chimni 2017). This drive takes place in an international system troubled by imperialism,[2] where colonialism has operated regimes of plunder and exploitation for the expansion of capitalism (Marx 2013 [1867]; Turner 2014 [1978]).[3] These forms of domination stand on the systematic violations of rights declared as universal and of which

[1] "And rights are taken, they are not requested; they are grabbed, not begged for. Even despots, if they are noblemen, like sincere and energetic language better than the timid and hesitant attempt." My translation from Spanish.

[2] Summarily put, imperialism is conceived as the phase of realisation of the capitalist tendency to monopolisation, when world powers rush to redivide areas rich in resources, seeking labour and new markets—often unfolding into war and (new) colonialism. These premises are discussed in Lenin's (1964 [1917]) *Imperialism, the Highest Stage of Capitalism*. See, for instance, with accounts of this and more angles, the volume edited by Rupert and Smith (2002).

[3] In Volume 1 of *Capital*, Chapter 33: "The Modern Theory of Colonisation", Marx (2013, 535–536) writes that in the colonies "the capitalist regime everywhere comes into collision with the resistance of the producer, who, as owner of his own conditions of labour, employs that labour to enrich himself, instead of the capitalist. [...] Where the capitalist has at his back the power of the mother-country, he tries to clear out of his way by force the modes of production and appropriation based on the independent labour of the producer. The same interest, which compels the sycophant of capital, the political economist, in the mother-country, to proclaim the theoretical identity of the capitalist mode of production with its contrary, that same interest compels him in the colonies to make a clean breast of it, and to proclaim aloud the antagonism of the two modes of production. To this end, he proves how the development of the social productive power of labour, co-operation, division of labour, use of machinery on a large scale, etc., are impossible without the expropriation of the labourers, and the corresponding transformation of their means of production into capital. In the interest of the so-called national wealth, he seeks for artificial means to ensure the poverty of the people".

oppressed peoples have demanded more than a promise. Sprouting in anti-imperialist convergences, including the 1955 Bandung Conference and the 1966 Tricontinental in Havana, the Third World "project" encompasses national states at the periphery of capitalism and engaged in the Non-Aligned Movement (NAM), national liberation movements (NLMs), and non-state actors such as social movements (Rajagopal 2003; Prashad 2007; Abi-Saab 2016). In different ways, these actors deploy international law and human rights in their claims for self-determination, their calls for protection and accountability for daily abuses, and in building new socio-political and economic regimes, as part of the hard task of decolonisation of institutions and of the minds,[4] as Frantz Fanon and other intellectual revolutionaries addressed ahead have urged.

A historical-materialist perspective of national emancipatory aims supports this chapter's effort to engage with the book's timely proposal of an assessment of emancipatory projects for human rights.[5] For this reason, it engages with discussions of rights and international law's limits and opportunities without ignoring incongruities between Marxist and certain 'third-worldist' approaches, notably regarding the roles of social movements/civil society and the state, but which cannot be fully explored here.[6] The chapter builds on an engaged research on Palestine's and Western Sahara's national struggles against colonisation by Israel and Morocco, including tactical-strategic assessments by critical scholars and by those active in networks of debate and campaigning. It tackles contradictions and avenues for NLMs particularly in the use of international human rights law (IHRL) and humanitarian law (IHL), as the situations addressed are sustained by protracted military occupation.

The research from which this chapter draws elements examines the challenges and the tactics adopted by Palestinians and Saharawis in their use of international law, namely IHRL. Since it could not do that in relation to each of those institutions where they have engaged, which are many, the analysis focuses on how they engage in the UN Human Rights Council. The chapter shows that, instead of complete

---

[4] On the risk of claims for decolonisation being co-opted for some sort of re-colonisation, Tuck and Yang (2012, 2) caution against turning the claim into a metaphor: "[d]ecolonization, which we assert is a distinct project from other civil and human rights-based social justice projects, is far too often subsumed into the directives of these projects, with no regard for how decolonization wants something different than those forms of justice".

[5] Formulations about the historical-materialist method are the best source of clarification of how Marxists see the relation between the concrete and the ideological structures of social forms and systems, including the international capitalist system, and of why consciousness of the historical contingencies of categories expressing them—instead of their supposed eternal validity—is necessary for emancipation as transformation and transcendence (Lukács 2014).

[6] For instance, Koskenniemi (2004, 242) ponders: "The redemption of civil society against the state by new social movements is today a routine aspect of transformative debates that take up the left-Hegelian themes of which Marx was profoundly critical. The call is for political emancipation in order to rid the international world of the distorting structures of statehood against which civil society is portrayed as an authentic realm of human spontaneity. Yet there is a danger that the critiques of the state—as much a part of international law as statehood itself—collapse into an uncritical endorsement of informal social power. Something that is said to exist 'naturally' is celebrated because that is what it appears to be". See also Wood (1990) on the "uses and abuses of civil society", addressed ahead.

adherence to essentialised and imposed concepts and procedures for organisation and mobilisation, a *conscientious engagement* with instruments informed by analyses of the concrete reality in which struggle is done is constantly urged for by activists and scholars concerned with tactics and emancipatory strategies as different—i.e., short to longer terms—yet co-dependent dimensions of action. The first part of the chapter explores categories of analysis and practice in these struggles and the problems of instruments and procedures in human rights advocacy. The second part addresses how these issues reflect on the strategic challenges of Palestinians and Saharawis in their struggles for self-determination, including their immediate concerns with protection from daily violations of human rights as policies sustaining the regimes that they seek to dismantle.

2 Strategising National Liberation and Human Rights

International law, namely IHRL and IHL, for the oppressed, has played the role of both a register of normative claims still being worked out and an instrument to be used in dealing with immediate predicaments, ranging from people's protection from daily abuses to implementation of the right to self-determination. National liberation from colonisation is fought for to this day, including through the operationalisation of international norms and institutions. Liberation goals—e.g., independence or autonomy, and emancipation, as institutional and cultural decolonisation and, for some, transcending into non-exploitative, socialist societies—require ponderation of historical dynamics and conjunctures, and the development of a new thinking for the transformation of reality. This means that engaged people must be aware of what the adoption of certain tactics in each period of their struggle entail, in the short to longer terms. Priorities or perspectives of the end goal may vary, which explains why actors are seldom unanimous about tactics too, but it is still necessary to chart a clear path by setting up a responsible strategy, by considering contextual geographic, social, political, historical particularities.[7]

These concerns have long infused critiques of the horizons and instruments that bourgeois and Western liberal 'utopias' have allowed peoples struggling for emancipation or rights to envision and mobilise, with procedural or technical moderation (Rajagopal 2003; Gordon 2004). They resonate, for instance, in 'principled opportunism' —using international law when it is useful and discarding it when it is not, although the idea that there is a *choice* to use or not to use law may be an illusion, as Robert Knox (2010) ponders; or in Abi-Saab's (2016) view of what issues and opportunities for gradual changes come with 'operating behind enemy lines'—in his

[7] Lukács (2014, 3) defines tactics as "a means by which politically active groups achieve their declared aims, as a link connecting ultimate objective with reality", in a fundamental distinction between "the immanent and the transcendent ultimate objective"—the strategy. While the former "accepts the existing legal order as a given principle" determining the scope of action, for groups with "a socio-transcendent objective that legal order is seen as pure reality, as real power, to be taken into account for, at most, *reasons of expediency*" (*Ibid*) (emphasis added).

case, sitting in the Appellate Body of the World Trade Organization.[8] From a broader perspective, Frantz Fanon (2001, 199) famously discussed the direction of struggles for national liberation, including the 'strength and weakness' of spontaneity in the organisation and practice of a national party, the 'pitfalls of national consciousness', or the 'practical realism' of the everyday fight, and the way forward after independence, considering what that nation operationalised in struggle will become. Challenges vary, and in many places, a pretense of (liberal) democracy is founded on the brutal repression of the new regime's opponents: in Morocco, for instance, after the 1956 independence from France, the regime of King Hassan II unleashed gruesome persecution of critics, such as that of Mehdi Ben Barka, a socialist leader forcibly disappeared in 1965 in France, later acknowledged as having been assassinated (Brittain 2001); and that of the communist Abraham Serfaty and his comrades, who were persecuted, imprisoned—in Serfaty's case, for 17 years—and tortured for opposing Hassan II's regime (Serfaty 1992).[9]

Also concerned with revolutionary processes for more than the overthrow of a ruthless dictatorship, with the aim of building a new society, Ernesto 'Che' Guevara (2005 [1965]) envisioned and strove to practice 'the new man' forged in the fight to defeat oppressive colonial, neocolonial, or authoritarian regimes. This process must hence lead to overcoming social, political and cultural/ideological categories and structures arising from and sustaining old social forms.[10] This is why consciousness of the real conditions in which people struggle is a requirement. Hence, calls for this conscientious engagement in mobilisation for anti-colonial and anti-imperialist struggles include the questions of what the nation is and is aimed at, and of rights-based approaches to these plights may accomplish; a combination expressed in the claim for implementation of people's right to self-determination against foreign domination and for independence and liberation. It is thus necessary to identify the contradictions and opportunities in the framework and tools available that can best work for the strategy outlined.

[8] Abi-Saab's (2016, 1968–1969) comments, on reformism: "If you accept to sit on a bench, you have to accept its terms of reference. And if you want to improve things, it has to be done within these terms of reference", and as long as the rules of law stand, "let us get the best out of them within the amenable margin of interpretation. If we can change them, that is all the better."

[9] An anti-Zionist Jew criticising Israel's colonisation of Palestine and Morocco's annexation of Western Sahara, Serfaty was again exiled and stripped of his Moroccan nationality in 1991, but then allowed back with his nationality re-instated in 2000. Serfaty is nicknamed as the 'Moroccan Mandela', e.g., in Bouazzaoui Mostafa (2018) "Abraham Serfaty: Morocco's Mandela", *Al Jazeera World*, at https://www.youtube.com/watch?v=jMG_ECewV5Y [20 Aug. 2021].

[10] Guevara (2005 [1965], 212) defines the individual as "the actor in this strange and moving drama of the building of socialism, in a dual existence as a unique being and as a member of society", in which "vestiges of the past are brought into the present in one's consciousness, and a continual labor is necessary to eradicate them".

3 National Liberation and Self-Determination

Establishing criteria to objectively define 'nation', for Hobsbawm (1992, 6), could be "trying to fit historically novel, emerging, changing and, even today, far from universal entities into a framework of permanence and universality". By the same token, 'nationalism' can take "a variety of forms and carr[y] with it a variety of political consequences", one of which reflects in the "interplay between 'nation' and 'state'", or "a relationship between national identity and political autonomy, between national integration and political sovereignty" (Rejai and Enloe 1969, 140). Different authors also challenge the Western-centric periodization of the history of nation that disregards how new forms of nationalism are created in "reaction against Western policies of imperialism and conquest", and that eventually rose to claim a national self-determination previously promoted for European countries (Rejai 1969, 21). For Rejai (*Ibid*, 22), this is a nationalism that aims "to terminate imperial rule and to create in its place a nation-state (more likely, a state-nation) on an equal footing with other sovereign states".[11] Still, Chatterjee (1986), replying to claims about the Indian case, ponders whether the nation-state in post-colonial contexts was indeed 'derivative' of a (European) model to argue that adaptations to overcome contradictions in contextual realities are as important as iterations, while Amin (1989, 256) deems it a "distinctive feature of Eurocentrism" to either "view the particular European way of articulating nation, state, and classes as a model that reveals the specificity of the European spirit [...] or the expression of a general law that will be inevitably reproduced elsewhere, even if delayed".

Amin also argues that the formation of nations "is closely linked with the crystallization of a state and the centralized circulation at this level of a specifically capitalist surplus (unification of the market, including markets for labor and capital)" (*Ibid*, 258). Therefore, as put by Visentini (2017), "the national question transcends the mere definition of what the Nation is because, beyond its definition in ethnic, linguistic and cultural characters, it is related to a structure of power, which in modern times is the State, the National State" (my translation from Portuguese). Still, Visentini ponders (*Ibid*), the coexistence of the 'national state' and international capitalism, which sought to move to more lucrative spaces, is a contradiction explained by differentiated development, a situation exploited by capital, which could at once move relatively 'free' while counting on the state as a 'fixed' power responsible for the territory and its population, able to isolate crises within certain boundaries, and responsible for protecting its own capitalists.

Hence, in the turn of the twentieth century,[12] 'the national question' and the challenge of imperialism gained relevance as "the imperial policies of the world powers

[11] In this argument, considering the state, the "crystallization of the structures of political authority", as *preceded* by the development of a sense of national identity in places like Europe and *succeeded* or rather co-constituted by or with such a development in Asia and Africa (Rejai and Enloe 1969, 140).

[12] In the Second International—Socialist (1889–1916) the national question was discussed at the intersection between class-struggle and internationalism and analyses of colonialism, and in the

and their 'civilizing mission' [...] forged opposing demands for struggles of national liberation and for the right to self-determination" (Pautasso et al 2019, 1–2). Debates among Marxists combined with the ensuing, anti-colonial development of Marxist reflections employed and transformed "according to the precedent of the greatest tricontinental anti-colonial intellectual politicians" (Young 2001, 6). Therefore, "the bulk of anti-colonialist activism and activist writing in the twentieth century has operated from a Marxist perspective", mostly "aware of the significance of subjective conditions for the creation of a revolutionary situation".[13] This perspective remains key when analysing struggles in their current conjuncture, in which discussion of 'the nation' and its goals are also ongoing.

Marxists have thus called for a cautious approach to nationalism as a possibly distracting bourgeois fetishization of nation (Davis 1967, 167). Addressing the national and colonial questions, Lenin (1965 [1920], 145) also criticises the abstract formulation of "equality in general and national equality in particular" of bourgeois democracy as masking structural inequalities, whereas "[t]he real meaning of the demand for equality consists in its being a demand for the abolition of classes." Hence, he argues (*Ibid*), the Communist Party's policy on the national question should rest,

> first, on a precise appraisal of the specific historical situation and, primarily, of economic conditions; second, on a clear distinction between the interests of the oppressed classes, of working and exploited people, and the general concept of national interests as a whole, which implies the interests of the ruling class; third, on an equally clear distinction between the oppressed, dependent and subject nations and the oppressing, exploiting and sovereign nations, in order to counter the bourgeoisdemocratic lies that play down this colonial and financial enslavement of the vast majority of the world's population by an insignificant minority of the richest and advanced capitalist countries, a feature characteristic of the era of finance capital and imperialism. (Lenin 1965, 145).

Many intellectual revolutionaries have thus mobilised nation in both popular agitation and strategic ponderation toward emancipation.[14] Among those eloquently articulating the relevance of nation and national consciousness, two instances of Fanon's

---

Third International—Communist (1919–1943), a more thorough debate of national liberation movements contrasted the bourgeois character of some uses of nation, reactionary nationalism, and its progressive uses (Davis 1965; Anderson 2016; Benner 2018).

[13] Marx and Engels engage with cases as diverse as India, Ireland, Indonesia, Russia, and Poland, promoting solidarity with peoples' struggles for national emancipation (*Ibid*; Davis 1968; Davis 2015). Some argue that developments in Marx and Engels' views on colonialism are disregarded by critics such as Edward Said, who includes Marx among Eurocentric orientalists. While recognising considerable erudition and eloquence in Said's work, Ahmad (1992, 222) contends such charges, like those of determinism and economism, as results of a misplaced emphasis on a premise that Marx ruled capitalism a necessary stage in historical progress, thus condoning colonialism as its bearer for 'backward' societies, and of the limited sample from which these conclusions are drawn then conveyed through a "dismissive hauteur [...] combined in very curious ways with indifference to—possibly ignorance of—how the complex issues raised by Marx's cryptic writings on India have actually been seen in the research of key Indian historians themselves".

[14] As Ahmad (2015, 13) puts it, regarding Fanon's caution, nationalism is "a two-edged sword: absolutely indispensable in uniting the whole people in the fight to overthrow colonial rule and creating a national solidarity out of various religious, linguistic, regional and ethnic groups inside

and Ernesto "Che" Guevara's stances must be recovered, as others, like Lebanon's Mehdi 'Amel, Peru's José Carlos Mariátegui and Guiné-Bissau's Amílcar Cabral, were equally engaged in radical praxis by reflecting on their nations' liberation processes, their societies' concrete realities, and their visions for the future, thus enriching the Marxist revolutionary theory and practice.[15]

Fanon develops a philosophical and practical examination to argue that the legitimacy of a claim made in the nation's name must not be taken for granted. These claims express a dispute for, more than the meaning, the horizon of struggle: "political parties start from living reality and it is in the name of this reality, in the name of the stark facts which weigh down the present and the future of men and women, that they fix their line of action" (Fanon 2001, 167).[16] Even if the idea of nation seems to change, what the party leading the liberation struggle is concerned with "is that the people who are listening understand the need to take part in the fight if, quite simply, they wish to continue to exist" (*Ibid*). In the meantime, "colonialism tries to disarm national demands" and "delay the crystallization of national consciousness", and since no social or economic reforms will ever satisfy the colonised people's aspirations, the regime will return to "its old reflexes, reinforcing police effectives, bringing up troops and setting up a reign of terror which is better adapted to its interests and its psychology" (*Ibid*, 167–168).

---

the national territory; but also an instrumentality that could be used for a transfer of power from the colonial masters not to the colonized people but to the newly emergent national elite, whether that elite was bourgeois or merely bureaucratic".

[15] For instance, Cabral (1979, 253) writes: "We are struggling to build in our countries, in Angola, Mozambique, in Guiné, in the Cape Verde Islands and in S. Tomé, a life of happiness, a life where every man will have the respect of all men, where discipline will not be imposed, where no one will be without work, where salaries will be just, where everyone will have the right to everything that man has built, has created for the happiness of men. It is for this that we are struggling. If we do not reach that point, we shall have failed in our duties, in the purpose of our struggle." For that, "[w]e have in Africa itself examples to follow and we have likewise in Africa examples we must not follow"; and "we are for the total liberation of the African continent from the colonial yoke, since we know that colonialism is an instrument of imperialism [...]; we want in the framework of our struggle to contribute in the most effective way to driving foreign domination from our continent for ever" (*Ibid*, 254).

[16] In this sense, Fanon (2001, pp. 30–31) argues that Marxist analyses of the colonial problem must be adapted due to the colonial arranging of people as 'belonging or not belonging' to a given race or species, with material manifestations: in the colonies, "[t]he cause is the consequence; you are rich because you are white, you are white because you are rich" (*Ibid*). Among Arab Marxists, Mahdi 'Amel—Hassan Abdullah Hamdan (1936–1987)—was also concerned with adaptation, including in relation to a "colonial mode of production" to be grasped. Travelling through the rural areas to talk to agricultural workers, for 'Amil the starting point was the (Arab and Lebanese) concrete reality "as a foundational movement", then engagement with the Marxist thought, not the reverse (Safieddine 2021).

In Africa, as in the Arab world,[17] Fanon writes, colonisers also work "to plant deep in the minds of the native population the idea that before the advent of colonialism their history was one which was dominated by barbarism" (*Ibid*, 168). Diagnosing the "native intellectual's" stages of anguish and emancipation, he argues that "the consciousness and organised undertaking by a colonised people to re-establish the sovereignty of that nation" also gives vitality and validity to culture, thus unleashed toward diverse and new paths —not to be anchored in past traditions, "accompanied by the discovery and encouragement of universalizing values" (*Ibid*, 198–199).[18] Hence, "there is not only the disappearance of colonialism but also the disappearance of the colonized man", and "[t]his new humanity cannot do otherwise than define a new humanism both for itself and for others. It is prefigured in the objectives and methods of the conflict" (*Ibid*). Therefore, against claims that the nation is "a phase that humanity has left behind", Fanon argues that the "national period" must not be skipped (*Ibid*). National consciousness "is the only thing that will give us an international dimension" and it is "national liberation which leads the nation to play its part on the stage of history" (*Ibid*, p. 199).

Che Guevara addressed the UN General Assembly in 1964, soon after the Cuban Revolution overthrew Fulgencio Batista's dictatorship, one that had strong ties to the United States.[19] In his speech, Che Guevara asserted the Cuban people's right to build another type of democracy for a new society and welcomed a new chapter in the history of the UN, which would gain more legitimacy as nations achieving their liberation finally began taking their seats. Noting that their struggles exposed the brutality of European colonialism —mentioning, for instance, the assassination

---

[17] This view resonates in Edward Said's (1978) and Bryan S. Turner's (2014 [1978]) discussions of *orientalism*—ideological and scholastic justifications for dominating foreign lands and peoples based on racial and cultural, essentialised features of backwardness. In 1925, Peruvian Marxist José Carlos Mariátegui (1964, 190) had also stated, rather condescendingly: "In its youthful vanity the Western civilization treated the oriental peoples with disdain and prepotency. The white man considered necessary, natural and legitimate his dominance over the colored man. He used the words oriental and barbarian as equivalents. He thought that only what was Western was civilized. Exploitation and colonization of the Orient was never a trade of intellectuals, but of merchants and warriors. [...] But now that the West, relativist and skeptic, faces its own decadence and foresees its impending twilight, it feels the need to explore and better understand the Orient. Mobilized by a feverish new curiosity, Westerns intern themselves passionately into Asian habits, history and religions" (my translation from Spanish).

[18] For Fanon, the "action of the native intellectual" may be 'limited historically', but it still "contributes greatly to upholding and justifying the action of politicians" (2001, 175). Yet, he cautions that these moves may usher a racialisation of African and Arab claims to the detriment of nationalisation (*Ibid*, 172). Africans and Arabs had to realise that the culture summoned is *national*, that each of "their geographical position and the economic ties of their region were stronger even than the past that they wished to revive" (*Ibid*, 174).

[19] The Revolution is itself inspired by the revolutionary-nationalist and internationalist ideals of the Cuban independence leader José Martí, with a vision of *Nuestra América* ('Our America') as the communion between the colonised peoples of Latin America in struggle for liberation from colonial and imperialist, in solidarity in the way toward emancipation. For that he also saw education as key in the elevation of an emancipatory consciousness. See, for instance, Nassif, Ricardo. 1984. 'Profile: José Martí, 1853–95'. In *Prospects: quarterly review of education* XIV, no. 2, 295–300. https://unesdoc.unesco.org/ark:/48223/pf0000060304.page=120.

of Patrice Lumumba in Congo, for which Belgium was admittedly responsible,[20] Guevara (1964) said: "Our free eyes today open up for new horizons and are able to see what yesterday our condition, as colonized slaves, prevented us from seeing: 'western civilization' hides behind a flashy façade a bunch of hyenas and jackals [...]. A murderous animal that feeds on defenseless peoples; this is what imperialism makes of man, this is what is distinct about the imperial 'white'". As a Marxist, he stated that "the majority is made of the peoples who have their skins burnt by different suns, colored by different pigments, these peoples who have come to fully understand that the difference among men is not on their skin color, but in the form of property of their means of production, in the relations of production".[21] For Che, the UN was under the 'obligation' of supporting the oppressed peoples by showing what the principle of 'peaceful coexistence' meant, instead of condoning the imperialists' version imposed on them (*Ibid*). Yet, he clarified, that principle could never apply to relations between exploiters and exploited, and solidarity was due to those fighting "all forms of colonial oppression" (*Ibid*).

Therefore, drawing from revolutionary explosions such as the French and Russian Revolutions, it is in the reality of struggle that many examine the dialectical development of the principle and right to self-determination (Bowring 2008; Chimni 2017), in contrast to accounts of the principle as written into a new world order inspired, or announced, by US President Woodrow Wilson's 1918 *Fourteen Points* speech, as some like Kissinger (1994) put it. By 1960, the UN General Assembly (UNGA) adopted the Declaration on the Granting of Independence to Colonial Countries and Peoples (A/RES/1514(XV)), giving national self-determination new impetus (Koskenniemi 1994, 241). The declaration deems alien subjugation, domination, and exploitation of peoples as violations of their human rights and of the UN Charter's principles. The right is then spelled out in the 1966 International Covenants on Civil and Political Rights and on Economic, Social, and Cultural Rights (ICCPR and ICESCR) in common Article I: "All peoples have the right to self-determination", meaning that they may "freely determine their political status and freely pursue their economic, social and cultural development", as well as "freely dispose of their

[20] The country's foreign minister admitted to Belgium's part in the assassination of the Congolese liberation leader and first prime minister in 1961; see for instance Ames, Paul. 2002. "Belgium 'sorry' for killing of Lumumba." *The Independent*, February 6, 2002. https://www.independent.co.uk/news/world/europe/belgium-sorry-killing-lumumba-9195253.html.

[21] Quotations from Che Guevara's speech at the UN in 1964 are my translations from Spanish.

natural wealth and resources".[22] UN resolutions and landmark cases in the International Court of Justice (ICJ), such as those related to Namibia, Western Sahara and East Timor, have also stated the right of peoples under foreign occupation to exercise their self-determination and classified this is as an *erga omnes* right (Van den Berg and Nowak 2020, 73), one owed to the entire "international community".[23] It is thus by emphasising this obligation that peoples struggling for national liberation demand other states' and, collectively, the UN's accountability for their situation and engagement for its termination.

Notwithstanding, for some, fundamental limits remain under scrutiny. For instance, the right being promoted was for colonial peoples to achieve independence, preferably leaving borders intact as drawn by colonial powers (Hannum, 1998). In this sense, Rajagopal (2003, 11) writes, 'traditional international law' only engaged with a resistance that is action "directed at the creation of states in the form of movements that asserted the right to self-determination" if it produces sovereignty.[24] Moreover, positing a difference between European and non-European cultures and peoples, "[i]t was only because of colonialism that international law became universal; and the dynamic of difference, the civilizing mission, that produced this result, continues into the present" (Anghie 2006, 742).[25] For that, the doctrine of sovereignty works as a mechanism of expulsion and later inclusion of the non-European into the realm

[22] In Van den Berg and Nowak's (2020) account, self-determination appears as a right in the UN Charter, but it is clarified in the 1948 Universal Declaration of Human Rights, the 1960 Declaration, the ICCPR and ICESCR, the 1970 Declaration on Principles of International Law Concerning Friendly Relations and Cooperation Among States in accordance with the Charter of the United Nations, GA Resolution, and the Declaration on the Occasion of the 50th Anniversary of the UN, GA Resolution 50/6 of 24 October 1995. Shaw (1983, 21) argues that the 1970 Declaration also demonstrates that self-determination has "through practice of a general and a specific nature, attained the status of a legal right and thus, consequently, a legal obligation with respect to the relevant parties". Every state, it was noted, had the duty to promote realisation of the principle and refrain from forcible actions depriving people of this right (*Ibid*).

[23] The idea of an 'international community' hegemonised by the categories and assumptions critiqued in the works cited—e.g., liberal perspectives of democracy and human rights as shared values, essentialising or crystallising these categories as eternally valid and absolute—must also be approached critically.

[24] Still, as pointed out by my anonymous reviewer, the ICJ Advisory Opinion on the Chagos Archipelago of 2019 has been examined, e.g., in its assertion that the right to self-determination was already customary international law by 1968 when Mauritius achieved independence from the United Kingdom, whereas Chagos had been separated from it and remained under British administration, which flouted the implementation of self-determination. See, for instance, Milanovic, Marko. 2019. "ICJ Delivers Chagos Advisory Opinion, UK Loses Badly". *EJIL: Talk!*, February 5, 20. Accessed October 5, 2022. https://www.ejiltalk.org/icj-delivers-chagos-advisory-opinion-uk-loses-badly/

[25] One of the key moments of this process is seen in the concept of *terra nullius* legitimising conquest of "lands inhabited by people regarded as inferior and backward" (Anghie 2006, 745). The concept is for instance used in one of the questions posed to the International Court of Justice (ICJ) in a request for an Advisory Opinion regarding Western Sahara, sent in by the UN at Morocco's initiative. See International Criminal Court, *Western Sahara: Overview of the Case*. Accessed August 15, 2021. https://www.icj-cij.org/en/case/61.

of the international system (*Ibid*).[26] This, Miéville (2006, 260) argues, is the 'empire of sovereignty': peoples' hard-won decolonisation translated into a "juridical form of independent sovereignty" that "imperialism itself tended to universalize".

Grappling with one consequence, Lightfoot and MacDonald (2020) argue that Indigenous peoples' struggle for recognition is set apart from other anti-colonial movements that seek independence. Oppression from settler-colonial states remained neglected, and only after negotiations and pushes from Indigenous councils was a UN Declaration on the Rights of Indigenous Peoples adopted in 2007. It establishes that states must heed to Indigenous peoples' demands for recognition and rights, whereas Indigenous communities adhered to principles of territorial integrity and national sovereignty, without relinquishing the right to self-determination (*Ibid*). Wider implications sought were "the inclusion of a broad set of collective rights into the human rights regime, alongside individual rights", in order to protect Indigenous peoples' "cultures, societies, and existence as distinct peoples" (*Ibid*, 40); to "create means of Indigenous self-determination that do not revolve around or rely on state structures" (*Ibid*, 41); and to provoke changes by "pointing the way toward a future beyond the current Westphalian international system, a liberal construction of human rights, and state-centric diplomacies" (*Ibid*, 43). This also shows how even after being written into international law, not only the right's reach but also its assumptions continue to be challenged through organised, non-state action.

4 Human Rights and Emancipation

The hegemonic liberal framework of human rights has been critiqued for fixing an ahistorical and eternal valence to individual rights that veil their categories' actual location as an exploitative system, capitalism, and their subjects' fundamentally unequal standing, masked in abstractions and generalisations such as 'citizens' (Koskenniemi 2004; Marks 2008 and 2011).[27] The traditional historical account of the emergence of human rights advocacy in the 1970s by the hand of international NGOs, the UN, and Western states and academics —some of "the main authors of the human rights discourse" (Mutua 2001, 202)—has also been problematised. For instance, Mutua questions the 'three-dimensional prism' that these actors constructed regarding a confrontation between 'savages, victims and saviors', pitting good against evil on the base of morality (*Ibid*), while Slaughter (2018, 735), sees that historical

[26] If such mechanisms of expulsion persist, Anghie (2006, 741) argues, "despite the official end of the colonial period, then it might become necessary to rethink the standard accounts of both colonialism and decolonisation".

[27] A Gramscian approach to hegemony considers it a supremacy of a social group and its ideas over others, not necessarily through force, but through concessions in aspects that are not essential to the ruling class's strategy; supremacy manifests through both domination and 'intellectual moral leadership' rested in 'civil society', which in turn is "a system of superstructural institutions that is intermediary between economy and State" (Anderson 1976, 35). For a broad account of the concept's many uses see Anderson (2017).

account in "a restricted Americo-Eurocentric perspective that disregards events and peoples in the rest of the world as makers of human rights history". What happened, he writes, was a "neoliberal hijacking of human rights that delegitimized national self-determination, narrowed international concern to the plight of individual political prisoners, and realigned the moral economy of human rights" (*Ibid*).

Yet, insisting on an agonistic character of rights as achievements of struggle,[28] Bowring (2008, 140) calls for recovering them as tools in a "fight to prevent and seek redress for the violations of human rights", which is, argues that "the principles of contemporary international law and human rights, emerging as they have from revolutionary struggles before and especially after World War II, are not simply rhetoric, nor utopian and impossible prophecies, but real, material weapons of offence and defence in the human fight for emancipation" (Ibid, 208). For Baxi (2008, 79–80), considering human rights 'as insurrectionary praxes', the "violence of the oppressed provide, as much as the violence of the dominant, a matrix for the emergence of human rights norms and standards", whereas "the jurisgenerative potential of violence directed to achieve better futures of human rights may be ignored at considerable peril".[29]

Hence, *consciousness* must be invoked for a strategic and thorough examination of normative assertions about those deemed the most progressive and even radical of claims advanced by forward-looking women and men.[30] Themselves the product of ongoing contention, normative views of human rights function as a sanctioned language (Rajagopal 2003), a discourse, "constitutive mechanisms that help shape relations among human beings" (Gordon 2004, 3). As proclaimed and used by the powerful to promote their agenda through diverse interventions, for Gordon, human rights can also serve to 'entrap' these powers and demand that they live up to their words (*Ibid*). Through this lens, the challenge is to oppose the marginalisation, on the one hand, and the co-optation of human rights "in the service of imperial wars", on the other, because marginalisation means not only retrocession from achievements of "long years of bloody struggle", but also "an attack on an egalitarian worldview" and its replacement "with a hierarchical worldview" (*Ibid*, 5). But since instead of abstractions, as in the liberal-universalist proclamations and discourse spelling rights out in declarations and conventions (*Ibid*, 6), Gordon argues, human rights must be

---

[28] Bowring (2008, 208) writes that "[i]nternational law contains within its principles and concepts the content of world-shaking movements"—i.e., the French and Russian revolutions and the post-World War II anti-colonial struggles, "a content that is capable, sometimes unpredictably, of reappearing with a terrible vengeance for injustice".

[29] Baxi (2008, 124–125) refers to Robert Cover's (1983) distinction between "jurisgenerative" and "jurispathic" violence, citing as examples the juridical translation of the fight and normative campaign against racism and apartheid into the 1963 UN Declaration on the Elimination of All Forms of Racial Discrimination, and the 1973 International Convention on the Suppression and Punishment of the Crime of Apartheid.

[30] For instance, women's push for inclusion in the Universal Declaration of Human Rights (UDHR), and not only that of the most prominent actor, Eleanor Roosevelt, but also women from the South such as Minerva Bernardino, from the Dominican Republic, Hansa Mehta, from India, Begum Shaista Ikramullah, from Pakistan, or in the case of women's inclusion in the 1945 UN Charter, Bertha Lutz from Brazil.

mobilised as the result of real struggle whose subjects' historical situation *is* liminal, so thus too are their views of human rights (*Ibid*, 7).

The contrast between liberal and radical views of rights is visible, for instance, in relation to emancipation as thought of in Marx's and Marxists' discussion of the goals of transformation of social reality. Responding to left liberals' promotion of secular politics and human rights, Marx argued that emancipation would go beyond the state and religion to reach the human relations constituting the reality of civil society (Koskenniemi 2004). First, a distinction must be made "between the material transformation of the economic conditions of production [...] and the legal, political, religious, aesthetic or philosophic—in short, ideological forms in which men become conscious of this conflict and fight it out" (Marx 2010, 92).[31] In this process, the ideological pillars of that social reality are transcended to give way to what Marx considers 'human emancipation', by transforming praxis as a reflexive unity between objectives and methods. This emancipatory praxis is also reflected upon through Gramscian approaches to a practice generating action and thought in and about reality with the aim to transform it (Freire 1978).

Whereas law and human rights are instrumentalised by the powerful to justify and legitimise interventions—colonial, military or otherwise—for some, they remain available for a dialectical development from the margins, the periphery of the capitalist system, and for instrumentalisation for emancipatory goals (Gordon 2004; Baxi 2008; Esmeir 2012; Chimni 2017). Legal rights, "like the other rules of the legal system, turn out to be open to strategic work designed to exploit or to generate gaps, conflicts, and ambiguities in particular cases, with the goal of making legal rules that will favorably dispose ideological stakes" (Kennedy 2002, 197). Knox (2010, 222) thus refers to Lukács' approach to tactics, where "law should always be openly invoked instrumentally and openly subordinated to political considerations, with the particular legal arguments changed whenever the particular political needs change", arguing therefore that "interventions should never be conducted directly in the name of legality". Yet, he ponders that Lukács' approach is a formalist and positivist view of law, and that, consequently, his critique of it "relies on an overly reified distinction between legal and illegal" (*Ibid*), whereas Lukács' legal strategy concerning the decision to 'use' or not to 'use' law thus "almost entirely ignores the fact that very

---

[31] Lukács (2017, 5), citing Marx, argues that in capitalist societies, the process of abstracting concepts from their concrete conditions is common due to the "fetishistic character of economic forms, the reification of all human relations, the constant expansion and extension of the division of labour which subjects the process of production to an abstract, rational analysis, without regard to the human potentialities and abilities of the immediate producers". This process transforms "the phenomena of society and with them the way in which they are perceived", e.g., by isolating facts into separate, specialised 'disciplines', whereas by contrast, "dialectics insists on the concrete unity of the whole" (*Ibid*). Hence the need for humans to become conscious of themselves as social beings, "as simultaneously the subject and object of the socio-historical process", and of reality, "the sensuous world", as "human sensuous activity", Marx argued in his *Theses on Feuerbach* (Ibid, 17). The question of praxis thus becomes clearer with the realisation that social forms have been mystified into natural relations that "appear to be fixed and can be manipulated and even comprehended, but never overthrown", and that social reality is the product of human activity, in turn understood as "crucial for the transformation of existence" (Ibid).

frequently this will *not* be a choice. We are always and already enmeshed in legal relations, and as such it cannot be said that there is a simple 'choice'" (*Ibid*, 223). Therefore, for Knox, "we need to carefully distinguish between law as an institutional phenomenon (or the terrain of juridical practices—courts, tribunals, lawsuits etc.), and the role of law in *framing* political mobilisations. This is because—simply put—law in its former guise is inevitable" (*Ibid*, 224). Others similarly argue that recourse to this instrument must be qualified as a principled, ethical use of a tool, considering its imbued contradictions and opportunities, and that peoples' struggles are not juridical, but political, even though some battles take the judicial form (Sultany 2014; Erakat 2014 and 2019).

As this chapter is concerned with the actual use of human rights as tools in the broader struggle for national liberation, and the ways and instances in which that occurs, it must briefly address another issue related to the judicialisation and bureaucratisation/depoliticisation of people's mobilisation by fitting prescribed forms and procedures. 'Civil society' enters this framework often as a depoliticised technical measure or representation of the collective that does advocacy, or an intermediate "public realm between state, business and family" (Spurk 2010, 8). As a generalising postulate goes, civil society "seen as a sector on its own [...] consists of a huge variety of mainly voluntary organizations and associations that maintain different objectives, interests, and ideologies" (*Ibid*, 6).[32] It is a mark of the liberal framework where the means for organising action are conceived[33] to abstract and essentialise categories that in practice are more diverse and contingent on historical processes that are foreign to the model. Hence, 'civil society' also surfaces as 'an all-purpose catchword for the left' and risks 'becoming an alibi for capitalism' and the associated "conceptual opposition of 'state' and 'civil society'" through the rising preeminence of the role of private property in structuring society (Wood 1990, 60). Yet, Wood (*Ibid*, 61) ponders, "any attempt to dilute the specificity of this 'civil society', to obscure its differentiation from earlier conceptions of 'society', risks disguising the particularity of capitalism itself as a distinct social form with its own characteristic social relations, its own modes of appropriation and exploitation, its own rules of reproduction, its own systemic imperatives".

The specific contours of 'civil society' are disregarded when it is conceptualised as a "universal condition of possibility, promoting a neo-evolutionary ranking of polities

[32] Debate about civil society, and transnational, or 'global civil society', and about democracy and international intervention, in which that category has a prominent place, are wide-ranging and cannot be covered here. For more, see: Kaldor, Mary (2003) *Global Civil Society: An Answer to War*. Cambridge, UK: Polity; Baker, Gideon, David Chandler, eds. 2005. *Global Civil Society: Contested Futures*. New York: Routledge; Colás, Alejandro. 2002. *International Civil Society: Social Movements in World Politics*. Malden, MA: Blackwell Publishers.

[33] For instance, considering how state is organised by the ruling class as 'above' society, civil society is also part of that structure sustaining the capitalist social form, whereas state is the form that represents attempts to crystallise a certain stage of development, a determinate situation, and a set of intellectual categories; representative liberal democracy hence works to legitimise this framework through popular vote, whereas the separation of powers remains of essential importance for political and economic liberalism (Gramsci 2012, 98–99).

according to their degree of 'civic development'" by ignoring its historical development (Bissell 1999, 124).[34] For instance, concerned with the de-historicisation of the concept, Bissell asks: "what shape might civil society assume in social formations that have been produced, to a greater or lesser extent, within the context of colonialism?" (*Ibid*, 125). Moreover, I would add, what are the impacts of a de-historicisation of 'civil society' as framed apart but still having state as a referential, in contexts where the state is not yet fully structured? Notwithstanding the apparent asynchronicity of 'civil society' as conceptualised in the liberal framework and applied to contexts of national liberation struggles, it encompasses various forms of people's organisation in those conditions—from national fronts formed by political parties, trade unions, popular committees, and other associations, to international campaigning networks and advocacy, and more specific tasks such as case-lawyering, all of which accounting for both strategic goals and concerns of daily resistance, or simply put, survival. For instance, from the perspective of legal workers, Lisa Hajjar (1997, 474) argues that differently from "'conventional' or 'client lawyering,' which is tailored to accommodate prevailing arrangements of power, cause lawyering involves the application of professional skills and services to transform some aspect of the status quo", which "implies agency, motivation, social identifications, political relations, and goals". On the other side—or rather because of that— "sociopolitical dynamics affect cause lawyering as opportunities for intervention expand or contract, political alliances shift, and causes become redefined by circumstance or deliberation" (*Ibid*). Hence, studying cause lawyering also "involves analysis of the contours of resistance through the medium of law within a given field of hegemonic relations" (*Ibid*).[35] Another way of framing the use of cases to promote broader goals is 'strategic litigation', whereby human rights organisations or local associations of various kinds

[34] Notably, NGOs and human rights advocacy have been examined as channels and methods/ language of interlocution —although other forms of associations also pass through the cracks— result in the professionalisation—often in an elitist, exclusive sense—and an *NGOization* of popular organisation—as 'technical', 'procedural' forms of organisation that often work to moderate or dilute political demands. For instance, Dianne Otto (2010, 120) writes, in international institutional settings, institutions can still 'turn' activists' ideas 'to their own purposes' (I thank the reviewer for mentioning Otto's work), and Emir Sader (2002, 92) cautions for the uses of NGOs as "agents for neoliberalism within civil society", as intermediaries of donor-countries and financial institutions such as the World Bank.

[35] Another type of practice in trials is that of disruption, or 'rupture', as performed by lawyer Jacques Vergès, who represented, among others, Algerian fighters in the anti-colonial struggle and Palestinian commandos involved in the hijacking of Israeli aeroplanes in the 1960 and 1970s. Vergès used trials to turn the table on courts representing the oppressive regimes by calling into question their own legitimacy, as shown in Barbet Schroeder's documentary film *L'avocat de la terreur* (France, 2007). The tactic is also aimed at shaking dominant narratives at court. See for instance, Hassellind, Filip S., and Mikael Baaz. 2020. "Just another battleground: resisting courtroom historiography in the extraordinary chambers in the courts of Cambodia." *Journal of Political Power* 13, no. 2: 252–267.

litigate an apparently individual case, whose results will benefit a wider endeavour, a community, a cause, and so on.[36]

In this sense, disputing the hegemonic framework of human rights is a task to fulfil in the course of resistance and struggle. Progressive social movements and parties, leftists and socialists, those in the margins, in the system's periphery or in the Global South, have also sought to instil alternative contents into the understanding of justice and rights that require a dispute of the entire ideological engine of that machinery, while fighting to transform the concrete conditions ushering those assumptions and being maintained by force. Yet, it has been emphasised that people often engage in this struggle including while their very survival is at stake, which calls for the "practical realism" noted by Fanon, above. As Angela Davis put it in an interview from prison caught in the 2011 documentary film *The Black Power Mixtape 1967–1975*, "if you're going to talk about a revolutionary situation you have to have people who are physically able to wage revolution, who are physically able to organize and physically able to do all that is done".

5 Palestine and Western Sahara in Struggle for Self-Determination

The cases of Western Sahara and Palestine have long been addressed as similar struggles for national liberation. Palestinians and Saharawis have resisted not only foreign domination and daily violations of their rights, life in forced displacement, exile, and refuge but also the hasty closure of the colonial chapter of world history.[37] As Rana Khoury (2011, 1) puts it, "colonial fumbling" originated both situations, which eventually created "significant refugee populations that would carry the mantle of their liberation movements". Palestine and Western Sahara remain non-sovereign entities even though dozens of countries have recognised the proclaimed State of Palestine and the Saharawi Arab Democratic Republic (SADR).[38] The concept of

[36] TRIAL International, for instance, engages in strategic litigation because "what is needed is systemic change for all victims of the same crimes". See TRIAL International. *Strategic Litigation.* Accessed August 15, 2021. https://trialinternational.org/topics-post/strategic-litigation/. Like TRIAL, some also have as a (meta)goal the progressive advancement of human rights per se, such as the Global Legal Action Network (GLAN), whose stated vision is "to challenge injustice through legal action and improve the lives of the disempowered", in GLAN. *About us.* Accessed June 5, 2022. https://www.glanlaw.org/about-us.

[37] In much of the literature in International Relations and Conflict Studies, and in the diplomatic jargon used by mediators, the cases addressed here are narrated as complex conflicts for opposing territorial claims, where diplomatic negotiations have supposedly been complicated by the parties' attachment to certain premises and other causes of regional and international geopolitical dimensions (Theofilopoulou 2006; Ojeda-García et al 2017).

[38] In SADR's case, it does have control over a smaller portion of Western Sahara, which it achieved through armed struggle, led from 1975 to 1991. In 2020 the Polisario Front decided to undertake efforts to reconstruct the area, as the state's institutions have been consolidated there and, mainly, in the refugee camps in southern Algeria.

terra nullius referred before is applied against claims made by people who, for those occupying their lands, are not really nations. The negation of Palestinians and Saharawis' nationhood was a central piece justifying colonisation of Palestine by the Zionists—aided by British occupation of the region and Mandatory Administration, bestowed by the League of Nations, followed by the proclamation of the State of Israel in 1948 (Masalha 1992; Said 2003; Sayigh 1997; Pappé 2006)—and the Moroccan take-over of the Western Sahara, after Spain hastily left following almost a century of dominance, in 1976, without fulfilling its duty of decolonisation or realisation of a self-determination referendum, as called for by the UN (Zunes and Mundy 2010; Omar 2017; Barreñada 2020).[39] Whereas the Zionist claim that Palestine was "a land with no people for a people without land" served to justify settlement of that 'promised land' by Jews from all over the world—especially from Europe and North America—and the Palestinians' expulsion (Masalha 1992; Pappé 2006), the Moroccan claim is that the Saharawis are a fictitious nation invented by its regional antagonist, Algeria (Ojeda-García et al 2017; Boukhars and Rousselier 2014).[40] For those governing Israel and Morocco's colonial land-grab, those resisting expulsion or compulsory assimilation have no claim or, for that matter, no right to self-determination on that land.

These situations are not identical, but they do share many attributes and goals worth tackling in a correlation. As peoples engaged in similar strategies, Palestinians and Saharawis organised in the Palestine Liberation Organization (PLO) and the Front for the Liberation of Saguía el-Harma y Río de Oro (Polisario) have once held closer ties, a shared history gradually recovered at the level of social movements and civil society associations ever since their antagonists, Morocco and Israel, signed one of the 'normalization agreements' mediated by then US President Donald Trump with Arab countries, in 2020.[41] Moreover, there has been continued support from part of the Palestinian groups, such as the People's Front for the Liberation of Palestine (PFLP) and other organisations and associations, and permanent support from Saharawis to the Palestinian struggle, even at the level of the Polisario Front.

---

[39] The UN had included Western Sahara in its list of non-self-governing territories in 1963, pending decolonisation. Spain instead agreed to and gave way to Morocco's and Mauritania's invasion and occupation (Omar 2017; Ojeda-García et al 2017).

[40] The ICJ was asked, among other things, whether Western Sahara was *terra nullius* when Spain occupied it, but in an Advisory Opinion issued in 1975, it found no evidence of a Moroccan sovereignty over it before the 1880s. Still, Morocco moved to annex and settle the territory through military intervention and the transference of thousands of its civilians (Zoubir 2007; Zunes and Mundy 2010; Ojeda-García et al 2017).

[41] Normalisation with Israel had been conditioned by the League of Arab States in a 2002 Peace Initiative on the end of Israel's occupation of Palestinian and other Arab territories. Allies' normalisation agreements with Israel have deemed by Palestinians as a betrayal; with Morocco's move, the Palestinian plight was brought closer to that of Saharawis. See for instance, Palestinian Center for Policy and Survey Research. 2020. *Public Opinion Poll No 77*, September 9-12, 2020. https://www.pcpsr.org/en/node/819; and Lmrabet, Ali. 2021. "Morocco Lost One of Its 'Sacred' Causes with the Israel Normalization". *Jadaliyya*, January 11, 2021. https://www.jadaliyya.com/Details/42223.

For Palestinians and Saharawis mobilising in advocacy and with whom my research engages, self-determination is the overarching right being violated by Israel and Morocco through the military occupation, colonisation and annexation of their territory[42]; and through the daily violation of a myriad of other civil, political, economic, social and cultural rights of the population under occupation.[43] The colonial roots of the Palestinian and Saharawi plights are not only well exposed but have, in different ways, very concrete manifestation in their daily lives. In order to tackle that as an ongoing process and a structure, the category of settler-colonisation has been growingly adopted in the (Western) scholarly literature to examine the Palestinian case. However, the Zionist movement had already been denounced as a colonialist enterprise by the Palestinians, as noted by the very British Mandate's authorities in reports of their commissions of inquiry into conflict between Arabs and incoming Jewish settlers as early as in the 1920s.[44] Notwithstanding the particularities of the realisation of Zionism, there are similarities between settler-colonialism in European colonies and Palestine, i.e., regarding the centrality of land to secure living conditions for settlers; the tendency toward a 'logic of elimination' of natives, even through 'accommodation'; the 'grammar of race' created to organise elimination and secure access to territory; and the reproduction of a structure "both as complex social formation and as continuity through time" for which 'the native repressed' must be eliminated but also remains (Wolfe 2006, 390). In this and other ways, there are many similarities between the regimes installed by the new occupiers, Israel and Morocco, and their means of population control and repression of continued resistance, as well as internal and external political factors, working to protract both situations (Khoury 2011).[45]

[42] Many have pointed out how these policies and practices constitute violations of IHL, namely the Fourth Geneva Convention's Article 49 about the transfer of population to and from occupied territory, among others, not to mention the very character of an occupation as temporary (Dugard and Reynolds, 2013; Kontorovich, 2017; Erakat, 2019).

[43] Adoption of the category of settler-colonialism has also been a dispute, with some opposing it in different grounds, as noted before—since pro-Israeli wide-ranging allegations that Jews have a promised right to the land, that Jewish institutions had previously bought lands being confiscated by Palestinians, that Palestinians were absent (itself a complicated category in Israeli jurisprudence) and thus abandoned their properties turned into (Israel's) state land, and so on, until apparently neutral or even well intentioned points made to the importance of not abandoning the IHL framework for military occupation, denouncing how Israel's 57-year-old regime on Palestine is already a permanent situation, and that this protraction has only been sustained through the systematic violation of the Palestinians' rights.

[44] Britain's Commission of inquiry on the "Palestine Disturbances of August 1929" reported that "racial animosity on the part of the Arabs, consequent upon the disappointment of their political and national aspirations and fear for their economic future, was the fundamental cause of the outbreak", and that "[t]he Arabs have come to see in the Jewish immigrant not only a menace to their livelihood but a possible overlord of the future" (United Nations Ad Hoc Committee on the Palestinian Question, 1947: para. 41).

[45] Israel occupied what remained of Palestine in the June War of 1967, making for the longest military occupation despite the fact that that is only deemed 'justified' under IHL if temporary and based on military necessity, and used military regulations to confiscate Palestinian land for Jewish

There are also several differences between both struggles, beginning with the place that each takes in the UN agenda (Zoubir 2007; Theofilopoulou 2006; Assis Crivelente 2020). Western Sahara is mainly addressed in the Special Political and Decolonization (Fourth Committee), whereas Palestine entered the agenda as a 'Question' addressed through dedicated items in the General Assembly and Human Rights Council, a special rapporteur on the situation, and a separate refugee agency, the UN Relief and Works Agency for the refugees of Palestine in the Middle East, UNRWA. The Palestine-Israel conflict has gotten much more prominence for various reasons, which include its span of over a century since British occupation and support for the establishment of a 'national home' for Jews in Palestine in 1917; the force of the Zionist movement and its reliance on Britain's then US support; the UN role in the process, starting with the 1947 General Assembly resolution 181 proposing a partition plan that had already been rejected by the Arab population, who saw it as legitimating colonisation and their marginalisation or expulsion by the Zionists; Jerusalem's significance for the Muslim world; and the regional dimension of the conflict between Israel and Arab neighbours such as Syria and Lebanon (Sayigh 1997; Khalidi 2006; Pappé 2006). On the other hand, after decades of armed struggle (1975–1991), a UN—African Union Peace Plan was initiated and a cease-fire adopted for the realisation of a referendum, to be overseen by the UN Mission for the Referendum on Western Sahara (MINURSO) then established. The consultation was never held and Morocco retracted from the commitment, instead offering autonomy to what would become a Moroccan Sahara (Zartman 2014, 66–67). Although world leaders such as US and UN representatives have welcomed the offer as a diplomatic effort from Morocco to overcome the stalemate, Saharawis have rejected the call to forfeit their right to self-determination by accepting a plan that eliminated independence as a choice (*Ibid*). Amidst growing frustration for the persistence of the status quo, the unheeded calls for international protection for Saharawis under Moroccan occupation and the continuing breach of the demilitarised zone between the occupied and the liberated territories by Moroccan trucks culminated in a protest by Saharawis in the liberated territory that was targeted by Moroccans, in November 2020, and Polisario's decision to return to armed struggle.

Yet, in similar practical terms, Palestinians and Saharawis, both as civil society, through various organisations and associations, and as national fronts—the PLO and the Polisario Front—have also adopted legal tactics, for instance, by bringing cases before European national and regional courts—challenging the commercialisation of their resources exploited by the occupiers, or of products manufactured on settlements in occupied lands (Barreñada 2020; Naili 2021); and human rights advocacy by denouncing arbitrary detention, torture, phony trials, land confiscation, the socio-economic consequences of discrimination, and much more, at the UN bodies and international agencies and organisations (Hajjar, 1997; Erakat, 2019).[46] Much

settlement and to contain the population in a "complex matrix of control" that include military orders inherited from the British Mandate (Halper 2015; Khalili 2010).

[46] These include the UN Human Rights Council—the work which I have accompanied in 2017 and 2018 for my research, the Committee on the Elimination of Discrimination against Women

of these tactics and their implications for strategy were and remain under consideration. In Palestine's case, for instance, Noura Erakat (2019, 97–98) describes as 'pragmatic revolutionaries' those leading the PLO's first official engagement with the UN in the 1970s, which she deems a move 'full of ambiguity' because while it "embodied the culmination of a struggle to achieve recognition as a people entitled to self-determination", it also "suggested the acceptance of a state-centric global order and a bid to establish a Palestinian state". Regarding Western Sahara, Meriem Naili (2021, 2) writes, "the battleground shifted from the international legal principle of self-determination to one of its components—the right to access natural resources—to the point of endangering the pursuit of the underlying goal of self-determination". Still, she underscores the relevance of contesting the exploitation of natural resources by the occupying Moroccan regime as a means to, e.g., reject the legitimacy regime's legitimacy—which attempted to use investment and development plans for its legitimation—and to expose the policy's effects on the prevention of Saharawi self-determination (*Ibid*, 4).

Another tactic centred on the juridical, but also political ground of struggle, is promoting the category of analysis and the legal framework of apartheid to describe Israel's discriminatory regime against the Palestinians, already conceived as a crime against humanity (Tilley 2012; Dugard and Reynolds 2013; Erakat 2019), as shown by Palestinian organisations such as Al-Haq, BADIL, and others (Al-Haq and Badil 2019); in reports, legal opinion or position papers issued between 2020 and 2022 by international and Israeli NGOs such as Human Rights Watch, Amnesty International, Yesh Din and B'Tselem[47]; as former and current UN Special Rapporteurs John Dugard, Richard Falk, Michael Lynk, and Francesca Albanese have discussed[48]; and previous reports and campaigns by Palestinian and solidary organisations and experts had been debating and denouncing (BADIL 2009; BADIL 2011). These endeavours have looked at "Israel's discriminatory laws, policies, and practices,

(CEDAW), the International Labor Organization (ILO), and more. See, for instance, Al-Haq. 2017. "Al-Haq Submits to the CEDAW Committee Regarding Israel's Sixth Periodic Report." *Al-Haq,* October 25, 2017. Accessed October 5, 2022. https://www.alhaq.org/advocacy/6312.html.

[47] For instance: Yesh Din. 2020. *The Occupation of the West Bank and the Crime of Apartheid: Legal Opinion.* July 7, 2020. Accessed October 5, 2022. https://www.yesh-din.org/en/the-occupation-of-the-west-bank-and-the-crime-of-apartheid-legal-opinion/; B'Tselem. 2021. *A regime of Jewish supremacy from the Jordan River to the Mediterranean Sea: This is apartheid.* January 12, 2021. https://www.btselem.org/publications/fulltext/202101_this_is_apartheid; Human Rights Watch. 2021. *A Threshold Crossed: Israeli Authorities and the Crimes of Apartheid and Persecution.* April 27, 2022. https://www.hrw.org/report/2021/04/27/threshold-crossed/israeli-authorities-and-crimes-apartheid-and-persecution; Amnesty International. 2022. *Israel's Apartheid Against the Palestinians: Cruel system of domination and crime against humanity,* February 1, 2022. https://www.amnesty.org/en/documents/mde15/5141/2022/en/.

[48] For instance, Falk, Richard. 2014. Report of the Special Rapporteur on the situation of human rights in the Palestinian territories occupied since 1967, Richard Falk (A/HRC/25/67). United Nations General Assembly. https://documents-dds-ny.un.org/doc/UNDOC/GEN/G14/101/98/PDF/G1410198.pdf; Albanese, Francesca. 2022. Report of the Special Rapporteur on the situation of human rights in the Palestinian territories occupied since 1967, Francesca Albanese (A/77/356). United Nations General Assembly. https://documents-dds-ny.un.org/doc/UNDOC/GEN/N22/598/03/PDF/N2259803.pdf.

as rooted in Israel's settler-colonial enterprise in Palestine through the definition of the crime of apartheid in international criminal law", a regime "embedded in a system of impunity" for crimes that "underpin Israel's continued domination over the Palestinian people as a whole, through erasure and fragmentation, including the denial of Palestinian refugee return, restrictions on freedom of movement and residence, and the closure of Jerusalem and the Gaza Strip, coupled with ongoing policies and practices of demographic manipulation and population transfer" (Al-Haq and BADIL 2019, 2). To sustain it, Israel has "create[ed] institutions, 'legal' pretexts, coercive environments, and violent means designed to drive population transfer and undermine the Palestinian people's will and capacity to challenge the apartheid regime" (*Ibid*). The regime encompasses what remained of the Palestinian territory under Palestinian Administration, Israel's Palestinian citizens or residents, and against those Palestinians physically absent, as refugees and as exiled, since their return is also either impeded or conditioned by Israel (Erakat 2019).

Applying apartheid as category of analysis and as legal framework, Lana Tatour and Yara Hawari (2021), like others, warn, brings both opportunities and issues for the continuing unveiling of the nature of the Israeli regimes' policies against Palestinians. Propelling the claim for rights by exposing their systematic violation within that regime, the move has also spurred concerns with at least two significant aspects: first, using the framework to demand civil rights can tend to the abstraction of a fight for equality under a reality of colonisation; second, the framework's adoption under certain terms—for instance, only in reference to the occupied West Bank, while the Palestinians in Gaza, in Israel and in the exile are also affected by this regime—has functioned to continue excluding those neglected and water down, or even dismiss, the denunciation of the settler-colonial structure that apartheid works to sustain.[49]

It is with these and related concerns in view that appeals for a conscientious use of international law and human rights continue to be heard, for the fulfilment of rights, hopefully "to counter hegemony if it is deployed strategically in furtherance of a broader political project" (Erakat, 2014: 1). Practitioners have thus been called on to consider that law's value and potential are "contingent on the broader political framework that gives it meaning", to beware of the "illusion of progress based on the approximation of rights without substance" (*Ibid*). This realisation affects the unveiling of the 'illusion of universality' (Reynolds and Xavier 2016, 961; Eslava

[49] Some of the reports and discussions mentioned focus on the territory under Israel's military occupation—thus neglecting the effects of Israel's policies on over six million refugees prevented from returning and on about 20% of its own population, Palestinians holding Israeli citizenship or residence permits to live in Jerusalem, but subjected to numerous forms of systematic discrimination, most clearly demonstrated in 2018 through the adoption of a Basic Law Israel: Nation-State of the Jewish People, which expressly stated that the right to self-determination was exclusive to Jews and, among other things, that settlement (on occupied Palestinian land) is a 'national value'. Palestinian Member of the Knesset (MK) Aida Touma-Sliman, of the Joint List coalition, writes for The Guardian that then Israel's Prime Minister Benjamin Netanyahu will be known as "the first prime minister of Israeli apartheid" (Touma-Sliman 2018): "For Netanyahu and his government, we are existential threats to be fought or internal enemies to be purged, never equal members in a democratic society".

and Pahuja 2011) and hegemonic views of legitimacy (Rajkovic et al. 2016), by acknowledging that law does play a role in political conflicts, although this role's nature remains under question (Sultany 2011).

6 Horizons to Strive for

Many have drawn attention to the necessary definition of the status of (international) law in struggles that are eminently political if they are to uphold a radical, transformative, and emancipatory strategy. Whereas the very goal of liberation in order to establish independent nation-states has been critiqued as one confined to the liberal-bourgeois form of national-statist organisation of societies, national liberation, from the perspective of many in the Global South, or the Third World, has also been pondered as a condition for further emancipation and for people's entrance into the international system as the subjects of their own history. This view involves identifying the particular histories and objective conditions of each case, i.e., the characteristics of social formations resulting from the stage of capitalist development in those places, the main characteristics of the process of colonisation or imperialist domination, and so forth. These are key topics that have been covered by Fanon and many others, mindful of the particularities of their own struggles and often rejecting models that ultimately hinder their strategies.

This chapter looked at the intersection between national liberation struggles as strategies and the mobilisation of international law and human rights as tactics for the accomplishment of that goal. In this sense, it set out to identify some of the main challenges that the choice for using international law and human rights brings to people currently mobilising in these struggles. As it was not a purely theoretical exercise, it drew from ongoing research on what has been termed as protracted, intractable conflicts: the struggles of Palestine and Western Sahara for self-determination against the military occupation and colonisation of their territories by Israel and Morocco. Still, the chapter explored conceptual and practical challenges that extrapolate these cases, by drawing on the examinations of the role of nation and of human rights in anti-colonial and 'third-worldist' struggles. It is inspired by the need for assessing contradictions and opportunities in hegemonic liberal conceptions of human rights in order to achieve substantive advancements in the way to overthrow enduring regimes of oppression. It hence overviewed practical issues aiming to contribute with discussions on the reasons for the tactical adoption or contestation of the hegemonic framework of human rights.

The issue has direct implication for international politics as ways to challenge narratives and procedures that keep people constrained in paradigms. This has been the case of both Palestine and Western Sahara, for which decade-long diplomatic processes have only worked to sustain and entrench colonisation, and gradually dilute the Palestinians' and Saharawis' right to self-determination. This has most visibly happened at least since the 1980s with the initiation of negotiations for the 1990s 'Oslo Accords', which have not culminated in the creation of the amputated but independent Palestine State by the end of that decade, as promised; and since the same period, when a cease-fire froze direct confrontation for the realisation of a referendum in Western Sahara, which was not held and has been reviewed for elimination of the option of independence in favour of autonomy. In both cases, Palestinians and Saharawis have been asked to make compromises in order to overcome a stalemate created by the very parameters of talks, beginning with bargaining the terms of self-determination and thus relativising that right. The fact that Polisario again took up arms against Morocco shows that the prevailing illusion of 'calm and stability' was really never that for Saharawis or the region. In Palestine, the repetition of Israel's military offensives against the besieged Gaza Strip; the looming threat of de jure annexation of Palestinian territory; and the blatant institutionalisation of Israel's oppression and discrimination of the Palestinian population, have propelled the regime's classification as one of apartheid. For those scrutinising Israel's policies and regulations for controlling the people through exclusion, expulsion, and fragmentation under ongoing colonisation, these practices and policies have nullified the solution pursued by the UN since 1947: the establishment of the State of Palestine beside Israel.

These are, hence, struggles for self-determination and resistance to military occupation and colonisation structured by national, racial, and class oppression, and sustained in an imperialist international system in which law has different implications in different cases. Considering some of these struggles' protraction, even when goals are apparently supported in international law and the established norm of modern international relations, such as national self-determination, this chapter engaged with discussions of tactics and strategy that question the limits and opportunities in hegemonic frameworks of international law, especially human rights. This chapter showed that critical scholars and practitioners of all types of activities geared to the transformation of oppressive realities have argued that this framework's concepts, rules and procedures are the products of historical processes, not eternally valid principles of natural law, and are thus open to instrumentalisation—for oppression or for emancipatory goals. Hence why international law, and human rights in particular, as a tool, must be mobilised conscientiously, with advocates minding its contradictions while taking or creating opportunities and the conditions for the advancement of the struggle for national liberation and for emancipation.

References

Abi-Saab, Georges. 2016. The Third World intellectual in praxis: Confrontation, participation, or operation behind enemy lines? *Third World Quarterly* 37 (11): 1957–1971. https://doi.org/10.1080/01436597.2016.1212653.

Achcar, Gilbert. 2013. *Marxism, orientalism, cosmopolitanism*. London: Saqi Books.

Ahmad, Aijaz. 1992. *In theory: classes, nations, literatures*. London and New York: Verso.

Al-Haq, Addameer, BADIL, Civic Coalition for Palestinian Rights in Jerusalem, Palestinian Center for Human Rights. 2019. *Joint Parallel Report to CERD on Israel's 17th–19th Periodic Reports*. United Nations Committee on the Elimination of Racial Discrimination—CERD. Geneva: Office of the High Commissioner for Human Rights. Accessed June 6, 2022. https://tbinternet.ohchr.org/Treaties/CERD/Shared%20Documents/ISR/INT_CERD_NGO_ISR_39700_E.pdf

Amin, Samir. 1989. *Eurocentrism: modernity, religion, and democracy. a critique of eurocentrism and culturalism.* Translated by Russel Moore and James Membrez. New York: Monthly Review Press

Anderson, Kevin B. 2016. *Marx at the margins: On nationalism, ethnicity, and non-Western societies*, 2nd ed. Chicago: The University of Chicago Press.

Anderson, Perry. 2017. *The H-Word: The Peripeteia of Hegemony.* London: Verso Books.

Anderson, Perry. 1976. The antinomies of antonio gramsci. *New Left Review* I, (100) (November-December): 5–78

Anghie, Antony. 2006. The evolution of international law: colonial and postcolonial realities. *Third World Quarterly* 27(5): 739–753. JSTOR. https://www.jstor.org/stable/4017775

Assis Crivelente, Moara. 2020. Self-Determination as Resistance: Sahrawis and Palestinians Struggle for the UN. In *The United Nations: Friend or Foe of Self-Determination?* ed Jacob R. Avgustin, 109–126. Bristol: E-International Relations. https://www.e-ir.info/publication/the-united-nations-friend-or-foe-of-self-determination/

Boukhars, Anouar and Jacques Rousselier, eds. 2014. *Perspectives on Western Sahara: Myths, Nationalisms and Geopolitics.* Lanham: Rowman and Littlefield

BADIL. 2009. Editorial: Holding Israel accountable—Yes we can. *Al-Majdal* 41: 2–3. Accessed October 5, 2022. https://www.badil.org/cached_uploads/view/2021/05/06/al-majdal-41-1620308679.pdf

BADIL. 2011. Editorial: Towards a comprehensive analysis of Israeli Apartheid." *Al-Majdal* 47: 2–5. Accessed October 5, 2022. https://www.badil.org/phocadownload/Badil_docs/publications/al-majdal47.pdf

Barreñada, Isaías. 2020. Los conflictos de larga duración no resueltos, un desafío para la comunidad internacional. Los casos de Israel-Palestina y de Marruecos-Sahara Occidental. In *El sistema internacional del siglo XXI. Dinámicas, actores y relaciones internacionales*, ed. Paloma González del Miño, 389–410. Valencia: Tirant Lo Blanch

Baxi, Upendra. 2008. *The future of human rights*, 3rd ed. New Delhi: Oxford University Press.

Benner, Erica. 2018. *Really existing nationalisms: a post-communist view from Marx and Engels.* London: Verso.

Bissell, William Cunningham. 1999. Colonial constructions: Historicizing debates on civil society in Africa. In *Civil Society and the Political Imagination in Africa: Critical Perspectives*, ed. John L. Comaroff and Jean Comaroff, 124–159. Chicago: University of Chicago Press.

Bowring, Bill. 2008. *The degradation of the international legal order? the rehabilitation of law and the possibility of politics.* New York: Routledge-Cavendish.

Brittain, Victoria. 2001. Ben Barka killed with French help. *The Guardian.* Accessed October 10, 2022. https://www.theguardian.com/world/2001/jul/02/victoriabrittain

Cabral, Amílcar. 1979. *Unity and Struggle.* Translated by Michael Wolfers. New York: Monthly Review Press

Chatterjee, Partha. 1986. *Nationalist thought and the colonial world: A derivative discourse.* London: Zed Books.

Chimni, Bhupinder. 2017. *International law and world order: a critique of contemporary approaches.* Cambridge: Cambridge University Press.

Davis, Horace B. 1965. Nations, colonies and social classes: The Position of Marx and Engels. *Science & Society* 29 (1) (Winter): 26–43. JSTOR. https://www.jstor.org/stable/40401093

Davis, Horace B. 1967. Lenin and Nationalism: The redirection of the marxist theory of nationalism, 1903–1917. *Science & Society* 31(2) (Spring): 164–185. JSTOR. http://www.jstor.org/stable/40401274

Davis, Mike. 2015. Marx's lost theory: The politics of nationalism in 1848. *New Left Review* 93 (May-June): 45–66

Dugard, John, and John Reynolds. 2013. Apartheid, international law, and the occupied Palestinian Territory. *The European Journal of International Law* 24 (3): 867–913. https://doi.org/10.1093/ejil/cht045.

Erakat, Noura. 2019. *Justice for some: law and the question of Palestine*. Stanford: Stanford University Press.

Erakat, Noura. 2014. What role for law in the Palestinian struggle for liberation?" *Al-Shabaka Policy Brief*. https://al-shabaka.org/briefs/what-role-law-palestinian-struggle-liberation/

Eslava, Luis, and Sundhya Pahuja. 2011. Between resistance and reform: TWAIL and the Universality of International Law. *Trade, Law and Development* 3 (1): 103–130.

Esmeir, Sameera. 2012. *Juridical humanity: a colonial history*. Stanford: Stanford University Press.

Fanon, Frantz. 2001. *The Wretched of the Earth.* Translated by Constance Farrington. London: Penguin Classics

Freire, Paulo. 1978. *Pedagogia do Oprimido*, 6th ed. Rio de Janeiro: Paz e Terra.

Gordon, Neve. 2004. *From the margins of globalization: critical perspectives on human rights.* Lanham: Lexington Books.

Gramsci, Antonio. 1971. *Selections from the Prison Notebooks.* Edited and translated Quentin Hoare and Geoffrey Nowell Smith. London: Lawrence Wishart

Gramsci, Antonio. 2012. *Gramsci: Poder, Política e Partido.* Translated by Eliana Aguiar and edited by Emir Sader. São Paulo: Expressão Popular

Guevara, Ernesto "Che". 2005. Socialism and man in Cuba." In *The Che Reader*, ed. David Deutschmann, 212–227. Wayside: Ocean Press. https://www.marxists.org/archive/guevara/1967/che-reader/che-reader.pdf

Guevara, Ernesto. 1964. Discurso ante la Asamblea General de las Naciones Unidas del Representante de la República de Cuba. Youtube video, 6:20, posted by "UNESCOenEspañol", May 14, 2012. https://www.youtube.com/watch?v=UgADsWjSxQo

Hajjar, Lisa. 1997. Cause Lawyering in Transnational Perspective: National Conflict and Human Rights in Israel/Palestine. *Law & Society Review* 31(3): 473–504. JSTOR. https://www.jstor.org/stable/3054043

Halper, Jeff. 2015. *War against the people: Israel, the Palestinians and Global Pacification.* London: Pluto Press.

Hannum, Hurst. 1998. The right of self-determination in the twenty-first century. *Washington and Lee Law Review* 55(3): 773–780. https://scholarlycommons.law.wlu.edu/wlulr/vol55/iss3/8

Hobsbawm, Eric. 1992. *Nations and nationalism since 1780: Program, myth, reality*, 2nd ed. Cambridge: Cambridge University Press.

Kennedy, Duncan. 2002. The critique of rights in critical legal studies. In *Left legalism/left critique*, ed. Wendy Brown and Janet Halley, 178–228. New York: Duke University Press. https://doi.org/10.1515/9780822383871-007

Khalidi, Rashid. 2006. *The iron cage: the story of the Palestinian struggle for statehood*. Boston: Beacon Press.

Khalili, Laleh. 2010. The location of Palestine in Global Counterinsurgencies. *International Journal of Middle East Studies*, 42: 413–433. https://doi.org/10.1017/S0020743810000425.

Khoury, Rana B. 2011. Western Sahara and Palestine: A comparative study of colonialisms, occupations, and nationalisms. *New Middle Eastern Studies*, (1): 1–20. http://www.brismes.ac.uk/nmes/archives/321

Kissinger, Henry. 1994. *Diplomacy*. New York: Simon & Schuster.

Knox, Robert. 2010. Strategy and tactics. *Finnish Yearbook of International Law* 21: 193–229.

Kontorovich, Eugene. 2017. Unsettled: A global study of settlements in occupied territory. *Journal of Legal Analysis* 9 (2): 285–350.

Koskenniemi, Martti. 2004. What should international lawyers Learn from Karl Marx? *Leiden Journal of International Law* 17: 229–246. https://doi.org/10.1017/S0922156504001803.

Koskenniemi, Martti. 1994. National self-determination today: problems of legal theory and practice. *The International and Comparative Law Quarterly* 43(2): 241–269. http://www.jstor.org/stable/761238

Lenin, Vladimir. 1965. Preliminary draft theses national and colonial questions—for the second congress of the communist international." In *Collected Works* 31, ed. and translated Julius Katzer, 144–151. Moscow: Progress Publishers. https://www.marxists.org/archive/lenin/works/cw/pdf/lenin-cw-vol-31.pdf

Lenin, Vladimir I. 1964. Imperialism, the highest stage of capitalism. In *Collected Works* 22, ed and translated Julius Katzer, 185–304. Moscow: Progress Publishers. https://www.marxists.org/archive/lenin/works/cw/pdf/lenin-cw-vol-22.pdf

Lightfoot, Sheryl and David MacDonald. 2020. The United Nations as both foe and friend to indigenous peoples and self-determination. In *The United Nations: Friend or Foe of Self-Determination?* ed. Jacob R. Avgustin, 32–46. Bristol: E-International Relations. https://www.e-ir.info/publication/the-united-nations-friend-or-foe-of-self-determination/

Lukács, Georg. 2014. *Tactics and Ethics, 1919–1929.* Translated by Michael McColgan. London and New York: Verso

Lukács, Georg. 2017. *History and class consciousness.* United States: Bibliotech Press. ISBN 978-1-61895-230-1

Mariátegui, José Carlos. 1964. *La Escena Contemporánea* 1. Lima: Biblioteca Amauta. https://www.archivochile.com/Ideas_Autores/mariategui_jc/s/Tomo1.pdf

Marks, Susan. 2008. Exploitation as an international legal concept. In *International Law on the Left: Re-examining Marxist Legacies*, ed. Susan Marks, 281–308. Cambridge: Cambridge University Press.

Marks, Susan. 2011. Human rights and root causes. *The Modern Law Review* 74 (1): 57–78.

Marx, Karl. 2010. Preface to A contribution to the critique of political economy. In *Marx today: Selected works and recent debates*, ed. John F. Sitton, 89–94. New York: Palgrave Macmillan.

Marx, Karl. 2013. *Capital: A Critical Analysis of Capitalist Production, Vol. 1.* Translated by Samuel Moore and Edward Avelin. Ware, Hertfordshire: Wordsworth Editions

Masalha, Nur. 1992. *Expulsion of the Palestinians: The concept of "transfer" in zionist political thought, 1882–1948.* Washington: Institute for Palestine Studies.

Miéville, China. 2006. *Between equal rights: a marxist theory of international law.* Chicago: Haymarket Books.

Mutua, Makau WA. 2001. Savages, victims, and saviors: the metaphor of human rights. *Harvard International Law Journal* 42 (1): 201–245.

Naili, Meriem. 2021. Defeating illegal trade in Western Sahara: corporations under pressure from NGOs. *The Journal of North African Studies,* 1-25. https://doi.org/10.1080/13629387.2021.1917124

Ojeda-García, Raquel, Irene Fernández-Molina, and Victoria Veguilla, eds. 2017. *Global, regional and local dimensions of Western Sahara's protracted decolonization: When a conflict gets old.* New York: Palgrave Macmillan.

Omar, Emboirik Ahmed. 2017. *El movimiento nacionalista saharaui: de Zemla a la Organización de la Unidad Africana.* Las Palmas: Mercurio Editorial

Otto, Dianne. 2010. Power and danger: Feminist engagement with international law through the UN Security Council. U of Melbourne Legal Studies Research Paper No. 497. *Australian Feminist Law Journal* 32: 97–121.

Pappé, Ilan. 2006. The 1948 ethnic cleansing of Palestine. *The Journal of Palestine Studies* 36 (1): 6–20.

Pappé, Ilan. 2008. Zionism as colonialism: a comparative view of diluted colonialism in Asia and Africa. *South Atlantic Quarterly* 107 (4): 611–633. https://doi.org/10.1215/00382876-2008-009.

Pautasso, Diego, Gaio Doria and Marcelo Fernandes. 2019. "Marxism and the National Question: Domenico Losurdo's Contribution to the Dialectics of the National and International". *International Critical Thought*: 1–s18. https://doi.org/10.1080/21598282.2019.1695533

Prashad, Vijay. 2007. *The darker nations: a people's history of the third world.* New York: The New Press.

Rajagopal, Balakrishnan. 2003. International law and social movements: challenges of theorizing resistance. *Columbia Journal of Transnational Law* 41 (2): 397–433.
Rajkovic, Nikolas M., Tanja Aalberts and Thomas Gammeltoft-Hansen. 2016. Introduction: Legality, interdisciplinarity and the study of practices." In *The Power of legality practices of international law and their politics*, ed. Nikolas M. Rajkovic, Tanja Aalberts and Thomas Gammeltoft-Hansen, 1–26. Cambridge: Cambridge University Press. https://doi.org/10.1017/CBO9781316535134.002
Rejai, Mostafa and Cynthia Enloe. 1969. Nation-States and State-Nations. *International Studies Quarterly* 13(2): 140–158. JSTOR. https://www.jstor.org/stable/3013942
Rejai, Mostafa. 1969. Periodization of nationalism: A Postscript. *Social Science* 44(1): 20–26. JSTOR. https://www.jstor.org/stable/41959421
Reynolds, John, and Sujith Xavier. 2016. The dark corners of the world': Twail and international criminal justice. *Journal of International Criminal Justice* 14: 959–983. https://doi.org/10.1093/jicj/mqw053.
Rupert, Mark, and Hazel Smith. 2002. *Historical materialism and globalization.* London and New York: Routledge.
Safieddine, Hicham. 2021. Mahdi Amel: On colonialism, sectarianism and hegemony. *Middle East Critique* 30 (1): 41–56. https://doi.org/10.1080/19436149.2021.1876397.
Said, Edward. 1978. *Orientalism.* London and Henley: Routledge & Kegan Paul.
Said, Edward. 2003. *The question of Palestine.* New York: Vintage Books.
Sayigh, Yezid. 1997. *Armed struggle and the search for state: the Palestinian national movement, 1949–1993.* Oxford: Clarendon Press.
Serfaty, Abraham. 1992. *Dans les Prisons du Roi: Écrits de Kenitra sur le Maroc.* Messidor Éditions sociales Paris.
Shaw, Malcolm. 1983. The international status of national liberation movements. *The Liverpool Law Review* 5 (1): 19–34.
Slaughter, Joseph. 2018. Hijacking human rights: Neoliberalism, the new historiography, and the end of the third world. *Human Rights Quarterly* 40 (4): 735–775.
Spurk, Christoph. 2010. Understanding civil society. In *Civil society and peace-building: a critical assessment*, ed. Thania Paffenholz, 3–28. Boulder: Lynne Rienner Publishers.
Sultany, Nimer. 2014. Activism and legitimation in Israel's jurisprudence of occupation. *Social & Legal Studies* 23 (3): 315–339.
Sultany, Nimer. 2011. Roundtable on occupation law: part of the conflict or the solution? (Part V: Nimer Sultany). *Jadaliyya.* Accessed August 15, 2021. https://www.jadaliyya.com/Details/24424
Tatour, Lana and Yara Hawari. 2020. Limitations and possibilities of the apartheid framework with Lana Tatour. *Rethinking Palestine,* Al-Shabaka podcast, 27:00. https://podcasts.apple.com/us/podcast/limitations-and-possibilities-of-the/id1537774938?i=1000507182508
Theofilopoulou, Anna. 2006. "The United Nations and Western Sahara: A Never-ending Affair." *Special Report* 166. Washington: United States Institute of Peace. https://www.usip.org/sites/default/files/sr166.pdf
Tilley, Virginia, ed. 2012. *Beyond occupation: apartheid, colonialism and international law in the occupied Palestinian Territories.* London: Pluto Press.
Touma-Sliman, Aida. 2018. "Netanyahu will be known as the first prime minister of Israeli apartheid." *The Guardian.* Accessed August 15, 2021. https://www.theguardian.com/commentisfree/2018/jul/23/netanyahu-israeli-apartheid-palestinians-nation-state-law
Tuck, Eve and K. Wayne Yang. 2012. "Decolonization is not a metaphor." *Decolonization: Indigeneity, Education & Society* 1(1): 1–40
Turner, Bryan. 2014. *Marx and the end of orientalism.* New York: Routledge.
Van den Berg, Charis and Tobias Nowak. 2020. "Alternative Approaches to Self-determination applied to the Cyprus Conflict." In *The United Nations: Friend or Foe of Self-Determination?*, ed. Jacob R. Avgustin, 70–85. Bristol: E-International Relations. https://www.e-ir.info/publication/the-united-nations-friend-or-foe-of-self-determination/

Wolfe, Patrick. 2006. Settler colonialism and the elimination of the native. *Journal of Genocide Research* 8 (4): 387–409. https://doi.org/10.1080/14623520601056240.
Wood, Ellen Meiksins. 1990. "The Uses and Abuses of 'Civil Society'." *Socialist Register 1990: The Retreat of the Intellectuals* 26: 60–84. https://socialistregister.com/index.php/srv/article/view/5574
Young, Robert J. 2001. *Postcolonialism: An historical introduction.* Oxford: Blackwell.
Zartman, I. William. 2014. "Morrocco's Saharan Policy." In *Perspectives on Western Sahara: Myths, Nationalisms and Geopolitics*, ed. Anouar Boukhars and Jacques Roussellier, 55–70. Lanham: Rowman and Littlefield
Zoubir, Yahia H. 2007. Stalemate in Western Sahara: Ending international legality. *Middle East Policy* 14 (4): 158–177.
Zreik, Raef. 2008. The persistence of the exception: some remarks on the story of israeli constitutionalism. In *Thinking Palestine*, ed. Ronit Lentin, 137–147. London: Zed Books.
Zunes, Stephen, and Jacob Mundy. 2010. *Western Sahara: war, nationalism, and conflict irresolution.* New York: Syracuse University Press.

Un Documents

A/RES/1514(XV). United Nations General Assembly. 1960. Declaration on the granting of independence to colonial countries and peoples. Available from https://www.un.org/ga/search/view_doc.asp?symbol=A/RES/1514(XV)
United Nations Ad Hoc Committee on the Palestinian Question. 1947. Political History of Palestine under British Administration—UK memorandum. Communication from the United Kingdom Delegation to the United Nations. https://www.un.org/unispal/document/auto-insert-185776/

Towards Decolonial Agenda for Transitional Justice: "The Old is Dying and the New Cannot Be Born"

Selbi Durdiyeva

Abstract It is argued that transitional justice is more culturally sensitive than its international human rights law counterpart. It is so due to the prominent role played by social movements in transitions and the relatively recent emergence of the field from what would be considered transitions in the 'Global South'. Moreover, individuals and civil society arguably play a greater role in norm creation in transitional justice than in international law. Nevertheless, the impact of coloniality and colonialism on societies reckoning with the past received only marginal attention in transitional justice practice and scholarship. Although critical approaches to transitional justice address the shortcomings of paradigmatic transitions to peace and liberal democracies, they fail to address the harm caused by colonialism, post-colonialism, and coloniality. When transitional justice is reluctant to engage with the decolonial agenda, it risks becoming complicit in promulgating colonial, post-colonial, and neo-colonial dynamics. Transitional justice's agenda should engage in the issues of decolonisation where decolonisation is viewed as a commitment that informs the practice and scholarship on all levels rather than looking at postcolonial situation symptomatically. To outline the state of the problem and suggest practical solutions, the chapter first examines why transitional justice needs a decolonial agenda. The chapter outlines suggestions of what could be done for the field to be decolonised. It argues that decoloniality should not be a metaphor (Tuck and Yang 2012) but a commitment to rethink the tenants of transitional justice and question its epistemic roots where modernity (understood as a Western enlightenment model) is taken as a baseline. The chapter makes a case for more radical alternative futures for transitional justice, enshrined in the tenants of decolonial theory.

S. Durdiyeva (✉)
Postdoctoral Researcher, Postcolonial Hierarchies in Peace and Conflict Project, Center for Conflict Studies, Philipps University Marburg, Ketzerbach 11, 35037 Marburg, Germany
e-mail: selbi.durdiyeva@staff.uni-marburg.de

T. Venthan Ananthavinayagan and A. Viswanath Shenoy (eds.), *The Wretched of the Global South*, International Law and the Global South,
https://doi.org/10.1007/978-981-99-9275-1_4

1 Introduction

Transitional Justice is a whole range of processes a society undertakes to reckon with the legacies of past atrocities (UNSG 2004). Rooted but not limited to international law, and particularly international human rights law, transitional justice became a *lingua franca* of societies dealing with mass-scale crimes. It is often associated with criminal trials, truth, reparations, guarantees of non-repetition, and memorialisation. Although the processes relating to rethinking the oppressive past can be traced back to many centuries ago, the field as we know it today has emerged from social movements in South America after the fall of military dictatorships and society's desire to break away from the past by seeking justice for crimes (Arthur 2009; Teitel 2015; Bell 2009; Leebaw 2008). Due to a historic situation at the end of the 1990s associated with the fall of the Soviet Union and with it, arguably a defeat of the socialist ideology, the paradigmatic transitions were viewed as the ones where countries transitioned from war to peace, and from authoritarianism to liberal democracy (Sharp 2015; McGill 2017; Nagy 2008). The field went through rethinking of its key tenants, with bourgeoning literature that invites to look 'beyond the end of history' (Sharp 2018; Bueno-Hansen 2018; Schulz 2020). A call to move from transitional, towards transformative justice has been made, with an emphasis on long-term change, local agency, and beyond heavy focus on the punitive justice (Gready and Robins 2014; Balasco 2018). The economic, social, and cultural rights as well as financial crimes such as corruption and unequal land distribution have been at the centre of attention of transitional justice scholarship for a number of decades now (Miller 2008; Evans 2016). A wealth of scholarship considers the gender dimension of transitional justice (Bell and O'Rourke 2007; Buckley-Zistel and Zolkos 2012; O'Rourke 2013). Yet, the field is at crossroads due to the challenges it encountered for over three decades of existence (Cheryl and Moffett 2016). The focus on symptoms rather than causes remain, while the ambitious critical scholarship represents an aspiration rather than a programme of action (Sharp 2019). The critical scrutiny the field has faced in the recent decade, as well as a global surge towards democratic decline, makes one question what the future of the past is (de Greiff 2020).

Even though a consensus exists in transitional justice theory and practice that transitional justice is no longer constrained by foundational paradigm, it is still the case that the newly emerging regimes are compared to 'the European threshold' of narratology of transitional justice—'progress, progression, procession' (Rothberg 2012, p. 4). The theory of transitional justice still deals with the 'master's tools', it uses the language of modernity (Tlostanova 2015). It is rooted in the paradox of the Western idea of progress that the oppressed should raise to the level of their masters and then continue oppressing others, rather than rethinking this form of relationship in the first place (Freire 2000). Transitional justice processes take place, for the most part, in the former Western European colonies. The violence committed in the aftermath of colonial administration and the foreign and artificial colonial structures are addressed by transitional justice institutions symptomatically, without considering how colonial dynamics allowed for the structures that led to violence in the first place.

The Truth and Reconciliation Commission of South Africa examined apartheid policies without paying due regard to the colonial roots of apartheid in the first place. The International Criminal Tribunal for Rwanda prosecuted the perpetrators of genocide, with no regard for the colonial administration that divided the population on ethnic principles that later led to the atrocities. Even if transitional justice tools are applied, violence is addressed, some form of justice and regime consolidation is achieved, still, in many contexts, "the settler colony remains a settler colony" (Park 2020, p. 267).

We thus have a case that transitional justice, as a field, received much scrutiny around repetitive claims that often seem to juggle the same questions—whether liberal inclinations should be kept, whether it should instead be transformative, whether it should fit somewhere in between radical and liberal (Sharp 2019). Postcolonial situation is taken as a given, with no attempt to challenge in it. Numerous scholars give a rather non-optimistic assessment of transitional justice processes to the date and their prospects (Nesiah 2016). The field is stuck when asking the same questions and providing the same answers, using the same case studies, where 'victim centric' and 'structural violence' are being repeated as an applauded mantra or cliché that is not being taken into consideration by practice. This forces the question, of why decolonial thinking does not penetrate through the field and what would decolonising transitional justice would mean.

A more nuanced and dedicated approach towards decolonisation is needed, where the questions of knowledge production, ontological and teleological premises of transitional justice are considered. Rather than speaking about trade-offs and compromises in transitional justice, decoloniality would imply a messy and difficult endeavour, where we rethink the norms and norm-creation and strive towards cocitizenship in a pluriversal and decentred world. It means acknowledging that multiple ways of knowing and knowledge-production exist. In this quest, decolonisation should not be merely a 'metaphor' (Tuck and Yang 2012) but rather a commitment to rethink the tenants of transitional justice as a field and question its epistemic roots where modernity (understood as a Western enlightenment model) is taken as a baseline. When considering colonial violence, both the understanding of 'transition' and 'justice' in transitional justice needs to be reconceived (Tuck and Yang 2012). Decolonisation in transitional justice should address the dynamics around land distribution, the economy, being, daily life, and imagination.

In the first section below, I discuss how transitional justice to date has been replicating the existent hegemonic discourses, hijacking, and promoting the ideas of justice, which does not address the fundamental harm caused by colonial situations around the world. This section also outlines the differences between 'de-' as opposed to 'post-' colonial approaches, arguing that it is the former that should be pursued in transitional justice. I then discuss what decolonising transitional justice would mean, first focusing on decolonising knowledge and norm production within the field and then the rethinking of transitional justice ontology and teleology to decolonise both. I conclude by arguing that a radical commitment to the decolonial agenda should be a way forward in transitional justice.

2 The Disregard for the Colonial in Transitional Justice

Transitional justice narratives are largely silent about Global North's complicity in creating, contributing, sustaining colonial violence, and protecting the image of the Western normativity. Post-colonial transitional justice scholarship points at the reluctance to engage with colonial violence and the fact that colonial violence is being fought using the masters' tools (Lorde 2018). A fall of colonial administration in different parts of the world did not result in the fall of colonial order, it persisted, and it is deeply embedded in 'Euro- North American—centric modernity' (Ndlovu-Gatsheni 2015, p 486). Transitional justice, thus, engages in a two-fold process of extending hegemonic and technocratic narratives with respect to reckoning with the past and, at the same time, it silences certain debates about the past, sustaining epistemic violence (Jamar 2019). Transitional justice measures have limited capacity to create 'conciliatory climate' in situations when grassroots groups working on questions of memory are continuously targeted, and when historical events relating to the colonial nature of conflict or oppression are whitewashed (Browne 2019).

To say that transitional justice is free of post-colonial concerns would not be accurate. A Belgian Parliament in 2020 established a Special Parliamentary Commission, to examine the country's colonial past in its overseas colonies, Congo, Burundi, and Rwanda (Gijs 2022). The Commission has a broad and a rather ambitious mandate in a short period of time to examine the colonial crimes from 1885 to 1962. Due to its nature and its mandate, the Commission is at risk of contributing to epistemic injustice due to omission of voices even though its impact could have far-reaching consequences (Destrooper 2022). In June 2022, the Belgian King Philippe 'expressed regret' for the colonial harm; and the country's Prime Minister apologised for Belgium's responsibility for the assassination of the DRC Prime Minister Patrice Lumumba (Gijs 2022). In May 2021, Germany officially apologised for the massacre of Herero and Nama tribespeople in Namibia that happened over a century ago, using for the first time, the term 'genocide' and offering to provide developmental aid as a form of reparation (Zoodsma 2022; Mazeingo and Nandi 2021). Transitional justice has also been used to address the harm inflicted on indigenous populations, for example relating to Indian Residential Schools in Canada and care institutions in Australia, where children were forced to study in a different language, adopt foreign cultural practices, and be separated from family and community (Park 2020). Such measures as inquiring on the events (truth dimension of transitional justice), reparations, public apologies were in place with respect to the settlers' policies towards indigenous populations in Australia and New Zealand, with a Waitangi Tribunal taking place to settle the disputes concerning land claims of Māori people (Park 2020, p 262). Even if these kinds of initiatives are laudable, they account for a colonial situation only to a limited extent, representing more compromises and easier 'fixes', which are not proportionate to the crimes perpetrated by colonisers.

The pursuit of justice remains in the hands of the powerful, as "liberal democracies that have the resources and political interest to mount a case" are more likely to engage in investigation and prosecution of perpetrators for international crimes (Nagy

2008, p. 282). An examination of 1,518 peace agreements that were concluded from 1990 until 2015 in 80 countries provided that "transitional justice dissemination displays a geographic discrepancy towards the Global South" (Jamar 2019, p. 56). The global project of transitional justice is thus asymmetric with "geographic 'zones of impunity'" located in the Global South (Nagy 2008, p. 282). Transitional justice represents a commodity of paying off the guilt of colonisers as well as an attempt to fight the 'collateral damage' of colonisation—the flow of refugees and migrants.

Transitional justice has been complicit in 'colonisation of time' and an imposition of 'miracle of the transition', which creates an illusion that with a transition of regime, previous structural injustice are gone (Madlingozi 2017, p. 126). Colonisation of time creates an artificial historical delineation, enforcing Western-centric linear understanding of time, engaging with a discourse of emancipation, whereas the reality for the 'forgotten', those who suffered due to the oppression, remains the same (Madlingozi 2017, p. 126). The 'transition' in this sense becomes an elite project even if it involves a few representatives of victims because these are usually the elite (Madlingozi 2017, p. 125).Transitional justice, thus, is complicit in insisting that there was a break between the past oppression and the present, whereas, in reality, one form of oppression flows into the other (Madlingozi 2017, p. 125).

The reason why transitional justice and decolonisation goals are incompatible is that the former tries to fix the rupture created by conflicts and authoritarianism, while the latter focuses on the very injustices of the regime transitional justice seeks to restore (Sesay 2022). Thus transitional justice is largely backwards-looking, whereas decolonisation is inherently future-oriented (Madlingozi 2017). Whereas transitional justice aims to identify the perpetrators and punish them, decolonisation focuses on the injustice that is of structural and cultural character (Madlingozi 2017). Transitional justice is involved in 'the assimilation politics', which are imposed on transitioning societies, which "always serve to reconfirm hierarchical social structures" (Madlingozi 2017, p. 129). Such actors as "humanitarians and other well-meaning dwellers of 'this side' of the colonial Line" engage in educating the colonised according to the canons of Western modernity, by which they "resolve the settler-problem", that is, they prepare and adjust people to the neo-colonial realities (Madlingozi 2017, p. 127). Those engaged in humanitarian work, activists, and academics working in transitional settings assume that 'political justice' has been done after the change of the regime and what 'the forgotten' need is 'social justice' as a panacea (Madlingozi 2017, p. 128).

The danger of excluding the decolonisation narrative and considering a country decolonised once a transitional justice package is implemented, is the exclusion of the colonised whose rights are not recognised and who do not have access to resources (Madlingozi 2017). Instead of a change, what we have is 'a reactive praxis of emancipation,' when the participation in politics becomes predetermined by the fact whether or not a colonised society has reached a certain level of 'development' and 'maturity' (Madlingozi 2017, p. 131). Transitional justice desideratum, the social justice is the opposite of liberation as social justice benefits elites (including the colonisers); whereas liberation brings about decolonisation (Madlingozi 2017, p. 131). Social justice is a promise, something that is to be granted if the conditions established by the coloniser are achieved, with strong civilising praxis, which is measured against the canons of European modernity (Madlingozi 2017, p. 131). Social justice debate leaves the issue of settler-colonialism untouched, it promotes the idea of the superiority of colonisers, and, most dangerously, it engages with identity politics, which is an inherent part of modernity and colonialism (Madlingozi 2017, p. 134).

Human rights order, on which transitional justice draws, played an instrumental role in validating a post-colonial situation, where a settler-coloniser remained a settler-coloniser who granted the rights to its subjects:

> With the UN human rights discourse, the universal dimension of those rights claims performed by different peoples everywhere were dismissed and repressed as violations of regulations and laws, or at best, approached as local demands that could be locally negotiated between long-time victims and their perpetrators, now figured as rioters and their employers (Azoulay 2019, p. 441).

The authors of these rights assumed that they can 'grant' people rights by first taking away their rights by ruining their worlds, forcing people to migrate, and then denying these rights in the communities where people migrated (Azoulay 2019, p. 438). The post-World War II ('WWII') situation was instrumentalised by the Allies, who covered up their colonial crimes with the newly established institutionalised framework of imperial rights (Azoulay 2019, p. 437).Imperial rights, or 'sovereign' discourse of rights, are opposite of what Ariella Aïsha Azoulay calls 'disabled rights' or 'civil rights', that is, "the rights of the dispossessed and their lost worlds, the rights validated not by state" (Azoulay 2019, p. 437). The minimal set of rights is "a preventive measure to keep people in bondage" in order "to protect and maximize the exploitability of their enslaved bodies" (Azoulay 2019, p. 446). They represent "a structure to secure the privileges of the few" (Azoulay 2019, p. 437). Even in the situation of subjugation, the dispossessed never ceased to create and re-create their own world, therefore, the meaning of Hannah Arendt's concept of 'worldliness' is not about the 'absence of a world', but rather "deprivation of the right to experience the world as one's unquestioned place" (Azoulay 2019, p. 445).

Colonisers were able to escape the responsibility, and even more so, driven by colonial guilt and the saviour complex, they embark on 'moves to innocence' and 'fantasies of easier paths of reconciliation' (Tuck and Yang 2012, p. 4). Colonial guilt or the desire to preserve the dominance of the European modernity remained among coloniser states, which became manifested in the need to educate and 'fix' the colonised and with that, promote this model to the other parts of the world. The colonial consciousness, thus, has never been changed and colonial structures in colonised states remained. The colonised, in turn, enchanted by the Western idea of progress, engage in internal colonisation, a belief that they themselves are inferior, and so are their language, culture, and consciousness (Maldonado-Torres 2007). This points to the need to rethink the core—that is, rather than generating the norms from the centre and spreading them to the periphery, transitional justice should instead allow the so-called periphery and marginalised to shape their own agenda. What we see instead is that transitional justice adopts easier 'easier fixes' and trade-offs.

One of such 'easier fixes' is adopting a hybrid model to address structural violence—mixing the 'local' with the sovereign international law discourse. It is often the case in transitional justice that "[t]he kinds of institutions transplanted and the legal assistance provided to transitional societies are often based on a given, preconceived template borrowed from the European legal tradition" (Vieille 2012, p. 68). Even though transitional justice is intertwined in the questions of power, it is surprisingly depoliticised (Nagy 2008). Depoliticisation is manifested in the fact that transitional justice mechanisms do not account for structural injustice permeated by 'colonial governance in postcolonial polities' (Yusuf 2018, p. 257). To dissolve colonising tendencies and pave away from decolonisation, hybridity is seen as an answer, where the local and international merge, while colonial structures remain.

Transitional justice to the date engaged in 'mimicry' of norms that were imposed by a coloniser after the fall of colonial administration, where people's agency has been taken away, fundamentally so when it comes to the questions of land and property rights (Moyo 2015). There is an overall sense that the independence of a colonised is not an endpoint or a teleological aim of transitions (Samset 2020), yet transitional justice framework is reluctant to evaluate critically and facilitate the change of the post-colonial situation. Both the universal discourse of human rights and transitional justice are oblivious to structural inequality (Azoulay 2015). The universal, in cultural relativism debates, is equated to globalised and colonising, while local is equated with indigenous (Azoulay 2015). 'Decolonisation', if any, then becomes a quest for the local and indigenous, with inconsiderate homogenisation and insertion of the 'local' into internationally generated norms to conceal the reluctance to deal with the consequences of colonialism and coloniality.

Most transitional justice scholarship that deals with the issue of colonialism and coloniality is anti-colonial or post-colonial as opposed to decolonial. One of the 'weakest' points of transitional justice as a field is "its engagement with the concept of decolonization itself" (Matsunaga 2016, p. 31). The terminology matters, as anti-colonialism "was largely an elite-driven project in which elites mobilized peasants and workers as foot soldiers in a struggle to replace direct colonial administrators" (Ndlovu-Gatsheni 2015, p. 488). Anti-colonial struggle did not result in a liberated world "marked by the birth of a new humanity as demanded by Fanon" (Ndlovu-Gatsheni 2015, p. 488). It would be more accurate to describe the current situation by what Gayatri Spivak (as cited in Ndlovu-Gatsheni 2015, p. 488) called 'postcolonial neo-colonised world'. Decolonisation, on the other hand, is "materialized as resistance, thought, and action" every time "the slave trade, imperialism, and colonialism were being launched" (Ndlovu-Gatsheni 2015, p. 488). Rather than embarking on decolonisation, transitional justice has been involved in shifting a balance of power where the post-colonial elite addressed to a limited extent the legacies of violence within the institutions inherited from the colonial administration.

The difference between postcolonial and decolonial theory is that "postcolonial theorists' horizon is universalism and cosmopolitanism, decolonial theory gestures towards pluriversality and new humanism" (Ndlovu-Gatsheni 2015, p. 491). Such indigenous approaches expressed through arts as threading and stitching are a good metaphor for the decolonial idea of re-existence, an attempt to create the world anew, through creating by redoing (Ndlovu-Gatsheni 2015, p. 491). The difference between the two theories is not properly accounted for in transitional justice, which limits the scholarship to the considerations of postcolonial failures only. At the same time, due to the attention paid to activism and 'bottom-up approaches' in transitional justice, "unlike postcolonial theory, decoloniality has a very strong activist and practical liberatory thrust" (Ndlovu-Gatsheni 2015, p. 492).

The reason why the post-colonial lens is unsuitable or satisfying, is that in post-colonialism, after the fall of direct colonial administration, a country's nationalistic elite recreates the system created by the coloniser (Ndlovu-Gatsheni 2015, p. 485). We thus still have colonial formation even after dismantling direct colonial administration. The postcolonial discourse is about the change of the boundaries and of the places of periphery and centre (Ndlovu-Gatsheni 2015, p. 485).Decolonisation, on the other hand, does not focus on reconstruction but rather on re-reading, re-writing, and re-thinking at the core (Ndlovu-Gatsheni 2015, p. 485). The decolonial theory is not about the substance, it is about the process and approach. In a similar vein, it is increasingly argued that transitional justice is about an ongoing process, which does not end when institutional transitional justice tools cease to exist (de Greiff 2012).

If transitional justice were to be decolonised, it would consider different types of colonialism—colonisation of being, internal, and external colonisation, colonisation of power, colonisation of the imagination, and colonisation in lived experience (Maldonado-Torres 2007, p. 240). It would focus on the difference between colonialism and coloniality:

Colonialism denotes a political and economic relation in which the sovereignty of a nation or a people rests on the power of another nation, which makes such nation an empire. Coloniality, instead, refers to long-standing patterns of power that emerged as a result of colonialism, but that define culture, labour, intersubjective relations, and knowledge production well beyond the strict limits of colonial administrations. Thus, coloniality survives colonialism (Samset 2020, p. 596).

Transitional justice enjoys a 'globalised presence' while on the other hand, it is unable to foster fundamental change (Nesiah 2016, p. 11). In the absence of decolonisation of norm creation in transitional justice, it risks transplanting "the colonial template of governance (colonial-style governance) in the postcolonial period" (Yusuf 2018, p. 257). We need to rethink key transitional justice goals, concepts, and assumptions not only to pave away from liberal democratic inclinations but also to decolonise them, which should be the priority of transitional justice, rather than democratisation in a liberal sense of a word. Walter Mignolo (2002, p. 57) perceptively referred to the bitter realisation that the state cannot be decolonised and democratised at the same time. Transitional justice scholarship reached a "rhetorical consensus—even within the mainstream—that new approaches are needed" (Sharp 2019, p. 589). This rethinking to the date has been shaped around compromises and trade-offs, attempting to reach a hybrid model of local and international, top-down together with bottom-up, with some considerations of economic and property rights. Colonisation and coloniality in a broader sense are not being addressed. As a result, we see a deadlock with re-emerging patterns of violence and a lack of change in the everyday lives of people. This condition was described by Nancy Fraser (2019) when referring to the crisis neoliberal condition imposed worldwide, paraphrasing Antonio Gramsci, "the old is dying and the new cannot be born".

3 What Embarking on Decolonial Agenda Entails for Transitional Justice?

Below, I outline some decolonising possibilities for transitional justice. The first section focuses on transitional justice epistemologies, drawing on the issues of how knowledge with respect to transitional justice norms is produced and accessed. The second section focuses on transitional justice ontology and teleology, that is, the rethinking of the tenants of the field and transitional justice aims. Both sections discuss possible ways forward and sketch what the decolonial agenda for transitional justice encompasses.

a. Decolonising Epistemology of Transitional Justice

When embarking on post-colonial agenda, transitional justice should adopt a 'decolonial turn' built on "post-colonial, feminist and cultural race geography" putting the question of knowledge production at its centre (Radcliffe 2017, p. 335). First, with respect to epistemology, transitional justice scholars and practitioners would need to ask deeper questions with respect to how the knowledge and norms that guide transitional justice practice and scholarship are created. The decolonial agenda demands us to reveal ourselves by making it clear where we come from (Mignolo 2002). It requires us to pose such questions as—how do we rethink the thinking (Mignolo 2002)? Despite the fact that increasingly more transitional justice scholars and practitioners are self-reflexive in their work, this should not be a stand-alone practice but rather a norm (Madlingozi 2010; Simic 2016; Brinton and van der Merwe 2019; Ní Aoláin 2012; Jones and Lühe 2021; Schultz 2021). Reflecting on positionality is even more pertinent since many of transitional justice scholars and practitioners work with vulnerable groups of a population in conflict or oppression-torn societies.

Radical approaches to research are characterised with acknowledgement of the agency of those who serve as a source of knowledge, amplification of their voices, challenging hegemonic narratives, and treating 'the respondents' in the 'field' not as a source of data or translators but rather as co-producers and co-creators of research. The field needs to be driven by those whom it concerns the most—the victims of colonial rule and its aftermath. As argued by Richa Nagar (2019, p. xii),

> We reject the Enlightenment-based approach to research, which typically views marginalized research subjects as "raw materials or suppliers of stories," and redefine these subjects as radical collaborators.

Walter Mignolo (2007, p. 449) suggests that we need to ask the 'why' question for the 'how' to follow. This practice has been well-documented in feminist and queer methodologies, notably, by Donna Haraway (1988) who drew on the notion of situated knowledge to other scholars who shed light on the dark sides of transitional justice-related research as Tshepo Madlingozi (2010).

Secondly, we need to consider how accessible transitional justice scholarship is. If we would do research in a decolonial way, it would mean that this knowledge would not be restricted to the academia of the Global North. It would also mean that sometimes the knowledge produced will not come in a logo-centric form but will draw on poetry, images, music, and storytelling, to name a few forms of knowledge production. For example, James Caron asserts that the readings and teachings done during Islamic Shia Holidays, could be equivalent to taking lectures at a university due to both the number of hours it takes and the depth of engagement—often this would be an overview of philosophical tenants starting with Socrates to the modern-day thinkers (Caron 2019; Caron and Khan 2022). In a similar vein, poetry could play a role of resistance and a way to share and produce knowledge (Caron 2019; Caron and Khan 2022). Respecting and drawing on these forms of knowledge production would be key if we were to decolonise transitional justice epistemologies.

The question of language and how we use it is also pertinent to decolonial methodologies. It means that we would need to pave away from the hegemony of English. At the same time, the silver lining of the colonising dynamics of English is that it has the potential (if not already) to become a language of solidarity and resistance shared and spoken around the world, erasing the physical borders of nation-states (Glasius 2012). The advent of "global English since 1950- … tied to global capitalism", it acquires also 'historical and political' significance of Gramsci (Glasius 2012, p. 684). English is also a language of "cooperative resistance and global struggle" (Glasius 2012, p. 684). Decolonising transitional justice epistemology would also imply not constraining ourselves to the limits of disciplines as prescribed in the Western academia. Even though transitional justice is claimed to be an inherently interdisciplinary field, beyond legalisms (McEvoy 2007); there are still disciplinary foundations that dominate the field. Strict boundaries of disciplines represent a colonising endeavour as they restrict access of people to knowledge (Pelletier 2009).

Thirdly, when we speak about knowledge production and decolonising it, we need to ask ourselves a question—who is in the room? We cannot speak about decolonisation in a true sense of the word if the room is filled mainly by white middle-class academics who do not speak the languages of the locations where they do the research; who have a sense of entitlement that they have a right to go to 'the field', which is a place of struggle for everyday existence for people who live there; and who speak on behalf of these people who are not more than a footnote in the economy of academic knowledge production. Even if the room is seemingly diverse, it would also mean reflecting, critically, on who gets to speak, how often, and how authoritatively. If structural and institutional hierarchies are maintained, if academia increasingly becomes a neo-liberal institution that runs on the shoulders of underpaid workers, we cannot speak about decolonising knowledge. A few fixes of curriculums and workshops on equality do not suffice as they do not speak to the commitment of incommensurability and creating a fugitive space within academia (Tuck and Yang 2012).

Decolonial agenda in transitional justice should be pursued by examining the experiences of violence within the structures that create the violence, using both the vocabulary as well as values and cultural lenses of that very context (Ndlovu-Gatsheni 2015, p. 485). Settler-colonialism is embedded in the logic of elimination: eliminating the people(s), their culture, history, traditions, language and replacing it with their own, while eliminating the traces of colonialism too (Park 2020, p. 264). We thus see dual attempts at elimination and silencing, the counterbalance of which would be challenging this culture of silence by 'resurgence', 're-empowerment', reclaiming of the cultures, traditions, and languages that have been erased (Park 2015, p. 275). The ideas stemming from the intersection of different cultures and backgrounds, the broader and more open cultural *milieu* should be considered. Thinking through the archaic lens of Europe vs Orient, Europe vs Asia, and other antagonistic regional divisions is not productive either. Imposing and sustaining binaries is a Western approach in itself. As argued by Derrida (Salmon 2020, p. 81), "… the history of Western thought relies on the apparent 'logic' of binary oppositions, where the first term is privileged over the second. But as Derrida points out, this is not a "peaceful coexistence of two terms, it is a violent hierarchy. The task of the deconstruction is to suspend the hierarchy at this moment and analyse and criticise it, in a sort of productive ambivalence… the task of deconstruction is not then to efface the difference through synthesis, but to mark it, to note its undecidability and explore its complex interplay". The focus in transitional justice should be shifted towards "amplifying the wealth of knowledge available within non-dominant and largely disregarded epistemologies of the global South that currently face destruction or, what Bonaventura de Sousa Santos terms, 'epistemicide'" (Ross 2017, p. 1063).

Decolonial theory has been overly focused on the questions of epistemology as many of the seminal decolonial scholars theorised at the time when the Soviet Union collapsed and hence the political remained a shaky question, while engaging with the question of epistemologies seemed like a safer recourse (Tlostanova 2015). We should be wary of an approach where one considers decolonisation of thinking to be the endpoint itself. Such claims as 'decolonise your thinking and the rest will follow' is a 'move to innocence', that is, unwillingness to commit to the true meaning of decolonisation with a goal to whitewash coloniser's guilt (Tuck and Yang 2012, p. 19). Frantz Fanon's approach to decolonisation, on the other hand, sees decolonisation as a messy project, where the return of land rather than re-occupying it is a goal: "[U]ntil the stolen land is relinquished, critical consciousness does not translate into action that disrupts settler colonialism" (Tuck and Yang 2012, p. 19). Decolonisation does not end with epistemology and, therefore, a less comfortable terrain of decolonising should be considered that involves the questions of the ontology and teleology.

b. Decolonising Ontology and Teleology of Transitional Justice

There is no one way of doing decolonisation, "numerous possibilities of thinking decolonisation" exist (Mignolo 2002). Decolonising transitional justice would involve imagining alternative futures of transitional justice but not in a way that is guided by Cold War thinking. Transitional justice followed colonising dynamics of its counterpart international human rights law—covering up with the discourse of human rights and 'granting the rights' to those who were deprived of these rights in the first place (Azoulay 2015). The WWII erasure of colonial harm introduced the framework of rights, which, among else, are the founding principles of transitional justice, and which "were materialized as a provision, a kind of gift—they could always be taken away or not given at all" (Azoulay 2019, p. 436). The post-WWII situation was used to create an ideological framework, which would airbrush the crimes committed because of colonisation:

> The binary paradigm of evil totalitarian regimes defeated by the good Allied liberators removed from sight the "internal" oppression of "minorities" and was soon after replaced by the Cold War framework (Azoulay 2019, p. 456).

Transitional justice should engage and foster understanding of the genealogies of decolonial thought in order not to enter the trope of hijacking the term because it is fashionable. A superficial adoption of the language of decolonisation serves solely for the purposes of addressing the settler's guilt and needs, and, as a result, hinders the possibility of decolonisation (Tuck and Yang 2012, p. 3). The "decolonizing projects and other social justice projects" are incommensurable as the work of decolonisation is both 'hard' and 'unsettling' (Tuck and Yang 2012, p. 4). As decolonisation of academia cannot be achieved by merely including a few names of authors of colour in reading lists in order to 'decolonise' the curriculums, transitional justice cannot be 'decolonised' in a true meaning of the word by including a few indigenous approaches into an otherwise liberal and externally-driven package of measures. Some ingredients of a radical approach to decolonisation in transitional justice could be: 'refusal, resurgence and prefiguration,' and "decentring of the settler state, internationalization of the justice relationship, challenging the legitimacy of the settler state, and abandoning liberal teleology" (Park 2020, p. 262).

Transitional justice should also focus on reparations for colonial crimes—this would involve providing compensation to the colonised for the harm suffered, which would involve but not be limited to pecuniary and non-pecuniary damage, restitution, return of the land, reparations for extracted natural resources and environmental damage, return of looted objects of "worldly environments and extracted objects that were repurposed" (Azoulay 2019, p. 455). Decolonisation presupposes the elimination of "settler property right and settler sovereignty". It requires the abolition of land as property and upholds the sovereignty of Native land and people (Tuck and Yang 2012, p. 26). Transitional justice, to date, has failed to address the complex entanglements relating to property rights arising out of colonial administration (Moyo 2015).

Since transitional justice deals with how to reckon with the legacies of violence, it is necessary to make links between the past and current border politics, which exacerbate the divide the between those who were born above the 'abyssal line' or 'Line of colonialism' and those who were born below it, with the latter being denied their humane status (Santos 2007). Migrants, asylum seekers, and refugees-related policies in the Global North are a continuation of colonialism. The colonial policies of the Global North and its contemporary forms need to be examined by transitional justice and how the Global North denies the very freedoms in the name of which it commits and committed colonial violence.

If transitional justice was to be decolonised, it would involve looking more closely, and there is an emerging scholarship with this respect, on the role of environment, as this affects the whole of humankind and some cultures have an intimate connection with nature, where nature is treated as an object of extractivism in the name of infinite growth. The daily practice of decolonisation would involve "embodying and living Indigeneity, honoring the longstanding relationships with the land and with one another" (Park 2020, p. 262).

Transitional justice, as part of a commitment to decolonisation, needs to examine the inequality, with which critical transitional justice scholarship continuously engages, but often it disregards the elephant in the room—the capitalist economy that causes and exacerbates inequality arguably to the same extent as any conflict or oppression (Quijano 2007). Crude capitalism is collateral of the liberal democratic model, which was favoured by transitional justice. Precarity is 'futureless', as "a systemic crisis is an epistemic crisis" (Mignolo 2002). Neoliberalism "or financial capitalism—privatization, austerity, global free-trade treaties, financialization, or any other top-down notions of adhering to an imperial timeline's major milestones" are used against people in 'colonies and offshore territories' to chase the 'fiction of Western progress' (Azoulay 2019, p. 35). The task of transitional justice as a field, if it would embark on decolonial agenda, will be to allow space for imagining an alternative future, outside of coloniality and outside of neoliberalism, as the two are interlinked.

Decolonising transitional justice would also mean putting the question of racial justice at the centre of its agenda:

> the abolition of slavery was equated with making it illegal, and not undoing the structures, institutions, and practices in which it was materialized: classification systems, human rights language, key political concepts, coercion and torture devices, expert knowledge, arts and crafts, waged and wageless labor, landscapes, museums, and archives' (Azoulay 2019, p. 447)

Although there has been a global surge of the removal of colonial monuments and calls for apologies and reparations for slavery, particularly after the Black Lives Matter protests, these efforts, nevertheless, reinforce the existing neoliberal order rather than challenge it (Sesay 2022, p. 5). Unless radicalised, transitional justice lacks the capacity to decolonise (Sesay 2022). The task of transitional justice, if it was to engage in decolonisation, would be undoing the model of 'emancipation-as-recognition', that is, the cases when settler colonisers recognise 'the settler-created states' (Madlingozi 2017, p. 134). It would mean to undo the consequences of "self-alienation, misrecognition and social death" of the colonised (Madlingozi 2017, p. 134).

Decolonial agenda in transitional justice and decolonising the field itself would involve a broader scope of action, taking into consideration less visible forms of coloniality persistent even in the states without colonial history. Imagining alternative futures in transitional justice would involve "decolonizing the mind, moving the center, re-remembering, and globaletics" (Thiong'o as cited in Ndlovu-Gatsheni 2015, p. 493):

> Decolonizing the mind speaks to the urgency of dealing with epistemicides and linguicides. Moving the centre addresses the problem of Euro-North American centrism. Remembering is about uniting a dismembered and fragmented continent. Globalectics gestures towards post-racial pluriversality as the home of new humanity (Ndlovu-Gatsheni 2015, p. 493).

Decolonial agenda for transitional justice would mean examining different forms of colonisation and coloniality, and internalised colonialism as well. Colonised people, reproduce colonial practices due to the feeling of inferiority, which has been forced onto them, through what Madlingozi (2017, p. 129) calls "teleological whiteness—the idea that being white and the attainment of whiteness are the highest ideals of emancipation and human progress". The internalisation of the norms imposed by the coloniser often subconsciously affects everyday behaviour and racism that is directed at oneself and the members of own community.

To think decoloniality within transitional justice would involve unlearning imperialism, embarking on 'non-imperial ontology' through "cocitizenship, a partnership against imperial citizenship", where people are given something more than abstract political categories of rights (Azoulay 2019, p. 34). We need to look at the absence, the stories, which are untold and the documents and photographs the archives do not show. Decolonisation means "the urgent need to thoroughly challenge the colonial situation" (Fanon as reproduced in Lemert 2017, p. 283) repairing the harm inflicted by colonialism, the process of unlearning, and dissociation (Azoulay 2019, p. 17).

4 Conclusion

Despite the proliferation of critical transitional justice scholarship that re-examines the goals and the state of the field in general, the engagement with the questions of decolonisation is limited. Mainstream scholarship on transitional justice fails to address the questions of imperialism, meaning-making, and epistemologies of transitional justice.

Transitional justice deals with transitions, sometimes these transitions result in a change of regime, in other cases, the changes of regimes do not happen; it also applies when conflict or oppression is ongoing or to the so-called 'established democracies. The change of a situation or ideology that allowed the atrocities to happen, as well as an aspiration to seek justice for past atrocity, are a *raison d'être* of the field. In light of this, it is puzzling that the question of decolonisation received little attention. Decolonisation in a true sense of a word would mean a change of conscience where the field would pave away from the colonial onto-epistemological project on the one hand and commit to rethinking and undoing the harm caused by colonisation, on the other. The question of land repatriation, wealth distribution, and structural violence has received much attention in the literature on transitional justice but what is missing is that this should be done with a decolonising mindset and praxis, that is, the return of what is owed, and non-imposition of the standards of modernity. As was coined by Fanon (Fanon as reproduced in Lemert 2017, p. 283), "Decolonisation never goes unnoticed, for it focuses on and fundamentally alters being…".

Decolonisation is everyone's business, not only of those who are oppressed and not only of the settler-colonial states, as different forms of coloniality exist in the increasingly globalised world, while indigenous knowledge and cultures are at risk of being lost. At the same time, the capitalist idea of infinite growth sweeps everyone under the same precarious structures where only a few reap the benefits of the system. Transitional justice, because it is the field that arguably connects the past and the present where both are not viewed in a linear way, should aim to become "an anti-imperial onto-epistemological framework through which everything and every place affected by western [note from author: and not only western] imperialism could be thought together" (Azoulay 2019, p. 17).

Acknowledgements This contribution was written as part of the research project "Postcolonial Hierarchies in Peace & Conflict" [grant number 01UG2205A], funded by the German Federal Ministry of Education and Research.

The author would like to thank the anonymous external reviewer, the editors—Thamil Venthan Ananthavinayagan and Amritha V. Shenoy, and Jeevan Justin for their invaluable assistance and insight.

References

Aoláin, Ní. 2012. Fionnuala, advancing feminist positioning in the field of transitional justice. *International Journal of Transitional Justice* 6 (2): 205–228.

Arthur, Paige. 2009. How transitions reshaped human rights: A conceptual history of transitional justice. *Human Rights Quarterly* 31 (2): 321–367.

Azoulay, Ariella. 2015. What are human rights? *Comparative Studies of South Asia, Africa and the Middle East* 35 (1): 8–20.

Azoulay, Ariella Aïsha. 2019. *Potential history unlearning imperialism.* London. New York: Verso Books.

Balasco, Lauren. 2018. Locating transformative justice: prism or schism in transitional justice? *International Journal of Transitional Justice* 12 (2): 368–378.

Bell, Christine. 2009. Transitional justice, interdisciplinarity and the state of the 'field' or 'non-field.' *International Journal of Transitional Justice* 3 (1): 5–27.

Bell, Christine, and Catherine O'Rourke. 2007. Does feminism need a theory of transitional justice? an introductory essay. *International Journal of Transitional Justice* 1 (1): 23–44.

Brinton, M Lykes and Hugo van der Merwe. 2019. Critical reflexivity and transitional justice praxis: solidarity, Accompaniment and Intermediarity. *International Journal of Transitional Justice* 13(3): 411–416

Browne, Brendan Ciarán. (2019). Transitional justice and the case of Palestine. In *Research Handbook on Transitional Justice*, eds. Cherly Lawther, Luke Moffett, and Dov Jacobs, 488–508. Cheltenham, Northampton: Edward Elgar Publishing

Buckley-Zistel, Susanne and Magdalena Zolkos. (2012). Introduction: Gender in transitional justice. In *Gender in transitional justice*, ed. Susanne Buckley-Zistel and Ruth Stanley. London: Palgrave Macmillan UK

Bueno-Hansen, Pascha. 2018. Decolonial feminism, gender, and transitional justice in Latin America. In *The Oxford handbook of gender and conflict*, eds. Fionnuala Ní Aoláin, Naomi Cahn, Dina Francesca Haynes, and Nahla Valj. Oxford: Oxford University Press

Caron, James. 2019. Pashto border literature as geopolitical knowledge. *Geopolitics* 24 (2): 444–461.

Caron, James, and Salman Khan. 2022. Writing war, and the politics of poetic conversation. *Critical Asian Studies* 54 (2): 149–170.

Cheryl, Lawther and Luke Moffett. 2016. Introduction—Researching transitional justice: The highs, the lows and the expansion of the field. In *Research handbook on transitional justice*, ed. Dov Jacobs. Cheltenham, Northampton: Edward Elgar Publishing

Derrida, Jacques. 1982. Positions, 77. Chicago, London: University of Chicago Press. as cited in Peter Salmon, An Event, Perhaps, A Biography of Jacques Derrida. London, New York, Verso

Destrooper, Tine. 2022. Belgium's 'Truth Commission' on its overseas colonial legacy: An expressivist analysis of transitional justice in consolidated democracies. *Journal of Human Rights* 2: 158–173.
Evans, Matthew. 2016. Structural violence, socioeconomic rights, and transformative justice. *Journal of Human Rights* 15 (1): 1–20.
Fanon, Frantz. 2017. Decolonizing, national culture, and the negro intellectual. In *Social theory. the multicultural, global and class readings*, reproduced in ed. Charles Lemert. Boulder: Westview Press
Fraser, Nancy. 2019. *The old is dying and the new cannot be born: from progressive neoliberalism to trump and beyond*. London, Brooklyn: Verso Books.
Freire, Paulo. 2000. *Pedagogy of the oppressed*. New York: Continuum.
Gijs, Anne-Sophie. 2022. Belgium is reviewing its colonial past in the DRC: it's a sensitive but necessary process. The Conversation https://theconversation.com/belgium-is-reviewing-its-colonial-past-in-the-drc-its-a-sensitive-but-necessary-process-186512
Glasius, Marlies. 2012. Gramsci for the twenty-first century: dialectics and translatability. *International Studies Review* 14 (4): 666–686.
Gready, Paul, and Simon Robins. 2014. From transitional to transformative justice: a new agenda for practice. *International Journal of Transitional Justice* 8 (3): 339–361.
de Greiff, Pablo. 2012. Theorizing transitional justice. *Nomos* 51: 31–77
de Greiff, Pablo. 2020. The future of the past: reflections on the present state and prospects of transitional justice. *International Journal of Transitional Justice* 14 (2): 251–259
Harasym, Sarah, and Gayatri Chakravorty Spivak ed. 1990. *The Post-colonial Critic: Interviews, Strategies, Dialogues*. Oxon, New York: Routledge, as cited in Ndlovu-Gatsheni, Decoloniality as the Future of Africa. *History Compass* 13(10): 485–496
Haraway, Donna. 1988. Situated knowledges: the science question in feminism and the privilege of partial perspective. *Feminist Studies* 14 (3): 575–599.
Jamar, Astrid. 2019. The crusade of transitional justice tracing the journeys of hegemonic claims in violence and democracy. *The British Academy*: 53–59
Jones, Briony, and Ulrike Lühe, eds. 2021. *Knowledge for peace: transitional justice and the politics of knowledge in theory and practice*. Cheltenham, Northapton: Edward Elgar Publishing.
Leebaw, Anne. 2008. The irreconcilable goals of transitional justice. *Human Rights Quarterly* 30 (1): 95–118.
Lorde, Audrey. 2018. *The master's tools will never dismantle the master's house*. Milton Keynes: Penguin Modern.
Madlingozi, Tshepo. 2010. On transitional justice entrepreneurs and the production of victims. *Journal of Human Rights Practice* 2 (2): 208–228.
Madlingozi, Tshepo. 2017. Social justice in a time of neo-apartheid constitutionalism: critiquing the anti-black economy of recognition, incorporation and distribution. *Stellenbosch Law Review* 28 (1): 123–147.
Maldonado-Torres, Nelson. 2007. On the coloniality of being: contributions to the development of a concept. *Cultural Studies* 21(2–3): 240–270
Matsunaga, Jennifer. 2016. Two faces of transitional justice: Theorizing the incommensurability of transitional justice and decolonization in Canada. *Decolonization: Indigeneity, Education & Society* 5(1): 24–44
Mazeingo, Nandiuasora "Nandi". 2021. Revisiting Germany's genocide apology to Namibia." AL JAZEERA. https://www.aljazeera.com/podcasts/2021/11/24/revisiting-germanys-genocide-apology-to-namibia
McEvoy, Kieran. 2007. Beyond legalism: towards a thicker understanding of transitional justice. *Journal of Law and Society* 34: 411–440.
McGill, Dáire. 2017. Different violence, different justice? taking structural violence seriously in post-conflict and transitional justice processes. *State Crime Journal* 6 (1): 79–101.
Mignolo, Walter D. 2002. The geopolitics of knowledge and the colonial difference. *The South Atlantic Quarterly* 101 (1): 57–96.

Mignolo, Walter D. 2007. DELINKING: The rhetoric of modernity, the logic of coloniality and the grammar of de-coloniality. *Cultural Studies* 21: 449–514
Miller, Zinaida. 2008. Effects of invisibility. In search of the 'economic' in transitional justice. *International Journal of Transitional Justice* 2 (3): 266–291.
Moyo, Khanyisela. 2015. Mimicry, transitional justice and the land question in racially divided former settler colonies. *International Journal of Transitional Justice* 9 (1): 70–89.
Nagar, Richa. 2019. *Hungry translations: relearning the world through radical vulnerability.* Transformations: Womanist Studies
Nagy, Rosemary. 2008. Transitional justice as global project: critical reflections. *Third World Quarterly* 29 (2): 275–289.
Ndlovu-Gatsheni, Sabelo J. 2015. Decoloniality as the Future of Africa. *History Compass* 13(10): 485–496
Nesiah, Vasuki. 2016. *Transitional justice practice: looking back, moving forward: scoping study.* Impunity Watch, Research Report
O'Rourke, Catherine. 2013. *Gender politics in transitional justice.* London: Routledge.
Park, Augustine S. J. 2020. Settler colonialism, decolonization and radicalizing transitional justice. *International Journal of Transitional Justice* 14(2): 260–279
Pelletier, Caroline. 2009. Rancière and the poetics of the social sciences. *International Journal of Research & Method in Education* 32 (3): 267–284.
Quijano, Aníbal. 2007. Coloniality and modernity/rationality. *Cultural Studies* 21 (2): 168–178.
Radcliffe, Sarah. 2017. Decolonising geographical knowledges. *Transactions of the Institute of British Geographers* 42 (3): 220–229.
Ross, Sara Gwendolyn. 2017. Review of Epistemologies of the South: Justice Against Epistemicide, by Bonaventura de Sousa Santos, *Alberta Law Review* 54 (4)
Rothberg, Michael. 2012. Progress, progression, procession: William Kentridge and the narratology of transitional justice. *Narrative* 20 (1): 1–24.
Salmon, Peter. 2020. *An event, perhaps: a biography of Jacques Derrida.* London, New York, Verso
Samset, Ingrid. 2020. Towards decolonial justice. *International Journal of Transitional Justice* 14 (3): 597–607.
Santos, Boaventura de Sousa. 2007. Beyond abyssal thinking: from global lines to ecologies of knowledges. *Review* (Fernand Braudel Center) 30(1): 45–89
Santos, Boaventura De Sousa. 2016. *Epistemologies of the South: Justice against Epistemicide.* London, New York: Routledge
Schulz, Philipp. 2020. Towards inclusive gender in transitional justice: gaps, blind-spots and opportunities. *Journal of Intervention and Statebuilding* 14 (5): 691–710.
Schulz, Philipp. 2021. Recognizing research participants' fluid positionalities in (post-)conflict zones. *Qualitative Research* 21 (4): 550–567.
Sesay, Mohamed. 2022. Decolonization of postcolonial Africa: a structural justice project more radical than transitional justice. *International Journal of Transitional Justice* 16: 254–271.
Sharp, Dustin. 2015. Emancipating transitional justice from the bonds of the paradigmatic transition. *International Journal of Transitional Justice* 9 (1): 150–169.
Sharp, Dustin. 2018. *Rethinking transitional justice for the twenty-first century: beyond the end of history.* Cambridge, New York: Cambridge University Press.
Sharp, Dustin N. 2019. What would satisfy us? taking stock of critical approaches to transitional justice. *International Journal of Transitional Justice* 13 (3): 570–589.
Simic, Olivera. 2016. Feminist research in transitional justice studies: navigating silences and disruptions in the field. *Human Rights Review* 17 (1): 95–113.
Teitel, Ruti G. 2015. *Globalizing transitional justice.* Oxford: Oxford University Press.
Thiong'o, Ngũgĩ wa, as cited in Sabelo Ndlovu-Gatsheni. 2015. Decoloniality as the Future of Africa. *History Compass* 13(10): 485–496
Tlostanova, Madina. 2015. Can the post-soviet think? on coloniality of knowledge, external imperial and double colonial difference. *Intersections. East European Journal of Society and Politics* 1(2)

Tuck, Eve and K Wayne Yang. 2012. Decolonization is not a metaphor. *Decolonization: Indigeneity, Education & Society* 1(1): 1–40
United Nations Secretary-General. 2004. The rule of law and transitional justice in conflict and post-conflict societies UN Doc S/2004/616
Vieille, Stephanie. 2012. Transitional justice: a colonizing field? *Amsterdam Law Forum* 4 (3): 58–68.
Yusuf, H.O. 2018. Colonialism and dilemmas of transitional justice in Nigeria. *International Journal of Transitional Justice* 12 (2): 257–276.
Zoodsma, Marieke. 2022. Examining the 'age of apology': Insights from the Political Apology database. *Journal of Peace Research* 59 (3): 436–448.

Forced Displacement and Borderlands in International Law: Perspectives from Below

Oreva Olakpe

Abstract African borders are contentious and arbitrary, shaped by both colonial and post-colonial events. How do communities that straddle borders experience the border and movement around it? The discourse around African borders in international law have often focused on border dispute resolution and delimitation between states or the impact of borders on state sovereignty. These discussions centre the state and sovereignty in the analysis of borders. However, borders have a profound impact on the daily lives and experiences of people and communities on the fringes of the state. This study aims to understand how border communities experience international law in their daily lives and under the limitations of borders using Mubi, Adamawa State in Northern Nigeria as a case study. Mubi is a borderland on Nigerian and Cameroonian lines, which is contentious and shaped historically by colonialism and contemporarily by insurgency and violence. The border between Nigeria and Cameroon has increasingly become securitised based on the anti-terrorism practices of Western countries towards the Boko Haram insurgency. This study is interested in studying accounts of people in Mubi of forced migration and the responses of Cameroon and Nigeria during the height of the insurgency in 2014. The objective is to derive an understanding of international law from below and to trace the link between the realities in border communities and international law. This study uses methods from Third World Approaches to International Law (TWAIL) to understand how border communities in the Global South are impacted by international norms and how they counter those norms at their level. TWAIL and legal ethnography has been used by scholars including Eslava, Sunter, and Parmar as a technique to document historical and ongoing struggles against colonialism and asymmetries of power in international law and uses local specificities and regional trends from the

This Chapter Is Based On Research That the Author Conducted With Funding From Heinrich Boll Stiftung Nigeria in 2019.

O. Olakpe (✉)
Canada Excellence Research Chair in Migration and Integration Program, Toronto Metropolitan University, Toronto, Canada
e-mail: oreva.olakpe@torontomu.ca

T. Venthan Ananthavinayagan and A. Viswanath Shenoy (eds.), *The Wretched of the Global South*, International Law and the Global South,
https://doi.org/10.1007/978-981-99-9275-1_5

Global South to change our understanding of international law. This chapter follows a similar path using perspectives from below to generate critique and significance.

1 Introduction

In this chapter, I focus on understanding how communities and people in borderlands in the Global South experience international legal norms and state practice from below.[1] I am particularly interested in how communities and individuals at borders experience international law and norms, as inhabitants of a space that is at the centre of state sovereignty, yet on the fringes of state protections. I study these communities to draw out what their realities say about approaches to international law at the different levels. This is essentially to unpack knowledge of the law from below, and the different manifestations of power imbalances and marginality in the Global South.

African borders are contentious and arbitrary, shaped by both colonial and post-colonial events. While decolonisation in its 'traditional' sense took place in the 1960s, communities and people in the Global South are stuck permanently within or outside borders and norms like *uti possidetis* that secure colonial boundary arrangements (Hlovor 2020, pp. 39–40). The long-term effects of political and legal decisions made at the international level on the Global South are felt in the daily lives of communities and people today. Simultaneously, local challenges stemming from these colonial and post-colonial events (including the delimitation of borders and the conflicts that arise because of them) also shape the daily lives of people and how they experience law and resist the from below.

Borders carry many contradictions. According to Mendez and Naples, "borders embody differing implications and meaning for those who confront them, depending on context and social actors' location within intersecting structures of power". This means that for some, borders can signify protection and for others, borders are violent and cruel (see Hebie (2015) and also Mendez and Naples (2014)). Borders empower state sovereignty, protect the interests of the elite within them and the exclusivity of citizenship, as well as signify safety for people escaping violence on one hand. On the other hand, borders are spaces of violence and cruelty for stateless people, displaced people, refugees, undocumented migrants, ethnic minorities, and other marginalised people. Borders are also spaces occupied by communities and individuals who are often caught between these extremes and where people live their daily lives (Deleixhe et al. 2019). Hlovor delves deeply into the nature of African borders and borderlands and argues that borderlanders must be key stakeholders in the bordering process, as well as the discourse on border and security because their lives and livelihoods are intricately tied to cross-border activities (Hlovor 2020, pp. 44–45). It is for this

[1] The phrase 'from below' is used in this chapter to reference both terms of local resistance, delineated by Balakrishnan Rajagopal in International Law from Below, as well as ethnography as a method to understand international law. See Rajagopal, B. (2003).

reason that I focus on borderlands from the perspective of people who experience life, insecurity, and state power struggles at borders, rather than from a state-centred or rule-focused perspective.

This chapter is focused primarily on the question: how do communities that straddle borders experience the border and movement around it in times of conflict? The discourse around African borders in international law has often been fixated on border dispute resolution and delimitation between states or the impact of borders on state sovereignty (Hlovor 2020, pp. 43–44). These discussions centre the state and sovereignty in the analysis of borders. However, borders have a profound impact on the daily lives and experiences of people and communities on the fringes of the state. This study aims to understand how border communities experience international law in their daily lives and their struggles to find protection despite the limitations of borders using Mubi, Adamawa State in Northeastern Nigeria as a case study.

Mubi is a borderland on Nigerian and Cameroonian lines, which has been contentious and shaped historically by colonialism and contemporarily by insurgency and violence (Duyile 2014). Borders between Nigeria and Cameroon have increasingly become securitised based on anti-terrorism practices of Western countries towards the Boko Haram insurgency including the increasing reliance on restrictive border policies and state-backed violence or hostility towards people crossing borders. This study is interested in studying accounts of people in Mubi of forced migration and the responses of Cameroon and Nigeria during the height of the insurgency in 2014. The objective is to derive an understanding of international law from below and to trace the link between border communities and the law.

This study uses ideas and concepts from Third World Approaches to International Law (TWAIL) to understand how international law is encountered in border communities in the Global South. TWAIL and legal ethnography have been used by scholars including Eslava, Sunter, and Parmar as a technique to document historical and ongoing struggles in the Global South against colonialism and asymmetries of power in international law and use local specificities and regional trends from the Global South to change our understanding of international law and its impact on people in the Global South. This chapter follows a similar path using perspectives from below to generate critique and significance.

1.1 Conceptual Clarifications

According to Anghie, international law can only be truly universal if legal theory derives from a wider range of legal traditions, systems, and conceptualisations (Anghie (2005) p. 320, also see De Sousa Santos (2018)). This means that the universality of international law will only be possible when it is opened to the diverse understandings and experiences of the law globally; this includes the legal conceptualisations from people and communities in the periphery of the Global South who are often the victims of international legal decisions and practices. At the same time, because these communities are the actual sites of the implementation of international law, we can learn about the direct implications, as well as the strengths and weaknesses of the legal and political decisions at the international level from below.

Woldemariam, Maguire, and Von Melding argue that human displacement, an issue of particular concern in the Global South, has been largely ignored because international law "lacks both adequate and responsive rules, and strategies to address its root causes" (Woldemariam et al. 2019). They use TWAIL to study the relationship between forced human displacement, international law, and the Global South. Their analysis roots displacement in the history of colonialism, the non-inclusion of the Global South in the decision and rulemaking processes of international law, and the resulting inequalities that feed widescale human displacement in the Global South. Colonialism and acts of hegemony and imperialism have historically led to displacement in the Third World but the historical underpinnings of the contemporary displacement we see are often ignored. Therefore, Woldemariam et al. focus on delineating the developments around forced human displacement in international law with the Global South in focus.

It is for these reasons that theoretical and methodological approaches that make the widening of international law beyond 'traditional' approaches possible are significant. It is also why TWAIL, which is a movement and a conceptualisation born out of the compelling desire for the inclusion and centring of the Global South in international law discourse, is a useful framework with which we can understand the impact of international law on peripheral communities including those located at borders. Scholars including Okafor, Mutua, Pahuja, and Eslava have argued that treating international law as a material object that goes beyond rules and state practice, manifests in the mundane, shapes people's daily lives and identities, and how they experience justice. This ideation sees the material nature of the law as the path towards the universal promise of international law. Because the law is larger than a theoretical exercise, it should be studied using methodologies that enable a materialist analysis (Mutua (2000), Eslava and Pahuja (2011), Okafor (2008)). Methods like ethnography that observe and document experiences of the impact of international law from below create the possibility for this type of analysis that can contribute to a richer understanding of the law through alternative lenses (Merry 2006).

Many critical scholars have suggested or used ethnography and other alternative research methods and methodologies to understand and critique the impact of international law on developing countries (see Okafor (2008) at p. 377; Burgis-Kasthala (2016) at pp. 13–14; Sunter (2007) at p. 489, 498; Eslava (2015); Thomas (2000); Parmar (2008)). Ethnography draws substance from experiences of international law from below, from the narratives and lived experiences of people and communities impacted by the law at the lowest levels. Traditional approaches to international law have been rigid, reliant on a statist focus, and relegating anything that is not deemed 'international enough' or between certain states to insignificance. This has created an international system that fails to protect vulnerable people all the time. However, understanding the local manifestation of historical, legal, and political decisions and the experiences of the impact of international law in the daily lives of people at the fringes of society in the Global South is the key to addressing the root causes of issues like forced human displacement and the capacity to effect real change therein.

For international law to manifest a transformative power, it must be able to address the impact of international norms and legal decisions on communities and individuals beyond international courts and processes in Geneva and the Hague. To embark on this project, it is necessary to close the distance between local-level realities and international law by unpacking those realities. This is the underpinning of this research of the case study that follows.

2 Background of Research in Mubi

My research in Mubi was conducted in 2019 in Mubi South and Mubi North Local Government Areas of Adamawa State with two three main objectives. Firstly, I wanted to investigate the experiences and migration narratives of people in Mubi, during the 2014 occupation of Mubi. Secondly, my research aimed to draw significance out of lived experiences at the border during and after the occupation about approaches to forced displacement and norms and practices of accepting refugees at borders during a crisis. Thirdly, I was interested in understanding the ways in which people in borderlands resist the obstructive policies and violent or hostile practices at the border.

2.1 Research Methods

My aim is to use ethnography to draw significance from below about international law, inspired by work that uses TWAIL as a research method as mentioned above. As a result, I utilised observation, listening, and informal conversations to understand the narratives of the communities in Mubi. I built a base of local contacts, including academic contacts at the Adamawa State University, Mubi, contacts in the Nigeria Police Force, contacts in the Army, contacts at the Mubi Transit Camp for refugees and internally displaced persons (IDPs), contacts at the Mubi Cattle Market including the traditional rulers of Markets and the leaders of the Fulani people on both sides of the border, contacts at Mubi Old Market, contacts at Mubi Union of Road Transport Workers, contacts in the Cameroonian community in Mubi North, contacts in the Igbo community in Mubi, and contacts in the bike transport association at the border between Mubi and Cameroon. This wide range of research networks was intended to enable me to have a better grasp of the security situation on the ground, as well as to get more balanced research by speaking to a diverse range of communities within the town about their experiences. My positionality as a female, non-Muslim Nigerian researcher situated me as both an insider and outsider; being a female researcher in male-dominated and religion-dominated spaces was a challenge. I had to have male chaperones to access certain spaces, for example.

The Mubi transit camp, the largest refugee camp in Mubi, is administered by both army and civilian personnel. The camp is located close to the border and was created to receive refugees temporarily for screening before they are moved to designated camps elsewhere or settle in the town. As a result, it was an important place to gain an understanding of the border and forced migration.

I interacted with 26 Mubi residents who either fled or attempted to flee to Cameroon on their experiences of the occupation of Mubi, crossing between Nigeria and Cameroon during the insurgency and on the future of Mubi. Listening sessions at the Mubi transit camp included over 20 people as well. In total, the research involved a total of 62 people including traditional rulers, religious leaders, security operatives, and cross-border business and transport associations. All the participants have been anonymised and de-identified for the purposes of this research.

3 Brief Historical Context of Mubi: From Colonial Boundary Delimitations and Territorial Transfers to Insurgent Occupation

Mubi is a town located at the contemporary northeastern border between Nigeria and Cameroon. People in the Mubi area have experienced a long history of foreign and armed occupations. In the precolonial era, the area was under the jurisdiction of the Sultanate of Mandara. By the late eighteenth century, the Fulani conquered Mubi in a jihad and incorporated it into the Fulani kingdom of Fumbina. European occupation of Mubi began in 1903 when Germany conquered the town and made it the administrative centre and border post of ‘German Kamerun’. Mubi remained under German colonial control until 1914, in the aftermath of the First World War when it was taken from Germany by the British. Germany lost its colonies including Cameroon, which was taken over by the British, French, and Belgian forces, and ‘German Kamerun’ was divided into the southern and northern parts. In 1922, the League of Nations designated Mubi and its environs to ‘British Cameroons’. None of these decisions involved the consent of the inhabitants of the town. Mubi became a part of Nigeria via a 1961 plebiscite after the independence of Nigeria and Cameroon from Britain and France respectively, southern Cameroon elected to join French Cameroon, whereas northern Cameroon chose to join Nigeria. Mubi is currently part of Adamawa State, northeastern Nigeria (see El Sudi 2019).

Northeastern Nigeria and the borderlands on both the Nigerian and Cameroonian sides are largely impacted by the Boko Haram insurgency. Isike and Isike give a detailed background of the history of terrorism and the rise of Boko Haram in Northern Nigeria through the lenses of transnational migration networks, globalisation, and geopolitics (Isike and Isike 2018). Onapajo and Uzodike analyse Boko Haram terrorism at the individual, state, and international levels; individual and group ideologies shaping the activities of the group, at the state level, the deep-rooted corruption, state-sanctioned violence, poverty, among other socio-economic and political challenges that both birthed and fed terrorism in the Northeast, and at the international level, the rise of religion-based terrorism and the terrorist networks across continents, regions, and national borders (Onapajo and Uzodike 2012). Otoghile dissects the origins of Boko Haram, rooting it in the colonial construction of ethnic consciousness in Northern Nigeria, and the dichotomies between the Southern and Northern parts of Nigeria by the colonial administration to further their 'divide and conquer' tactics. According to Otoghile (Otoghile & Igbafe 2014):

> The amalgamation of 1914 did not result from any agreement between the various ethnic and religious groups that make up the Nigerian society. This diversity has continued to reflect in the polity of the country with the north always wanting to have control of political power. The country is violently divided along regional, ethnic, linguistic and religious lines...These ethnoreligious identities have constituted instruments of mobilization and contestation in the struggle for power and resources… Following the amalgamation of North and South by the British, divisive tendencies were created and it existed alongside the colonial state.

Without looking at the national and subnational levels of analysis, we will be unable to see the colonial roots of the contemporary problem. The border hostilities between Nigeria and Cameroon caused by multiple colonial delimitations and territorial transfers also impact people at the borders who are fleeing from insurgents. In addition to creating the foundations for ethnic and religious divisions that led to the rise of insurgency, colonial-era decisions have also shaped the politics around the Nigerian-Cameroon border in Mubi. Abiodun delves into the complex boundary relations between Nigeria and Cameroon in Northern Nigeria. Like Otoghile, Abiodun shows how the errors of colonial agreements including the 1931 Anglo-French Declaration created a faulty delimitation of the border in Northern Nigeria, affecting places in Borno, Taraba, and Adamawa states (which includes Mubi) (Abiodun 2014). Abiodun discusses how numerous border demarcation issues in the Northern part have remained unresolved until today. Coupled with the international legal decision about the delimitation of the border in Southern Nigeria at the Hague, which designated the Bakassi Peninsula to Cameroon based on colonial agreements, rather than local realities and pre-colonial history, this has created a hostile relationship between the two states contemporarily.[2]

This chapter does not focus on analysing the roots of Boko Haram because there are numerous references that delve into that context (see Aghedo & Osumah 2012; Osumah 2013; Hansen & Aliyu 2013; Ibanga and Archibong 2018; Agbiboa and Egiegba 2013; Agbiboa 2015; see also Umukoro 2016), but instead on how Mubi inhabitants experienced the border and what it tells us about how people who have been displaced experience the impact of practices and rules stemming from the international level. Nevertheless, it is important to highlight the calamitous impact of the insurgency. Since the rise of Boko Haram in 2002, Boko Haram insurgents have

[2] International Court of Justice. 2002. Land and Maritime Boundary between Cameroon and Nigeria, Cameroon and Equatorial Guinea (intervening) v Nigeria, Judgment, Merits, [2002] ICJ Rep 303, ICGJ 63, para 25. See also Wikileaks. 2009. New Wave of Nigerians Return from Bakassi. Accessed at https://wikileaks.org/plusd/cables/09LAGOS465_a.html on June 25, 2021; See BBC News Africa. 2013. Bakassi Residents to pay tax under Cameroon Sovereignty. Accessed at http://www.bbc.co.uk/news/world-africa-23710733 on June 25, 2021.

killed tens of thousands of people, displaced over two million people in Nigeria and hundreds of thousands in Cameroon, kidnapped thousands of women, and children, and destroyed hundreds of villages, schools, and infrastructure (see Mukhtar et al. 2020). Mubi has been particularly targeted by Boko Haram because of its economic and political significance in the northeast and its strategic location on the frontier. Isike and Isike hold that Boko Haram has been able to "sustain and expand itself by developing sophisticated social networks" by focusing on conquering border towns and villages and taking advantage of porous borders, ethnolinguistic relations across borders, and the ECOWAS Protocol on the Freedom of Movement, which they state, "facilitates easy movement into Nigeria" (Isike and Isike 2018, p. 45).

3.1 Armed Occupation of Mubi: A Brief Timeline

Adamawa State has faced repeated attacks from Boko Haram in recent years and Mubi has been a target. Mubi was eventually occupied by Boko Haram, forcing many of its inhabitants to flee (Vanguard 2012; Reuters 2012; The New Humanitarian 2013; France24 2014; Aljazeera 2014; UNHCR 2014; BBC News 2014; United Nations 2014).[3]

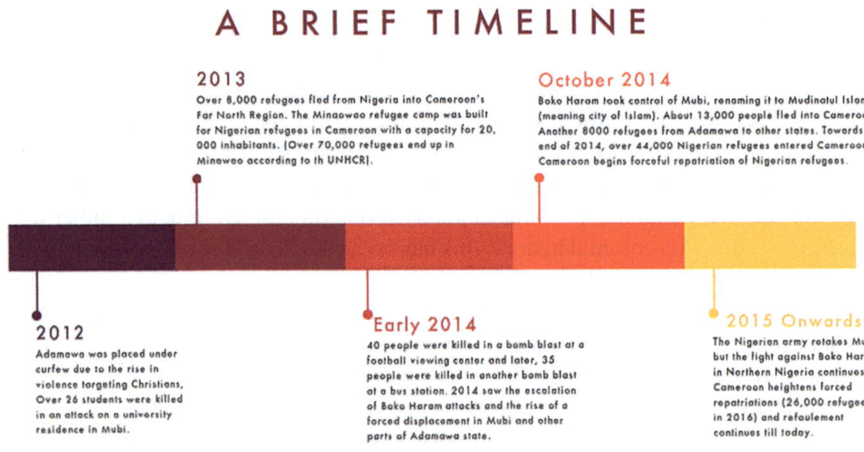

Kasuwan Tike, the Mubi Cattle Market, is central to the experience of the border and the movement of people and goods into and from Mubi. The market is also a key contributor to the Gross Domestic Product and internally generated revenue of Adamawa State. It is believed to be the largest cattle market in West Africa and the source of all the cattle in Nigeria, with estimates of tens of thousands of cows

[3] Many refugees fled to the towns of Guider and Gashiga in the North region of Cameroon and to Bourha, Mogode and Boukoula in the Far North.

coming into Nigeria weekly from Chad, Niger, Cameroon, and the Central African Republic.[4] The market sees a minimum of 200 truck conveyances of cattle daily and the employment of hundreds of Mubi residents as drivers, loaders, cattle marketers, herders, motorboys, conductors, and others (Sajo 2018). According to a leader of the market, the market was destroyed by Boko Haram insurgents in 2014. Boko Haram was eventually repelled and pushed out of the territory by the collaboration of civil militia and the Nigerian army in 2015.

Mubi is one of the three towns in northeastern Nigeria to be under a state of emergency for more than a year, as a result of Boko Haram activities. In 2016, the Cameroonian government forcefully repatriated over 26,000 Nigerian refugees in total, going against their obligations under the 1951 Refugee Convention and the 1969 OAU Refugee Convention, both of which Cameroon has ratified.[5] By early 2017, the number of Nigerian refugees in Cameroon had increased to 85,000. Cameroon is said to have forcefully repatriated another 2,600 Nigerian refugees to northeastern Nigeria from border towns in the Far North region of Cameroon such as the town of Amtide and Mora (BBC News 2017). The Far North region in Cameroon hosts an estimated 85,000 Nigerian refugees including 62,000 who were in Minawao refugee camp as of 2017, excluding people who had not been reached by humanitarian organisations.[6] Due to the increasing practices of *refoulement* by Cameroon, the UNHCR facilitated a tripartite agreement between Cameroon and Nigeria about the conditions of the return of Nigerian refugees in Cameroon to Nigeria.[7] The agreement laid out the legal framework for the voluntary return of the refugees in the Far North region in Cameroon, with specifications on the importance of the voluntary character of repatriation (Art.2), safe and dignified repatriation processes (Art. 3), and freedom of choice of destination (Art. 5).[8]

Boko Haram attacks in Mubi continued in 2017, with a mosque bombing that killed 50 people (Aljazeera 2017). In 2018, another mosque and market bombing in Mubi claimed 86 lives (Aljazeera 2018). The UNHCR estimates that a total of 110,000 Nigerians in total fled to Cameroon due to Boko-Haram's insurgence. 87,600 of these refugees have been registered by the UNHCR. The Minawao camp hosts over 70,000

---

[4] Conversation with a leader of the Mubi Emirate Council, January 2019, on file with Author.

[5] United Nations General Assembly. 1951. Convention Relating to the Status of Refugees. United Nations, Treaty Series, vol. 189, p. 137 accessed at https://www.refworld.org/docid/3be01b964.html on July 5, 2021 (referred to as UN Refugee Convention), and Organization of African Unity. 1969. Convention Governing the Specific Aspects of Refugee Problems in Africa ('OAU Convention'), 10 September 1969, 1001 U.N.T.S. 45. Muma delves into details of the principle of nonrefoulement in the Refugee Convention and the OAU Refugee Convention and how it applies specifically to the Nigeria and Cameroon case, as a result, I will not delve into that matter here. See Muma (2018) p. 350–353. See also Bueno (2006).

[6] UN High Commissioner for Refugees. 2017. Tripartite agreement for the voluntary repatriation of Nigerian refugees living in Cameroon between the Government of the Republic of Cameroon, the Government of the Federal Republic of Nigeria and the UN High Commissioner for Refugees (referred to as the Tripartite Agreement). Accessed at https://reliefweb.int/report/cameroon/tripartite-agreement-voluntary-repatriation-nigerian-refugees-living-cameroon, on June 20, 2021.

[7] Ibid.

[8] Ibid., Arts 2, 3, and 5.

refugees and over 30,000 refugees live in surrounding towns (Reliefweb 2018). In 2018, over 2000 Nigerian refugees were forcefully repatriated from Cameroon, despite the tripartite agreement. The UNHCR holds that Cameroon has forcefully repatriated about 90,000 refugees to Nigeria since 2015, whereas Human Rights Watch estimates 100,000 forceful repatriations from Cameroon to border towns like Mubi.[9] These repatriations were a breach of the Refugee Convention, the OAU Refugee Convention, and the Tripartite Agreement. Additionally, these forced returns have impacted the social, political, and economic configurations of the town, as the research ethnography will show below. At the time of the research (2019), forced repatriations were still ongoing. While I was at the Mubi Transit Camp, I witnessed the arrival of 21 people who had been removed from Cameroon, and camp officials confirmed that every day, people are sent back from Cameroon.[10]

Beyond expounding the context and the details of the occupation of Mubi and the forced displacement of its inhabitants, I now set out to unpack the narratives of people who experienced the occupation and forced repatriation at the Cameroonian border. My intention is to centre the narratives from below about the impact of international and state practices and highlight the struggles of people against the violence and obstructive practices of states in borderlands.

4 Narratives and Experiences of the Border at Mubi: Identity and Forced Return During an Insurgency

Most of the people in *Kasuwan Tike*, including the leader of the market fled into Cameroon during the attack in 2014 and faced varying degrees of difficulty at the Cameroonian border.[11] The leader of the market stated that that he had only a few difficulties at the border, but this experience was not like less privileged members of *Kasuwan Tike* and regular inhabitants of Mubi who wield no political power or have no official documentation. All the participants in the research fled out of Mubi when Boko Haram occupied the town. They include farmers, herders, traders, bike riders, and students. They also experienced refoulement when they tried to cross the Cameroonian border for safety at the height of the insurgence and occupation of Mubi.

[9] UN Refugee Convention Art. 33; The OAU Refugee Convention Arts 2 and 5, and the Tripartite Agreement Arts 2, 3, and 5.

[10] Conversation with officials in Mubi Transit Camp, Adamawa State, Nigeria, January 2019, on file with Author.

[11] Listening Session at Kasuwan Tike, Mubi, Adamawa State, Nigeria, January 2019, on file with Author.

4.1 The Normalisation of Refoulement in West Africa

A resident of Mubi, S. recounted that he was working on the farm when he heard that Mubi was now under the control of Boko Haram. People were stuck in Mubi because there was no movement from Mubi to other parts of Nigeria and so he was forced to trek from Mubi to the Cameroonian border with his wife R. and their two children. S. recounts his experience trying to seek entry into Cameroon:

> We found a corn farm along the border, but as we were talking with the owner of the farm, we were told that there was a registration going for people to enter Cameroon. We did the registration; we wrote our names and the names of our wives and children.... But they took us to a big river that separates Nigeria and Cameroon along Gerie Road and dropped us there. I put my wife and children on a motorbike so that they can enter Yola that night, but I could not join them because I did not have sufficient funds to pay the bike man. There was also a curfew in Yola, and it was too late for me...[12]

Yola is the capital of Adamawa State. S. and his family were among the thousands of Nigerians who were not allowed to enter Cameroonian villages or towns. Rather, after their details were taken at the border, they were transported back to Adamawa at a time when the entire state was under attack by Boko Haram. This counts as refoulement because Cameroonian officials knew that people including S. and his family were fleeing from the ongoing occupation of Mubi by Boko Haram and registered them. As a party to the 1951 Refugee Convention and the 1969 OAU Refugee Convention, transporting them back to Adamawa at that time was an act of bad faith and a contravention of both conventions.[13] Globally, states in the Global North have normalised the practice of being hostile to refugees at borders and reducing the protections refugees can access within their borders. States in the Global South are increasingly following this trend. The experiences in Mubi are an example of this trend developing in West Africa. Furthermore, as Mbizoyo (2017) argues, by violating international human rights law and sending refugees back to danger, Cameroon legitimises Boko Haram's claims that states will not protect people (see Mbizoyo 2017).

B., an elderly resident of Mubi fled was able to enter Cameroon because he had identification documents with him when he fled. However, his refuge was short-lived. He states that:

> We had to use the bush to run for our lives to reach to the border, after we have entered Cameroon, we got to a place called Burha where we were put in an abandoned classroom by government officials there that night. The Cameroonian government provided trucks that conveyed us back to the border the next day.[14]

E., a student at Adamawa State University recounted that he tried to get to the Cameroonian border with his brother and classmates but was turned back because of a lack of permission to enter:

---

[12] Conversation with S. and R., January 2019, Mubi North Local Government Area, on file with Author.

[13] UN Refugee Convention, Art. 33.

[14] Conversation with B., January 2019, Mubi North Local Government Area, on file with Author.

> We were at the Uni on the 29th when we heard Boko Haram was in Mubi, we were not able to leave because communication lines were shut down and there was no means of transportation. We couldn't communicate with our parents to know exactly where they were or what was going on. We heard that people were running to Cameroon and when we heard that Boko Haram was heading towards the Uni, we decided to leave. Our first attempt at leaving failed because insurgents were on the road towards the border, so we sneaked by to the Uni and slept that night. The next day, we were able to make it to the border, but the Cameroonian officials told us that we cannot cross over until they get permission from the governor. It appears that the day before, some people were allowed to enter Cameroon, but we weren't so lucky. Because they refused to allow us to enter, we trekked to Mubi South Local Government. There were many dangers on the way, but we met some family members there. Together, we trekked along the border through Maiha to get to Yola.

The Mubi Old Market is the largest commodity market in Adamawa, and it is not surprising that this has attracted traders and businesspersons from all over the region. Boko Haram looted and destroyed the market during the occupation of the town (Sajo 2018, p. 64). P., a trader in the market experienced the limitations of lack of identification when he tried to enter Cameroon. He recounts that:

> We trekked from Mubi to Maiha Local Government and tried to enter Cameroon from there. My mother and younger siblings had identification on them, and they were able to enter Cameroon. I was not able to enter and so we were forced to split up at the border. I ended up trekking for many days until I got to Yola. I had no food or water and I saw so many bad things on the way. I found out that my mother and siblings were later removed from Cameroon even though they had IDs. They were sent back to the border at Maiha, and they ended up paying their way to get to Yola.

While concerns about security and the potential influx of insurgents at borders are valid, requiring people to possess and show identification at the border at the height of an insurgency can also be interpreted as an act of bad faith.[15] The UNHCR has detailed refugee screening procedures to ascertain the status of asylum seekers, however, these procedures are often left to the discretion of the state, which is often at odds with the protection of refugees.[16] The insurgency and occupation of Mubi being an extreme circumstance, forced people to seek refuge, leaving their homes and belongings. As a result, they were highly unlikely to have proof of identity at the time they showed up at the Cameroonian border.

Additionally, many people do not own a passport but are able to carry out their daily activities informally across the border. For example, many of the cross-border motorbike transporters do not own international passports, instead, they get special permits that serve as identification cards to cross into Cameroon, and they pay a tax each time they carry a passenger into Cameroon. Most of the cross-border activities are informal in nature. Instead of an international passport, it was more important for the bike riders to be taxpaying members of the cross-border bike transporters

[15] UN Refugee Convention, Art. 27 and 28.

[16] United Nations High Commission for Refugees. 1992. Handbook on Procedures and Criteria for Determining Refugee Status under the 1951 Convention and the 1967 Protocol relating to the Status of Refugees HCR/IP/4/Eng/REV.1.

association and to pay their fees on both sides of the border.[17] The cross-border bike permits did not work at the height of the occupation of Mubi, so bike riders were not able to use their identification at that time, nor transport people across. Conversations with traders, bike transporters, and herders showed that it is usually the leaders of these communities and associations, as well as the political, cultural, and religious elite that had international passports and used them in their daily cross-border activities.[18] The privilege of owning an international passport impacts the daily lives of poorer Mubi inhabitants and the insurgency compounded it.

4.2 *The Hardening of Borders*

The relationship between those in Mubi and those on the other side of the border in Maroua and Garoua in Cameroon, including their shared language, culture, history, and cross-border trade remains relevant today but the borders, the stiff relations between Nigeria and Cameroon, and insecurity have made these relationships tenuous.[19] The hardening of the practices of exclusion and discrimination heightened during the insurgency when many people needed to seek refuge across the border. Borders harden for political reasons and become barriers to the protection of the rights of people who live within or across those spaces.

The creation of the border by colonial actors split the communities in the area, and created and systemised discrimination between the two states that dictate state practice even in times with extraordinary circumstances that should create humanitarian grounds for ignoring border delimitations and exclusions. Difficulties at the Cameroonian border forced most people to find alternative routes out of Mubi, whereas some of those who had passports were able to enter Cameroon to seek refuge in the Minawao refugee camp. Many people with documentation were turned away at the border.

The UNHCR addresses the issue of identification of people seeking refuge:

> For a refugee, the lack of identity documents may be far more than a source of inconvenience. in almost all countries an alien must be able to prove not only his identity but also that his presence in the country is lawful. In some countries aliens without appropriate documentation are subject to detention and sometimes even to summary expulsion. Such measures are particularly serious for a refugee, for whom they could also involve the risk of being returned to his country of origin. Even where the consequences of being without documentation are less drastic, the refugee, in order to benefit from treatment in accordance with internationally

[17] Listening session with members of the Bike Rider's Association, January 2019 at Gidan Madara between Cameroon and Nigeria, on file with Author.

[18] Ibid., Conversation with members of the Mubi Motor Park, January 2019, on file with Author. Conversations with herders at Mubi Cattle Market, January 2019, on file with Author.

[19] Conversation with security operatives in Mubi South Local Government Area, Adamawa State, Nigeria, January 2019, on file with Author.

> accepted standards, needs to be able to establish vis-à-vis government officials not only his identity but also his refugee character.[20]

If in order to benefit from treatment in accordance with international standards, refugees need to establish their identity, this means that according to international law, identification remains more important than refugee protection. Placing the burden of proof of identification on people fleeing conflict and insurgency is setting them up for refoulement. Additionally, what would suffice as 'refugee character'? The Cameroonian government was aware that Boko Haram had occupied Mubi and was killing its inhabitants, destroying their homes and belongings, and taking over public and private spaces. Would this context count as sufficient proof of the characters of the people fleeing to the border?

T., a farmer, describes the issue of character and the response of border officials as they came to the border:

> They knew we were all from Mubi, we were with our children, and they knew we were running from Boko Haram. We tried to enter at Dembo, but the government refused to give us permission. They packed us like animals with our children in trucks and sent us to Yola. When we got to Yola, we heard that the insurgents were coming and so Yola would not be safe for long.[21]

The Cameroonian government did not consider the mass displacement due to the occupation as sufficient proof of refugee character. The international community was also silent about these practices because the refugees and internally displaced people fleeing Boko Haram are not elevated in the politics and the discussions and developments around armed occupations and international refugee law. In a 2017 report, Human Rights Watch claims that since 2015, Cameroon has been carrying out one of the largest illegal deportations globally but at the international level, there is very little reaction to these serious claims (Human Rights Watch 2017). The cases that garner more international action to push for changes in state practice are often those where powers in the Global North have stakes. People in border towns in the Global South are forgotten or ignored in international legal discourse as well, even though their daily existence is shaped by the borders created by international law and its history of colonialism. International legal norms and accepted practices are not fit for purpose in real-life situations because they are created with the interests of the states in mind, rather than those of the people in situations of forced displacement. The stakeholders also determine the international response to the plight of those who have been forcefully displaced. What is unfolding on the ground in borderlands in the Global South informs our understanding of the realities of the international legal order and TWAIL enables us to see beyond the high-level stuff for a clearer view of what international law is permitting.

Mbizoyo (2017, p. 8) states that:

---

[20] See United Nations High Commission for Refugees. 1984. Identity Documents for Refugees EC/SCP/33. Accessed at https://www.unhcr.org/excom/scip/3ae68cce4/identity-documents-refugees.html on July 5, 2012.

[21] Conversation with T. in January 2019, Mubi South Local Government Area, Adamawa State, Nigeria, on file with Author.

> Delegitimising governments as ruling entities is a central Boko Haram narrative, as are regular claims of state illegitimacy and inability or unwillingness to protect people. Boko Haram messaging repeatedly calls for the suspension of national constitutions and the democratic process (including in Cameroon, specifically).

The disillusionment with the state and its failure to protect people as well as the failure of international law to address the negative impact of harmful norms and state practices is one of the root causes behind the rise and legitimacy of groups like Boko Haram and the cause of forced displacement.

5 Resisting Violence and Obstructive Borders in Mubi

Beyond the narratives of forced displacement and refoulement, communities in borderlands in the Global South are also involved in doing the work of rebuilding, as well as resisting the violence and obstructiveness of the borders that define their existence. The narratives of people in Mubi show how forced migrants actively seek protection and seek to counter the refoulement through other networks and resources and through informal border crossing practices and informal protection mechanisms.

After Mubi was recaptured by the Nigerian military, many of its inhabitants did not return immediately out of fear that Boko Haram would return. All the research participants who are residents of Mubi stayed away for months, returning from 2018 onwards. However, some people never returned to Mubi and some of them left the north permanently.[22] Those who returned to Mubi indicated that on arrival, many of them found their houses and schools burned down or robbed, banks were emptied and destroyed, churches and mosques were razed, and businesses were levelled. Sajo (2018, p. 64) estimates that financial institutions in Mubi lost 2.7 billion Naira during the insurgency and occupation of Mubi in 2014. At the time of the research in 2019, Mubi still bore the scars of Boko Haram's occupation, with the skeletal remains of homes, offices, and businesses lining the streets. However, people had rebuilt their lives, the town was bustling with people, and the markets were alive again.

E., one of the research participants stated that it took his family about 3 years to rebuild and recover from the losses of forced displacement, and people in the Old Market pooled resources together to start again.[23] People in Kasuwan Tike also lost all their possessions. The operations of the cattle market were hindered during the period of the conflict and when Mubi was recaptured from Boko Haram, the market faced severe challenges. Members of the community also did not have the capital to buy cows in order to restart their businesses. According to a leader of the market, the market community came up with strategies to rebuild. The strategy of the cattle market was to forgive debts that came as a result of the loss of cattle. Over the course

[22] Listening session with students who left Mubi and resettled in Yola, at Nas Meridien Hotel, Jimeta, Yola, North Local Government Area, January 2019, on file with Author.

[23] Conversation with E. in January 2019, Mubi South Local Government Area, Adamawa State, Nigeria, on file with Author.

of 4 years, people raised capital to purchase cows and some of them have been able to recover portions of their investments in the market. The act of returning, rebuilding, and pooling resources together to help members of the community bounce back shows the agency of the people in Mubi and their determination to protect their interests and rights and to return to their everyday lives and cross-border activities. This is because even though the border is unpredictable and hostile, the border remains the home and source of livelihood for the communities that live around them.

The security situation had not improved in Mubi and around the border as of 2019. However, the inhabitants of Mubi have come up with ways to protect the town to prevent a repeat of 2014. According to security operatives, the security in Mubi now relies heavily on community policing in both Nigerian and Cameroonian communities along the border due to the long-standing pre-colonial ties that exist across borders.[24] Local vigilantes and civil militias involved in cross-border policing are a kind of 'police without borders'; they are able to go across the border to places where the state cannot go and assist them with solving crimes and protect the town and border from Boko Haram. This level of informal cross-border cooperation is filling the gaps where international law and regional and bilateral frameworks have failed to provide solutions or succour. Local-level, informal cross-border community protection is an understudied aspect of how people at borders are fighting against violence and marginalisation in borderlands, where states guard sovereignty fiercely but offer weak protections.

Finally, the issue of forced return remains a matter of concern, years after Mubi was recaptured from Boko Haram but people in Mubi have made created space for other refugees. Every day, the Mubi Transit Camp receives people who fled from other parts of the northeast that remain under the control of Boko Haram to Cameroon. These people are still being forcefully returned to dangerous places, but they are transferred to the camp in Mubi. The refugees in the camp are women and children from other places in Adamawa, Borno, and Yobe like Madagali, Michika, Dula, and small communities like Fadama, Dabu, and Gata, where Boko Haram still exerts control over territory. Mubi Transit Camp had about 500 returnees in 2018 but the camp has been gradually and consistently releasing them into Mubi and the city of Yola for resettlement. According to a camp manager, the number of incomers has been on the decline in comparison to 2014 and 2015 but people are still being turned away by Cameroon.[25]

Refugees from Cameroon are often repatriated first to Sagoda, a border transit camp located about 3 kms from Cameroon, which was constructed to only receive returnees. From Sagoda, they are transferred to Mubi Transit Camp. Another route through which Nigerians are repatriated from Cameroon is from camps in Cameroon to Madagali, from where they are transferred to Mubi.[26] Madagali is currently still

[24] Listening session with security operatives in Mubi North Local Government Area, Adamawa State, Nigeria in January 2019, on file with Author.

[25] Interview with a camp manager at the Mubi Transit Camp, Mubi North Local Government Area, Adamawa, January 2019, on file with Author.

[26] Madagali is one of the towns in Adamawa still struggling with the presence of Boko Haram.

facing attacks from Boko Haram, as a result, it is a contravention of the Refugee Convention to repatriate Nigerians there. Most times, refugees are not moved to Mubi Transit Camp until they are large in number. According to camp officials, they are gathered in Madagali and when they are a substantial number, they are transported by the Nigerian Army to Mubi.

As of January 21, 2019, there were 13 refugees in Mubi Transit Camp and that same day, another 26 refugees joined them from Madagali while another 35 were expected from Cameroon that day.[27] Camp officials explained that Mubi Transit camp only receives women and children because young women and men are separated at Madagali and taken to Chibok and other locales where they are screened to ascertain whether they are either missing Chibok girls or male members of Boko Haram. After screening, if they are not Chibok girls, they are sent to the transit camp but if they are members of Boko Haram, they are sent for 'rehabilitation'. Camp officials hold that the Nigerian refugees who are still in Minawao and other camps in Cameroon are from Borno State because Borno is still a Boko Haram stronghold.

The refugees being repatriated from Cameroon to Mubi are non-indigenes of Mubi. Most of them cannot return to their homes and are forced to build new lives in Mubi. Camp Officials state that most of the refugees struggle to resettle in Mubi and find it hard to find jobs, shelter, food, and other necessities. Repatriation to Madagali from Cameroon endangers the lives of refugees because Madagali is not free from insurgency. However, people in Mubi have made space for people who are being forcefully returned to Madagali and this is changing the configuration of the town. According to one of the oldest inhabitants of Mubi:

> I see Mubi having peace in the future and what is even happening now is that after the insurgence the population in Mubi have almost multiplied the previous. People have come to stay in Mubi, from places like Maiduguri, Madagali, and Michika because of their experience in Cameroon. I don't think they would like to go back because of the fear of the insurgence in their various localities. We are now one big community.

These actions in the communities in Mubi give us insight into how people in the borderlands are involved in doing the work to address the injustices of international law and abuses of state sovereignty.

6 Conclusion

There is still a lack of collaboration between neighbouring countries to address conflict, security, and displacement issues, and a failure to practice international refugee law norms in good faith. It is evidence of the fragmentation within the Global South as a result of colonial hangovers. The conflicting approaches of the Nigerian government and the Cameroonian government towards their borders, forced migrations, transportation of people and goods, and cross-border business greatly

[27] Interview with a Health Officer at Mubi Transit Camp, Mubi North Local Government Area, Adamawa, January 2019, on file with Author.

affect how people in Mubi and those fleeing conflict in other parts of Northeastern Nigeria experience the border. It reflects the current state of intra-African relations, security, and trade, and an example of how people's daily lives today are still impacted by the colonial legacy of strict and exclusionary borderlines. The Mubi example gives insight into how Nigeria and Cameroon practice their obligations under international refugee law, where security concerns still trump international human rights law and humanitarian principles. It is also an indication of the growing trend of states in the Global South, like their counterparts in the Global North, to undermine international law by minimising refugee protection under the guise of fighting against terrorism.

This chapter documents some narratives of people in Mubi to understand how factors including contentious borders stemming from colonialism, and contemporary terrorism impact their lives and their struggles to maintain their homes between hostile states. These narratives are not amplified beyond local or regional levels due to disregard of the issues that concern many African communities, particularly those in borderlands on the fringes of the state. Studying the ways in which international legal and state-level norms unfold at the local level in the daily lives of people has demonstrated a few things. The local level (particularly border communities) is where historical and contemporary international legal decisions and failures of international law play out in the Global South. It is also at this level that individuals and communities are doing the important work of protecting their rights and interests, securing their communities, and rebuilding. This is the reason why more research on international law must go beyond the courts, the statutes, and the conventions and should also consider the daily manifestations of the law in the lives of people and communities as well.

It is tempting, and even expected, to discuss borders as hot spots for state sovereignty contests or to study the decisions on border disputes at the Hague as lessons on how international law works. However, by focusing on the people who live there, we understand that borders are not abstract- they represent home, a place where people actualise their goals and fight for their rights. Family and business ties existed before colonialism and these ties continue today under the pressure of the limitations of border delimitations and the protection of state sovereignty. This is where we can learn how things work, whether they work or not. It is also where the limitations or the latitude of state power and citizenship are tried and tested in real time.

The study of Mubi shows that the relegation of international border issues to a regional or local event because it is happening between African states, remains bad for the transformative capacity of international law. The problem of scale, i.e., what is international and deserves international-level action remains one of the biggest problems of international law (Riles 1995). International law can only be transformative if these ongoing struggles and challenges at borders against violence and hegemony are acknowledged, documented, and understood in the first place. The narratives of people in Mubi show that international law is still not fit for purpose because it has failed them so many times. Daily displacement and refoulement are unacknowledged and unaddressed by the international community. Their struggles and efforts to normalise and rebuild in their town and to create space for other displaced people are unrecognised and a lot of the ongoing local-level work, including informal cross-border security work is an attempt to right the wrongs of colonialism and international law, and the failures of Nigeria and Cameroon.

By looking at the realities on the ground, it has been possible to learn and understand the dynamics of the refugee situation in Mubi better. The refugee population is decreasing, however, there are indications that many refugees from Borno and Yobe are still in Cameroon and will eventually migrate to Mubi. This is significant considering the context of the displacement between Cameroon and Nigeria; it means that the refugee migrations across the borders are far from over. Refugee migration and settlement in Mubi remains a very important subject for future research, as most of the refugees are unlikely to return to their places of origin and their presence in Mubi will have a significant impact on Mubi. The population of Mubi has been increasing since the insurgency and this will have future implications.

Finally, Mubi remains the economic nerve of Adamawa, not only because of its proximity to the border but also because neighbouring towns and villages, both in Nigeria and Cameroon have come to rely on Mubi for goods and services, as well as refuge in times of conflict. For these reasons, an understanding of the daily life in Mubi and the narratives around the border and displacement remains crucial. Mubi holds answers to some of the big questions about the evolution of borders, contemporary intra-African migrations, and alternative sources of knowledge that challenge the dominant narratives and perspectives of Africa and African people. The work of local researchers and ethnographers is essential to uncovering these contemporary manifestations of the gaps in international law and state practice. In the study of international law, TWAIL makes this possible because it opens the possibility to decentre dominant narratives and practices of international legal scholarship and foregrounds the use of non-traditional research methods and methodologies to gain an understanding of the impact of the law in the Global South.

References

Abiodun, Duyile. 2014. Nigeria-Cameroon boundary relations in the North of Nigeria, 1914–94. *International Affairs and Global Strategy* 27: 35.

Agbiboa, Daniel Egiegba. 2015. The social dynamics of the "Nigerian Taliban": fresh insights from the social identity theory. *Social Dynamics* 41 (3): 415–437. https://doi.org/10.1080/02533952.2015.1100364.

Agbiboa, Daniel Egiegba. 2018. Eyes on the street: civilian joint task force and the surveillance of Boko Haram in Northeastern Nigeria. *Intelligence and National Security* 33 (7): 1022–1039. https://doi.org/10.1080/02684527.2018.1475892.

Agbiboa, Daniel Egiegba. 2013. The ongoing campaign of terror in Nigeria: boko haram versus the State. Stability. *International Journal of Security & Development* 2(3): 52 1–18. https://doi.org/10.5334/sta.cl

Aghedo, Iro, and Oarhe Osumah. 2012. The Boko Haram uprising: how should Nigeria Respond? *Third World Quarterly* 33 (5): 853–869. https://doi.org/10.1080/01436597.2012.674701.

Aljazeera. 2014. Scores killed in bus station blast, November 28, 2014. Accessed at https://www.aljazeera.com/news/2014/11/28/scores-killed-in-nigeria-bus-station-blast on June 25, 2021

Aljazeera. 2017. Suicide bomber kills worshippers at Mosque in Mubi, November 21, 2017. Accessed at https://www.aljazeera.com/news/2017/11/21/suicide-bomber-kills-worshippers-at-mosque-in-mubi on June 30, 2021

Aljazeera. 2018. Nigeria mosque death toll rises to 86, May 2, 2018. Accessed at https://www.aljazeera.com/news/2018/5/2/nigeria-mosque-attack-death-toll-rises-to-86 on June 30, 2021

Anghie, Anthony. 2005. *Imperialism, sovereignty and making international law (Cambridge studies in comparative and international law)*. Cambridge: Cambridge University Press. https://doi.org/10.1017/CBO9780511614262.

BBC News Africa. 2013. Bakassi residents to pay tax under Cameroon sovereignty. Accessed at http://www.bbc.co.uk/news/world-africa-23710733 on June 25, 2021

Bueno, Olivia. 2006. Perspectives on refoulement in Africa. International Refugee Rights Initiative. Accessed at http://refugee-rights.org/perspectives-on-refoulement-in-africa/ on July 5, 2021

Burgis-Kasthala, Michelle. 2016. Scholarship as dialogue? ICL, TWAIL and the politics of methodology. *Journal of International Criminal Justice* 14 (4): 921–937. https://doi.org/10.1093/jicj/mqw044.

Chimni, Bhupinder. 2011. The World of TWAIL: Introduction to the special issue. *Trade, Law and Development 3*(1): 14–25

de Sousa Santos, Bonaventura. 2018. The end of the cognitive empire: The coming of age of epistemologies of the South, Durham: Duke University Press

Deleixhe, Martin, Magdalena Dembinska, and Julien Danero Iglesias. 2019. Securitized borderlands. *Journal of Borderlands Studies* 34 (5): 639–647. https://doi.org/10.1080/08865655.2018.1445547.

El-Sudi, Ibrahim Tukur. 2019. The Nigerian states that formed parts of Northern Cameroon. PR Nigeria. Accessed at https://prnigeria.com/2019/04/20/nigerian-states-northern-cameroons/, on June 25, 2021

Eslava, Luis. 2015. *Local space, global life: the everyday operation of international law and development*. Cambridge: Cambridge University Press.

Eslava, Luis, and Sundhya Pahuja. 2011. Between resistance and reform: TWAIL and the universality of international law. *Trade, Law and Development Trade, Law and Development* 3: 1103–1130.

Eslava, Luis. 2019. TWAIL coordinates. Legal critical thinking. Accessed at: http://criticallegalthinking.com/2019/04/02/twail-coordinates/ on June 17, 2021

France24. 2014. Football stadium blast kills scores in Northern Nigeria. Accessed at https://www.france24.com/en/20140601-football-stadium-blast-kills-scores-northern-nigeria-mubi on June 25, 2021

Hansen, William W., and Musa Umma Aliyu. 2013. Fanon, the wretched and Boko Haram. *Journal of Asian and African Studies* 48 (3): 281–296. https://doi.org/10.1177/0021909612467277.

Hebie, Mamadou. 2015. Was there something missing in the decolonization process in Africa?: The territorial dimension. *Leiden Journal of International Law* 28:529–556. https://doi.org/10.1017/S092215651500028X

Hlovor, Ishmael K. 2020. Inclusion of borderlanders in border management in Africa: Toward an emancipatory framework for the study and management of African borders. *International Studies Perspectives* 21: 37–53.

Human Rights Watch. 2017. Cameroon: Force mass returns of Nigerian Refugees: Military deports 100,000, Torture and abuse in remote border area. Accessed at https://www.hrw.org/news/2017/09/27/cameroon-mass-forced-return-nigerian-refugees on July 7, 2021

New Humanitarian. 2013. Refugee influx causes unease in Cameroon. Accessed at https://www.thenewhumanitarian.org/news/2013/10/30/refugee-influx-causes-unease-cameroon on June 25, 2021

Ibanga, Michael, and James Archibong. 2018. The Boko haram insurgency: characterization and implications under municipal and international laws. In *Boko Haram and International Law*, ed. John-Mark Iyi and Hennie Strydom, 137–153. Cham: Springer, International Publishing. https://doi.org/10.1007/978-3-319-74957-0_7

International Court of Justice. 2002. Land and maritime boundary between Cameroon and Nigeria, Cameroon and Equatorial Guinea (intervening) v Nigeria, Judgment, Merits, [2002] ICJ Rep 303, ICGJ 63

Isike, Christopher, and Efe Isike. 2018. Migration and the geopolitics of boko haram terrorism in Nigeria. *Strategic Review for Southern Africa* 40(2): 34–51. https://doi.org/10.35293/srsa.v40i2.183

MacEachern, Scott. 2020. Boko Haram, bandits and slave-raiders: Identities and violence in a Central African borderland. *Canadian Journal of African Studies* 54 (2): 247–263. https://doi.org/10.1080/00083968.2019.1700142.

Mbiyozo, Aimée-Noël. 2017. Cameroon's forceful repatriation of Nigerian refugees. Institute for Security Studies Policy Brief, pp. 1–10

Mendez, Jennifer Bickham, and Nancy A. Naples. 2014. Contests over Territory, Nation, Identity, and Belonging. In *Border Politics: Social Movements, Collective Identities, and Globalization,* ed. Nancy A. Naples, and Jennifer Bickham Mendez. New York University Press. https://doi.org/10.18574/nyu/9781479898992.003.0001

Merry, Sally Engle. 2006. Anthropology and International Law. *Annual Review of Anthropology 35*(1):99–116. https://doi.org/10.1146/annurev.anthro.35.081705.123245

Mukhtar, Sadiq, Rosniza Aznie Che Rose, Lam Kuok Choy, and Amina Ummulkhair Ibrahim Bibi-Farouk. 2020. Boko haram and the geopolitics of forced migration in Nigeria. *Journal of International Studies14*: 51–63. https://doi.org/10.32890/jis.14.2018.7998

Muma, Eric Che. 2018. The principle of non-refoulement and the obligations of the united nations in ensuring the accountability of states toward refugee protection: lessons from Nigeria and Cameroon. In *RAIS conference proceedings—the 11th international RAIS conference on social sciences*. https://doi.org/10.2139/ssrn.3303552

Mutua, Makau. 2000. Critical race theory and international law: the view of an insider-outsider. *Villanova Law Review 45*(5): 841–853. https://digitalcommons.law.buffalo.edu/journal_articles/568

BBC News. 2014. Boko haram renames seized town in Adamawa State November 5, 2014. Accessed at https://www.bbc.com/news/world-africa-29921047 on June 30, 2021

BBC News. 2017. Boko haram crisis: Cameroon forcing Nigerian refugees home. Accessed at https://www.bbc.com/news/world-africa-39343514 on June 30, 2021

Okafor, Obiora Chinedu. 2008. Critical Third World Approaches to International Law (TWAIL): theory, methodology, or both. *International Community Law Review 10*: 371–378. https://digitalcommons.osgoode.yorku.ca/scholarly_works/892

Onapajo, Hakeem, Ufo Okeke Uzodike, and Ayo Whetho. 2012. Boko haram terrorism in Nigeria. *African Security Review* 21 (3): 24–39. https://doi.org/10.1080/10220461.2012.740319.

Organization of African Unity. 1969. Convention governing the specific aspects of refugee problems in Africa ("OAU Convention"), 1001 U.N.T.S. 45

Osumah, Oarhe. 2013. Boko haram insurgency in northern Nigeria and the vicious cycle of internal insecurity. *Small Wars and Insurgencies* 24 (3): 536–556. https://doi.org/10.1080/09592318.2013.802605.

Otoghile, Aiguosatile, and Afeaye A. Igbafe. 2014. Colonial construction and boko haram insurgency in Nigeria: relating the present to the past. *Public Policy and Administration Research* 4: 12.

Parmar, Pooja. 2008. TWAIL: An epistemological inquiry. *International Community Law Review* 10 (4): 363–370.

Rajagopal, Balakrishnan. 2003. International law from below: development, social movements and third world resistance. Cambridge: Cambridge University Press. https://doi.org/10.1017/CBO9780511494079

Reliefweb. 2018. Cameroons forced returns puts Nigerians at Risk. Accessed https://reliefweb.int/report/cameroon/cameroon-s-forced-returns-put-nigerian-refugees-risk on June 30, 2021

Reuters. 2012. Gunmen kill at least 26 students at Nigerian College. Accessed at https://www.reuters.com/article/us-nigeria-shooting-college-idUSBRE8910IK20121002 on June 25, 2021

Riles, Annelise. 1995. The View from the international plane: perspective and scale in the architecture of colonial international law. Cornell Law Faculty Publications. p. 1072. https://scholarship.law.cornell.edu/facpub/1072
Sajo, Salama. 2018. An impact assessment of boko haram insurgency on commercial activities in Mubi Town. *Journal of Social Science and Humanities Research 3*(5): 58–82. https://doi.org/10.53555/sshr.v3i5.2025
Xavier Sujith. 2016. Learning from below: Theorizing global governance through ethnographies and critical reflections from the global South. Windsor Yearbook of Access to Justice 33: 3 229–255. https://doi.org/10.22329/wyaj.v33i3.4918
Sunter, Andew F. 2007. TWAIL as naturalized epistemology. *Canadian Journal of Law and Jurisprudence* 20: 2.
Thomas, Chantal. 2000. Critical race theory and postcolonial development theory: observations on methodology. *Villanova Law Review* 45 (5): 1195–1220.
Umukoro, Nathaniel. 2016. Thermodynamics: application of its principles to the effects of cross-border migration and boko haram crisis on security challenges in Africa. *Journal of Applied Security Research* 11 (1): 44–60. https://doi.org/10.1080/19361610.2016.1104279.
UN High Commissioner for Refugees. 2017. Tripartite agreement for the voluntary repatriation of Nigerian refugees living in Cameroon between the Government of the Republic of Cameroon, the Government of the Federal Republic of Nigeria and the UN High Commissioner for Refugees. Accessed at https://reliefweb.int/report/cameroon/tripartite-agreement-voluntary-repatriation-nigerian-refugees-living-cameroon, on June 20, 2021
United Nations General Assembly. 1951. Convention relating to the status of refugees. United Nations, Treaty Series, vol. 189, p. 137 accessed at https://www.refworld.org/docid/3be01b964.html on July 5, 2021
United Nations High Commission for Refugees. 1984. Identity documents for refugees EC/SCP/33. Accessed at https://www.unhcr.org/excom/scip/3ae68cce4/identity-documents-refugees.html on July 5, 2012
United Nations High Commission for Refugees. 1992. Handbook on procedures and criteria for determining refugee status under the 1951 Convention and the 1967 Protocol relating to the Status of Refugees HCR/IP/4/Eng/REV.1.
United Nations High Commission for Refugees. 2014. Boko Haram attacks in Nigeria force 13,000 to flee to Cameroon, November 11, 2014. Accessed at https://www.unhcr.org/news/latest/2014/11/546228896/boko-haram-attacks-nigeria-force-13000-flee-cameroon.html on June 30, 2021
United Nations. 2014. UN Agency reports growing number of refugees as Nigeria Insurgency Continues. Accessed at https://www.un.org/africarenewal/news/un-agency-reports-growing-number-refugees-nigeria-insurgency-continues on June 30, 2021
Vanguard. 2012. Adamawa imposes curfew after boko haram killings. Accessed at https://www.vanguardngr.com/2012/01/adamawa-imposes-curfew-after-boko-haram-killings/ on June 25, 2021
Wikileaks. 2009. New wave of Nigerians return from Bakassi. Accessed at https://wikileaks.org/plusd/cables/09LAGOS465_a.html on June 25, 2021
Woldemariam, Samuel Berhanu, Amy Maguire, and Jason Von Meding. 2019. Forced human displacement, the third world and international law: A TWAIL perspective. *Melbourne Journal of International Law* 20 (1): 248–276.

The Global South and Forgotten Voices

The Children of Kuveni: A Critical Analysis of the Derogated Status of Vedda Community in Post-independent Sri Lanka

Punsara Amarasinghe

Abstract This chapter critically examines the challenges faced by Sri Lanka's indigenous community, Vedda's in the post-colonial setting of the island nation and it further unfolds the long-term impacts created by neoliberal agendas on the well-being of the Vedda people. This chapter astutely looks into the land and socio-economic rights of Sri Lanka's indigenous community as they have been challenged in the aftermath of the independence before the populist steps taken by the successive governments. The analysis emerging from this chapter unveils how Sri Lanka has failed in safeguarding the rights of the indigenous community: Veddas regardless of country's pretext in complying with international law standards.

Keywords Vedda · Sri Lanka · Neoliberalism · Rights

1 Introduction

The whole notion of human rights and international law developed under the guise of the intellectual upheaval of the West and its initial understanding was confined to Europe as its founding fathers excluded the rest of the world community into the peripheral stage of incivility. Nonetheless, it is a palatable factor that such a parochial view existed in international law and human rights began to wane in the aftermath of the Second World War, particularly before the steeping rise of decolonising movement which ended the colonial yoke over Afro-Asian countries. The Universal Declaration of Human Rights in 1948 and the emergence of the non-aligned movement at the Bandung Conference in 1955 embodied the broader significance of international law and human rights discourse beyond its Eurocentric antecedents. However, the empathy for the 'indigenous community' in the realm of international law and human rights scholarship arose in the 1970s (Philips 2015, p. 120). The proclivity toward indigenous rights transformed from a prosaic description into a concept with

P. Amarasinghe (✉)
Institute of Law, Politics and Development, Scuola Superiore Sant Anna, Pisa, Italy
e-mail: punsaraprint10@gmail.com

T. Venthan Ananthavinayagan and A. Viswanath Shenoy (eds.), *The Wretched of the Global South*, International Law and the Global South,
https://doi.org/10.1007/978-981-99-9275-1_6

a considerable agency as a basis for subaltern studies. The definition of the term 'indigenous people' played a highly contentious role as there was no consensus among the international community and organisations to categorise it. Given such ambiguity, the definition stemmed from the UN Special Rapporteur on Discrimination against Indigenous Populations, Martinez Cobo in 1983 can be regarded as a widely accepted one. Cobo describes indigenous people as follows:

> Indigenous communities, peoples and nations are those which, having a historical continuity with pre-invasion and pre-colonial societies that developed on their territories, consider themselves distinct from other sectors of the societies now prevailing in those territories, or parts of them. They form at present non-dominant sectors of society and are determined to preserve, develop and transmit to future generations their ancestral territories, and their ethnic identity, as the basis of their continued existence as peoples, in accordance with their own cultural patterns, social institutions and legal system (Cobo 1983).

In tracing the indigenous communities hobnobbing with the international law, the idea of excluding the indigenous people from the terrain of self-determination or sovereign rights seems to be a recent one as indigenous people had been regarded as a subject of international law and holders of sovereignty for centuries. One of the founding fathers of international law, Spanish theologian Francisco Vittoria was a proponent in the early epoch of sixteenth century international law who admitted the indigenous Indian tribes' right to comprehend natural law (Anghie 1996). In the early phase of organising its state structure, the US alone entered into more than 800 treaties with Indian tribes between 1776 and 1871. The treaty of Waitangi which came into force between the British crown and the 540 Maori chiefs in New Zealand in 1840 made an indispensable impact on the concept of the sovereignty of the indigenous people. In Wantangi Treaty, Maori explicitly ceded soverignity over New Zealand to the Crown (Matson 1991).

Notwithstanding the discontents and views prevalent in international law regarding the right to self-determination of the indigenous community, this paper seeks to examine the impoverished status of the Veda community in Sri Lanka whose existence has been detrimentally affected by various development mechanisms in the post-independent Sri Lanka. In particular, this paper gives special attention to the rapid neoliberal agenda embraced by Sri Lankan governments, which continues to marginalise and derogate the Vedda community from enjoying their rights as the only indigenous community in Sri Lanka. The task of this paper is threefold. First, it traces the intrinsic status of Vedda Community in Sri Lanka imbued with the historiography of the island. In analysing the sui generis role of Vedda community in Sri Lanka, this article unfolds the post-colonial trajectories of Sri Lanka that gradually curtailed the participation of Veddas in the state apparatus. Secondly, this article elaborates how Neoliberal agenda, which engulfed Sri Lanka after introducing open economy transformed the outlook of Vedda's heritage as an oriental depecition to the foreign tourists while ignoring the real needs of the Veddas. This analysis simply reflects the ignominy that has befallen the Vedda community as a marginalised community who confronts the state authoritarianism in safeguarding their rights for lands and other necessities. Thirdly, this article traces the defective nature of the Sri Lankan legal system, which has not safeguarded the rights of the Vedda community as it has ensured the customary laws of the other ethnic minorities on the island.

2 Story of Veddas in Sri Lanka

Everything that is natural-god given.

The sun, the moon, the wind, the trees.

And the beauty of the blowing wind, the wild animal.

Who is a part of nature itself belongs to us the vannilathho.

The men of the jungle.

Our forearms possess the strength of a steady rock.

Our minds are filled with beauty.

That can be compared to the serenity of the jungle.

Our hearts contain the rhythms of the running water.

We are the men of the jungle (Fernando 2019).

The abovementioned two verses known as the anthem of the Vedda community in Sri Lanka echo the same ethos propounded by Chief Seattle in his famous letter to the 13th President of the USA.

The saga of the Vedda community in Sri Lanka is imbued with the general history of the island and it even traces beyond the recorded history of Sri Lanka. The term Vedda has derived from the Sanskrit word *Vyadha*, which denotes the bearer of the bow and arrow (Dharmadasa 1974, p. 92). Dr Nandadeva Wijesekere, who devoted his whole academic life to researching the ethnographical features of the Vedda community in Sri Lanka states:

> The Veddas have been considered a distinct human type known as ‘Veddoids’. This type though mixed can be recognized as persisting to this day. The vedda is a shy quiet human being short in stature and dark in complexion except the Mediterranean type which is lighter in colour. He has a long and narrow head with a cephalic index of 72.6, a cranial capacity of 1227 and a nasal index of 73.1. The average height of a Vedda is 15788 mm. The majority of Veddahs belonged to the ‘O’ blood group. Woman are petite with fine features and are comparatively short in stature (Wijesekara 198, pp. 38).

Besides the physical anthropological explanation written by Dr. Wijesekera, the history of the Vedda community in Sri Lanka has been a rather fascinating one. The general belief among the historians is that Veddas descend from a direct line of Sri Lanka’s Neolithic community. Nonetheless, according to Dr. Shiran Deraniyagala their origin exceeds beyond 16,000 B.C. (Deraniyagala 1985). The *Mahawamsa,* which is regarded as the primary canonical text narrating the history of Sri Lanka, links Veddah community to the lineage of Prince Vijaya who arrived in Sri Lanka in the sixth century BC. Vijaya later went on to become the first king of Sri Lanka, met Kuveni on the shores of Thambapanni. Kuveni was the queen of the Yakka's, one of the two tribes, the other being the Nagas that had settlements in Sri Lanka. Vijaya, fell in love with the queen and they had two children, a girl and a boy. The marriage was short-lived, as Vijaya, by then king of the island, left Kuveni for a Pandya princess. The children had then, according to the chronicle, departed to the valleys of the Rathnapura District where they had multiplied giving rise to the Veddahs of today. There is strong academic opinion in favour of the above narration and anthropologists such as Seligmann as far back as, 1911 believed that there were similarities between the genetics of the Yakkas and modern-day Veddas (Selighman 1911).

It is true that the Vedda community persistently secured their homogeneity in Sri Lanka for centuries regardless of the various challenges they faced. Especially, it was rather remarkable that this community did not cease to exist even after the deadliest military invasions came from South India and then the European invaders who altered the geopolitical structure of Sri Lanka. Indeed, the linguistic distinction was well preserved by the Vedda community in Sri Lanka as they occupied a transition area as the buffer between the Sinhala and Tamil speaking Vedda people (Stremuer 1997). However, the life of the Vedda community began to drastically change after Sri Lanka gained independence from the British in 1948. The successive majoritarian governments consisting of the Sinhala community showed less concern about the ecological conservation in formulating its development structure, which mainly paved the path for the steeping decline of the autonomy of the Vedda community as an independent sect. The systematic violation of the Vedda community's right to their lands began exactly one year after the independence in 1949 with the populist agenda initiated by Sri Lanka's first Premier D.S Senanayake who went on to build the largest man-made lake in Sri Lanka called 'Senanayake Samudraya' (Farmer 1963). In the modern socio-political history of Sri Lanka, the reservoir built by D.S Senanayake aggrandises his vision of transforming the island nation into a self-sustained country in its post-colonial venture. But the very position advocated by Sri Lanka's first premier and his political party disdained the certain rights enjoyed by another community. Ironically so many vocal opponents lampooned D.S Senanayake and his government when he went on to disfranchise the Indian Tamil community in the hill country as it was generally viewed as a clear ethnic demarcation. But none of those vocal opponents showed enthusiasm for safeguarding the well-being of the indigenous community in Sri Lanka. From a post-colonial point of view, this incident exposes the gravity of 'otherness' shown by the ethnically divided government of newly independent Sri Lanka where the majority of Sinhalese and Tamils were involved in deciding the structure of governmentality. In this ethnically divided quest to attain their political rights under the guise of so-called 'Modernity' implanted by the British, the ruling class of Sri Lanka excluded the Veddas as a community from the primitive past. The exodus of the Vedda people from their traditional settlements due to the construction of Senanayake Samudraya and Gal Oya colonisation created a fatal effect on the lifestyle they preserved for the centuries. Despite the government's efforts to portray Vedda's resettlement as an act of safeguarding their basic needs, none of the leaders from the Vedda community liked the government's decision (Jayasena 2015, p. 291).

3 Vanishing Veddas: Marginalisation of Vedda Community After Independence

According to renown Sri Lankan anthropologist Prof. Gananath Obeysekere, the knowledge and the perception of the Vedda community in Sri Lanka in its post-colonial context were based on the colonial view developed by British colonial administrators who gazed at Vedda from the Saidian lenses of 'Orientalism' (Said, 1974). In Obeyaskere's view, the successive governments that came into power in post-independent Sri Lanka followed the colonial practice of considering the Veddas as an inferior race regardless of their fervent existence in Sri Lankan history. Comparing Sinhalese-Tamil rivalry with Sinhalese view on the Vedda community Obeyasekere writes:

> Nowadays, we are accustomed to think that the main structural opposition in the history is between Sinhalese and Tamils. Yet, this appositional relationship is a historically contingent one, that is, it depends on particular historical circumstances such that period of Sinhala Tamil opposition might be followed by alliances expressive of amity; or both opposition or amity co-exist in the same time span; at other times neither nor amity seem to matter and both communities went on living and partly living. By contrast, as Mahavasma clearly recognizes the opposition between Veddas and Sinhalese was much stable and permanent though not a hostile one. Right through history, even when Veddas practiced agriculture, they were depicted as a different ethnic group, that is as hunters (Obeyasekera 2003, p. 61).

By neglecting the autonomy enjoyed by the Vedda community, the Sinhalese dominated government excluded Veddas from the post-independent state formation. This was further manifested in the way how Sri Lanka adopted its Constitution. 1947 Constitution commonly known as Soulbury Constitution was not a document embodying the intrinsic values of the compatriots in Sri Lanka. On the contrary, it is a constitution imposed upon the nation as a document that is intended to form the governmentality for a new nation. The architect of the 1947 Constitution, Sir Ivor Jennings drafted the Constitution under the gamut of Westminster constitutional doctrines that he revered as a colonial constitutional maker (Amarasinghe 2017). As a mechanism addressing the concerns of the ethnic minorities of the island, Jennings included Article 29 (2) in the Constitution, which ensured protection for the ethnic minorities. However, Jennings' constitutional experiment in Sri Lanka did not include directive principles chapter to the Constitution to ensure the social and economic development which particularly affected the welfare of the Vedda community. Under Jennings' Constitution, Veddas were devoid of constitutional protection that applied to other ethnic minorities and the robust agricultural development implemented by the successive governments compelled this vanishing Vedda community to assimilate into Sinhalese culture. It was in this context that Dr Nandaveda Wijesekere deplorably stated "In 1963 I saw the phase of a vanishing race. In 1980 there are no true Veddas to see. The real Veddas have vanished" (Wijesekere 1981).

Nonetheless the salient guarantee of welfare to the indigenous tribes in the Indian Constitution in 1950 stands in contrast to the constitutional failure visible in Jennings' Constitution in Sri Lanka. The Constitution of India in 1950 primarily distinguished itself from Sri Lankan Constitution under two stances. First, it was an autochthonous constitution echoed the aspirations of a newly independent nation striving to overcome its haunted colonial past and secondly it was dedicated to addressing the socio-economic grievances prevalent in the marginalised communities. Indian's authentic doyen of its constitutional making B.R Ambedkar was a not vocal supporter of safeguarding the rights of India's Adivasi tribes as he devoted himself to the annihilation of caste. He was lampooned by his critics for not including the term 'Scheduled Tribes' in the Constitution along with the term 'Scheduled Areas' (Guha 2007). Yet, Ambedkar's intention went much further as he expressed the need for a separate commission for Adivasi tribes (India's indigenous community). Even though, the Constitution does not enshrine the term 'Adivasi' explicitly Article 342 included by Ambedkar provides a certain guarantee for the scheduled tribes. This protection has been further bolstered by the Fifth and Sixth Schedule of India's Constitution which widely speaks about the rights of the scheduled tribes. In addition to that, the Directive Principles of the State Policy (Article 36–51) specify in the guidelines to the states that every possible action must be undertaken to improve the conditions of all the citizens, which includes the scheduled tribes (Adivasi) (Menon 2007).

The constitutional making process in Sri Lanka in the aftermath of its colonial rule under British made no satiable efforts in safeguarding its indigenous community Veddas. Instead, the state apparatus of Sri Lanka intensified various policy makings for the sake of sheer development, which resulted in further decline of Veddas. In particular, both homegrown constitutions that Sri Lanka adopted in 1972 and 1978, respectively, failed in enshrining the aspirations of the Veddas or at least including satisfactory provisions in safeguarding their rights.

When Sri Lanka embraced the open economy as the first country to do so in South Asia under J.R Jayewardene, the country's remaining Vedda population became more susceptible to the robust changes. Especially, the intensified Mahavali development project appeared to be a nemesis for their existence as the development tasks carried out by the administrative officers curtailed Vedda's ownership of the lands (Peebles 1991). One of the biggest pitfalls in those development projects was the apathy of the government in cooperating with the Vedda community for the progress of the Mahaweli development project. On this issue Sri Lankan anthropologist Jayantha Perera comments:

> The Mahaweli agencies have not consulted Veddas regarding development projects. I was a resident anthropologist in the Mahaweli H region in the 1970s where I met many of them. They were worried about how fast they were losing their land, identity, and culture. In the late 1980s, I was in System B of the Mahaweli as an irrigation water management specialist. The Vedda community complained that the state had established large wildlife parks such as Madura Oya Sanctuary and relocation sites without consulting them or engaging them in decision-making. International law prescribes that the state or project owners should obtain

their 'free, prior, informed consent. But no such consent-seeking exercises have ever been conducted among Veddas (Perera 2021).

As Perera rightly commented the biggest pitfall of Mahaweli project was rooted in its inability to understand the primary concerns of the Sri Lanka's indigenous population. The biggest goal that Sri Lankan government under J.R Jayewardene focused was to attain rapid economic development based on Singapore model (Gnanarajah 1981). It negated the concern for social development towards the marginalised communities and mainly focused on encouraging market-oriented entrepreneurs. It was rather a notable factor the government patronage for the private land developers for various development projects resulted in a massive loss of the traditional lands possessed by Veddas. The Neoliberal principles idealised by the government tended to transform many forest lands into national sanctuaries or agricultural colonies aiming at the wealth accumulation, whereas Veddas were resettled in areas which completely altered the culture, traditions, and livelihood of the Vedda community mainly in Dimulagala and Henanigala. The market ideology which is an integral part of the Neoliberalism played a pivotal role in the early phase of open economic policies adopted by Sri Lanka. For example, some of the development projects increased the contacts between Veddas and the outside world, which paved the path for the internal degeneration of the Vedda community. In writing a report on the Vedda community in post-independent Sri Lanka, De Silva and Punchihewa discuss how Ramba Ken Oya project in Sri Lanka jeopardised the peaceful existence of Vedda community by the influx of outsiders to their territories. They state:

> Due to the Ramba Ken Oya Project attracting many labourers from outside the village, there are lot of services that are granted from the people in the village. Unfortunately, some of the services include providing sex for benefits that is not considered morally correct by the cultural settings. Due to the economic deprivation, women and even young girls have become sex workers. The culture has altered itself to a situation where there are pimps who connect such sex workers with prospective customers. As they are unaware about the preventive and precautionary methods used by conventional sex workers in urban settlements, those women that engage in sex work have become exposed to the risk of becoming victims of sexually transmitted diseases. It is said that there have been instances where such women have opted abortion as a last resort, some of which have been done using traditional and life threatening methods as they are unable to afford expensive professional services (de Silva Punchihewa 2011).

4 Loopholes in the Legal System in Safeguarding Vedda Rights

The question that comes to the fore is the duplicity of the Neoliberal state outlook toward the common interests. The recognition given to the Indigenous communities under the state patronage was depicted as an offer and Jakeeth Singh describes it as a recognition from above in which the state plays the role of an arbiter for just and unjust claims for recognition from subordinate groups (Singh 2015). The doggy side of this relationship between the state and those subordinate groups is that it is the state that measures the terms of that recognition. This argument shows how the state utilises the existence of the marginalised minorities such as indigenous communities for the economic interests of the Neoliberal age while patronising their welfare for them. The keen interest shown by the Sri Lankan governments after 1977 seemed to be a candid one ensuring the protection of the Vedda community and their social welfare. For example, the establishment of a museum of the Aboriginal culture in 1996 in Dambana in Sri Lanka, which happens to be the province where the Vedda community leader resides denotes the interest of the government in preserving and recognising the Vedda people as the earliest settlers in Sri Lanka. But the paradoxical reality stemming from this great exhibition is nothing more than a sheer attempt made by the Sri Lankan state machinery based on its Neoliberal agenda. On one side, the inclusion of the Vedda community as a key pillar in its tourism sector boosted the revenue of the government. On the other side, it was an act that resembled the colonial practice of displaying African people in human zoos in Europe during the late nineteenth century (Vandenbussche 2014). In the mind of nineteenth-century imperialists, the notion of presenting African people in human zoos perpetuated the difference between enlightened Europe and primitive Africa, which consoled the Western masses to be content in their socio-economic advancement. However, the display of the Vedda community as an exhibition in Sri Lanka is akin to wealth accumulation to the government in the age of Neoliberalism. It further proves Jakketh Singh's contention of 'recognition from above as a reality in the neoliberal state organisation'.

It may be worth examining the recent development regarding the indigenous rights in international law. Before forming a consensus on the indigenous rights in the UN system, it was International Labour Organization that defended the social and economic rights of groups whose customs, traditions, institutions, or language set them apart from other sections of national communities. In 1953, ILO published a study on indigenous peoples and in 1957 adopted C107 and Recommendation No.104 on the Protection and Integration of Indigenous and Tribal Populations. To a certain extent, the Article 27 of the ICCPR (International Covenant on Civil and Political Rights) in 1966 provided a minimal protection in securing the indigenous people's rights. The Article 27 of the ICCPR states:

> In those States in which ethnic, religious or linguistic minorities exist, persons belonging to such minorities shall not be denied the right, in community with other members of their group, to enjoy their own culture, to profess and practice their own religion, or to use their own language (UN General Assembly, 1966a, Article 27).

These were the first international legal instruments specifically created to protect the rights of peoples whose ways of life and existence were—then, as now—threatened by dominating cultures. But none of those implicit references fortified the whole set of rights of the indigenous communities around the world. Regarding the discontent between modern society and the indigenous communities, Richard Falk argues indigenous people are in a situation where their claims for protection cannot be coherently understood except when treated separately (Falk 2006). However, the conflicting views in framing the indigenous community and national ethnic minorities continued till the ratification of the United Nations Declaration on the Rights of Indigenous People that came into effect in 2007. This constitutes a crucial moment in framing the standards for the treatment of the indigenous communities by the state. Ostensibly the key tenants of the UNDRIP are akin to a well-balanced document consisting of anti-colonial objectives in safeguarding the rights of the indigenous people. But the glorified idea of the 'right to self-determination' in the UNDRIP in 2007 has been evasively framed under certain constraints which uphold the state centrism over the self-determination of the indigenous people. For example, the Article 3 of the UNDRIP states:

> Indigenous peoples have the right to self-determination. By virtue of that right they freely determine their political status and freely pursue their economic, social and cultural development

The abovementiBut this right has been sharply limited by the Article 46(1) of the convention which states:

> nothing in this Declaration may be interpreted as implying for any State, people, group or person any right to engage in any activity or to perform any act contrary to the Charter of the United Nations or constructed as authorising or encouraging any action which could dismember or impair totally or in part, the territorial integrity of political unity of sovereign and independent States.

> oned article is a defensive clause protecting the interest of the state, which categorises the indigenous self-determination as a domestic or internal right that can be only exercised within the boundaries of the state. When considering the position of Sri Lanka towards the UNDRIP, it is notable that Sri Lanka voted in favour of adopting UNDRIP in 2007. But, the dualist nature that Sri Lanka holds in international law prevents the country from taking the general international legal principles into the domestic law. Nonetheless, it is a fact beyond any dispute that activism nourished under the astute caring of the upper benches of the Sri Lankan judiciary brought international legal principles into consideration in the domestic context regardless of the dualist nature. The position held by the Supreme Court of Sri Lanka in the famous Tikiri Banda Bulankumala case reflects the judicial proclivity among the judges in adopting international legal principles to manifest the common good, which internationally uplifted the reputation of the Sri Lankan judiciary. Therefore, it is reasonable to argue that Judicial interpretation of international law might harbour the Vedda community in upholding their rights. But the stark reality that one needs to comprehend related to the situation in Sri Lanka on the indigenous rights is that its legal apparatus is akin to a mechanism that continues to curtail the rights of the subaltern.

One of the biggest challenges that befell the whole Vedda society is the submission of their authentic identity to the Sinhalese society, which has been described by Prof. Premakaumara de Silva as the sinhalisation of the Veddas (de Silva 2011). Contrary to the interests of the old generation Vedda community leaders, the Vedda youth has been driven by the interest of cooperating with Sinhala society leading to a greater cultural erosion. The legal mechanism in the county was set in favour of the hegemonic view that prevailed in the Sinhalese-dominated government, which systematically ignored the customs preserved among Vedda's by penalising them under law. The acquisition of the Vedda settlements and banning their traditional hunting were antithetical to the peaceful existence of Veddas. After the series of

Sinhalese colonisation in the Vedda inhabited areas, the last remaining Veddas were turned into the Maduru Oya National Park in the 1980s. Indigenous Peoples were banned from entering the park without a permit and forbidden from hunting in the park—even fishing requires a permit (Peebles 1990). The loss of their forests robbed the Wanniyala-Aetto of their means of subsistence, and of much of what gave their lives meaning. The Environment and Natural Resources Ministry was supposed to issue special Maduru Oya National Park identity cards for the Wanniyala-Aetto, but very few permits were ever issued, leaving many Wanniyala-Aetto vulnerable to the whims of the park guards. The central argument arising from this situtaion is whether law enforcement authorities have shown an equal treatment to all the communities in safeguarding their interests. The last ramparts that survived among the Veddas from their bygone era are at stake due to their incompatibility with the modernity that emerged in the state of Sri Lanka after the departure of the British. The modernism inherited by the Sinhalese dominant governments in Sri Lanka from the British rule beholds the Veddas in awe as to how their colonial masters did in the past and the legal barriers imposed upon them deprive their existential rights. From a vantage point, this legal mechanism pushes the Vedda community to the extinction of their race and their vulnerability exposes them to adopt the modernised life.

The Neoliberal economic framework encouraged by the policymakers has further impeded Vedda community in securing their land rights and harmonious existence with the nature as the land reforms intended to acquire lands under the guise of development. It is worth noting that the concept of national park and the laws related to the forest conservation were made by the British colonial rulers who looked at the nature conservation system from their point of view (Cormier 2017, pp. 45). During the colonial period in Sri Lanka, British administrators often tended to take over forest lands and it has been argued by many subaltern scholars in South Asia that the concept of '*terra nullius*' was widely used in those colonial ventures to expropriate the indigenous lands (Banner 2005, pp. 95–131). After the acquisition of those lands was utilised by them mainly for the financial gains and it continued by the governments in post-independent Sri Lanka. The ideas of Michael Foucault and Humphreys can be relevant in locating the Neoliberalist position in indigenous community in Sri Lanka. Foucault's views are quite antithetical to glorifying neoliberalism as believed that in the neoliberal tradition state policies are even in the social sphere strongly influenced by the market forces (Audier 2015, pp.30). Humphrey argues that the neoliberal governments are interested in introducing market-based disciplines to new areas, which can be used by the private sector. Furthermore, Humphrey has pointed out how neoliberal policies have influenced upon international legal mechanisms to harmonise the private sector's cooperation with the forest conservation, which has baptised Forest as a market-oriented object. In Humphrey's argument International Convention of Biological Diversity which came into effect in 1993 was widely influenced by Neoliberal influences such as the Convention encouraged the private–public partnership as a mechanism to enhance private companies' participation in the natural resource conservation (Humphrey 2009).

The prolonged and still ongoing conflict between Vedda people who are determined to preserve their traditional lands and the government of Sri Lanka is not a mere offshoot of colonialism or the Vedda people's incompatibility of complying with modernity. It is a crisis endemic to the neoliberal socio-economic upheaval in Sri Lanka, which has forged the convulsion of the Vedda community. The formations of National Parks by expelling the Veddas from their traditional territories and penalisation of hunting as a criminal offence deteriorated the Vedda's social progress in the post independent Sri Lanka and the legal system which is inexplicable for the minds of Veddas have imposed various boundaries which are not in safeguarding the rights of the Vedda tribe. In addressing the UN Working Group on Indigenous People in 1996, Vedda chieftain Uru Warrige Wannila Aththo profoundly stated.

> On 6th of November 1983 the central government of Sri Lanka turned the last of our forest territory into a national park. The Maduru Oya national park, and thereby transformed us from being hunters into poachers. Our traditional way of life became a criminal offence in the eyes of the English Common Law, a law from a foreign county that we do not understand. (UN report 1993)

This letter written by Vedda chief highlighting the deprivation of his community urged the UN working group on indigenous communities, which finally aspired the committee to pressurise the Sri Lankan government regarding their policy toward the Vedda community. However, the government apparatus and the staunch state bureaucracy of Sri Lanka showed no genuine interest in securing the indigenous rights. On the contrary, the Sri Lankan authorities continued to restrict Vedda's inherent rights such as hunting and bee honey gathering under the criminal law of the country impeding the accustomed lifestyle of the Veddas. To some extend, the authorities took rather harsh measures in taming the resistance that came from the Veddas. For instance, Sri Lankan government of Immigration and Emigration refused to issue passports to the Vedda delegates claiming that they are not real Sri Lankans and also the Swedish anthropologist Dr. Wiveca Stegeborn, an academic who closely associated Vedda community since 1977 was expelled from the county as '*persona non grata*' (Stegeborn 1987). This was one incident clearly showing the authoritative nature of Sri Lankan government in its reluctance to admit Vedda rights.

5 Conclusion

The overarching aspects of ingenious rights have largely been constructed through Eurocentric lenses in which the Indignity is viewed in an alluring charm and admitted by Western scholars as present-day relics from the past. Anthropologists such as Gananatah Obeyesekere have vehemently opposed this stereotyped conception (Obeyesekere 2003, pp.81). The status of Veddas in Sri Lanka and their reception have been followed by this archetypical colonial model, which is pushing the Vedda population to the brink of primitively. By emulating the colonial or Eurocentric attitude toward the original inhabitants of the island, the state apparatus of post-independent Sri Lanka simply categorised the Vedda as the distinct 'other'. As this paper discussed, the post colonial state developments were implemented without direct or indirect participation from the Vedda community. From a Foucauldian point of view, the role of the legal system has further displaced the Vedda community as the law has been used to legitimise the power and aspirations of the Sinhalese dominant governments. Regarding the anathema prevalent among the Vedda community towards the state legal system, Sri Lankan legal scholar G.L Peiris states.

> So, there is this deep cynicism which characterises the attitudes of Vedda people to the established courts of the Republic. There is a certain perceived sense of alienation from their experiences and from their priorities of what is important to them in life. So, there is this process of alienation which I think one needs to be conscious of (Peiris 1994).

It is a pivotal fact that Sri Lanka should take bold steps in extending certain recognition to the Vedda community through the Constitution. The current Indian legislation Forest Rights Act in 2006 is a model enactment that Sri Lankan can reckon with to set up a standard of legal protection for its Vedda community. The colonial practices emanated from the Dutch period of continuing the customary laws that were intrinsic to ethnic minorities such as Tamils and Muslims were not granted to the Vedda community in Sri Lanka as they were excluded from the national discourse. Subsequently, the Veddahs had to abide by the general law of the country consisting of Roman-Dutch and English legal elements as their final jurisdiction, which is entirely alien to their ken. The acknowledgement of Vedda's own dispute settlement as the ground rule for their land entitlement is a just solution before the complete extinction of Veddas by their hybridisation with the major ethnic communities of Sri Lanka.

References

Academic Journals

Anghie, Anthony. 1996. Francisco de Vitoria and the Colonial Origins of International Law. *Social and Legal Studies* 5 (3): 321–336.

Serge, Audier. 2015. Neoliberalism through Foucault's eyes. *History and Theory* 54 (3): 404–418.

Banner, Stuert. 2005. Why Terra Nuillus? Anthropology and Property Law. *Law and History Review* 23 (1): 95–131.

Cobo, Martinez Cobo. 1987, Study of the Problem of Discrimination against Indigenous Population. Vol.5, United Nations.

Cormier, Paul 2017, British Colonialism and Indigenous People. *Peace Research* 49:2: -39–60.

David, Humphreys. 2009. Discourse as ideology: Neoliberalism and the international forest policy. *Forest Policy and Economics* 11 (5): 319–325.

De Silva, Premakumara, Punchihewa, Asitha. 2011, Socio Anthropological Research Project on Vedda Community in Sri Lanka. Submitted to University of Colombo.

Dharmadasa, K.N.O. 1971. The Creolization of an Aboriginal Language: The Case of Vedda in Sri Lanka. *Anthropological Linguistics* 16 (2): 79–106.

Farmer. 1952. Peasant Colonization in Ceylon. *Pacific Affairs* 25 (4): 389–398.

Falk, Richard. 2006. International Law and the Future. *Third World Quarterly* 27 (5): 727–737.

Gnanarajah, A. 1981. Some Comparative Perspectives: Sri Lanka and Singapore. *Southeast Journal of Social Sciences* 9 (2): 86–99.

Guha, Ramachandra. 2007. Adivasis, Naxalites and Indian Democracy. *Economic and Political Weekly* 42 (32): 3305–3315.
Jayasena, Asoka. 2015. The Changing Life Pattern of Veddahs in Sri Lanka. *Counterpoints* 500 (1): 285–317.
Gananath, Obeyaskere. 2003. Representations of the wild men in Sri Lanka. *Beyond Primitivism* 03: 34–51.
Matson.J.N. 1991. The Language, The Law and the Treaty of Waitangi. *The Journal of Polynesian Society* 100 (4): 343–361.
Stegeborn, Wiveca. 2004. The Disappearing Vedda in Sri Lanka: A Case Study. *Nomadic Peoples* 8 (1): 43–63.
Peebles, Patrick. 1990. Colonization and Ethnic Conflict in the Dry Zone of Sri Lanka. *The Journal of Asian Studies* 49 (1): 30–55.
Phillips, James. 2015. The Rights of Indigenous People under International Law. *Global Bioethics* 26 (2): 120–127.
Wijesekera, Nandadeva. 1981. Vanishing Veddas. *Journal of the Royal Asiatic Society* 26 (1): 1–22.
Vandenbussche, Liselotte. 2016. The Other Power Relation and Zoo "Humane." *Journal of Diversity and Gender Studies* 3 (2): 75–90.

Books

Selighman, C.G. 2011. *The Veddas*. Cambridge: Cambridge University Press.

Book Chapters

Singh, Jakeet. 2014. Recognition and Self Determination: Dilemma of Emergency Politics. In *Recognition Vs Self-Determination*, ed. Jeremy Webber, 47–62. Toronto: UBC Press.

Online Sources

Ferando,D.L. 2019, Indigenous Community in Sri Lanka: The Veddas. https://www.dilmahtea.com/tea-inspired-ebooks/free/veddha/veddha-book.pdf Accessed 20th of May 2022.
Pieris, G.L. 1994, What we can learn from Indigenous People. http://vedda.org/glpieris.htm. Accessed 26th of May 2022.
Perera, Jayantha, 2021. Land Rights of the Veddas. https://island.lk/land-rights-of-veddas. Accessed 21th of May 2022.

Nomads and Forest Rights, Is It a Myth? An Indian Perspective on the Forest-Dependent Pastoral Communities and Their Practices in Protected Areas

Kumarjeeb Pegu

Abstract A peripheral observation of the Indian legal regime on the Indigenous Peoples' right to the forest provides a tale of progression made particularly in the past two decades. The present regime provides a resolute case for the protection of rights of indigenous peoples including their right to own, use, develop, and control the lands, territories, and resources that they possess by reason of traditional ownership or other traditional occupation and practices.

It indeed seems that the enactment of forest management legislation furthers India's intent towards moving towards a serious discourse on realising the rights, particularly that of the forest-dependent tribal. Accordingly, these national frameworks are intended to confer grassroots democracy through institutions of community forest management on these groups. Further, this process is to be supported by the concept of Community Forest Resource Rights (CFR). Herein, within the CFR also enshrined are the traditional pastoral rights of these communities passed on through generations. In reflection, a substantial part of the present literature hints towards a systemic failure on the part of the state in maintaining the due process required in preserving the pastoral rights of these communities as the growing reality of conservation-induced human displacement takes shape in India. The chapter examines the critical questions pertaining to the social efficacy of state's legal instruments in restricting pastoral rights of Indigenous communities in the Indian forest landscape. Also, within the above scope the chapter seeks to understand where the limits of legal centralism lie.

Keywords Community forest resource · Pastoral rights · Tribal rights · Grassroots institutions

---

The original version of the chapter has been revised: The belated corrections have been incorporated. A correction to this chapter can be found at
https://doi.org/10.1007/978-981-99-9275-1_14

K. Pegu (✉)
National Law University Odisha, Cuttack, Odisha 753015, India
e-mail: kumarjeebpegu@nluo.ac.in

T. Venthan Ananthavinayagan and A. Viswanath Shenoy (eds.), *The Wretched of the Global South*, International Law and the Global South,
https://doi.org/10.1007/978-981-99-9275-1_7

1 Introduction

The literature provides a strong implication that law and policy have significantly influenced the identity of the pastoral communities vis-à-vis their traditional forest rights in both pre and post-independent India. Herein, a timeline is drawn from 1865 (the inception of the first Colonial Forest Act) to the present. The author relies his faith on this exercise as it is estimated that both pre and post-colonial forest legislation have led to enforcement of state ownership of forests including on the tribal occupied forest lands without due acknowledgement of the pre-existing land rights of the forest-dependent communities. The enactment of the Scheduled Tribes and Other Traditional Forest Dwellers (Recognition of Forest Rights) Act 2006 (FRA) was seen as a step towards undoing the past alienation of forest rights including the right to pastoral practices. Its preamble in fact proclaims that historic injustice was done against forest-dwelling communities while the forests were legally consolidated into State forests during the colonial and post-independent periods. The legislation reiterates that such wrongs led to the denial of adequate recognition of rights to their ancestral lands and habitat. The provisions of the legislation itself provided for granting more rights to the Scheduled Tribes and people residing in the forests of India than was ever achieved in earlier periods.

This chapter focuses on the state-sponsored restrictions on the pastoral rights of the 'forest-dwelling communities' and the 'forest-dependent postural communities'. Firstly, this chapter will provide a brief assessment of The United Nations Declaration on the Rights of Indigenous Peoples, 2007 vis-à-vis its implications on India for the purpose of examining the various layers attached to the understanding of how indigenous land rights discourse is evolving in the contemporary times. Then, the chapter will explore the impacts resulting from such restrictions on these groups and their sustenance and cultural rights. Secondly, this will provide an evaluation of the purpose, the result, and the impact of such restrictions.

The paper examines the impact of Indian laws from the context of access to forest resources for Indigenous and tribal peoples with a particular emphasis on the Scheduled Tribes and Other Traditional Forest Dwellers (Recognition of Forest Rights) Act, 2006. Also, the very nature of Community Forest Resource Rights as provided within the national framework will be evaluated through the manuscript.

The methods applied are a critical study of case laws particularly reflecting the grey area of implementation fault lines within the governmental machinery.

1.1 A Reflection of the Indigenous Peoples' Rights Discourse Under UNDRIP and the Indian Approach

Mearns maintains that when settled agriculture is not sufficient, the commons (common resources) such as forest lands become an important additional resource (Mearns 1999). However, in the case of forests, there remain major challenges to local access and management (Oskarsson 2018). In this context, Levien (2011) reflects on the rising phenomenon of increasing land acquisitions by the Indian state. He further emphasises that the primary stakeholders losing ground here are often the farmers, forest dwellers, herders, and many other impoverished groups fighting to keep hold of their land against the state and private entities over increasingly scarce pockets of land (Levien 2011). Guha observes that Adivasis[1] across India have been unable to participate directly in the political discourse for protecting their rights and have instead been organised through social movements, engaging directly with the bureaucracy or the judiciary (Guha 2007). Although the indigenous peoples' struggle for political and cultural rights under international law has existed for some time now, it has only in recent decades built the required momentum. Today under the discourse of international law, norms exist that furthers the interests of indigenous peoples (Phillips 2015). Also, an argument is made that soft law declarations passed receive widespread support as their principles have been derived from customary international law and in the same light also found under general principles of law recognised by civilised nations (Hadden 2007; Anaya 2009: 79–82, 124, 151). Perhaps a major event remains the adoption of the United Nations Declaration on the Rights of Indigenous Peoples on 13th September 2007 (GA Res. 2007). The resolution was able to achieve a high margin of support from the comity of states.[2] The Declaration was in the making for over thirty years and went through a series of long processes passing through layers of channels and committees within the UN. Champagne (2013) notes

---

[1] C R Bijoy, Ratnaker Bhengra and Shimreichon Luithui in their report titled 'The Adivasis of India. (1999) published by Minority Rights Group International, provides that the term adivasi means 'original inhabitants' corresponds largely, to the 'Scheduled Tribes (STs) of India, who are geographically dispersed and culturally diverse. The authors on the distinct aspects such as language, religion, a profound bond between the individual to the community and towards nature, minimal dependence on money and markets, a tradition of community-level self-government, and an egalitarian culture that rejects the rigid social hierarchy of the Hindu caste system. Also, Dash and Khotari in their work 'Grabbing: Dangers of the Green India Mission' published as book chapter, in Banking on Forests: Assets for a Climate Cure?, writes that some tribal groups listed in the Indian Constitution are accorded differential status in different states, such as being scheduled tribes in one state but not in another.

Also, designation of Scheduled Tribe status under the Constitution of India is provided as follows;

Article 342(1) of Constitution of India, 1950 states: 'The President may with respect to any State or Union territory, and where it is a State, after consultation with th Governor thereof, by public notification, specify the tribes or tribal communities or parts of or groups within tribes or tribal communities which shall for the purposes of this Constitution be deemed to be Scheduled Tribes in relation to that State or Union territory, as the case may be.'.

Also, Bijoy et al. in their work India and the Rights of Indigenous Peoples (2010) maintains that the term 'Indigenous Peoples' is not designated to any specific community or group of people in India as the Indian Government officially maintains that all Indians are Indigenous.

[2] The Declaration was adopted by the General Assembly dated 13 September 2007, with the majority vote of 144 states in favour, 4 votes against (Australia, Canada, New Zealand and the United States) and 11 abstentions (Azerbaijan, Bangladesh, Bhutan, Burundi, Colombia, Georgia, Kenya, Nigeria, Russian Federation, Samoa and Ukraine). Later, the four nations voting against have reversed their votes in support of the Declaration.

that many of the arguments by indigenous peoples and non-governmental organisations set against arguments from nation-state governments were reflected in the Declaration and yet it was passed with an unexpectedly high margin (Champagne 2013). The UNDRIP itself is not void of criticisms. Champagne also observes that the Declaration does not include any 'special rights' and upholds a primary focus of contemporary nation-states that all citizens were equal before the law. This position denies the indigenous people protection of their rights and equally the autonomy of their cultural and political community while forcing their participation as citizens, often without their consent. This proposition particularly withholds one's right who elects to remain within indigenous communities and reject the choice to join the national culture and economy (Champagne 2013). Furthermore, while within international law, UNDRIP continues a legacy of preserving indigenous peoples' struggle for their cultural rights, particularly the right to self-determination based on land rights, an important challenge remains the rapidly growing phenomenon of resource exploitation by the state in lands otherwise claimed by the indigenous peoples. For instance, Brysk (2000) claims that there exists a 'global triad of modernity', consisting of the states, markets, and Western ideology. This only furthers the rise of the supporting movement for indigenous peoples' 'trio of core demands i.e. self-determination, land rights, and cultural survival' (Brysk 2000). An implication of this conflict and the attempt at a resolution is reflected in the multiple references within the text of the declaration insisting on states providing paramount interest in preserving the land tenure rights of indigenous groups. Similar implication is also drawn from the Sustainable Development Goals 2015–2030 (herein forth SDGs). The Major Group for Indigenous Peoples[3] in its reference to the SDGs explains, i.e.

> For Indigenous Peoples around the world, 'leaving no one behind' means respecting subsistence economies and promoting nonmonetary measures of well-being. For instance, the financial measure of $1.25/day for extreme poverty is inappropriate for Indigenous Peoples, for whom security of rights to lands, territories and resources is essential for poverty eradication. From this perspective, the linear monetary measure of poverty can contribute to further impoverishing Indigenous Peoples under the guise of the theme 'leaving no one behind'.
>
> (High Level Political Forum 2016)

In fact, under 1.4 of the Goal i.e. 'End Poverty in all its forms everywhere', member states of the U.N are required to ensure that,

> all men and women, in particular the poor and the vulnerable, have equal rights to economic resources, as well as access to basic services, ownership and control over land and other forms of property, inheritance, natural resources, appropriate new technology and financial services, including microfinance.
>
> (UN General Assembly, 2015)

Here, the assessment of Goal 1 of the SDGs also allows a reference to the availability of land as a source of livelihood to the indigenous communities dependent on forests. On a similar note, In India, the protection of the community forest rights of

[3] The Indigenous Peoples Major Group is one of nine sectors of society that have been identified as stakeholders in sustainable development and have been involved in the processes at the UN level.

the tribal peoples under the law has been vastly strengthened in recent decades and shall be provided with a detailed examination in the later sections.

Herein, it is pertinent to mention that international law has not succeeded in providing a concrete shape to which groups are to be classified as 'indigenous' and for that matter a particular definition. It is further observed that the diversity of legal notions of indigeneity makes it rather difficult to construct a legal notion of indigeneity that could serve as a sound analytical instrument to be employed across the boundaries of states' legal and political systems (Gosart 2012). It may also be emphasised here that paragraph 1 of Article 33 of the UNDRIP states that such peoples have the right to 'determine their own identity'. In the Indian context, the Xaxa Committee report (2014) in its recommendation has maintained that the Scheduled Tribes or STs should be provided with the right to say 'no' to the acquisition of their land and to access and manage forests and other common property rights, be recognised. The Committee further adds that the concept of eminent domain does not apply equally in all territories within India, particularly considering the rights of tribal communities to land in Scheduled Areas having specifically been treated as 'distinct' from other private holdings of land (Xaxa et al. 2014). Also, internationally, India has remained adamant in not defining a set of people as indigenous within its territory, including when the opportunity was provided during the adoption of the text of the UNDRIP. Still, it has been noted that for internal administrative requirements and purposes, the Scheduled Tribes are deemed 'indigenous people' (Bijoy et al. 2010).

Within the debates on India's interaction with international law, the foremost pressing need remains in observing India's approach to defining who constitutes the 'indigenous peoples' internally. Undoubtedly, this exercise can further help in tracing the traits of the tribes of India and their relation to the forest. Else in India, a contextually comprehensive definition of tribal peoples remains incomplete.

1.2 The History of Forest Legislation and Their Impact on Forest Communities

State forests, consist of the greater share of the total forest cover in India and are directly under the control of the respective state governments in India. The increase in the control and management of such forests by the state administration has only intensified the conflict between state's priorities vs. that of the traditional practices of the forest dwellers and the dependent communities (Paquet and Kuroyedov 2021; Springate-Baginski et al. 2008).

The displacement of traditional forest rights of the tribal communities as a process took shape during the period of the British Raj. The literature accords such approach[4] on part of the state to its ambitions of turning the forest resources into a commodity

[4] The British colonial rule applied the regime of 'terra nullius' ('land belongs to no-one') for establishing its claims particularly over the forested geography of India. More on the events that shaped the experience is discussed later in the paper.

for revenue generation. In the same light, such act of the state has been described as exploitation (Gilbert and Doyle 2011; Springate-Baginski et al. 2008; Domínguez and Luoma 2020).

The first attempts to claim ownership of the state's forests were seen between 1864 and 1865, wherein the first set of forest legislation was initiated. Particularly the enactment of the 1878 Act rapidly solidified the colonial government's ambitions of en masse reservation of forests as properties of the state (Guha 1983; Springate-Baginski and Blakie 2007). During this process, the tribals rebelled against such dictates by the state, although it only resulted in their suppression (Sinha 2007).

Also, in 1874, the colonial government declared all adivasi areas to fall under scheduled areas, i.e. outside the jurisdiction of normal administration and which were later incorporated in the Indian constitution.[5]

Such areas were brought under the purview of the Scheduled District Act of 1874, (1874 Act) and later the Government of India (Excluded and Partially Excluded Areas) Order 1936. These legal instruments ousted the operation of the general Acts and Regulations enforced in British India from these areas. Also, the aforementioned general laws could only be enforced in these areas with the previous sanction of the Governor-General in Council as sought by the Local Government under section 5 of the 1874 Act. The resulting implication was not any lessening of the British exploits on the Tribal rights to land resources. Even the removing of the general land revenue laws from the Adivasi areas could barely provide a truce between the tribal dissident and the British Indian State. Also, the Government of India Act 1919 continued the legacy of the 1874 Act by continuing the policy of non-application of general Acts in the Scheduled areas. In today's post independent India, these areas fall under the Fifth and Sixth Schedules of the Indian Constitution. The above events influenced the legal discourse in the post-colonial period i.e. to reinforce control of the forest department over forest-dependent communities and forest dwellers through legal instruments such as the Wildlife Protection Act (1972), the Forest Conservation Act, (1980), the National Forest Policy (1988) and the Joint Forest Management programme initiated through it, etc. (Sigamany 2017; Springate-Baginski et al. 2008; Dash and Khotari 2012).

1.3 Pastoral Communities and the Colonial Experience: An Indian Lens

Pastoralism is not defined under Indian law, although there remains the presence of various pastoralist communities in India.

Sutton and Anderson define pastoralism as a form of agriculture wherein its practitioners specialise and obtain their primary subsistence from, the husbandry of one or a few herbivorous animal species domesticated, albeit in some cases such as the reindeer herding practiced by the Sámi', the species of focus is not domesticated

[5] For more, see Article 244 (1) and 244 (2) of the Indian Constitution, 1950.

(Sutton and Anderson, 2010). LIFE Network et al. (2016) provide that pastoralism has been categorised as "dependence on common pool resources, mobility, primary income from livestock, the existence of traditional knowledge systems and association with specific breeds". Also, around 80% of India's livestock are dependent on common pool resources[6](herein forth CPRs) i.e. implying that CPRs form a vital element of pastoralist in India (LIFE Network et al., 2016). The existence of traditional knowledge systems is not a necessity for pastoralism in certain parts of today's India as new communities many nontraditional pastoralists are adopting pastoralism.

A recent report (2020) estimates the Indian pastoralist population to be around 1% of the Indian population, or about 13 million people. A variety of pastoralist within 46 castes and communities having specialised pastoralist identities, including transhumance and nomadic, semi-nomadic, and village-based herding exist in India (Kishore and Köhler-Rollefson 2020).

Bhattachariya (2018) explains that during the British period, the state sought to settle pastoralists since they did not own any land and therefore could not be taxed. Further emphasis is provided on the point that during the period many of the nomadic pastoralists were classified as 'criminal tribes'[7] (Bhattachariya 2018).

The colonial regime discriminated between settled communities and the nomads by recognising the occupation of land by the former and not vice versa., who in turn were characterised as 'wild and lawless' (Bhattacharya 1995; Saberwal 1999). The colonial narrative of 'overgrazing' to limit pastoralism had brought about various restrictions on the rights of the pastoral communities. For instance, The Cattle Trespass Act of 1871 introduced legal regulations for impounding cattle under claims of trespass and imposition of a fine on the owners for the release of the cattle to supplement the above narrative.

Bhattacharya provides that the cattle trespass law became a tool in the hands of the imperial government in restricting traditional pastoral rights in areas now converted into farmlands. He states;

> The problem was particularly acute in places where pastoral lands were being taken over for plantations or settled agriculture. In these transitional landscapes, the new order of rights could not be established without the trauma of dispossession and without negotiation and conflict.
>
> (Bhattacharya 222, 2018, p 405)

---

[6] Chopra and Dasgupta (2002) in Common Pool Resources in India: Evidence, Significance and New Management Initiatives (Final Report of DFID sponsored project on Policy Implications of Knowledge with respect to Common Pool Resources undertaken jointly with University of Cambridge, UK.), provide that Common pool resources in the Indian context maybe defined as non-exclusive resources belonging to a number of owners based on their membership of some group such as a village or a tribe or a particular community and includes the distribution of the use of the rights to the CPR among themselves.

[7] From 1871 onwards, when the first Criminal Tribes Act 1871 (imperial legislation of India) was passed, and the subsequent passing of a series of such legislations (in 1911 and 1924) provided for the legal framework for criminalization of entire communities through the process of legally classifies them as habitual criminals engaging in non-bailable offences, to enforce state imposed restriction and monitoring on their movement and activities.

The enactment of the 1878 Forest Act gave the colonial government vast powers in declaring any forest land as government property, and hence the resultant reservation of forests without proper acknowledgement of tribal rights which included restrictions on the customary practices of the pastoral communities in terms of accessing the forests (Springate et al. 2007).

In hindsight, contrary to the claims of the colonizers, it has been proven that the pastoralist had a positive impact on the natural environment as well as the society before the pre-colonial period. The nomadic pastoralists particularly in Himachal Pradesh were deemed to be an essential part of the larger socio-economic system based on an integrated and well-tuned system of agriculture and mobile pastoralism, and its links to the sustainable use of the mountain environment (Gooch 2009).

1.4 *Forest Right and the Law: Present Indian Stance and the Implementation Gaps*

While the Indian Forest Act, 1927 provided preservation of 'rights' to forest-dependent peoples,[8] this was also the legislation that introduced the attempt on part of the state to control the accessible forest resources by branding them as 'forest produce' (See section 2.4 of the Act). These forest resources which provided fodder to the herds of the pastoral people were otherwise accessible previously. Gooch (2009) explains that through the Indian Forest Act of 1927, the state initiated legalisation of its monopoly over such forest produce by 'presumption' of its ownership, sharpening the concept of 'forest offence' and authority of forest officers to hold an inquiry into forest offence and, in the course of such enquiry, to receive and record evidence's. Gooch also maintains that the state's increased authority under the Act only helped in achieving a system of corruption and bribery which continues to prevail in today's India. She further notes the impact of the legislation on pastoral rights, particularly that of the pastoral Van Gujjars of Central Indian Himalayas, since they were forced into discontinuing their communal forest management rights as a result of the introduction of individual lopping and grazing permits given to the head of a household.[9] This, led to the interactions of the community with the forest department as individuals and not as a group, which further weakened their position. The aforementioned problem is further aggravated for the reason that the Van Gujjars due to their nomadic traits did not hold land or domicile rights before their mobilised agitations took shape in the 1990s (Gooch 2009).

Environmental legislations in the post-independent era before the implementation of the Scheduled Tribes and the Other Traditional Forest Dwellers (Recognition of Forest Rights) Act, 2006, also commonly referred to as the Forest Rights Act (Herein forth FRA) were heavily tilted towards environmental protection at the cost

---

[8] For more see Sects. 11, 12, 17 and 18 of the legislation.

[9] Such permit came with designated forest area for use by the household along with a number of buffaloes allowed in the permit and the tax to be paid.

of Indigenous rights to forests. For instance, only in 2006 through an amendment to the Wildlife (Protection) Act 1972, the preservation of forest rights of Indigenous communities in Critical Tiger Reserves under section 38 (V) of the legislation was provided to coincide with the enforcement of the FRA.

Also, while the Indian Parliament had passed the Panchayats (Extension to the Scheduled Areas) Act in 1996 which franchises grassroots democracy to the tribals in the scheduled areas, the question of such self-governance rights in protected areas remained blurred which undoubtedly with the enactment of the FRA was provided more clarity.

Meanwhile, the tribal struggle for forest rights continued, and so did the stories of the evictions of forest dwellers without the recognition of their rights even though the FRA was already enforced (Springate-Baginski et al. 2008).

Springate-Baginski et al. (2007) inform that even post-independence, power remained centralised under the state's bureaucratic Forest Department. Accordingly, legal centralism without dialogue with the forest-dependent tribes can be traced to the first National Forest Policy of independent India in 1952. The policy monopolised forest resources under the control of the state. Similar trends were witnessed with further consolidation of the forest bureaucracy under the Forest Conservation Act of 1980. Hence, leading to further solidification of the tribal struggle (Springate et al. 2007). Its impact can be witnessed in the added attempts on part of the state to appease the tribals through a gradual shift in the policy and law outlook. One being the National Forest Policy of 1988 as well as various other reports presented to the Government of India providing a changing perspective in the political discourse i.e. to finally accept the implication that forest and wildlife conservation can be linked together with the forest rights discourse. However, the efforts remained far from ideal in resolving the conflict since state bureaucracy in the forests hardly implemented the much needed changes (Bandi 2014).

With the implementation of the FRA, it was anticipated that the Act will swiftly provide for regularising of the claims of the forest dwellers to the forest through the redistribution of land titles (Kumar and Kerr 2012). After all, the preamble of the FRA recognises the existence of the forest rights of the forest dwellers who have resided in the forests for generations, without having their rights previously recorded. The FRA provided for an institutionalised process for the documentation of such rights of the forest dwellers i.e. both individual and community rights. The FRA also provided norms for responsibility and sustainable use, conservation of biodiversity and maintenance of ecology by the forest dwellers, to be monitored by the grassroots institution in the form of Gram Sabhas (local decentralised village-level institutions of governance) (Pegu 2021). However, structural weaknesses such as the exclusion of women and special minority groups from forest rights committees, although the same is mandated under Rule 3 of the Scheduled Tribes and Other Traditional Forest Dwellers (Recognition of Forest Rights) Rules 2007 and the implementation gaps had prevented the legislation from truly achieving its set objectives (Kothari 2011). Further discussions on the legislation follow ahead. Also, while individual forest rights (herein forth IFRs) under FRA are limited to four hectares of the land as claimed under the Act (see section 4.6 of FRA), no such restriction exists under

Community Forest Rights (herein forth CFRs). Hence, the CFR rights are particularly of crucial interest to the pastoral communities as they use land extensively (Paquet and Kuroyedov 2021).

Section 2 (a) of the FRA provides the definition of 'community forest resource' as

> customary common forest land within the traditional or customary boundaries of the village or seasonal use of landscape in the case of pastoral communities, including reserved forests, protected forests and protected areas such as Sanctuaries and National Parks to which the community had traditional access;

Such CFRs and its recognition under the FRA provide a new boon for the pastoral communities who were otherwise forced to interact with forest officials as individuals and not as a community for grant of permit and the tax paid thereupon for grazing rights in the protected areas as seen above. However, due to the implementation gaps under FRA as discussed above, there has generally been a low acceptance rate of both IFRs and CFR claims across India with indications based on official reporting pegging such defects on the acute shortage of trained manpower at the ground level (Mohanty 2015).

Previously, identification of pastoral rights has also been undertaken in the Indian Forest Act, 1927 (herein forth IFA). The Forest Settlement-officer under the Act is provided with the authority to pass an order admitting or rejecting the claim to rights of pasture or to forest produce in whole or in part made by the forest-dependent communities including the forest dwellers (See section 12 of IFA). Also, under section 25 of the Wildlife (Protection) Act, 1972 (herein forth WLPA) if the land acquisition proceedings for creating protected areas such as sanctuaries and national parks, lead to the extinguishing of previous rights exercised over the land such as right of public way or common pasture, the collector[10] with the previous sanction of the State Government, may provide alternative public way or common pasture, as far as may be practicable or convenient. Herein, accordingly, alternate land for common pasture in the event of land accusation may not always be granted as the ultimate discretion remains under the state administration. Also, section 24 of the WLPA further provides that, during the acquisition of rights to the land including that of pastoral rights for the creation of sanctuaries, the collector in the event of being satisfied that a claim to such right exists, may immediately pass an order in which either such land over which right is claimed is excluded or to proceed to acquire such land or to allow in consultation with the chief wildlife warden appointed by the respective state government, the continuation of the right of any person in or over such land to be otherwise assigned within the limits of the sanctuary. Herein, again, the discretion remains with the officials of the state to decide if the rights shall continue albeit where by an agreement between the owner of such land or holder of rights and the state, the owner or holder of such rights has agreed to surrender their

[10] Section 3 (g) of the Right to Fair Compensation and Transparency in Land Acquisition, Rehabilitation and Resettlement Act, 2013 (India) defines collector as follows; ~"*Collector means the Collector of a revenue district, and includes a Deputy Commissioner and any officer specially designated by the appropriate Government to perform the functions of a Collector under this Act.*".

rights, in or over such land, and on payment of compensation (See section 24 (2) (b) of the WLPA). Importantly section 24 (2) (b) does not apply in the case of acquiring of land over which one may exercise traditional rights for the setting up of national parks (See section 35 (3) of the WLPA).

After the implementation of the Forest Rights Act, the forest rights including pastoral rights practiced by the forest-dependent indigenous communities in protected areas including national parks can no longer be taken away by the state except for in the case of creation of 'Critical Wildlife Habitats (Herein forth CWHs) (See section 4(2) of the FRA) or for creation of 'Critical Tiger Habitats' (Herein forth CTHs) in such sanctuaries or national parks. More discussion on CWHs and CTHs under the FRA follows in the subsequent part of the work.

While observing S.2 (a) of the FRA, the reference to words—customary common forest land within the traditional or customary boundaries of the village or seasonal use of landscape in the case of pastoral communities,' and 'national park', allows for an assurance within the law that a claimant under the FRA should have access to a forest land which comes within traditional boundaries. The verification of the evidence claimed for such legal right is provided under Rule 13 of the Scheduled Tribes and Other Traditional Forest Dwellers (Recognition of Forest Rights) Rules, 2007 or the Forest Rights Rules. However, when the terms 'customary boundaries' and 'seasonal use of landscape in the case of pastoral communities' are taken into consideration, it becomes evident that indigenous populations who have dependence on national parks for generations should be provided access to the same.

According to a recent status report on the implementation of the FRA prepared by the Tribal Affairs Ministry, Indian Government (2021), the state of Sikkim had stated that there are no Forest-Dwelling STs and Other Traditional Forest Dwellers 'in the true sense of the terms' within the territorial boundaries of the state. The state further explains that most of the Scheduled Tribes (Herein forth STs) (see footnote 1) of Sikkim already hold revenue land in their own name and they are not solely dependent on the forests for their livelihood. Singh et al. observing the pastoral rights of Livestock herder in the Khanchendzonga National Park of Sikkim State writes that the wildlife and park officials had restricted the traditional access of the pastoral communities to the grazing areas in the park, under state sponsored pastoral evictions carried out in the state between 2000 and 2002 (Singh et al. 2022). The abovementioned report by the Tribal Affairs Ministry provides a similar story for the non-enforcement of the FRA in the North eastern states of India barring Assam and Tripura. As a matter of fact, the government of Mizoram has provided that the State being a Sixth Schedule state,[11] with nearly '100% of the population' being STs with common ownership of non-reserved forest land in its villages, no issue of deprivation or rejection of forest rights exist as forest ownership rights since time

[11] The Sixth Schedule of enshrined in Articles 244(2) and 275(1) of Provisions of the Indian Constitution provides for administration of Tribal Areas in the States of Assam, Meghalaya, Tripura and Mizoram through creation of Autonomous districts Councils (ADCs) with the aim of protecting and preserving tribal culture in these areas. The ADCs are provides with authority to make laws in the areas under their jurisdiction, which cover the land, including the right to collect land revenues and certain other taxes.

immemorial continue to be vested in the hands of the community of every villages (Indian Ministry of Tribal Affairs 2021).

In the case of Assam, the Gauhati High Court had previously held that no traditional forest dwellers existed in Assam, which only further propelled the Assam states' ambitions of evicting forest-dwelling communities including denial of grazing rights in the forest lands during the time (Pegu 2021). Presently, The Assam state is reviewing the implementation status in the state. Bijoy (2019) explains that the FRA extends to the northeastern states of India since unclassified-forests[12] as found in these states are included under the FRA i.e. the definition of 'forest land' in section 2(d), in addition to the inclusion of a northeast-specific provision under section 3(1)(j) allows for unclassified forests to fall within the ambit of FRA.[13] Also, he refers to the Indian Supreme Court's judgment in T.N. Godavarman Thirumulpad versus Union of India & Ors dated 12 March 1947,[14] wherein the court held that while 'forest land' occurring in section 2 of the Forest Conservation Act 1980, includes 'forest' as understood in the dictionary sense, and also covers area otherwise recorded as forest in the government record irrespective of the ownership", and hence allowing the forest laws to be legally extended to unclassified forest areas of the North East.[15] His remarks are of particular importance since he empathises that attempts had been made by the ruling Bharatiya Janata Party government at the Centre to bring 'unclassed' or 'unclassified' forests' under the purview of the Indian Forest Act with a proposed amendment, the proposal of which was also circulated through its environment ministry on March 7, 2019, with the state governments. It is held that the proposition is unpopular among the forest communities including the fact that such an amendment has the tendency to confer arbitrary powers with bureaucracy including the use of unabated violence, arrests without warrants, imposing of collective punishments, taking away of forest rights, etc. Bijoy finally maintains that such arbitrary centralisation of power could turn forests into veritable war zones and

---

[12] While the above category is recorded as forest, they are not included in reserved or protected forest category under the Indian Law. Accordingly, the north-East Indian states of Arunachal Pradesh, Manipur, Mizoram and Nagaland claimed such forests within their geographical territorial are under the control of community ownership by the indigenous tribal.

[13] The provision states as follows; 'rights which are recognised under any State law or laws of any Autonomous District Council or Autonomous Regional Council or which are accepted as rights of tribal under any traditional or customary law of the concerned tribes of any State'.

[14] Supreme Court of India (1995), Writ Petition (Civil) No. 202.

[15] Under a major amendment brought to the Forest (conservation) Act, 1980 in 2023, a new section i.e. 1A. (1), has been added. A per critics, the provision stands to alter the definition of forest as mandated by the Supreme Court. Section i.e. 1A. (1), reads.

"The following land shall be covered under the provisions of this Act,

namely:—

(a) the land that has been declared or notified as a forest in accordance with the provisions of the Indian Forest Act, 1927 or under any other law for the time being in force;

(b) the land that is not covered under clause (a), but has been recorded in Government record as forest, as on or after the 25th October, 1980:".

The present chapter do not focus on the above amendment since the chapter was prepared before the above stated amendment was made.

only the FRA's implementation can keep away the forest bureaucracy from grabbing community forests, particularly in the northeast (Bijoy 2019).

In reflection, the above arguments may also be extended in the case of Sikkim, and apart from the obvious reasons for the debate on the centre-state power play politics, since presently as observed in the preceding part, there seems to be a lack of formal regime for protection of pastoral rights especially in the protected areas in the state, which otherwise under the FRA is provides as an integral right of such communities along with the mechanism for determining such rights by state authorities particular under section 6.

1.5 Implications

Gooch's work (2009) already shows the hardships previously faced by the pastoral Van Gujjars while migrating across their traditional routes between the northern Indian states of Uttar Pradesh, Uttarakhand and Himachal Pradesh. Also, her work explores the complexities of administrative divisions of the aforementioned states, which led to the community being deemed 'intruders' for the reason of not having a permanent state belonging. She also maintains that the Forest Rights Act through its approach to community forest management rights provides the Van Gujjars with the hope to continue pastoralism in the forests in the future, which otherwise was previously untenable (Gooch 2009).

Presently, the community has realised domicile rights including access to state-sponsored welfare schemes, registration under the state voter's list, etc. in several locations nearby the protected areas in Uttarakhand state. However, their experience also evokes an imperative thought i.e.

> For availing benefits under the FRA, is it mandatory that the persons claiming the forest rights including in the case of pastoral rights, be granted to them only if they can prove their domicile to the respective state wherein the right is to be applied?

Herein, since FRA is applicable to the forest-dwelling Scheduled Tribes (Herein forth FDSTs) and other traditional forest dwellers (Herein forth OTFDs), it is pertinent to observe their definitions under the Act. A simple reading of section 2 (c) of the FRA, which defines FDSTs implies that members belonging to the group both as individuals or collectively should 'primarily reside' and 'depend on the forest for their bona fide livelihood needs' and includes the Scheduled Tribe pastoralist communities. In the case of OTFDs, section 2 (o) defines them on similar lines to FDSTs albeit, they must have primarily resided and depended on the forest land for bona fide livelihood needs for at least three generations through family lineage (75 years) prior to the 13th day of December 2005 i.e. from the initiation date of 13 December 1930. Section 4 (3) of the Act further provides that both FDSTs and OTFDs must have occupied the forest land before the 13th day of December 2005 to be eligible to claim rights under the Act.

Firstly, the above phase i.e. 'primarily reside' is not explained in the legislation and hence leaves a point of ambiguity. It has been held earlier that if the phase is narrowly interpreted, it may help in defending forests against land grabbers but equally may also exclude most rightful claimants (Springate-Baginski et al. 2008). While no explanation has been provided in the FRA through either an amendment or in the Forest Rights Rules, 2007, there was a clarification circular[16] released by the Union Ministry of Tribal Affairs (Herein forth MoTA) dated 9th June 2008 wherein it was held that 'primarily resides in' implies such FDSTs and OTFDs who are not necessarily residing inside the forest but are depending on the forest for their bona fide livelihood needs under sections 2(c) and 2(o) of the FRA. The MoTA further provides that in the case of OTFDs, continuous exercise of forest rights for 75 years without interruption need not be proved (Indian Ministry for Tribal Affairs, 2015, p. 8).

The clarification comes as a vital relief especially since nomadic pastoral communities may not be 'technically' residing within the forests.

This issue was further clarified by MoTA, as the ministry accepted that pastoralist and nomadic communities usually practice grazing rights in forest land while residing in permanently settled villages in revenue lands located outside the forest land. It was held that although nomadic or pastoralist communities may not primarily reside in forests, they are still eligible for rights under the FRA, if the grazing rights sought are in forest lands. It is further explained that the specific provision for protection of the grazing rights, both settled or transhumant, and traditional seasonal resource access of nomadic or pastoralist communities under section 3(1) (d) of FRA only substantiates the above argument. Herein, direct examples of the traits of the semi-nomadic pastoralist communities in the Himalayan region are taken, with emphasis laid on the fact that they may even engage in agricultural activities, alongside seasonal nomadic pastoral activities which are traditional in nature and shall continue to be included under the FRA i.e. in reference to their traditional customary pastoral practices (Indian Ministry for Tribal Affairs 2015, pp. 9–10). However, the immediate need to insert the above clarification or policy approach of the state under the FRA remains. Such a step will ensure the complete and permanent resolution to the question of protecting of rights of these communities.

Coming back to the above question, under the FRA if the persons claiming the grazing rights belong to an ST pastoral community, it is required that the claimant must be a registered ST in the relevant area within the state as per the Constitution (Scheduled Tribes) Order, 1950.[17] Depending on the state, one's FDST status may be restricted to a particular District or may apply to the entire territory of the state (Indian Ministry for Tribal Affairs 2015, p. 7). Accordingly, it is provided that pastoral rights can be claimed by the nomadic pastoralists across states based on the production of any two pieces of evidence specified in Rule 13 (Indian Ministry for Tribal Affairs 2015, p. 8). However, it is to be noted that in general forest rights claims are provided

[16] Ministry of Tribal Affairs (2008), Circular no. No.17014/02/2007-PC&V (Vol.VII).

[17] The Order provides for the list of tribal communities of India recognised as Scheduled Tribes under the Constitution of India.

based on the domicile of the claimant and subject to the further condition that FRA is applicable in the state. Also, if such claimants are recognised as an FDST in a particular area within a given state and covered under section 2 (c) of the FRA, then in those districts of the state where they are not recognised as STs including in the bordering states where they claim pastoral rights, they shall be regarded as OTFDs for the purpose of the Act and accordingly shall fall under the definition of section 2 (o) of the FRA. Hence, technically, while domicile certificates are means of evidence that may be produced under Rule 13 of the Forest Rights Rules, yet the possibility of using other means of evidence under the said Rule including evidence of the traditional grazing grounds as part of Community Forest Resource remains. Accordingly, it can be deciphered that the FRA does not restrict or confine the traditional practices of the pastoralist to only the area where they claim their domicile especially within the state boundaries. However, depending on the administrative area, they may be considered as OTFD in one location, although FDST in another.

Today, Conservation-induced displacement and eviction of forest-dependent communities from protected areas remain a hallmark in India (Fanari 2019). Herein, particularly area of concern remains the removal of forest dwellers including curtailment of the rights to grazing land of the pastoral communities in the protected areas such as sanctuaries and national parks during declaration of such areas as CWHs (See. S.2. b of the FRA). While the provision was inserted as an attempt to placate the wildlife conservationists, it remains pertinent to note that evictions or curtailing of traditional rights of the forest-dependent indigenous communities must only be performed when their presence in the area causes irreversible damage to the forest habitat or when no option for human–wildlife co-existence remains as provided under clauses ‘b’ and ‘c’ of sub-section 2 to section 4 of FRA. Similar view on CTHs as notified under section 38 V (4) (i) of the Wildlife (Protection) Act, 1972 was also maintained under Provision 7B of a ministerial clarification (Ministry of Environment and Forest 2011). However, another letter by the National Tiger Conservation Authority, dated March 28, 2017; referring to the above provision of the WLPA on CTHs provides that in the absence of guidelines for notification of CWHs (as required under the FRA), no rights shall be conferred in CTHs which otherwise is mandated under the WLPA (Ministry of Environment, Forest and Climate Change 2017). The aforementioned letter is not only contradicting the objective of the FRA and the Union Environment Ministry’s own clarification of 2011, but also sets a dangerous precedence for erroneous application of law by the state at will and hence ultimately defeats the objective of preserving traditional forest rights of the forest-dependent communities. At the time of writing, the letter containing the Order on denial of rights in CTHs has been withdrawn as Guidelines for Notification of Critical Wildlife Habitats, 2018 have been implemented. However, several criticisms remain on the contents of the Notification (Kukreti and Agarwal 2018). Also, a problematic situation exists since CWHs can be notified only after the consent of the Gram Sabha in the area, while in the case of CTHs, no such requirement exists as they are notified by the National Tiger Conservation Authority (Herein froth NTCA) created under the WLPA. However, the Guidelines for Notification of Critical Wildlife Habitats 2018 make no mention of the requirement of free and informed consent of the Gram

Sabha. Yet, the 2018 Guidelines at guideline 3.4 mentioned that no forest rights of the STs or the OTFDs can be modified or resettled unless all provisions of section 4(2) (a) to (f) of FRA are complied with. Section 4(2)(e) provides for the free and informed consent of the Gram Sabhas in the areas concerned with the proposed resettlement and to the alternatives package that has been obtained in writing.

Again, as the guidelines are meant to supplement the main legislation i.e. the FRA, the 2018 guidelines should be read in consonance with the FRA and not otherwise. Since currently there are no CWHs in India, and though Maharashtra has been in the process of implementing CWHs in the state since 2018, the state high court of Bombay halted the CWH process in 2019 after it was found that the forest rights claims of the people in the proposed CWHs were being denied and illegally rejected, further exemplifies the implementation lack of forest rights. The 2018 guidelines itself is criticized for lack of clarity in many areas, with one being the guidelines' failure to explain what constitutes evidence for 'irreversible' harm as caused by the forest dwellers to wildlife in the CWH (Gokhale 2020).

Also, even as CTHs are not falling in the areas covered under the FRA, the NTCA has a responsibility while issuing directions for the protection of tiger or tiger reserves to ensure that no such direction shall interfere with or affect the rights of local people, particularly the Scheduled Tribes (See section 30-O (2) of WLPA). Equally, the State Government while preparing a Tiger Conservation Plan is required to ensure the agricultural, livelihood, developmental, and other interests of the people living in tiger bearing forests or a tiger reserve[18] (See section 38 V (4) of WLPA). Finally, section 38 V (5) of WLPA also provides that the no Scheduled Tribes or such other forest dwellers shall be resettled or have their rights adversely affected for the purpose of creating inviolate areas for tiger conservation unless co-habitation is not feasible between them and the wildlife and that the practices of the people in the area causes irreversible damage and threaten the existence of tiger population and their habitat in the area. On technical grounds, once the CTH falls in an area otherwise covered under the FRA, the determination of the rights of the forest communities in such areas under section 4 (2) of FRA becomes applicable, as previously admitted by the Union Ministry for Environment and Forest.

Eviction of indigenous forest-dependent communities from CTHs without considering the question of the forest peoples' socio-cultural links to the area will be tantamount to denying them their basic rights.

It may be recalled that in the Vedanta judgment, the Supreme Court of India providing an emphasis on the Particularly Vulnerable Tribal Groups[19] under the FRA held that:

---

[18] The CTHs are including in the expression the Tiger Reserve.

[19] A 'Particularly Vulnerable Tribal Group', previously known as 'primitive tribal group' is a classification provided by the Government of India for providing support for the uplift of certain tribal groups with the lowest level of socio-economic development. For more see the Report of the Scheduled Areas and Scheduled Tribes Commission, 1960–1961, Government of India. The previously employed term 'primitive' used to denote official choice, is seen as reflecting bias against the tribal communities of India. This term is frequently associated with a negative connotation, whether expressed consciously or unconsciously.

> Primitive Tribal Groups need some emphasis, as very few communities in India in general and Orissa in particular come under the ambit of such a category. Their dependence on the forest being almost complete, the violation of the specific protections extended to their habitat and habitations by the Forest Rights Act, 2006 are simply unacceptable.
>
> (Supreme Court of India 2013)

Furthermore, Lele et al. write that despite the safeguards as provided for in CWH areas under the FRA, illegal evictions have taken place in the past due to the state's lack of due diligence. Lele et al. maintain that the use of 'scientific and objective criteria' and consultative processes must be the norm in determining whether co-existence is possible through a modified set of rights or management practices. Same needs to be decided by a multi-stakeholder expert committee with the informed consent of the concerned Gram Sabhas (Lele and Upadhyay 2020).

Also, an assessment of the FRA only highlights the fact that there is no clarity on the processes involved for recognizing the pastoral rights and particularly the issues on the set of such rights which is covered across various Gram Sabhas and districts as well as state borders. Although a response on the same was provided by the MoTA in 2015, i.e.

> Claims can be filed before their own Gram Sabhas. If the rights are exercised in forests traversing number of villages, they should also file before all the Gram Sabhas through which they traditionally have rights of passage and temporary grazing. This can be done as a community through traditional community institutions, or through individual members. Correspondingly, according to Rule 12(1)(c) of the FR Rules, the Forest Rights Committee has to ensure that the claims from pastoralists and nomadic tribes for determination of their rights are verified when such individuals, communities or their representatives are present, and no decision on these rights should be taken in their absence.
>
> (Indian Ministry of Tribal Affairs 2015, p. 10)

However, the same was published as a clarification in a booklet by MoTA, implying that the provisions within the FRA lack clarity and are missing explanations to resolve such discrepancies. Also, the impetuous act of the MoEFCC in denial of forest rights in CTHs will only adversely impact the rights of the forest-dependent communities (Agarwal and Shrivastava 2017). Particularly, keeping in mind that these pastoral communities mainly benefit from CRFs as it does not come within limitations of geographical area, it is vital that an amendment is made to the FRA. Accordingly, such amendment must provide provision for the inclusion of CTHs falling in areas where the FRA is applied to require the free and informed consent of Gram Sabhas before its notification to ensure institutional security and a democratic process in the discussion making related to the continuance, subsequent modification or resettlement of the forest rights as provided under sub-section 2 to section 4 of FRA.

Also, as the number of CTHs will continue to grow across protected areas in India, one may consider that the MoEFCC had already provided in 2011 that CTHs require at the minimum at least an inviolate area[20] of 800–1200 km^2 to sustain a

[20] 'Inviolate' or inviolate spaces imply that such space or area should be devoid of human settlement and usage as human-wildlife conflicts can be reduced and wildlife conservation can be achieve.

viable population of tigers. If more of such habitats are built on traditional forest land otherwise used by the pastoralist, it could have a severe impact on these communities (Thomas 2022). Ultimately these apprehensions exist as pastoral rights mainly rely on CFRs.

It can be concluded that the FRA requires amendments and further clarity in its guidelines. It also remains to be seen if the respective governments of states wherein the FRA is applicable shall ensure that there remains no lag in its thorough implementation. Also, for the interest of the pastoralist communities, the emphasis needs to be on their community rights even as they cross over from their domiciled state to the neighbouring state where their traditional rights are located. The implementation of the FRA by the state machinery has been criticized for its excessive emphasis on individual rights in the past (Gadgil 2008). It is high time; the attitude needs to change.

References

Agarwal, S. 2017. Community forest rights in critical tiger habitats under threat: NTCA's order to deny forest rights in tiger habitat has become a contentious issue Downtoearth.org. https://www.downtoearth.org.in/news/forests/community-forest-rights-in-critical-habitats-face-hurdle-due-to-lack-of-legal-roadmap-57602

Anaya, J. 2009. International human rights and indigenous peoples. Kluwer Publications.

Bandi, M. 2014. Forest Rights Act: Towards the End of Struggle for Tribals? *Social Scientist*, 42, No. 1/2.

Bhattachariya, N. 2018. *The great agrarian conquest*. Permanent Black.

Bijoy, C.R. 2019. Forest rights in the north east inching towards exclusion. *Economic & Political Weekly IIV*(45), 17–19.

Bijoy, C.R. et al. 2010. India and the rights of indigenous peoples constitutional, legislative and administrative provisions concerning indigenous and tribal peoples in India and their relation to international law on indigenous peoples. Asia Indigenous Peoples Pact Foundation.

Brysk, , A. 2000. From tribal village to global village: Indian rights and international relations in South America, Stanford: Stanford University Press. Champagne, D. 2013. UNDRIP (United Nations declaration on the rights of indigenous peoples): human, civil, and indigenous rights. *Wíčazo Ša Review* 28 (1): 9–22.

Dash, T., and A. Khotari. 2012. Grabbing: dangers of the green India mission. In *Banking on forests: assets for a climate cure?*, eds. K. Kohli and M. Menon. Kalpavriksh and Henrich Boll Stiftung.

Domínguez, L., and C. Luoma. 2020. Decolonising conservation policy: how colonial land and conservation ideologies persist and perpetuate indigenous injustices at the expense of the environment. *Land*, 9(3): 65. https://doi.org/10.3390/land9030065

Fanari, E. 2019. Relocation from protected areas as a violent process in the recent history of biodiversity conservation in India. *Ecology, Economy and Society–The INSEE Journal* 2(1): 43–76. https://doi.org/10.37773/ees.v2i1.55

Such consequently implies that CTHs must be devoid of human settlement including relocation of people living in such areas. However, as analysed above, protections provided to the Scheduled Tribes or such other forest dwellers under both the WLPA as well under the FRA must be ensured including considerations to the possibility of human-wildlife co-habitation while establishing CTHs provided such co-habitation is feasible and that the practices of the people in the area do not cause irreversible damage and threaten the existence of wildlife species and their habitat in the CTHs.

Gadgil, M. 2008. *Let our rightful forests flourish.* (NCAS Working Paper No. 27). National Centre for Advocacy Studies, Pune. https://dokumen.tips/documents/let-our-rightful-forests-flourish-by-madhav-gadgi.html

Gilbert, J., and C. Doyle. 2011. A new dawn over the land: shedding light on collective ownership and consent. In *Reflections on the UN declaration on the rights of indigenous peoples*, eds. S. Allen and A. Xanthaki, 289–328. Oxford, UK: Hart Publishing.

Gokhale, N. 2020. Critical wildlife habitats advisory augurs future conflicts in national parks. *The Wire Science*. https://science.thewire.in/environment/critical-wildlife-habitats-environment-advisory-national-parks/

Gooch, P. 2009. Victims of conservation or rights as forest dwellers: Van Gujjar pastoralists between contesting codes of law. *Conservation & Society* 7(4): 239–248.

Guha, R. 2007. Adivasis, naxalites and Indian democracy. *Economic and Political Weekly* 42 (32): 3305–3312.

Guha, R. 1983. Forestry in British and Post-British India: A historical analysis. *Economic and Political Weekly*, 18(44): 1882–1896. http://www.jstor.org/stable/4372653.http://www.pastoralpeoples.org/wp-content/uploads/2020/09/Accounting4pastoralists-in.pdf

Hadden, T. 2007. The United Nations working group on minorities. *International Journal on Minority and Group Rights* 14: 285–297.

High Level Political Forum. 2016. Ensuring that no one is left behind. International Indian Treaty Council, Global Organizing Partners for the Indigenous Peoples Major Group.

Indian Ministry of Tribal Affairs. 2021. Status report on the implementation of the Scheduled Tribes and Other Traditional Forest Dwellers (Recognition of Forest Rights) Act, 2006 for the period ending 30 September, 202. Government of India. https://tribal.nic.in/downloads/FRA/MPR/2021/(B)%20MPR%20Sep%202021.pdf

Indian Ministry for Tribal Affairs. 2015. *Frequently Asked Questions on the Forest Rights Act*, Government of India. https://tribal.nic.in/downloads/FRA/FAQ/FAQ%20ENGLISH_Approved_compressed.pdf.

Phillips, James S., and S. J. 2015. The rights of indigenous peoples under international law. *Global Bioethics* 26 (2): 1–8. https://doi.org/10.1080/11287462.2015.1036514.

Kishore, K., and I. Köhler-Rollefson. 2020. Accounting for pastoralists in India. League for Pastoral Peoples and Endogenous Livestock Development. Ober-Ramstadt, Germany.

Kothari, A. 2011. The Promise of The FRA Remains Largely Unfulfilled, says a Committee set up by the Ministries of Environment and Forests and Tribal Affairs. *Frontline* 28(05). https://frontline.thehindu.com/social-issues/article30174735.ece

Kukreti, I., and S. Agarwal. 2018. Critical Wildlife Habitat guidelines issued; NTCA order superseded. *DownToEarth.org*. https://www.downtoearth.org.in/news/governance/critical-wildlife-habitat-guidelines-issued-ntca-order-superseded-59934

Kumar, K., and J. Kerr. 2012. Democratic assertions: The making of India's recognition of Forest Rights Act. *Development and Change* 43 (3): 751–771.

Levien, M. 2011. Rationalising dispossession: The land acquisition and resettlement bills. *Economic and Political Weekly* 46 (11): 66–71.

Lele, S., A. Joshi, and P. Upadhyay. 2020. Hardline conservationists fail to see possibilities of people-wildlife coexistence. The Indian Express. https://indianexpress.com/article/opinion/critical-wildlife-habitat-forest-rights-act-wildlife-conservation-6553692/#:~:text=CWH%20is%20a%20provision%20under,assuage%20concerns%20of%20wildlife%20conservationists

LIFE Network, LPPS, LPP and RLN. 2016. *Kullu call for the recognition of the importance of common pool resources (CPRs) and pastoralism for India's livestock sector* [Brochure]. http://rln.org.in/wp-content/uploads/2019/04/Kullu-Call-Brochure.pdf

Mearns, R. 1999. Access to Land in Rural India. World Bank (Policy Research Working Paper 2123).

Ministry of Environment and Forest. 2011. *Clarification by Minister of State for Environment and Forests on Tiger Reserves, Critical Wildlife Habitats and Forest Right Act, 2006*, Government of India.

Ministry of Environment, Forest and Climate Change. 2017. Conferring Rights under Scheduled Tribes and Other Traditional Forest Dwellers (Recognition fo Rights) Act, 2006 in Critical Tiger Habitats- reg., 2017, Government of India. https://tribal.nic.in/FRA/declarationsClarifications/CRTigerHabitats28032017.pdf)

Oskarsson, P. 2018. Adivasi land rights and dispossession. In *Landlock: Paralysing Dispute over Minerals on Adivasi Land in India*, ed. Oskarsson, P.. ANU Press. https://doi.org/10.22459/10.22459/L.09.2018

Paquet, P.A., and A. Kuroyedov. 2021. Everyday forest rights: claiming territories NAD pastoral livelihoods in Uttar Pradesh and Uttarakhand, India. *Conservation & Society* 19 (4): 236–247.

Pegu, K. 2021. Tribals and forest rights in India: A critical appraisal of the legal literature. In *The role of law in governing sustainability*, 1st edn, ed. Mauerhofer, V. Routledge. https://doi.org/10.4324/9781003158837

UN General Assembly. 2015. Transforming our world: the 2030 Agenda for Sustainable Development, UN Doc. A/RES/70/1: 2015.

Saberwal, V.K. 1999. *Pastoral politics: Shepherds, bureaucrats, and conservation in the western Himalayas*. Oxford University Press.

Sigamany, I. 2017. Land rights and neoliberalism: An irreconcilable conflict for indigeneous peoples in India? *International Journal of Law in Context* 13 (3): 369–387. https://doi.org/10.1017/S1744552316000392.

Sinha, A.K. 2007. Implementation of forest law: A case study in East Singhbum of Jharhand in Paty in C.K. Paty (Eds.), Forest Government and Tribe. Concept Publishing Company, New Delhi.

Springate-Baginski, O., and P. Blaikie. 2007. Introduction: Setting up key policy issues in participatory forest management. In *Forests, people and power: The political ecology of reform in South Asia*, eds. O. Springate-Baginski and P. Blaikie. Earthscan.

Springate-baginski, O., M. Sarin, S. Ghosh, P. Dasgupta, Bose, A. Banerjee, K. Sarap, P. Misra, S. Behera, M.G. Reddy, and P.T. Rao. 2008. *The Indian Forest Rights Act 2006: Commoning Enclosures*. Norwich: Overseas Development Group, University of East Anglia.

Supreme Court of India. 2013. Orissa Mining Corporation Ltd vs Ministry of Environment & Forest, Civil Original Jurisdiction Writ Petition (CIVIL) NO. 180 OF 2011.

Sutton, M.Q., and E.N. Anderson. 2010. *Introduction to cultural ecology*, 2nd ed. Lanham, Md.: AltaMira Press.

Tomas, R. 2022. Is a tiger reserve in Rajasthan's Kumbhalgarh a bad idea? *Mongabay*. https://india.mongabay.com/2022/04/is-a-tiger-reserve-in-rajasthans-kumbhalgarh-a-bad-idea/

Impacts of Sinosphere on Ensuring Equal Rights of Ethnic Minority Women in Southeast Asian Countries: Barriers, Challenges and Recent Developments

Nguyen Toan Thang, Nguyen Thi Hong Yen, and La Minh Trang

Abstract The Sinosphere culture has specific effects on the role of women in society. Moreover, along with the development of human rights standards, Southeast Asian countries have achieved changes in ensuring human rights and gender equality. Since the Sinosphere has influenced gender equality in Southeast Asian countries, what are the effects on gender equality of ethnic minority women (EMW) from there to now? It is necessary to figure out gender equality in Southeast Asian countries and the impacts of the Sinosphere in these countries. This chapter will identify the values of the Sinosphere/Eastern Asian Cultural sphere and its impacts on awareness of the position of EMW in Southeast Asian countries. Then, the chapter will clarify the effects of the values of the Sinosphere on the gender equality of EMW in these countries.

Keywords Sinosphere · Chinese culture · Equal rights · Ethnic minority women · Southeast Asian countries

1 Introduction

Asia is the world's largest and most populous continent and has produced great cultural heritages of humankind. The Sinosphere or East Asian Cultural Sphere or 'the Chinese cultural area' is deeply influenced in many Asian countries, including Japan, Korea, Singapore, and Vietnam by historical evolutions and migration (Emery

N. T. Thang
Comparative Law Institute, Hanoi Law University (HLU), Hanoi, Vietnam
e-mail: ngthang@hlu.edu.vn

N. T. H. Yen (✉) · L. M. Trang
Department of International Law, Hanoi Law University (HLU), Hanoi, Vietnam
e-mail: hongyennguyen.hlu@gmail.com; nguyenhongyen@hlu.edu.vn

L. M. Trang
e-mail: laminhtrang@hlu.edu.vn

T. Venthan Ananthavinayagan and A. Viswanath Shenoy (eds.), *The Wretched of the Global South*, International Law and the Global South,
https://doi.org/10.1007/978-981-99-9275-1_8

1999). In traditional Chinese culture, women always took a lower position than men then they were not allowed to decide on family and societal issues; their life purpose was to be a wife/mother and care for their households and children instead (Van 2019). With the absolute emphasis on the role of men and husbands in the family and society, there was no role-sharing between husband and wife in the family; women were often dependent on their husbands and accepted to let husbands decide for them because they were passive and resigned to their fates; thus, they had little desire to enjoy their fundamental human rights.

Although there are significant efforts to eliminate gender stereotypes and the gender gap, the internal contradictions within Eastern societies regarding gender equality still exist, even quite deeply in several countries. That is also a fact that Southeast Asian countries are currently facing (Molony 2004). The average income of Asian women is only 70–90% of that of men; more than 75% of all jobs are informal, without access to welfare policies such as sickness or maternity benefits. Poor conditions and low-paid jobs in informal employment led women to live in poverty more than formal workers (ILO 2011; ILO 2015).

The chapter will begin with identifying the values of the Sinosphere and its effects on awareness of the position of women and the EMW in Southeast Asian countries. The following sections will discuss the impacts of Sinosphere's values on gender equality, especially the EMW in these countries. After the chapter, we will raise issues to continue the discussion on the need to change the perception of the position of the EMW in East Asian countries to improve the role of women in society.

2 The Influence of the Sinosphere in Shaping the Status of EMW in Southeast Asian Countries

2.1 The Values of the Sinosphere in Southeast Asian Countries' Society

The Male Chauvinist

The Sinosphere, with excellent schools of philosophy that have shaped modern Chinese society's unique character, has spread and significantly impacted many cultures in the region, such as Vietnam, Singapore, Malaysia, Thailand, and Indonesia. Buddhism, Taoism, and Confucianism have strongly influenced the formation process of state structure, cultural life, ideology, religion, and beliefs in Asia and Southeast Asia (Fan 2000; Wan and Henry 2011). In addition, Confucianism strongly influences how to educate people on respect for the rule of law and family disciplines to stabilise social order, thereby affirming women's position in the family and society.

Confucianism is one of the leading philosophical schools of China, dating back to the Zhou Dynasty, the most culturally significant of the early Chinese dynasties.

Confucianism was born at the end of an era known in Chinese history as the Spring and Autumn period—Warring States (551 BC–3 BC) when the socio-economic situation was the most volatile in Chinese history. Faced with that situation, Confucianism thinkers, starting with Confucius, explained social problems and purpose measures to manage a society that was later considered 'rule of the country' during the feudal period in China. In essence, Confucianism draws attention to the control of personal desires and emotions and self-interest restraint for the benefit of the group to avoid conflict and maintain harmony (Yan 2006). In Confucianism, women in society must follow the rules of 'Three Obedience' and 'Four Virtues'. Accordingly, the 'Three Obedience' are three things a woman must follow: a woman's first obedience is to her father before she is married to her husband while she is married, and to her son, after her husband dies. The 'Four Virtues' refer to the four basic standards of a woman, including gong (doing well), dung (beautifying beauty), language (soft speech), and conduct (gentle character). These are the moral characteristics that any woman needs to cultivate to improve herself. In the ethical contents of Confucianism, the theory of 'Three Obedience' and 'Four Virtues' are the fundamental moral norms used to evaluate a woman. While the 'Five Constant Virtues' are things that a man must have in his life, including benevolence (love for all living things), righteousness (behaving with everyone in a righteous manner), propriety (respect, being gentle in dealing with people), wisdom (reasonable), and trustworthy (reliable) (Berling 1982). The 'Five Constant Virtues' in Confucianism create traditional moral norms to govern the family by emphasising the decision-making power of the father, husband, and the children or the wife must follow. Therefore, the limitation of Confucianism is that women are not considered independent subjects but must depend on the man in their family. (Nguyen and Nguyen 2012). As a moral system, Confucianism focuses on five cardinal role relations between the emperor- subject, father-son, husband-wife, elder-younger brothers, and friend-friend. All these relationships involve a set of defined roles and mutual obligations. Each individual should conform to his or her role and act properly to perfect society (Berling 1982; Thang et al. 2021).

EMW in the Southeast Asian Countries

Southeast Asia is heterogeneous, with diverse ethnicities, cultures, and religions. From a broad perspective, the term 'minority' may include ethnic and linguistic minorities, religious minorities, and indigenous peoples. Generally, those three groups are distinctive from each other. The indigenous peoples have a dynamic of people living initially and primitively in a particular sovereign territory (United Nations 2021). The religious minority is identified based on religion to distinguish it from the beliefs held by the majority. For instance, in the Philippines, the minority religion is Muslim, as the major religion in this country is Catholic. In Indonesia, the minority religion is Catholic, while the Muslim's major religion is Muslim (Clarke 2001).

As of the date hereof, there has been no authoritative definition for 'ethnic minority', and this term has not been defined under any international legal document. In an advisory opinion in 1930, the Permanent Court of International Justice viewed that:

> The 'community' is a group of persons living in a given country or locality, having a race, religion, language and traditions of their own and united by this identity of race, religion, language and traditions in a sentiment of solidarity, to preserve their traditions, maintain their form of worship, ensuring the instruction and upbringing of their children by the spirit and traditions of their race and rendering mutual assistance to each other (PCIJ 1930).

In the Declaration on the Rights of Indigenous Peoples (UNDRIP) 2007, the regulations on indigenous peoples were created based on the features of ethnicity, race, culture, religion, and language. Despite the lack of one authoritative definition for indigenous peoples, in human rights documents of the United Nations, this term is usually used to describe a minority group of people with distinctive features in ethnicity, race, language, and religion, which are different from the remaining populations of a nation (OHCHR 2013). The ethnic minority in Southeast Asia is defined based on the same understanding.

Each Southeast Asian country has multiple indigenous peoples with a different number of people. For instance, the Cham ethnic group in Cambodia has about 200,000 people; the Hmong ethnic group in Laos has about 231,168 people; The OrangAsli ethnic group has about 80,000 people (Clarke 2001). Among Southeast Asian countries, Vietnam has the most ethnic minorities, including 53 ethnic minorities with over 14 million people (General Statistics Office and Committee for Ethnic Minority Affairs 2020).

Factors Create Discrimination Against EMW in Southeast Asian Countries' Society

If Asia is a continent with varied and diverse ethnicities, religions, and beliefs, Southeast Asia is a multi-ethnic and multi-cultural region; furthermore, the diversity is also reflected in each country. However, a common feature in this region is usually one leading ethnic group, accounting for the most significant number in each country. For example, in Laos, the 'Lao Lum' accounts for 70% of the population, the 'Kinh' accounts for 90% of the population of Vietnam and the 'Javanese' account for 70% of the population of Indonesia, etc. (Nguyen 2008). In this region, cultural diversity is reflected in every country's identity; however, Chinese culture influences them more or less.

Currently, although the legal frameworks on gender equality in ethnic minority areas are developed in Southeast Asian countries, the EMW are still facing discrimination and suffering from '*dual*' hardship in both ethnicity and gender inequality due to the influence of the following factors:

The first factor is the Sinosphere's influence on the traditional moral principles, which were educated publicly. The 'Five Constant Virtues', 'Three Obedience' and 'Four Virtues' theories as mentioned above put women in a lower position and have less self-control than men. Today, women are still in a disadvantaged position because gender norms in Southeast Asian cultures are still strong that women should be 'keepers of the peace' in the family, or men still have the property right, especially land or other valuable assets (Van 2019).

In terms of the EMW, suppose there is a lack of participation of minorities in the policy and law formulation (Truong 2018). In that case, they will have little opportunity to express their will and protect their rights in the decision-making process. The EMW who are inherently disadvantaged in gender when forced to be mothers and housewives; also have difficulties accessing education for development and access to services and justice because of geographical distance and limitations of mobility. EMW, therefore, are more vulnerable.

The second factor is the influence of the habits and experiences of agricultural production activities. In Eastern culture, to increase agricultural productivity, the role of collectivity seems to be more important than the individuals, and the behaviour culture of the Eastern often attaches to collectivity over the individuals. Therefore, everyone must know how to close themselves and integrate their ego with the majority instead of manifesting their ability in front of the collective (Kaplan 2015). Besides, the community's cohesion also makes the interests of the minority group gradually replaced by the majority group (Robison 1996a, b). The idea of "the few keep up with the majority" creates prejudices about ethnic groups in the society in Sinosphere areas. At that point, ethnic minorities will have prejudices or lose confidence because they are afraid of non-conformity with the expected standards of society. It leads to the 'minority' community becoming further away from the 'majority' group and refusing to participate in activities to protect their rights (ISEE 2018).

The third factor is the inaccurate labelling of the 'majority' to the 'minority'. In the history of Southeast Asian countries, these countries understood that close solidarity with all classes of people was always valued because of invasions. In governing states in which the Sinosphere is highly influenced, unity would create stability in social orders, mainly when the country fought against foreign invaders. When people share the same ideology and the common, the government would defeat foreign invaders and maintain territorial sovereignty (Choe 2006). It could be the reason for the common characteristic in the ethnic structure is that there is one leading and largest ethnic group in Southeast Asian countries because a part of the ethnic minorities gradually turned into the majority after the wars against aggression (Shin 2006; Karmel 2002). Those who kept their ethnicity would be inaccurately 'labelled' as unpatriotic, inferior, disloyal, etc. According to the theory of 'labelling' discrimination by Link and Phelan (2001), social prejudice is an unfair discriminatory process, leading to the resistance and exclusion of a social group towards those possessing attributes that are not similar to the 'majority' group. This process generally goes through five stages: (1) Labelling, (2) Stereotyping, (3) Separation, (4) Status Loss (5) Discrimination (Link and Phelan 2001). Thus, 'labelling' people belonging to ethnic minorities with a faulty view of ethnic minorities with a disrespectful attitude will turn them into victims of discrimination.

Finally, the 'Asian values' in the process of economic development are assessed in such issues as the responsibility of individuals to society, or the role of the family and the maintenance of law and order (Dellapenna 1995). Traditionally, Confucianism focuses on relations between father-son and husband-wife as a moral system involving defined roles and mutual obligations. Therefore, Confucianism requires a broad commitment in society that each individual should conform to his or her proper role and act properly to perfect the society (Berling 1982). From 1960 to 1990, the Four Asian Tigers, including Hong Kong (China), Taiwan (China), Singapore, and

Korea, made the world admire exports and rapid industrialisation. These four countries have maintained consistently high levels of economic growth since the 1960s and have become the wealthiest countries in the world (Leipziger 2001). During this period, a wave of '*Asian values*' emerged in many Asian countries, which was said to be the reason behind the rapid economic development of the Four Asian Tigers and countries in Southeast Asia such as Malaysia, Thailand, Indonesia, and Vietnam (Wan 2011; Lin 1995; Landes 2006).

In 1965, Singapore became an independent country after the separation from Malaysia. Lee Kuan Yew engineered Singapore's economic miracle and was considered a successful modernising leader who promoted Confucian quintessence by selectively absorbing Western culture (Liang 2010). The Confucian doctrines were applied to stabilise society and create a premise for economic development. At the same time, Lee Kuan Yew developed Western economic theories to manage and develop the country's economy combined with the advanced technology system of developed countries (Robison 1996a, b). Besides, in a multi-ethnic society like Singapore, the governing policy of Lee Kuan Yew was "imposing harmony in the top-down society", which was undoubtedly compatible with the idea of ruling according to Confucian (Ian 2015). At the same time, community and family are core values in Confucianism that also play an essential role in the development of Singapore (Nguyen and Trinh 2018). Compared to the West, although there is no country denying values enshrined in the Universal Declaration of Human Rights, cultural diversity is an argument for gross violations of human rights (Dellapenna 1995). At the same time, community and family are core values in Confucianism that also play an essential role in the development of Singapore. The Confucian thought also heightened a cult of learning and thrift, a spirit of self-sacrifice based on common social standards, and Lee said it was '*Asian values*'. This idea held that a society built on '*Asian values*' was a stable and orderly society with loyalty (Schuman 2009). Thus, until now, this view deeply rooted in 'Chinese culture' has made waves in many countries, causing many debates because of the notion that the position of women is not guaranteed (Schuman 2009).

2.2 The Impacts of the Sinosphere on Awareness of the Position of EMW in the Southeast Asian Countries

Southeast Asia is a region with a long-standing culture, made up of many relationships and unique identities of each nation. The cultural values in the transaction process have brought Southeast Asia a diverse, unique, and meaningful culture. In Southeast Asia, besides the patriarchal family system that exists in most of the region, the matriarchal regime is also recognised in some communities living in Vietnam, Cambodia, Thailand (Cham group), Minangkabau group (Indonesia) (Deutsche Welle The Nation 2017). Given those mentioned above, compared to other neighbouring regions such as East Asia or South Asia, women's position in Southeast Asian society is relatively high. Then, over time, the promotion of new concepts and religions emphasised the importance of men, resulting in women gradually becoming dependent on men. Confucianism emphasises maintaining social order by connecting emotional feelings between family members as a moral system. In the Confucian culture, the role of each family member was hierarchically placed and clearly defined; therefore, the order and harmony achieved through hierarchical familial relationships should be the basis for establishing wider social order (Sangwha 1999: 19). "The patriarch of a family is in some sense himself subsumed under the category of familial order as one of the 'role-performers' in that order. Yet, in the Confucian conception, the particular manner he plays that role remains crucial to maintaining the familial order. The father and ruler bring the 'creative power' of their persons to bear precisely by acting wholeheartedly in ways that correspond to preordained sacred prescriptions rather than acting in ways that make them the 'interesting' protagonists of stories" (Schwartz 1985).

In the Confucian framework, people believe that men should be educated to take part in examinations and make their way up society by academics, but women should only concern themselves with housework. Contrary to boys, girls are not allowed to go to school: this fact comes from the concept of respecting men and disrespecting women, and girls should make sacrifices for the sake of the family. Confucianism inherently emphasises the word 'filial' because 'filial piety', according to Confucianism, is considered a moral standard and a central and first-class moral quality of people in family relations. In addition, ethnic minority women cannot participate in political life but can only stay at home. Confucian principles require a woman to love and take care of her husband and children and be submissive to her husband to keep a peaceful and happy family in a marital relationship. It creates prejudices which place women in a dependent position in the family; meanwhile, men are considered the owners and the primary decision-makers. These perceptions deprive ethnic minority women of their right to access knowledge, work, and participate in political life. Regarding the division of labour, men took responsibility for public and outside work, while females were private and inside work. Sangwha argued in the patriarchal framework, men's labour was defined in social activities for the state, such as politics, diplomacy, and defence, while domestic work was engaged for women.

However, not all perceptions of women are in the direction of downplaying their role. In the flow of history, Southeast Asian countries, tolerating imported cultures, have made changes to suit their customs, practices, and national traditions. Although influenced by China's Confucianism, Vietnamese society mainly received Confucianism as an instrument for the emperor to rule the country, calm the people and build a proper social order (Hoang and Hoang 2015). If China's Confucianism favours men and despises women and imposes strict ethical standards such as "to be submissive to her father at home, to her husband during marriage, and to her son, after her husband's death," or "one boy means one, ten girls mean none," the Confucianism in Vietnam is not quite like that. History has proven that the Vietnamese people and Vietnamese Confucianists greatly appreciate the glorious victories of national heroines fighting against foreign invaders such as Hai Ba Trung (40 AD) and Ba Trieu (248 AD). In the Ly Dynasty, when Emperor Ly Thanh Tong left to fight the

Southern invaders in 1069, he gave one of his imperial consorts—Y Lan Nguyen Phi, the regent power to rule the court affairs (Nguyen 2011).

At the end of the nineteenth century, the feudal regime in the country began to decline. As Chinese civilization gradually degraded, Western culture began to penetrate Vietnam with the invasion of the French colonists. In the 1920s–1930s, Marxism-Leninism ideology was introduced into Vietnam. This ideology, combined with patriotism, has become the driving force for historical transformation leading the country towards independence, democracy, and socialism. However, Confucian thought in the twentieth century still influences social life. Ho Chi Minh, the Vietnamese revolutionary leader from a Confucian family, paid great attention to the position of women in general and ethnic minority women in particular in society and their essential role in the revolution. Ho Chi Minh always emphasised that the women's force was an integral part of the revolution, one of the crucial factors in ensuring all benefits of the fight for independence and freedom of the nation and the people's happiness. Ho Chi Minh gave Vietnamese women four golden words: "Heroic, Unconquerable, Loyal, and Capable" (Nguyen 2011).

3 The Sinosphere and Gender Equality of EMW in Vietnam and Other Southeast Asian Countries

As mentioned above, Southeast Asia is a region of multiple societies with cultural diversity. Unlike European countries with a unity mission, Southeast Asian countries aimed to unite in diversity (Johnson 2010). Cultural diversity impacts families and their point of view on gender equality, which analyses the fact that no direct approach is applied to all Southeast Asian countries. For example, China's Confucianism impacts Malaysian-Chinese families, they still wish to have a son because of the heavily gender-biased (United Nations, Department of Economic and Social Affairs 2015; The Economist Intelligence Unit 2019). The heavy influences of the Sinosphere show gender inequality in two aspects: gender inequality in the family and the workspace.

3.1 Male Chauvinism—Gender Inequality in the Family

Despite remarkable achievements regarding gender equality, Southeast Asia is a region where there is still male chauvinism in sharing household chores and participation in socio-economic development. (The Economist Intelligence Unit 2019). Happiness in the family is built upon three principles: self-financing growth, raising good kids, and maintaining and developing good relationships in the community. Women tend to take an active role in managing family wealth nowadays. However, the thoughts of "men build the houses and women make it home" are generally believed by most people (UNFPA, Ministry of Labour, War Invalids and Social Welfare 2020). As an example of gender inequality in Thailand, Thai women have spent most of their lives caring for their children and parents. As a result, they lack time for social work. Hence, women always expected their family burdens to be helped by men. Professor Prachuabmoh insisted that the inequality in the household between men and women would be conflicted with higher education for women. (The Economist Intelligence Unit 2019).

In Vietnam, the patriarchy in Confucianism has played an essential role in society as it experienced more disruptions than any other Southeast Asian country. During the feudal system period, Confucianism attempted to spread across the country, which resulted in an ideology of law, rules, and customs, imposing valuing men above women (Gupta et al. 2003). However, K. Marx and Lenin's thoughts on Equality in the early modern period positively influenced gender equality in Vietnam. During the 1930s, the primary tasks of the Vietnamese Communist Party focused on national liberation, class, and women's liberation as being conducted and supported at the same time. Women's role in Vietnamese women's liberation was an essential part that they engaged in direct action for the success of the August Revolution in 1945. It contributes to empowering gender equality and decreasing Confucian practices (Quy 2013).

Respect towards women has become a new lifestyle of gender equality. Hence, Socialist ideology has affected Vietnam's policies and laws regarding gender equality regarding changing the status and role of women. Vietnamese women in the present are expanding their capacity for economic independence, participating, and being recognised in every aspect of life, such as family, economics, politics, and society (Vu and Pham 2021). The 1946 Constitution of Vietnam states that both men and women can share equality, and it continues to be noted in the Constitution of Vietnam of 1959, 1980, 1992, and 2013. Then, many laws of Vietnam, such as the Law on Marriage and Family 2014, the Labor Code 2019, the Law on Gender Equality in 2006, and the Law on Domestic Violence Prevention and Control 2007, concretised the spirits from these Constitutions. These laws have the objective of eliminating gender discrimination and building gender equality in the family and all areas of social life. By codifying the provisions of the CEDAW into national laws, this Convention is implemented in Vietnam smoothly, without obstacles and difficulties (LQ 2013). Currently, Vietnam is among ten countries in the Asia Pacific region regarding gender equality (World Economic Forum 2020).

However, in reality, ethnic minority women are still vulnerable and subject to gender inequality. The most noticeable inequality is that men are considered the head of the household when up to 74% of men in ethnic minority households have independent names regarding land ownership and credit. After marriage, men still prioritise going to school, while women must stay home to fulfil motherhood and wife duties. Therefore, ethnic minority men know much more about reading and writing than women. In some ethnic minorities such as Mong, Ha Nhi, La Hu, and Lu, only about 20–30% of women can read and write. In addition, domestic violence in ethnic minorities is quite common, especially among patriarchal ethnic groups. The analysis results show that 58.6% of ethnic minority women aged 15–49 believe that a husband has the right to beat his wife if she goes out without permission, argues with her husband, or refuses to have sex, which is rare for Kinh women to accept this. Patriarchal attitudes and stereotypes regarding the roles of women and men are the cause of discriminatory behaviour (UNFPA 2020).

Making a change in gender equality is still challenging for the Vietnamese government. The country has made significant achievements in gender equality but remains far from full equality as women's appearance to be dedicated and willing to sacrifice one. Women continue to be unpaid workers at home. The position of women in society is affected by socio-economic status resulting from discrimination between men and women. Confucianism's discrimination against gender and patriarchy has been rooted for many years. Women need to work hard in both fields: family and society. They spend hours in the workspace while being back home, and they still have the responsibility of being a wife, a mother, a helper, a financial manager, and a tutor. Such household things waste time and effort, so women have no time for self-care. It leads to the widening gaps between men and women in every society; therefore, promoting the role of women in the community and the family may cause the opposite effect, which contributes to reinforcing gender stereotypes. (VU and Pham 2021; Thang et al. 2021).

3.2 Gender Inequality in Economics, Labour, and Workspace

The participation of women in many fields, especially in the labour market, has increased significantly in recent years (World Bank 2012; Thang et al. 2021). However, the number of women who work at home is still the majority because women have fewer opportunities in the labour market and are more at risk of unemployment than men. The female labour force participation rate was ranked differently in each country, depending on various factors such as culture, customs, economic growth, education level, birth rate, salary rate, and other services (Chaudhary and Verick 2014).

In modern living, the participation of women in the labour market in Malaysia contributes to the development economy (Ismail and Sulaiman 2014). Over the last few decades, Malaysia's labour market has increased female participation in the labour market and narrowed the gender wage gap between men and women (Milanovic 2001). Surprisingly, Malaysia's female labour force participation rate was low compared to other Southeast Asian countries, with around 44–48% annually (Qinfen 2017). This rate, however, increased to 54.7% in 2017 (Department of Statistics 2017) and 55.4% in the first quarter of 2021 (Department of Statistics 2021).

In Vietnam, the female labour force participation rate was relatively high among Southeast Asian countries' labour markets, around 70.9% in 2019. This rate was 47.2% globally, and the average rate in the Asian—pacific was 43.9%. There was a gender gap in the labour participation rate; however, the average rate was only 9.5% during the past decade compared to the ASEAN and global. Data from the 2018 labour force survey showed that nearly half of the females chose not to participate in the labour market for 'personal or family-related reasons'; meanwhile, only 18.9% of males (ILO 2021). Ms. Valentina Barcucci—ILO Vietnam's labour economist, cites: "Women Inequality in terms of job quality and career goal also comes from their dual responsibility." Women spend twice as much as men doing housework (Tuoitre 2021). The ILO 2021 also showed that women spent an average of 20.2 h per week cleaning up the house, washing clothes, cooking, and doing other household jobs while men only have 10.7 h for these jobs; moreover, nearly one over five of men who took the survey never spend times to do house job. Thus, despite having a tremendous female labour force participation rate, women in Vietnam still face unequal opportunities in the labour market. Dr. Chang Hee Lee—Director of ILO Vietnam, said that inequality in the labour market starts from traditional prejudice towards women's roles, reinforced by expected standards. In this way, Confucianism still exists and has affected Vietnamese society (Vu and Yamada 2020). In Vietnam Labour Code 2019, aims to ensure the opportunity to narrow the gender gap between men and women by tackling gender equality. For example, bridging the retirement age gap or removing restrictions on women's participation in the workplace are changing effectively. And the most challenging task that takes more effort to complete is to change behaviours and mindsets for all men and women in the Vietnam labour market (Hanoitimes 2020, Tuoitre 2021, Thang et al. 2021).

In ethnic minority areas, the employment rate of men is higher than women, though this difference is not the same among ethnic groups. Some ethnic groups have a much higher percentage of men in employment than women. Specifically, the top is the Ngai ethnic group, with 76.4% of employed workers male. The higher rate of men employed in this ethnic group is strongly related to cultural factors. It is an ethnic group where men play a decisive role in significant family affairs. Male workers are also high in other ethnic groups such as Pu Peo, Co Lao, O Du, Khmer, Tho, Chut, Cho Ro, and Cham, accounting for about 55%. There are some ethnic groups where the percentage of female workers is higher than that of men, but the difference is not significant (Ro Mam, Si La, Lo Lo, Gie Trieng, Gia Rai, Cong, Phu La, Xinh Mun) (UNDP, Irish Aid and Committee for Ethnic Minority Affairs 2017).

The possibility of ethnic minorities getting paid jobs is lower than that of Kinh people, and the likelihood of women getting paid jobs is also lower; only 17% of working non-Kinh women have a paid job, compared with 22% of Kinh women and 32% of men from ethnic minorities. In addition, ethnic minority women in paid jobs also earn significantly lower wages than non-ethnic minority women or men. These women earn 17% lower than ethnic minority men, 35% lower than Kinh women and 50% lower than non-ethnic minority men. Instead, ethnic minority women focus on self-employed farming with lower wages and less stability. For example, 59% of women from certain ethnic minority groups are engaged in farming, compared with 40% of women from the majority ethnic group.

Among Southeast Asia countries, the proportion of female labour force participation rate in Cambodia is the highest at 80% (Asian Development Bank 2015). The gender gap between male and female participation in the labour market is only 10%. In the last two decades, the rapid development in Cambodia's economy has accompanied an essential step towards gender equality in the labour market (Asian Development Bank 2013). In the Philippines, Indonesia, Malaysia, and Myanmar, we can see low female labour force participation rates compared to these rates in Vietnam, Laos, and Cambodia (Gavalyugova and Cunningham 2020).

Overall, different factors affect gender inequality in Southeast Asian countries, such as cultural diversity, religion, belief, economy, education level, and health, but the element that most affects gender inequality and discrimination is the role of women in society. As a woman, they must spend more time on family, household responsibilities, and jobs at the workplace than men (Asian Development Bank 2015). Inequality in household chores leads to gender-based imbalances in the workspace, while the male statistic at work is higher than females. It can be clearly shown in the Sinosphere countries like Vietnam (Vu and Yamada 2020). Therefore, to achieve full gender equality and non-discrimination, changing one's mindset and behaviours in all aspects of life is necessary. The Sinosphere with Male chauvinism has still influenced and created such barriers for women in ASEAN (Grosse 2015).

4 Conclusion

In contrast to many areas where much progress has been made, inequality against women, especially ethnic minority women, persists in some areas, such as inequality in economic activities, gender inequality in income, and gender inequality in doing housework and taking care of the family. Progress in these areas is sometimes hard to see, even though Southeast Asian countries have achieved positive results. So what is the cause? In addition to reasons related to institutions and policies, the convergence of many factors that prevent progress, the perception of women's status over many generations is a factor that has a strong impact and is not easily removed in a short time. Gender inequalities are long-lasting when deeply rooted in long-standing gender functions and social norms, such as who is responsible for taking care of housework or what is "acceptable" for women and men to learn, do, and desire. This inequality tends to recur from generation to generation (World Bank 2012; Thang et al. 2021).

In Eastern culture, women are the main ones responsible for household affairs. This pattern is shown more clearly after women get married and give birth. Regardless of income, women have to take charge of most housework and take care of the family, while men are mainly responsible for incurring income. Even if women spend more time working outside than their husbands, they are still primarily responsible for taking care of the family and doing housework. That leads to disparities between women and men in the issue of time spent, limiting women's opportunities and affecting their leisure time and happiness (UN Women 2016; Thang et al. 2021).

To promote women's participation in today's social life, removing barriers, especially barriers of perception, culture, and customs, is an essential key to unleashing women's potential as they are a vital factor for the development of society. Women's second-class status and inequalities of opportunity have not historically been permanent. In removing these obstacles, on the one hand, it is necessary to change social relationships and social prejudices and build political institutions and an authoritative and progressive legal framework. On the other hand, it is necessary to change women's perspectives, psychology, and actions. Women must overcome themselves, meet the requirements of modern society, and contribute to the development of society. The goal of a just society for women is not only for women but for the sustainable development of nations and ethnicities in the twenty-first century. This goal cannot be achieved without changing the gender prejudice against men in the family and society. A just society for women is a new height in awareness and implementation of social justice today. Changing perceptions and unfair behaviour towards women requires drastic reforms in leadership and social management to achieve the goal of social justice (Thang et al. 2021).

References

Barbara Watson Andaya. 2021. Women in Southeast Asia. Asia Society, Centre for Global Education. https://asiasociety.org/education/women-southeast-asia. Accessed 24 Jul 2021.

Brunell, L., and Burkett Elinor. 2021. Feminism. Encyclopedia Britannica. https://www.britannica.com/topic/feminism. Accessed 24 Jul 2021.

Chaudhary, R., and Verick, S. 2014. Female labour force participation in India and beyond. Genève, Switzerland: International Labour Organization.

Choe, H. 2006. National Identity and Citizenship in the People's Republic of China and the Republic of Korea. *Journal of Historical Sociology* 19 (1): 84–118. https://doi.org/10.1177/1468796819834951.

Clarke, G. 2001. From ethnocide to ethnodevelopment? Ethnic minorities and Indigenous Peoples in Southeast Asia. *Third World Quarterly* 22 (3): 413–436.

Dellapenna, J., D'Amato, A., and Kausikan, B. 1995. An Asian Approach to Human Rights. In *Proceedings of the Annual Meeting (American Society of International Law)* (pp. 146–152). The American Society of International Law.

Deutsche Welle The Nation. 2017. Asia's matrilineal societies where women rule. National Thailand. https://www.nationthailand.com/perspective/30308589. Accessed 24 Jul 2021.

Emery, G. A. 1999. Chinese Business and Confucianism. http://collection.nlc-bnc.ca/100/202/300/moral_musings/v3n1/Emery.html

Fagbongbe, Mosope. 2008. The Future of Women's Rights from a TWAIL Perspective. *International Community Law Review* 10: 401–409.

Fan, Y. 2000. A classification of Chinese culture. *Cross-Cultural Management: An International Journal*. https://doi.org/10.1108/13527600010797057

Freeman, M. 1996, Human rights, democracy and 'Asian values. *The Pacific Review*, 9(3): 352–366, p 359. https://doi.org/10.1080/09512749608719191.

Fung, A. 2000. Feminist philosophy and cultural representation in the Asian context. *Gazette (leiden, Netherlands)* 62 (2): 153–165.

Gavalyugova, D., Cunningham, W. 2020. Gender Analysis of the Cambodian Labor Market. World Bank, Washington DC. © World Bank. https://openknowledge.worldbank.org/handle/10986/34201. Accessed 26 Jul 2021.

General Statistics Office and Committee for Ethnic Minority Affairs. 2020. Survey on the Socio-economic situation amongst 53 Ethnic Minorities in 2019. https://www.gso.gov.vn/wp-content/uploads/2020/07/01-Bao-cao-53-dan-toc-thieu-so-2019_ban-in.pdf. Accessed 08 Jan 2024.

Grosse, I. 2015. Gender values in Vietnam—Between Confucianism, communism, and modernization. *Asian Journal of Peacebuilding* 3 (2): 253–272.
Gupta, M., J. Zhenghua, L. Bohua, X. Zhenming, W. Chung, and B. Hwa-Ok. 2003. Why is son preference so persistent in East and South Asia? A cross-country Study of China, India and the Republic of Korea. *Journal of Development Studies* 40 (2): 153–187. https://doi.org/10.1080/00220380412331293807.
Hanoitimes. 2020. Vietnam advances greatly in gender equality but remains far from full equality: UN Women. September 21, 2020. http://hanoitimes.vn/vietnam-advances-greatlyin-gender-equality-but-remains-far-from-full-equality-un-women-314263.html. Accessed 08 Jan 2024.
Hoang N.V., and Hoang T.N.N. 2015. Confucianism—One of the Eastern cultural roots of Ho Chi Minh's thought /Nho giáo—Một trong những cội nguồn văn hóa phương Đông của tư tưởng Hồ Chí Minh. Journal of Science and Technology/Tạp chí Khoa học và Công nghệ. http://joshusc.hueuni.edu.vn/upload/vol_3/no_2/102_fulltext_3.8.LLCT%20-%20Hoang%20Ngoc%20Vinh.pdf, Accessed 24 Jul 2021.
Ian, B. 2015. Asian Values RIP, Project Syndicate. https://www.project-syndicate.org/commentary/asian-values-lee-kuan-yew-by-ian-buruma-2015-04. Accessed 24 Jul 2021.
ILO. 2011. Women and labour markets in Asia—Rebalancing for gender equality, ISBN: 9789221247074. https://www.ilo.org/wcmsp5/groups/public/---asia/---ro-bangkok/documents/publication/wcms_154846.pdf. Accessed 5 May 2022.
ILO. 2015. Women in business and management: Gaining momentum. Geneva. https://www.ilo.org/wcmsp5/groups/public/@dgreports/@dcomm/@publ/documents/publication/wcms_334882.pdf. Accessed 08 Jan 2024.
ILO. 2021. Gender and the labour market in Viet Nam: An analysis based on the Labour Force Survey. Viet Nam.
Institute for Social Development Studies. 2015. Social Determinants of Gender Inequality in Vietnam: Findings of a research study between 2012–2015. Hanoi.
IR. 2011. Non-Discrimination in International Law: A handbook for practitioners. The international centre for the Legal Protection of Human rights. http://adapt.it/adapt-indice-a-z/wp-content/uploads/2014/08/interight_non-discrimination_in_international_law_2011.pdf. Accessed 18 Jul 2021.
ISEE. 2018. Minority need to grow up to the significant Prejudice in ethnic relations in Vietnam/Thiểu số cần tiến kịp đa số - Định kiến trong quan hệ tộc người ở Việt Nam, http://isee.org.vn/wp-content/uploads/2018/11/thieu-so-can-tien-kip-da-so-dinhkien-trong-quan-he-toc-nguoi-o-viet-nam..pdf. Accessed 24 Jul 2021.
Ismail, R., and N. Sulaiman. 2014. Married women labor supply decision in Malaysia. *Asian Social Science* 10 (3): 221–231.
Jönsson, K. 2010. Unity-in-diversity? Regional identity-building in Southeast Asia. *Journal of Current Southeast Asian Affairs* 29 (2): 41–72.
Kaplan, R.D. 2015. Asia's rise is rooted in Confucian values. *The Wall Street Journal*, 6.
Karmel, S.M. 2002. *Ethnic nationalism in mainland China.* In Asian Nationalism: Routledge.
Landes, D.S. 2006. Why Europe and the west? Why not China? *Journal of Economic Perspectives* 20 (2): 3–22.
Leipziger, D.M. (Ed.). 2001. Lessons from East Asia. University of Michigan Press, pp. 6–7
Liang, M.Y. 2010. Confucianism and the East Asian miracle. *American Economic Journal: Macroeconomics*, 2(3): 206–34, p 209
Lin, J.Y. 1995. The Needham puzzle: Why the industrial revolution did not originate in China. *Economic Development and Cultural Change* 43 (2): 269–292.
Link, B.G., and J.C. Phelan. 2001. Conceptualizing stigma. Annual review of. *Sociology* 27 (1): 363–385.
Milanovic, B. 2001. Inequality and determinants of earnings in Malaysia, 1984–97. Paper Presented at the Asia and Pacific Forum on Poverty: Reforming Policies and Institutions for Poverty Reduction Asian Development Bank, Manila, 5–9 February 2001.

Molony, B. 2004. Frameworks of gender: Feminism and nationalism in twentieth-century Asia. A companion to gender history, 513–539

Nguyen, T.T., and Trinh, X.T. 2018. Confucianism in the process of modernization in some East Asian countries, Tạp chí Văn hóa/Journal of Culture and Art, no 406, 4/2018, 39–43. http://vhnt.org.vn/tin-tuc/van-hoa-duong-dai/30816/nho-giao-trong-tien-trinh-hien-dai-hoa-o-mot-so-nuoc-dong-a. Accessed 24 Jul 2021.

Nguyen, T.T., and T.B. Nguyen. 2012. Filial piety and the implementation of taking care of elderly people in Vietnamese families at present time. *Journal of Educational and Social Research* 2 (3): 227–227.

Nguyen, T.B.T. 2011. Tư tưởng Hồ Chí Minh về công tác phụ nữ trong xây dựng chủ nghĩa xã hội/ Ho Chi Minh's thought on women's work in building socialism, Party Building Journal. http://www.xaydungdang.org.vn/Home/tutuonghochiminh/2011/3478/Tu-tuong-Ho-Chi-Minh-ve-cong-tac-phu-nu-trong-xay.aspx. Accessed 18 Jul 2021.

Nguyen, T.D. 2008. Southeast Asians—Research, Collect and Introduce cultural diversity in the Southeast Asia/Người Đông Nam Á – Nghiên cứu, sưu tầm và giới thiệu về sự đa dạng văn hoá ở khu vực Đông Nam Á, Journal of Cultural Heritage/Tạp Chí Di Sản Văn Hóa, 01/2008. http://dsvh.gov.vn/Upload/files/Tap%20chi%20DSVH/So%2022/2211_Nguoi%20Dong%20Nam%20A%20nghien%20cuu%20suu%20tam%20va%20gioi%20thieu%20ve%20su%20da%20dang%20van%20hoa%20o%20khu%20vuc.pdf. Accessed 24 Jul 2021.

OHCHR. 2013. The United Nations declaration on the rights of indigenous peoples: A manual for national human rights institutions. https://www.ohchr.org/Documents/Issues/IPeoples/UNDRIPManualForNHRIs.pdf. Accessed 08 Jan 2024.

PCIJ. 1930. Greco-Bulgarian "Communities". Advisory Opinion of 31 July 1930. https://www.icj-cij.org/public/files/permanent-court-of-international-justice/serie_B/B_17/01_Communautes_greco-bulgares_Avis_consultatif.pdf. Accessed 26 Jul 2021.

Qinfen, M. 2017. Femail labor force participation in Malaysia: time-series evidence. *South-East Asia Journal of Contemporary Business, Economics and Law* 14 (3): 1–7.

Quý, L.T. 2013. Bình đẳng giới ở Việt Nam hiện nay. *Tạp Chí Khoa Học Xã Hội Việt Nam* 2: 76–80.

Robison, R. 1996a. The politics of 'Asian values. *The Pacific Review* 9 (3): 309–327. https://doi.org/10.1080/09512749608719189.

Robison, R. 1996b. The politics of 'Asian values. *The Pacific Review*, 9(3): 309–327, p 310

Sandra Lovelace v. Canada, Communication No. 24/1977: Canada 30/07/81, UN Doc. CCPR/C/13/D/24/1977.

S. W. M. Broeks v. The Netherlands, Communication No. 172/1984, U.N. Doc. CCPR/C/OP/2 at 196 (1990). http://hrlibrary.umn.edu/undocs/newscans/172-1984.html

Schuman, M. 2009. *The miracle: the epic story of Asia's quest for wealth.* Harper Collins.

Shin, G.W. 2006. *Ethnic nationalism in Korea: Genealogy, politics, and legacy.* Stanford University Press.

Thang, N.T., Yen, N.H., and Trang, L.M. 2021. Impacts of Confucianism on ensuring gender equality in Viet Nam: challenges and developments. *Papers of Canadian International Conference on Gender & Women's Studies 2021.* Unique Conferences Canada. https://imrjournal.info/wp-content/uploads/2021/08/Paper-Proceedings-CGWS2021.pdf.

Truong, L. T. 2018. An analysis of the gaps in current government policies relating to ethnic women in Vietnam. *CTA Experience Capitalization Series.*

Tung, P.D., and Trang, D.T. 2014. 54 ethnic groups: why different? Hanoi, Vietnam: Mekong Development Research Institute.

Tuoitre. 2021. ILO: The rate of Vietnamese women participating in the labor force is more than 70%, less than 50% globally. https://tuoitre.vn/ilo-ti-le-phu-nu-viet-tham-gia-lao-dong-hon-70-toan-cau-duoi-50-20210304120619536.htm. Accessed 08 Jan 2024.

UN Women. 2015. Progress of the world's women 2015–2016 – Transforming economies, realizing rights, https://progress.unwomen.org/en/2015/pdf/UNW_progressreport.pdf. Accessed 5 May 2022.

UN Women. 2016. Towards Gender Equality in Vietnam: For inclusive growth to benefit women. Ha Noi.
UN Women. 2017. Data on women and men of all ethnic groups in Vietnam in 2015 through the survey on the socio-economic status of 53 ethnic minorities in Vietnam in 2015. Ha Noi.
UN Women. 2020. A 5-year review report on implementing the Project Reducing child marriage and consanguineous marriage in ethnic minority areas in the period 2015 - 2025. Ha Noi.
UNFPA. 2020. *Independent review report ten years of implementing the Law on Gender Equality*. Ha Noi: Hong Duc Publishing House.
United Nations. 2018. Report on the World Social Situation 2018, Promoting Inclusion through Social Protection. https://www.un.org/development/desa/dspd/wp-content/uploads/sites/22/2018/11/SD-Brief_7_Indigenous_and_ethnic_minorities-.pdf. Accessed 24 Jul 2021
United Nations. 2021. Indigenous Peoples at the United Nations. https://www.un.org/development/desa/indigenouspeoples/about-us.html. Accessed 08 Jan 2024.
United Nations, Department of Economic and Social Affairs. 2015. World Fertility Patterns 2015—Data Booklet (ST/ESA/SER.A/370). https://www.un.org/en/development/desa/population/publications/pdf/fertility/world-fertility-patterns-2015.pdf. Accessed 08 Jan 2024.
Van, V.H. 2019. The view of Confucianism about the importance of men, disregard for women and its influence on Vietnam. *International Journal of Advance Research, Ideas and Innovations in Technology* 5 (3): 1912–1917.
Vu, M.T., and Pham, T.T.T. 2021. Still in the shadow of Confucianism? Gender bias in contemporary English textbooks in Vietnam. Pedagogy, Culture & Society. https://doi.org/10.1080/14681366.2021.1924239
Vu, T.M., and Yamada, H. 2020. The legacy of Confucianism in gender inequality in Vietnam. MPRA Paper No. 101487. https://mpra.ub.uni-muenchen.de/101487/. Accessed 26 Jul 2021.
Wan Jr, H. Y. 2011. Economic Development in a Globalized Environment: East Asian Evidences. Springer Science & Business Media.
Weiwei, L. 2004. Equality and non-discrimination under international human rights law (pp. 1–26). SMR.
Bank, Working. 2009. *Country Social analysis: ethnicity and development in Vietnam*. Washington, D.C.: Social Development Unit, East Asia and Pacific Region.
World Bank. 2013. *2012 Vietnam poverty assessment: well begun, not yet done-Vietnam's remarkable progress on poverty reduction and the emerging challenges*. Washington, D.C.: World Bank.
World Economic Forum. 2020. Global Gender Gap Report 2020. http://www3.weforum.org/docs/WEF_GGGR_2020.pdf. Accessed 26 Jul 2021.
Yan, J., and R. Sorenson. 2006. The effect of Confucian values on succession in the family business. *Family Business Review* 3: 235–250.

The Wretched of the World: TWAIL, Casteism and the Global South—A Critique

Thamil Venthan Ananthavinayagan, Jeevan Justin, Kanak Mishra, and Omkar Hemanth

1 Introduction

Let us ask at the very outset the obvious question. What is caste? It is a social construct that allows and enables rigid social stratification—the inequalities it perpetuates allow for hegemony in society, law, and politics. Caste has fostered and maintained poverty and deprivation, prevalent among lower caste populations in the face of historical injustice and justified by socio-religious traditions (Pellisserya et al 2015). In the words of Hugo Gorringe, Surinder S. Jodhka and Opinderjit Kaur Takhar:

> the inequalities of caste are as much about power as are those of race, ethnicity, or gender. Following Ambedkar, we understand caste as a relational system, such that 'caste in the singular number is an unreality. Castes exist only in the plural number. There is no such thing as a caste: there are always castes' while one is born into a particular caste, there are no physical markers that delineate status. Caste, instead, 'is etched into the social fabric by codes of conduct governing modes of address, attire...physical positioning', and forms of social interaction. (Gorringe et al 2017, p. 232)

With my best thanks to my students Samara Baboolal and Syania Binte Muhammad Shaharuddin for their invaluable help to finish this chapter.

T. V. Ananthavinayagan (✉)
Researcher Department of Justice, Dublin, Republic of Ireland
e-mail: thamil.ananthavinayagan@woxsen.edu.in

Law Woxsen University, Kamkole, India

J. Justin
National Law University Odisha, Cuttack, India

K. Mishra
International Collaborations, O.P. Jindal Global School, Sonipat, India

O. Hemanth
Bangalore, India

T. Venthan Ananthavinayagan and A. Viswanath Shenoy (eds.), *The Wretched of the Global South*, International Law and the Global South,
https://doi.org/10.1007/978-981-99-9275-1_9

Despite the developments the world has faced, the caste system withstood these various developments either from within or from outside (Jogdanda 2016). Neither colonialism, industrialisation nor 'modernisation' were capable of collapsing the caste system—as a matter of fact, caste is an instrumental feature in elections (for example in India) while it is justified to this day for the sake of societal organisation (Bapuji and Snehanjali 2020). Here, the aforementioned influential social thinker and lawyer B.R. Ambedkar theorised resistance to the caste system on the Indian subcontinent from the point of moral knowledge (Yadav et al. 2020). He argued that the lived narratives and experiences of the people within the caste system are amplifying the moral wrongs and the overarching injustices (Yadav et al. 2020). The intellectual impetus for his movement against the caste system was the fight against injustice. This strikes very much with the tenor of this article. As one scholar ascertains, caste is defined through the homogeneous social corporation bearing a common name and distinguished by the following four characteristics: (i) it is hereditary, that is, its members belong to it by right of birth, a man being born, not made, a member of a caste; (2) it is endogamous, that is, its members marry within its own circle only; (3) its members profess to follow the same occupation; and (4) its members do not eat with members of other castes and in varying degrees even avoid contact with them. The caste is controlled by a council or standing committee, whose rules are enforced by penalties and excommunication (Macdonell 1914).

The subordination of men and women through an organisational system, justified by religion, maintains patriarchy, hierarchy, and dependency. It justifies injustice and turns our eyes blind to the heritage of discrimination that we have accepted as part and parcel of a larger societal structure. Pre-colonial societies have benefitted from the injustices the caste systems had generated, so has colonial rule. Against this background, the caste systems in the colonised states were the animating spirit for colonial capitalism that had helped to generate wealth through indentured labour, slavery, and land dispossession (Manjapra 2020). To expand on this thought, '*(…) British conceptions of racial purity were interwoven with the categorization of communities based on censuses results. (…) The myriad associations with the caste division benefited colonizers the most when it came to labor*.' (Kudekallu, 2020).

Today, the caste system with all the injustices it creates is conveniently used by the Third World elite as a bargaining tool during election campaigns (Jogdanda et al 2016). It was only in 2002 when the Committee on Elimination of Racial Discrimination adopted its General Comment 20 on descent-based discrimination flowing from Art. 1.1 of the Convention (International Convention on the Elimination of All Forms of Racial Discrimination), stating that "*steps to identify those descent-based communities under their jurisdiction who suffer from discrimination, especially on the basis of caste and analogous systems of inherited status […]*."

And here it is necessary to address the failure of Third World Approaches to International Law (TWAIL). TWAIL has failed to adequately respond and give an analytical methodology to rectify the ills created and perpetuated by the caste system. Against this backdrop, Srinivas Burra argues that—despite the fact that TWAIL presents itself as a progressive force within international law—'*certain third world voices and issues are pushed into oblivion. Non recognition of these third world voices and issues leads to the suspicion of emancipatory potential of the TWAIL scholarship despite its well-intentioned challenge to the European and North American voices.*' (Burra 2016).

In addition, the caste system works in a way that excludes and falls beyond the ambit of Western vigilance. We can observe spatial limitations of the moral value-system of the West, but also due to the fact that the caste system operates within a non-racial paradigm. This means then that, in short, the discussion that we have on caste is reproducing an archaic system (and that the historical disadvantages are remedied through legalised compensation as a form of gift). We have seen, however, the mobilisation of caste politics: the use of caste at election campaigns, promises of betterment through market access and legalised means of emancipation. (Mosse 2018) In the larger discussion on discrimination, it would be therefore misplaced to equal caste with racial differences in the United States, as the nature and the historical injustices are juxtaposed to each other. Yet, there is shared suffering and discrimination rooted in oppression.

In consequence, the article will -first- discuss in a critical fashion how the history of caste system has impacted the making of societies. It will then examine the failures of Third World Approaches to International Law to rectify the ills caused and sustained by the caste system in the Global South. It will then outline visions for rectifying the ills within the realm of international law and sixth and finally, provide a conclusion to this article.

2 History of Caste System in Different Countries

Castes can be broadly defined as "hereditary, endogamous, hierarchically ranked and sometimes occupationally defined groups" (Boivin 2007). This section will attempt to unpack the historiography of caste systems in four regions of the Global South - namely: South Asia, South East Asia, Africa and Latin America. All of these regions harbour some kind of caste system which fits the definition above. Each of these regions will be discussed in turn, compared in their structures and analysed.

2.1 Africa

In Africa, while there are various forms of discrimination based on descent, a caste system is observed in West Africa and some parts of East Africa. While there is debate regarding the origins of this system, it is possible that the system developed within one society or a small cluster of areas, and diffused through migration (LaBrack 1973). There is a hierarchical division between three social categories (McNaughton 1988) the nobles or freeborn, the caste communities, and slaves. The nobles are the most common category, and are engaged in agriculture, or in some cases, herding. Even though they form the majority of the population, only a few of them aspire to political power. Slaves can be of two kinds, either hereditary, or acquired through conquest. Nobles could become slaves as a result of capture in war (Tal 1991).

Where does this leave the caste communities? In this context, caste can be understood to mean an "endogamous ranked specialist group". This occupational specialisation can be grouped into three simple categories: bards, blacksmiths, and tanners, but related crafts also fall under each category. This social category only tends to be a small minority of the population. The number of such groups also varies from community to community, ranging from one, or at most, three. In all of these communities, however, they are considered to be above slaves, but below the freeborn. This does not, however, mean that they are free of discrimination.

Social distance between these groups is maintained and regulated by the concept of pollution (Tuden and Plotnicov 1970). In Senegal, for instance, the Wolof society contains a caste community called the ñeeño, who form 10–20% of the population (International Dalit Solidarity Network Report). The members of this community are seen as polluting, because of the work that traditionally undertook (including circumcision and midwifery, though this is no longer the norm) and because they are descended from those who performed those tasks. As a result of this taboo, there is forced endogamy and restrictions on commensality. Further, those from the freeborn communities who marry a ñeeño may be ostracised (Human Rights Watch 2001). This discrimination based on purity is a common theme among West African communities. Perceptions of impurity not only arise from traditional occupations but also from myths (International Dalit Solidarity Network report).

In East Africa, caste discrimination is observed in Somalia, Ethiopia, and Nigeria. Similar considerations of purity are found here as well. In Somalia, non-noble castes are discriminated against on the basis of mythical narratives that claim that they are of unholy origin and because they engage in lowly occupations (Eno et al. 2014). Caste discrimination in Ethiopia is similar to what was observed in West Africa. In Nigeria, the 'Osu' system is rather unique. Osu people were traditionally 'owned' by Nigerian deities. They were dedicated and sacrificed to these gods, and forced to live on the outskirts of villages (Research Directorate, Immigration and Refugee Board Canada 1999).[1]

Despite the various forms this discrimination might take, the communities that are discriminated against are invariably denied their human rights. The stigma these groups face prevents them from freely mingling with their local communities, and also holding positions of responsibility.

[1] *Nigeria: Osu caste system in the Igbo community and whether: an Osu is someone chosen by community to serve God and the people; as an Osu one will not eat, play or associate with non-Osu people; when a Chief Highness dies three Osu members are chosen to be sacrificed and buried with him; and, Osu are sacrificed to appease the gods.*

2.2 South East Asia

Caste systems appeared in South East Asia mainly because of the influence of Indian culture. The implantation of Hindu-Buddhist culture was an initiative of warriors and settlers, traders or local rulers, or some combination of them (Mabbett 1977a, b). Scholars such as H.G. Quaritch Wakes have also observed a marked dominance of Indian culture in the western part of Southeast Asia, from which it diffused eastwards (Wales 1951).

The Indian culture that was so diffused was given a high status. The initial exodus of Indians who had converted to Buddhism, was followed by the Brahmans and Kshatriyas. There is evidence to suggest that local kings held brahmins in high regard, as it was believed that they possessed magical powers. The Hindu Kings exalted and rewarded handsomely the ritual duties of the Brahmans. In Cambodia, Brahmans formed and maintained a powerful hierarchy (Wales 1931; Quaritch 2011; Brockhurst 2011). In Thailand, though the kings were Buddhist, they recruited their court Brahmans from Cambodia.

Despite the fact that a good number of Indians moved eastwards, and the fact that the upper castes undoubtedly had political influence, the caste system underwent significant changes when it came into contact with Southeast Asian people (Coedes et al. 1968). The concept of racial purity was loosened, and Brahmins who wanted to start families were given the daughters of native kings, which indicates that endogamy was not strictly enforced. What can be observed is that, as was in Indonesia, the three highest castes formed seven percent of the population (they possessed both Indian and Indonesian blood) and the mass was Indonesian, and were classified as servants or sudras (Stutterheim 1929). In Thailand, the caste system was only found within the king's palace, where the servants were grouped into different castes based on their duties (Mabbett 1977a, b) However, despite all this, there was never a stringent caste system as there was in India, and the only remaining traces of it is a keen feeling of social rank.

2.3 Latin America

In Latin America, the caste system, called *casta*, is of a much more recent origin. Casta was a product of Spanish colonisation, created in an effort to secure the colonisers' wealth, power, and privileges (Martinez 2010). In the New World, around the year, 1570, Spanish households only numbered 25,000. In order to establish and maintain the status quo with Spanish colonists at the top, they created the Sistema de Castas. This system had its main determinant as descent, the amount of Spanish blood a person had. It was intended to be a comprehensive system, as it sought to account for all the possible kinds of unions between Spaniards and natives, and also included the Africans, most of whom were slaves (Mcalister 2021). The slaves, of course, occupied the lowest rung of society. There were four overall racial categories, namely, the Europeans, those with mixed native and European blood, natives (called Indians), and slaves. Among the Spaniards, those who were born in Spain had higher social standing than those born in the New World, who were called Creoles (Burton 2000). Among those of mixed descent, there was a distinction between mestizos which included mixtures of Indians and Spaniards and mulattos, who were mixtures of Africans and Spaniards, Zambo or Zambaigo, who were mixtures of Indians and Negroes. This caste system, however, was never as rigid and closed as the Indian one is (Roncal 1944). This can be inferred from the fact that, as time went on, new terms of reference were invented to refer to descendants of unions between the castes (Caldas 2014) mentioned above. The Sistema de Castas, determined access to social, political and economic privilege. Laws were designed to restrict access to those who were mainly of pure Spanish blood. However, as it became more difficult to establish a person's ancestry, the less rigid the system became. This enabled upward mobility within the *Sistema de Castas* (Castleman 2001).

In the nineteenth century, most of the Spanish colonies gained independence. However, remnants of the concept of racial purity ingrained by the Sistema still remained. The elites that emerged tended to have lighter skin and belonged to a more privileged class of people. They were those who had, before independence, been second in the hierarchy only to Spaniards and Portuguese born in their homelands (Torres 2017). The relationship between inequality and ethnic composition still remains quite strong within Latin America n (Hoffman and Centeno 2003).

2.4 South Asia

While a mention of the four varnas could be found even in the ancient *Rig Veda* (Macdonell 1914), the hierarchical system and the emphasis on purity became popularised only in the post-Mughal period, just prior to colonisation (Bayly 1999). Bayly argues that in India, the modern form of caste experience arose only during the colonial period, when Brahmins became widely deferred to, and "the pollution barrier became the defining feature of everyday caste experience". This is important to note, as in its ancient iteration, the system was one of the social classes, between which mobility was possible (Ambedkar 1916).

A unique feature of the caste system in South Asia is its particular rigidity. Ambedkar attributes this rigidity to the transformation of the four major castes into multiple endogamous groups. The Brahmins at a certain point in history detached themselves from the rest of society and became a caste by 'closing the door', that is, enforcing endogamy. The lower castes began imitating the endogamous practice of the Brahmins. As different castes closed their doors and became rigid endogamous groups, others were forced to do so, as exogamy does not remain a possibility any longer. This resulted in the formation of the myriad, stringently endogamous groups, which we call castes.

Despite the debates around origin, the defining characteristics are clear. Caste is translated to the Hindi word Jati, which means something similar to genus (Boivin

2007). Each jati is an endogamous group. The wider term, varna, refers to the occupational division of society into four, namely the Brahmins, the Kshatriyas, the Vaishyas and the Shudras. The untouchables, who traditionally worked with impure substances such as hide, meat, or human refuse, are not included in the caste system. These untouchable castes, now known as Dalits, face the brunt of the discrimination, and almost complete social ostracisation.

Caste systems of similar forms are found in Nepal, Pakistan, Bangladesh and Sri Lanka. Dalits remain the lowest of the low, and face the most discrimination, despite their large numbers in the region.

In Nepal, there is an almost identical varna structure as India. Nepali Dalits make up 21% of the population.[2] In Sri Lanka, there are two separate systems, one among the Sinhalese majority, and the second among the Tamil minority. The Sinhalese contain a segregated community known as the Rodiyas, who were historically excluded from the villages and forced into begging, scavenging, and roving. Among the Tamils, members of lower castes who were brought into Sri Lanka as labourers in the tea plantations face oppression, as a traditional division of labour is perpetrated and marriages between castes are strongly proscribed. Plantation workers remain marginalised from economic, social and political opportunities, and suffer from poor healthcare and an inability to participate in political life (Gooneskere 2001). The driving force behind the migration of the Tamils was colonial capitalism. Coffee and tea plantations were established with the help of violence, that is, the forced subjugation and the use of indentured labour (Sassen 1998). In the case of Sri Lanka, Tamil migrant labour was imported when the members of the Sri Lankan Kandyan caste refused to keep working for foreign landowners (Ahmad 2014). Better wages as compared to what they would have received in their home state in India was a sufficient pull factor. These labourers formed a part of the colonial coolie system, which replaced the slave trade (Hardy 2009). This coolie system was a convenient source of cheap labour, as it relied on short term contracts, enforced through penal sanctions, and which were linked to debts incurred in transit (Kale 1998). In addition, the working conditions were invariably barbaric, and the workers were paid very little. Caste divisions do not fail to find their place here. The labourers were purposefully recruited from lower castes, and their supervisors from higher castes. This led to the maintenance of caste hierarchies, and tasks such as sanitation were reserved for the workers of the lowest castes. As such, it is apparent that the caste system and its inherent divisions of labour allowed the colonisers to simply import existing structures to their places of choice, much to their convenience and advantage.

In Pakistan, Punjabi Christians of a sweeper caste are treated as untouchables. In India, they belonged to a low-caste Hindu group called the Chuhras. After partition, they moved to Pakistan and took up polluting jobs like sweeping and scavenging. They are segregated and forced to live in areas which are extremely poor and squalid (Streefland 1979). Sanitation jobs—including street cleaning and the handling of

[2] Discrimination against Dalits in Nepal. 2004. *Human Rights Watch.* https://www.justice.gov/sites/default/files/eoir/legacy/2013/06/14/HRW_Dalits.pdf. Accessed 20 September 2022.

human waste and animal carcasses—are functions almost exclusively performed by Dalits in India, Sri Lanka, Bangladesh, and Nepal.

Dalits in Bangladesh—who originally migrated from India under British rule and remained after the partition of the subcontinent in 1947—work principally as municipal cleaners and domestic workers,[3] lowly jobs that are shunned by the country's majority Muslim Bengali population. As we can clearly see, all these areas, which were formerly colonised, exhibited some form of caste system. It is pertinent now to look at caste discrimination and its effects in the present day.

3 Caste Discrimination in the 21st Century

It is quite clear that caste discrimination is a widespread and damning problem that affects a significant portion of the world. The question one must ask oneself at this juncture is why, even in the era of International Human Rights, caste discrimination still persists. The answer is thus: caste discrimination is a structural problem, but only its manifestations are being treated, with an over-reliance on the state as the neutral agent of change.

The problem with this approach is that the state, or rather, the individuals capable of exercising the state's power are inherently casteist. In other words, the maintenance of the caste system is advantageous to the social, economic, and political interests of such individuals. This manifests in the unfair treatment of lower caste groups by the very institutions tasked with their protection. Examples of this abound, from all over the world. For instance, the victims of caste-based violence face many obstacles to justice at every level of the criminal 'justice' system. Fear of reprisal prevents them from reporting attacks, and even when reported, most crimes go unpunished and unaddressed by the Governments.[4] Political participation, which can increase representation and hold a way to mitigating injustices, is closed off to people of lower castes, by the denial of their right to vote.[5] There is institutionalisation of caste-based labour division, evidenced by the Government of India's employment of manual scavengers.

It is evident from these examples that state machineries, which within the traditional enforcement paradigm, are tasked with the protection of human rights, *are the very ones that propagate them.* Further, because of the respect for sovereignty, and non-interference with internal affairs (Charter of the United Nations Art 2(7) 1945)

---

[3] The human rights situation of Dalits in Bangladesh, their socio-economic problems, legal and constitutional protections, and the issues of discrimination on the basis of caste and lower status, para.7, Submitted to OHCHR 2009, https://lib.ohchr.org/HRBodies/UPR/Documents/Session4/BD/IDSN_BGD_UPR_S4_2009_InternationalDalitSolidarityNetwork_JOINT_upr.pdf.

[4] Report of the Special Rapporteur on minority issues, A/HRC/31/56. 2016. https://digitallibrary.un.org/record/831487?ln=en.

[5] *Id.* CERD. 2007. Concluding observations of the Committee on the Elimination of Racial Discrimination CERD/C/IND/CO/19. https://tbinternet.ohchr.org/_layouts/15/treatybodyexternal/Download.aspx?symbolno=CERD/C/IND/CO/19&Lang=En.

that the International Human Rights system affords even in the face of massive violations, such violations cannot be stopped. States have the ability to block, delay, and divert focus from their Human Rights violations. India serves as an excellent example of this. The Indian Government's firm position during the 2001 Dublin World Conference on Racism was to reject any international interference with the issue (Iyer 2001). Arguments ranged from the issue being a purely internal one, to a refusal to equate caste with race, which would have removed caste issues from the ambit of the Convention on the Elimination of Racial Discrimination. A more recent example would be India's continuing impunity for the systematic Human Rights violations in Kashmir. This seems to have been ensured quite easily by merely delaying or refusing periodic reports. India currently has 5 overdue reports to various Human Rights Bodies.[6] Further, India has also systematically denied access to Kashmir to UN Special Rapporteurs (Haider 2019). It is clear that without the cooperation of the State in question, the enforcement of human rights is close to impossible. Unfortunately, in the case of caste, it is well within the State's interests to refuse such cooperation. As a consequence of this, the current human rights enforcement paradigm is woefully insufficient to tackle caste-based discrimination.

Alternative enforcement paradigms are the need of the hour. One that can possibly help is the model based on social and political mobilisation proposed by Prof. Abdullahi Ahmed An-Na'im (Ahmed An-Na'im 2016). He argues that in order to fulfil the universality of human rights, they must be defined and realised through a global consensus building process, whereby communities of people can decide for themselves the content of various rights based on their local contexts. Enforcement would take place through the empowerment of local actors to protect their own rights, with the objective of gradually reducing dependence on external systems. In essence, this would empower civil society organisations and smaller human rights organisations that work to protect human rights locally, giving them greater strength to resist State sanctioned violations.

Such a paradigm would be infinitely more useful in combating caste discriminations than the existing one. This radical departure from the traditional understanding of human rights enforcement is required if we are ever to achieve the political and social democracy (Ambedkar 1949) that is a prerequisite for the complete abolition of caste systems.

4 The Failures of TWAIL

TWAIL has evolved as a legal scholarship from theory to method to movement (Al Attar 2019) and now into a counter-hegemonic term (Hyppolyte 2016) to deconstruct and reform the Eurocentric and colonialist foundations of international law. The move away from self-proclaiming TWAIL as each of the above has happened in a

---

[6] List of State Parties without overdue reports. *United Nations*. https://tbinternet.ohchr.org/_layouts/15/TreatyBodyExternal/LateReporting.aspx.

measured fashion. Ascribing the terminology of a 'theory' to TWAIL was deemed to be restrictive of the praxis it sought to undertake in reforming international law (Narajan et al. 2016). Its reference solely as a 'method' would restrict TWAIL to a mere enquiry of 'what the law is.' (Anghie and Bhupinder 2003). The usage of the word 'movement' for TWAIL still follows, however, very cautiously, so as to not denote allegiance to any ideology or party for being a part of TWAIL. Thus, from the first generation of TWAILers to the budding and upcoming generation of TWAILers, the movement has largely ignored caste oppression and has thus faltered upon its promises of emancipation.

Despite TWAIL's many attempts at being the 'chorus of voices' (Okafor 2005) of the marginalised and oppressed third world, it continues to grapple with issues within itself that need considerable restructuring. For a legal project that aims to foster mutual understanding, shared responsibilities, and common political commitment against the colonial impositions, TWAIL has failed to create a network of solidarity and support that gives voice to the silenced or underrepresented strata of the society. Srinivas Burra notes that TWAIL largely ignores the pre-colonial complexities such as the caste system (Burra 2021). This is because TWAIL originated as a movement to critique the colonial project. However, fixating itself to colonialism, TWAIL was implicitly or explicitly bound to lose sight of more complex struggles (Attar 2019) like caste-based prejudices, gender and race.

One such issue that happens to be the focus of this paper is that of caste-based oppression. This section seeks to use the existing critiques of the TWAIL scholarship to point out its failures in representing the many struggles of those in the global south, facing caste oppression. In undertaking this analysis, the author's aim is to make TWAIL an inclusive movement. To enable active participation of the people of the lower castes and the indigenous people who have historically remained excluded from transformative scholarship and institutional resistance.

Gajendra Ayyathurai, a researcher at the Centre for Indian Studies at the Göttingen University, Germany, describes caste as a 'durable inequality.' His reference to the term comes from the persistence of caste oppression within societies to be a social crisis, deeply rooted within and yet at the heart and mouth of every institution and structure. He states that Brahmanism has been glorified throughout all these years with the collaborative effort of the state, civil society and the academic forums. The state and its institutions like the executive and the police legitimise violence. The civil society has created the caste system and continues to shield it. Academic forums on the other hand have failed in their duty to bring out the voices of the marginalised and the most vulnerable. Scholars sugarcoat Brahmanism and casteism and even intentionally ignore or let the academic collusions between Westerners and Brahmins pass at the cost of the scholarship of the marginalised. This practice further distances the idea of international law's promise of justice. It makes the theory and praxis discourse of the TWAIL movement a farce. It is one of the blind spots of TWAIL according to Mohsen al-Attar that even when Anghie and others seek to reform international law to promote justice, it is ironic how IL can then be "hopelessly prejudicial and yet a beacon of justice". This is what Chimni famously refers to as the structural indeterminacy of international law (Chimni 2017).

To map the evolution of TWAIL as a generational movement aiming for the emancipation of the third world people it is imperative to locate the TWAIL scholarship in the field of TWAIL movement. In an attempt to locate TWAIL's theoretical underpinnings, Mohsen al Attar establishes that TWAIL exists on the spectrum of the identity of the self in relation to that of the other. TWAIL began as a movement against the mainstream international law. It sought to uncover the linear narratives of history that are essentialist Eurocentric and colonial legacies. In exposing this Eurocentric nature of international law, TWAIL 'otherizes' the Global North from the Global South. Thus, TWAIL finds its identity in otherising the self against the other i.e. the West. TWAIL's inability to theorise in the absence of the self-other dichotomy leads to its self-subjugation such that the excuse of all world happenings seems justifiable under the domination of the Global North (Sreejith 2016). In this manner, TWAIL perpetuates class and caste struggles in the name of the giving of the West to the Global South.' This approach is not solution-oriented but rather merely accusatory in nature. As a consequence of authorisation, what follows is a homogenous self as against a homogeneous other. This homogenisation of both sides, works in tandem to suppress many intersectionalities and more often than not, leads to silencing of marginalised identities. As a direct consequence of silencing marginalised voices TWAIL falls into the same trope it seeks to fight against (i.e. the silencing of the third world by the West). Therefore, the TWAIL movement with its binary of the East-West should not seek to silence the West as: "it must not do unto them what they did unto us".

S.G. Sreejith in his piece on the Autocritique of TWAIL refers to this opposition between the self as opposed to the other as TWAIL's 'dialectic of otherness.' He notes the motto of the first and second generation of TWAIL- 'global forces against capitalism.' In doing so he applies the Hegelian Dialectic and establishes TWAIL's subjectivism based on the hope for the objectivity of the other's power. This optimism and hope for an objective power from the very same authority that continues the systemic exploitation of the third world, reproduces the power dominance. Applying the same analysis to the self of TWAIL, caste hierarchies are reproduced every time TWAIL forces its optimism at the expansion of the West. This universalising binary of the Global North as against the Global South does not just erase many intersectional oppressions of people, but also goes one step ahead in forming a human social as against the human ontological. Sreejith points out the importance of the relativism of the social as against the monism of the ontological. The inherent ideas driving TWAIL are opposition, resistance, and suspicion against the West. However, the selfless ideas of love, empathy, and kindness lack in the movement as it stands today. These ideas can promote caste inclusion. The lack of such ideas acts as an impediment in TWAIL's quest to create a just world where emancipation exists for all, even the downtrodden. It is only in giving up the binary of the self versus the other that there lies the renewal of selfhood in relation to its own existence in the broader spectrum of life. A movement devoid of binaries would then introspect into itself rather than hoping from the other. Self-introspection of TWAIL, to include the caste oppressed will furnish new grounds for the renewal of both theory and praxis to voice the concerns of those who were historically and continue to be deliberately silenced and excluded from scholarship.

TWAIL also remains oblivious to the caste hierarchies as the movement is centred to protect the interests of the marginalised class. TWAIL revolves around critiquing the Transnational Capitalist Class that shapes international law and institutions (Chimni 2010). Thus, TWAIL's analysis of domination and subjugation remains fixated on the class struggle instead of the struggles of caste and gender, etc. This predilection towards the domination of the TCC represents the extent to which TWAIL represents and builds on the horizontal past i.e. of the Global North and Global South binary. It is this reason why the vertical past, ridden with gender and caste oppression, receives less to no attention from TWAILers who deem it easy to cherry pick and assimilate arguments in favour of TWAIL. Bachand has previously recognised TWAIL's failure to problematise certain categories of oppression like 'race and religion' due to TWAIL's preoccupation with the Europe and third world binary (Bachand 2013). However, even Bachand's analysis of TWAIL's shortcomings remains oblivious to the caste struggle that continues to remain one of the strongest internal divisions.

An issue with TWAIL is also the scholars' dedication to theory and analysis of TWAIL in bringing down the West while compromising on the normative and reformative alternative to international law that TWAILers hope for. The distance between TWAIL's analysis versus TWAIL's advocacy that as Hilary Charlesworth (Charlesworth 1995) mentions, ignores the intersections of gender and consequently also glosses over caste. The scholarly criticism and continuous deconstruction of international law by TWAILers prohibits any reformative or solution-based approach towards international law. This reductionism of TWAIL to a scholarship rather than an inclusive movement seeking justice for the whole of the third world is tantamount to 'TWAIL elitism.' Thereby making TWAILers fall prey to the very same hegemony and dominance they oppose.

The absence of any methodological tools for theorising TWAIL is another persistent problem that reduces TWAIL to a mere analytical inquiry instead of a reformative, solution-based approach. Early scholars have expressed reluctance regarding the use of Western methodological tools in measuring the progress of a movement. However, TWAIL needs some micro-tools, albeit non-western, to undertake a conscious analysis of its self sans the other. A move away from TWAIL's existing rhetorical tools of suspicion against the West would enable a structural analysis of the vertical past and present hierarchies and domination that continue to plague the marginalised castes.

5 Visions for the Future

The reformation of International Law in general, and TWAIL in particular (in order to find solutions to the problem of caste) is a project that has overlaps, but also must be considered as two separate branches. The reformation of international law requires a focus on enforcement mechanisms and institutions. The reformation of TWAIL requires imagining a new future for the movement, a more inclusive and introspective one. The reformation of TWAIL is beneficial for the project of reformation of international law, as TWAIL scholars aim to make the voices of the subaltern heard in the international realm. Since it is the subaltern we are concerned with, the greater representation of their issues has the potential to bring solutions through the reformation of international law and institutions.

Regarding the TWAIL movement, the first consideration is the representation of lower castes within TWAIL itself. To illustrate this point, a discussion on access to legal education in India is pertinent. There is, and always has been a chronic under-representation of lower castes in Indian law schools, and the legal system. In the top law schools of India, a considerable number of students hail from the Brahmin caste (Desai et al. 2012).[7] Only around 13 percent of the students hail from Scheduled Castes. This trend holds in every level of the legal system. Even a disproportionately large number of Supreme Court Judges have been Brahmins, with a vanishingly small number of judges from lower castes (Saxena 2021). Therefore, by default, socio-legal and legal theory will primarily be built on the patterns of knowledge and ignorance of those people of privilege. As Charles Mills says, the structures of domination and subordination in any given society result in a conceptual apparatus shaped by the biases of the dominant groups (Mills 2007). Clearly, this will not only exclude caste considerations, at its worst, because of the necessity to maintain the hierarchy, might also be actively harmful.

All barriers to access are increased manifold in the realm of international law. Speaking generally of the Global South, the accumulation of symbolic capital is one of the primary factors that determine success within the international legal field (Farid 2016). That is, in order to project claims from the Third World, a 'legal scholactivist' must acquire credentials and master intellectual tools. In order to do this, scholars study and eventually move to universities in the Global North. Only the elites of the global south can avail such access, barring certain exceptional cases.

Therefore, only global south elites, of higher castes will become international law scholars and TWAIL scholars. Their blind spots will be reflected in the TWAIL scholarship. Therefore, there must be a radical increase in inclusion in the TWAIL fraternity of non-elites. Without this, the objectives of TWAIL will be rendered meaningless, as we will merely advocate for the maintenance of oppressive hierarchies in the global south, by shifting attention away from such hierarchies.

The second aspect of the reformation of the TWAIL movement is to redefine the role of TWAIL scholars themselves. Traditional intellectuals are the tools of the ruling class and use their intellectual production to legitimise the ideas that contribute to oppression (Bodenheimer 1976). As seen above, TWAILers criticise the transnational capitalist class, but generally belong to the dominant classes of their own nations. As such, while they may be called organic intellectuals with respect to the Transnational Capitalist Class, and the international realm, they resemble traditional intellectuals

[7] IDIA. 2019. Diversity Survey. https://www.idialaw.org/wp-content/uploads/2020/04/diversity-survey-2018-19.pdf.

within their own nations. This is further evidenced by the ignorance of issues such as caste within their own nations. TWAIL, as a movement of resistance against the global north, must first unify/represent the issues and marginalised communities within the global south itself. But above that, it must redeem itself, rather than being consumed into the elitist academic litany of the Global North. They must not only include within their ranks organic intellectuals from the non-elite communities of the global south, they must also act to share their knowledge and resources with them, and improve access to knowledge that will nurture more such intellectuals. Only if this occurs will TWAIL be able to find holistic solutions and reformations to international law and institutions, not only breaking the shackles of neo-colonialism, but also mould the institutions to the benefit of the oppressed within the global south.

Regarding the future of international human rights law, one must ask a difficult question before choosing a pathway for change. One must consider whether to continue to trust existing laws and institutions, or work for radical change. If one chooses the former option, the path is relatively straightforward. The main objective would be to further empower human rights organisations to pierce the shield of sovereignty and to reduce the importance given to State consent in human rights enforcement. If however, one chooses to work for radical change, quite naturally, the path taken must also be radically different.

Drawing on the ideas of Prof. Abdullahi Ahmed An-Na'im. discussed above, radical change can happen when the oppressed exercise their own agency and organise and struggle for their own rights. This happens in the form of social movements, defined as sustained collective mobilisations for social change by civil society actors through extrainstitutional routes (Tsutsui et al. 2012). Human rights law must find its place in these movements as a tool to be wielded by the oppressed, and as a source of legitimisation and support.

As scholars such as Neil Stammers have noted, in the past, social movements have played a key role in originating human rights (Stammers 2009). Not only have they helped in redeeming and enforcing the rights available to groups of people, but they have also formed the basis for the development of new human rights. This understanding has been lost in contemporary scholarship, both among the supporters and critics of IHRL. The effect has been that IHRL is not viewed enough as a tool for bottom-up social change. This is the understanding that must be eliminated, which in turn gives new hope to the oppressed.

IHRL can be used in social movements in various ways. The institutions can form a support system for social movements, and the law itself can be vernacularised by translators, leading to the law becoming the part of the movement. This does bring with it multiple benefits. As noted by Tsutsui, international human rights law has opened up new venues for contestation. Secondly, these movements have benefited from competition between superpowers as to who had the most legitimate social system. Thirdly, contacts with elites in third world governments or UN institutions have helped these movements. There is also a huge benefit in terms of resource mobilisation, as institutions and fora serve as conduits for flows of material and human resources for human rights advocacy work. In other words, these social movements can turn into a de-facto human rights enforcement mechanism, more readily available and able to address human rights violations on the ground. This, in turn, would help in addressing the major flaw in the current IHRL system.

6 Conclusion

This chapter has outlined, from a critical perspective, the values of resistance to hierarchy and oppression. Hegemony persists in the Global South against subaltern voices which strive to participate in the post-colonial societies. Ambedkar ascertained prominently:

> (…) there is a community economically poor, socially degraded, educationally backward and which is exploited, oppressed and tyrannised without shame and without remorse, disowned by society, unowned by Government and which has no security for protection and no guarantee for justice, fair play, and equal opportunity. Such a community is told that it can have no safeguards, not because it has no case for safeguards but only because the bully on whom the bill of rights is presented thinks that because the community is not politically organised to have sanctions behind its demand, he can successfully bluff". (Moon 1979)

The TWAIL movement, to this end, was too focused to otherwise the Global North as the hegemon, while neglecting the malaise at home. TWAIL methodology, however, can as outlined in this chapter be helpful to provide the safeguards, resist tyranny, and provide ideas and visions to access justice. The moment is now.

References

Ahmed An-Na'im, Abdullahi. 2016. The Spirit of Laws is Not Universal: Alternatives to the Enforcement Paradigm for Human Rights. *Tilburg Law Review* 21.
Ahmad H., Ilyas. 2014. Estate Tamils of Sri Lanka: A socio-economic review. *International Journal of Sociology and Anthropology* 6.
Al Attar, Mohsin. 2019. TWAIL: A Paradox within a Paradox. *Int'l Community Law Review.*
Attar, Mohsin Al. 2019. Paradox of TWAIL. *International Community Law Review.*
Ambedkar, B.R. 1916. *Castes in India.* True Sign Publishing House.
Ambedkar. 1949. Debate from the Constituent Assembly of India. http://parliamentofindia.nic.in/ls/debates/vol11pl.htm.
Anghie, and, Chimni. 2003. Third world approaches to international law and individual responsibility in internal conflict. *Chinese Journal of Int'l Law* 2: 1.
Bachand, Remi. 2013. Les Third World Approaches to International Law: Perspectives Pour Une Approche Subalterniste Du Droit International. In Droit International et Nouvelles Approches sur le Tiers-Monde: Entre Répétition et Renouveau. eds. Toufayan, Mark, Emmanuelle Tourme-Jouannet and Helene Ruiz Fabri.
Bapuji, and, Snehanjali. 2020. Understanding economic inequality through the lens of caste. *Journal of Business Ethics* 162: 536.
Bayly, Susan. 1999. *Caste, society and politics in India from the eighteenth century to the modern age.* Cambridge University Press.
Bodenheimer, Thomas. 1976. The Role of Intellectuals in Class Struggle.

Boivin, Nicole. 2007. Anthropological, historical, archaeological and genetic perspectives on the origins of caste in South Asia.

Burra, Srinivas. 2016. *TWAIL's others: A caste critique of TWAILers and their field of analysis.* Windsor Y B.

General Recommendation, Committee on Elimination of All Forms of Racial Discrimination, CERD/C/61/Misc.29/rev.1, 22 August 2002.

Burra, Srinivas. 2021. Interview by Jinken Newsletter. International Review of Human Rights Law. https://irhrl.com/forum/jinken-newsletter-may-2021-edition-issue-vii/. Accessed 20 Sep 2022.

Caldas, Natalia. 2014. Casta painting and the characterization of colonial Mexican identities. *Electronic Thesis and Dissertation Repository.*

Castleman, B.A. 2001. Social climbers in a Colonial Mexican City: Individual mobility within the Sistema de Castas in Orizaba. *Colonial Latin American Review.*

Charlesworth, Hilary. 1995. Feminists Critiques of International Law and Their Critics. *Third World Legal Studies.*

Chimni, Bhupinder. 2017. Concluding Response from Professor Chimni: International Law and World Order. https://www.ejiltalk.org/concluding-response-from-professor-chimni-international-law-and-world-order/.

Chimni, B.S. 2010. Prolegomena to a Class Approach to International Law. *European Journal of Int'l Law.*

Coedes, Vella, and Cowing. 1968. *The Indianized States of Southeast Asia.* University of Hawaii Press.

Concluding observations of the Committee on the Elimination of Racial Discrimination CERD/C/IND/CO/19. https://tbinternet.ohchr.org/_layouts/15/treatybodyexternal/Download.aspx?symbolno=CERD/C/IND/CO/19&Lang=En.

Desai, Sonali, and Dubey. 2012. Caste in 21st Century India: Competing Narratives. *EPW* 46(11).

Eno, Mohamed A. and Kusow. 2014. Racial and Caste Prejudice in Somalia. *Journal of Somali Studies.*

Gorringe, Hugo, and Jodhka Takhar. 2017. Caste: Experiences in South Asia and beyond. *Contemporary South Asia* 25: 3.

Farid, Cynthia. 2016. *Legal Scholactivists in the third world: between ambition, altruism and access.* Windsor YB.

Haider, Suhasini. 2019. India cuts of UN panel after Jammu and Kashmir Report. The Hindu. https://www.thehindu.com/news/national/india-cuts-off-un-panel-after-jammu-kashmir-report/article27190445.ece. Accessed 20 Sep 2022.

Hardy, Jane. 2009. Migration, migrant workers and capitalism. *International Socialism* Issue 122. http://isj.org.uk/migration-migrant-workers-and-capitalism/#122hardy_4. Accessed 20 Sep 2022.

Hoffman and Centeno. 2003. The lopsided continent: Inequality in Latin America. *Annual Review of Sociology*. https://doi.org/10.1146/annurev.soc.29.010202.100141. https://www.amherst.edu/system/files/media/0598/Lopsided%2520continent.pdf.

Human Rights Watch. 2004. Discrimination Against Dalits in Nepal. https://www.justice.gov/sites/default/files/eoir/legacy/2013/06/14/HRW_Dalits.pdf.

Human Rights Watch. 2001. Caste Discrimination: A Global Concern. https://www.hrw.org/reports/2001/globalcaste/caste0801.pdf.

Hyppolyte, A.R. 2016. Correcting Twail's Blind Spots: A Plea for a Pragmatic Approach to International Economic Governance. *Int'l Community Law Review.*

IDIA. 2019. Diversity Survey. https://www.idialaw.org/wp-content/uploads/2020/04/diversity-survey-2018-19.pdf.

Immigration and Refugee Board of Canada. https://www.refworld.org/docid/3ae6ab348c.html.

International Convention on the Elimination of All Forms of Racial Discrimination, Adopted and opened for signature and ratification by General Assembly resolution 2106 of 21 December 1965, entry into force 4 January 1969.

International Dalit Solidarity Network Report, "Discrimination Based on Descent in Africa, p. 4. https://idsn.org/wp-content/uploads/user_folder/pdf/Old_files/africa/pdf/Africafull.pdf.
Iyer, Lakshmi. 2001. India confronts contentious issue of Dalit atrocities at Durban conference on racism. https://www.indiatoday.in/magazine/nation/story/20010903-india-confronts-contentious-issue-of-dalit-atrocities-at-durban-conference-on-racism-774118-2001-09-03
Jogdanda, A., Yashpal, and Khanb, and Kumar Mishra. 2016. Understanding the persistence of caste: A commentary on Cotterill, Sidanius, Bhardwaj and Kumar. *Journal of Social and Political Psychology* 4: 555.
Goonesekere, Rajendra Kalidas Wimala. 2001. Prevention of Discrimination and Protection of Indigenous Peoples and Minorities. New York: United Nations. E/CN.4/Sub. 2/2001/16, para. 38.
Kale, Madhavi. 1998. *Fragments of Empire: Capital, Slavery and Indentured Labour*. University of Pennsylvania Press.
Kudekallu, Ramya Jawahar. 2020. Race, Caste, and Hunger. *Fordham International Law Journal* 43:4.
LaBrack, Bruce. 1973. The concept of caste: Cross-cultural applications. *Transactions of the Nebraska Academy of Sciences and Affiliated Societies.* 383: 51.
Mabbett, I.W. 1977a. Varṇas in Angkor and the Indian caste system. *The Journal of Asian Studies* 36: 429.
Mabbett, I.W. 1977b. The 'Indianization' of Southeast Asia: Reactions on the historical sources. *Journal of Southeast Asian Studies* 8: 143–161.
Macdonell, A.A. 1914. The early history of caste. *The American Historical Review* 19: 231.
Manjapra, Kris. 2020. *Colonalism on a Global Perspective.* Cambridge University Press: First Edition.
Martinez, Maria Elena. 2010. Social order in the Spanish New World. https://inside.sfuhs.org/dept/history/Mexicoreader/Chapter3/Social%20Order%20in%20the%20Spanish%20New%20Wo
Mcalister, L.N. 2021. Social structure and social change in New Spain. *The Hispanic American Historical Review* 43: 349–370.
McNaughton, Patrick R. 1988. *The Mande blacksmiths: Knowledge, power and art in West Africa.* Bloomington.
Mills, Charles. 2007. White Ignorance. In Race and Epistemologies of Ignorance. Eds. *Shannon Sullivan, Nancy Tuana. Albany.* NY: State University of New York Press.
Moon, Vasant. 1979. Dr. *Babasaheb Ambedkar Writings and Speeches*, Vol. 1. Dr. Ambedkar Foundation: New Delhi. https://www.mea.gov.in/Images/attach/amb/Volume_01.pdf.
Mosse, David. 2018. Caste and development: Contemporary perspectives on a structure of discrimination and advantage. *World Development* 110: 424.
Natarajan, Usha, Bhatia Reynolds, and Xavier. 2016. Introduction: TWAIL—On Praxis and the intellectual. *Third World Quarterly* 37: 11.
Okafor, Obiora, C. 2005. Newness, imperialism, and international legal reform in our time: A TWAIL perspective. *Osgoode Hall L. J.* 43: 1.
Pellisserya, Sony, Pampackala, and Bopaiah. 2015. Caste and distributive justice: Can social policy address durable inequalities? *Social Policy & Administration* 49: 786.
Rentas, Jonathan Torres. 2017. Race, culture, and identity: an exploration of dominican identity and race-based discriminations against Haitians in the Dominican republic. https://ruor.uottawa.ca/bitstream/10393/36990/1/Rentas_Jonathan%20Torres_2017_researchpaper.pdf
Research Directorate, Immigration and Refugee Board, Canada. 1999. Nigeria.
Roncal, Joaquín. 1944. The Negro race in Mexico. *Hispanic American Historical Review* 24: 530–540.
Sassen, Saski. 1998. *The mobility of labour and capital: A study in international investment and labour flow.* Cambridge University Press.
Sexena, Namit 2021. Disproportionate Representation at the Supreme Court: A perspective based on Caste and Religion of Judges. *Bar and Bench.* https://www.barandbench.com/columns/disproportionate-representation-supreme-court-caste-and-religion-of-judges.

Sreejith, S.G. 2016. An auto-critique of TWAIL's historical fallacy: Sketching an alternative manifesto. *Third World Quarterly* 38: 7.

Stammers, Neil. 2009. *Human rights and social movements*. London: Pluto Press.

Streefland, Pieter H. 1979. The sweepers of the slaughterhouse: Conflict and survival in a Karachi Neighborhood. *Assen, the Netherlands: Van Gorcum.*

Stutterheim, W.F. 1929. *Indian Influences in the Lands of the Pacific*. Weltevreden.

Tamari, Tal. 1991. The development of caste systems in West Africa. *The Journal of African History* 32: 221–250.

The human rights situation of Dalits in Bangladesh, their socio-economic problems, legal and constitutional protections, and the issues of discrimination on the basis of caste and lower status, para.7, Submitted to OHCHR 2009. https://lib.ohchr.org/HRBodies/UPR/Documents/Session4/BD/IDSN_BGD_UPR_S4_2009_InternationalDalitSolidarityNetwork_JOINT_upr.pdf.

Tuden, A., and L. Plotnicov. 1970. *Social stratification in Africa*. New York: The Free Press.

Tsutsui, Kiyoteru, Claire Whitlinger, and Alwyn Lim. 2012. International human rights law and social movements: States' resistance and civil society's insistence. *Annual Review of Law and Social Science* 8: 1.

United Nations, List of State Parties without Overdue Reports. https://tbinternet.ohchr.org/_layouts/15/TreatyBodyExternal/LateReporting.aspx.

United Nations, Charter of the United Nations, Art 2(7), 24 October 1945, 1 UNTS XVI. https://www.refworld.org/docid/3ae6b3930.html. Accessed 20 September 2022.

Wales, H.G.Q. 1951. *The making of greater India: A study in south-East Asian culture change*. London: Bernard Quaritch.

Wales, H.G.Q. 1931. *Siamese state ceremonies: Their history and function*. London: Bernard Quaritch.

Brockhurst, Johannes. 2011. *The Spread of Sanskrit in Southeast Asia, in Early Interactions between South and Southeast Asia*. ISEAS Publishing.

Yadav, Vivek Kumar, Shomik Dasgupta, and Bharath Kumar. 2020. All human beings are of equal status since birth: Caste, inequality and B.R. Ambedkar's universal claim for human equality. *Indian Journal of Human Development* 14: 484.

The Global South's Vision for the Future

Has 'The Law Found on the Street' Reached the Inter-American Court of Human Rights? A Socio-Legal Analysis of the Communal Property Right Recognition

Tatiana Cardoso Squeff and Jackeline Caixeta Santana

Abstract In this paper we first discuss the content of the '*O Direito Achado na Rua*', its precursors and assumptions, questioning why this theory has not yet been recognised properly as an important alternate dialectical perspective of Law. Secondly, we verify the 'encounter' between this framework and the 'International Law from below' theory, pointing to its similarities, particularly with regard to the importance of marginalised social movements for the (re)construction of Law, and for battling against colonial and imperial remnants. Then, after highlighting property as a human right of liberal tradition prescribed for in the American Convention of Human Rights, we analyse four Inter-American Court of Human Rights cases on indigenous communities aiming at verifying if this Court applies '*O Direito Achado na Rua*'. At last, we conclude that by comprehending indigenous land as communal property, as advanced by the communities themselves before the Inter-American System, that is, *desde abajo*, the Court may indeed bring those forgotten by the Law to the centre of its construction.

T. C. Squeff (✉)
Federal University of Rio Grande do Sul, Porto Alegre, RS, Brazil
e-mail: tatiana.squeff@ufrgs.br

J. C. Santana
Federal University of Uberlandia, Uberlandia, MG, Brazil
e-mail: caixetajackeline@hotmail.com

T. Venthan Ananthavinayagan and A. Viswanath Shenoy (eds.), *The Wretched of the Global South*, International Law and the Global South,
https://doi.org/10.1007/978-981-99-9275-1_10

1 Introduction

'*O Direito Achado na Rua*' (The Law Found on the Street)[1] is an expression coined by the late Brazilian jurist Roberto Lyra Filho (1926–1986). It stands for a theoretical conception that fights against the State's monopoly on normative enunciation, instigating the rupture with the dogmatic-positivist vision in the sense of promoting an expansion of norms arising from other social spheres—'the street'. This conception is usually referred to as a form of true realisation of participatory democracy. It understands these *other* public locations as both (a) legitimate places of social organisation (since they are not in the typical communal space, especially those marginalised and forgotten ones that are renegades by the centres of power), and (b) where the manifestation of ample freedom is possible (in which the individual is duly/fully recognised as a person of the margins, of vulnerable bodies, full of colours and marks acquired precisely because one does not fit the Europeanised standard).

This theory promotes (a) a dialectical technique aimed at opposing ideas to promote the emergence of others[2]; (b) legal pluralism, for enabling normative variety[3]; (c) critical theory, for not accepting the standards vertically (and colonially and/or imperially) imposed within society[4]; and (d) historical materialism, seeking to understand the changes in society arising from its needs.[5] Hence, when used as an epistemological foundation, this theory allows for the recognition of rules from a bottom-up perspective.

Taking the above into account, this paper aims at exploring the possibility of this theory to have been used by the Inter-American Court of Human Rights—IACHR—when it recognises the communal property of indigenous and traditional populations—an intrinsic right that derives from their way of living and as understood by them as such. The contention here is that the Court has made an implicit use of '*O Direito Achado na Rua*' by formally recognising such property *ultra legem*, taking it to the international level.

For that, our intention is not only to describe the theoretical conception above mentioned, but also to analyse four precedents of the Inter-American Court, so that the comprehension of communal property set forth by marginalised groups is drawn, seeking to confirm that the mentioned theory has, indeed, materially reached the international arena by bringing the forgotten voices to the centre of the construction of law. We believe this is a way to not only assert the possibility of law to emerge

[1] It is important to clarify that one of the forerunners of the theoretical-political line of thought under analysis, José Geraldo de Sousa Júnior, translates the expression himself into English as both "The Law Founded in the Street", and "The Right Found in the Street", in his text entitled "The Law Founded in the Street: social conditions and theoretical foundations" (2019). Despite this, we chose to translate it to "The Law found on the Street" because it seems semantically closer to the original term of the movement.

[2] Dialectics according to the Hegelian mode. See Hegel (2011).

[3] Legal pluralism as in the works of Wolkmer (1997), Hoekema (2002), López (2014).

[4] Critical theory as in the works of Santos and Menezes (2010), Wolkmer (2017), Akal (2015), Lander (2003).

[5] Historical materialism as in the works of Sartre (1971).

from alternative means, but also a way to 'free' the subject from the margins of/in the Global South, and finally *see* (i.e. recognise) them in the system.

2 Between *the Law Found on the Street* and International Law *from Below*: Perspectives in (Mis)encounters

2.1 A Theoretical-Political Line of Thought Created Within the Social Struggles and Legal Criticism: History and Assumptions of the Law Found on the Street

Although it has been more than three decades since the original release of the first edition of the series '*O Direito Achado na Rua*' (The Law Found on the Street) (1987), its resonance and its national and international recognition are still not equivalent to the importance of its proposal. Collectively drafted as a project coordinated by the Center for Studies for Peace and Human Rights and by the Distance Education Center of the University of Brasília, this theoretical-political line of thought embraces, from the outset, a programmatic turning point in the form of dispersion of legal knowledge, leading the dialogue with social movements, with popular legal consultants and with citizens' agents.[6]

As Sousa Júnior explains, this line of thought was an offshoot of a set of concerns and practices of a group of intellectuals who called themselves the New Brazilian Legal School, which was organised by Roberto Lyra Filho.[7] Among them, the heterodox and non-conformist nature of this line of thought stands out, guided by an alternative thinking that is concerned with social transformation from a legal trajectory.[8] In Lyra Filho's own terms, the "New School is juridical, because it aims, above all, to re-examine Law, not as a stagnant order, but as the positivisation, in struggle, of liberating principles, in the social totality in movement".[9] It therefore reveals the legal field as a historical process where a plurality of antithetical orders coexist, but not mutually exclusive.

As a legacy of this New School, *O Direito Achado na Rua* is designed to move away from the dogmatic conceptions to assert itself as a project that forms a "live warehouse of intellectual exchanges" that recognises the sources of Law beyond those chosen by the hegemonic doctrines.[10] Thus, contrary to what we usually observe, *O Direito Achado na Rua* carries out an upward movement: instead of flowing from institutions to the people, it emerges as a provocation of urban and rural organisations, popular lawyers, and human rights commissions to the university agendas, that are

---

[6] Sousa Júnior (2017).

[7] Sousa Júnior (2019).

[8] Sousa Júnior (1993).

[9] Lyra Filho (1982).

[10] Ibid.

detached of "reflection on social praxis constituted in their common experience of struggle for justice and rights".[11]

This umbilical link between NAIR and the aforementioned line of thought makes the *Lyrian* philosophy to act as a substrate for the development of both projects. According to Costa and Coelho, Lyra Filho aimed to "build an alternative to the current law" and not "offer an alternative interpretation of law", which she sought to do from a process triggered by the affirmation of a thesis that, when denied, would be overcome, presenting a positive character.[12] This process, conceived by Lyra Filho as *negation of negation*, consists of what remains known as theory and/or dialectical perspective of Law—an analytical and practical lens that, once inspired by Marxist historical materialism, checks its cracks and challenges itself to overcome it.

Similarly, Lyra Filho examines Brazilian legal criticism and notices gaps that need to be addressed. In Ferraz Júnior's studies, although he verifies notable renovations of the philosophy of language through the pragmatics of legal-normative communication, he also perceives the insufficiency of this criticism regarding its propositional capacity.[13] Regarding the *waratian* philosophy, based on the semiology of power and hermeneutic philosophy,[14] Lyra Filho points out the limitation of criticising the hegemonic narratives without, on the other hand, suggesting trajectories for the rupture with the current order. As a result, the creator of *O Direito Achado na Rua* continually demonstrates to care for the propositional nature of his line of thought, given that he did not intend to empty the credibility of the legal field without, in return, offering an analytical and theoretical framework capable of revealing its hidden and potentially emancipator facets.[15]

In view of this, the political-theoretical framework offered by him highlighted the need to strengthen the connection between social justice and the procedures understood as essential to its realisation, which should be carried out from critical and disruptive thinking. It strives for the "widening of the understanding of the legal phenomenon, beyond the restricted limits of its positive capture", inserting the "social groups in their historical appearance and in the cultural, subcultural and countercultural affirmation of their respective projects of political organisation".[16]

We can thus say that *O Direito Achado na Rua* is a movement that is at the forefront of the process of opening up the Law, since, by raising a contextualised legal practice, it is dedicated to giving greater security to regulation's intelligibility and application.[17] In Campilongo and Faria's words,

> As the name of the initiative indicates, there is a concern not so much with the law of codes, taught in faculties, but with the different legal forms effectively practiced in social relations. Opting for a "critical" analysis of state law, questioning the strategies of neutralization and

[11] Sousa Júnior (1993), 71.

[12] Costa and Coelho (2017).

[13] Ferraz Júnior (2006).

[14] Warat (1981).

[15] Costa and Coelho (2017).

[16] Sousa Júnior (1984).

[17] Sousa Júnior (2019).

> depoliticization established by legal dogmatics and privileging social transformation to the detriment of the permanence of legal institutions, that is, treating legal experience from an admittedly political angle—from not only from the exploration of the antinomies of positive law and gaps in the law by popular movements, but also from the different alternative rights forged by marginalized communities in social and economic terms – this UnB [University of Brasilia] project aims to act as a transmitter of information in favor of a more legitimate, deformalized and decentralized normative order.[18]

It is inferred from this excerpt that the aforementioned political-theoretical line of thought places in the public arena a political agenda aimed at subjects that are somehow invisible to the social dynamics of power,[19] removing them from the simplified condition of abstract holders of rights and leading them to the position of active participants in the spheres of normative elaboration and decision-making. Thus, it becomes noticeable that the displacements promoted by the *O Direito Achado na Rua* transit, as Borges and Santana conclude, through the fact that "legality is not above society as an entity that hovers under it, but, on the contrary, it from society emanates and finds in it the reasons for its constant renewal".[20]

Therefore, it is important to emphasise that this theory is not a mere analytical deconstruction, but rather a claiming platform that demands firm and continuous dialogues and efforts, towards the institution of a liberating *praxis* derived from creative contributions.[21] It aims, therefore, at the formation of *other* sociabilities, based, above all, on the reciprocal recognition of autonomous actions that aim to exercise, without hindrance, citizenship.[22]

It is at this point that the rearrangement of people individualised by Western modernity occurs, given that '*O Direito Achado na Rua*' integrates them into "conscious collective identities, more or less autonomous, arising from different social strata, with the capacity for self-organisation and self-determination, interconnected by ways of life with common interests and values".[23] It can be seen that the aforementioned thought rescues some premises forgotten—or annihilated—by the policies of modern-colonial social domination and exploitation, such as, for example, collectivity, self-organisation, self-determination, and political action directed to a common sense, of something that is shared.

Then, *O Direito Achado na Rua* has as its main objectives (i) the identification of the political space where the enunciative practices of rights—especially in their extra-legal conformation—are developed; (ii) the understanding to define the legal nature of this new subject capable of designing a political project of social transformation, understood here as a collective subject of law; and (iii) mapping and framing the data emerging from these practices in order to establish new legal categories, paved by

---

[18] Campilongo and Faria (1991).

[19] The subjects who, whether by ethnic-racial, cultural, gender identity, location, sexual orientation, among others, diverge from the Euro(north)centered hegemonic model underlying the project of modernity and the colonial enterprise in the world-system.

[20] Borges and Santana (2021).

[21] Costa and Coelho (2017).

[22] Sousa Júnior (2008).

[23] Wolkmer (1997).

solidary relationships capable of realising the law as "a project of legitimate social organisation of freedom".[24]

The *street* is, therefore, a symbolic space articulated in order to sensitise the legal field and invite us—as subjects—to overcome the State monopoly in the construction and application of Law. In doing so, the metaphor echoes the importance of recognising the strength of social movements and subjects "who, in the daily practice of a political-institutional culture and a particular socioeconomic model, [...] are affected in their dignity by the perverse and injustice of the living conditions imposed by the rejection of the process of participation and social development".[25]

The *street* is chosen as a figure of speech, in view of this, not only because it is a public space, but, above all, because it is fertile ground for the development of social practices that transform destinies and carry out the experiences of these subjects towards emancipation. It manifests itself, in this sense, as a *locus* capable of encompassing the collectivity that, in a solidary way, undertakes the task of breaking with the oppressions and spoliations suffered in a non-isolated manner.[26] The paradigm introduced in this conception is, therefore, the community and peaceful resolution of conflicts in favour of the most immediate demands and needs of those denied by the centres of power, involving an emancipating cultural project.[27]

Still, it is noted that *O Direito Achado na Rua* is based on a conception of legal pluralism, since it gives prominence to collective subjects and political-social actors in the normative elaboration, as well as criticises the static, vertical, and monolithic Law typical of the Modern State.[28] Equally, it is observed that there is also an epistemological approximation between *O Direito Achado na Rua* and decolonial studies.[29]

In both, the strengthening of dialogical competences—whether between institution and subject, or in society among themselves—is an indisputable trajectory for bringing Law closer to the social complexities it neglects. Furthermore, the two political projects present ways to dismantle the processes of dehumanisation engendered by the colonial power around the globe, giving back to the historically subordinated expectation of finding in the legal field the materialisation of social justice.[30]

In view of the proposed discussions, we realise that *O Direito Achado na Rua* reverberates both in the content and in the legal structure. This is because, when questioning the premises of hegemonic Law, vertical, elaborated in restricted spaces, where only a small group of addressees of the norms is allowed to enter (or, better, it

---

[24] Sousa Júnior (1993).

[25] Wolkmer (1997).

[26] Sousa Júnior (2008).

[27] Catusso (2007).

[28] Ramos (2012).

[29] José Geraldo de Sousa Júnior, along with Fonseca, even transports *O Direito Achado na Rua* to a theoretical-conceptual framework called "Constitutionalism Found on the Street", whose axiological matrix consists of positioning itself as "a practice of building rights that expresses this *decoloniality of Law*" (emphasis added). See Sousa Júnior and Fonseca (2017).

[30] Borges and Santana (2021).

was placed in it at the end of colonialism, and there it remained, now, under the cloak of internal coloniality), the normative content is strained by losing its foundation of legitimacy, by what is (re)produced by a group that holds the monopoly of power.

Regarding the structure, what this theoretical-political line of thought constrains us to reflect and modify are the reasons why only State Law is recognised in its juridicity, leaving thus on the margins the plurality of legal manifestations that do not derive from the State or any of its institutions and that, because of it, are relegated to the condition of subalternity.

2.2 Mirar desde la calle es pensar desde abajo*: Possible Legal Transformations in the International Arena Through the Brazil/India Connection*

If, on the one hand, we identify in South America a theoretical-political proposal based on social movements, such as *O Direito Achado na Rua*, on the other hand, in South Asia, we also verify *another* thought that seems similar and complementary to it—although the inequities of dispersion between the proposals around the globe are notorious. We specifically quote the research developed by the Indian intellectual Balakrishnan Rajagopal who, when discussing an International Law from below (*desde abajo*), shares common denominators with the *Lyrian* philosophy, as both investigate, primarily, the power of action and collective subject in the legal field.

These analytical encounters occur as Rajagopal stresses the legitimacy, coherence, and efficiency of legal literature in the face of the challenges posed by social movements. For him, it is important to unveil the narratives made invisible on the global stage by the power dynamics that reverberate the mainstream while erasing Third World resistance and its ability to impact, mobilise, and propose more appropriate ways of operating International Law.[31]

One of the questions that interest him is, specifically, the possibilities of interaction between plural forms of resistance and institutions—what he calls "dialectic between Law and social movements".[32] For this reason, he studies several aspects that are transversal to the forms of social mobilisation, such as (i) the pressures exerted by social demands on justice administration bodies, (ii) the institutionalisation of emerging agendas of social movements, (iii) the coherence of these institutionalisation mechanisms and their final product with the demands pointed out by the people, and (iv) which issues are more assertively inserted in these debates.

For Rajagopal, resistance is situated, therefore, in a place of analytical category in International Law, since, without it, the impossibility remains that this field ceases to be delineated, applied, and thought *by* and *for* the hegemonic groups legitimised by the colonial power and its imperial past,[33] which raised them to the centre of the

---

[31] Rajagopal (2003).

[32] Rajagopal (2005a).

[33] Rajagopal (2003).

World-System and still keeps them in this environment.[34] Thus, we perceive that, from the author's point of view, Law can play two dichotomous roles: at the same time, it can operate as an instrument of domination; it can *also* be transformed into a space of resistance and contestation.[35]

We observed, then, that the author sees the social movements as agents that preserve the implicit autonomy of the positivist vision in its aspects that take advantage of them and, at the same time, abandon the conception of the Nation-State as a collectivity able to watch over this autonomy. Consequently, social movements reveal themselves as agents that catalyse the multiplication of political-social arenas and actors, establishing new frontiers for political issues insofar as they oblige International Law to recognise that identity as a survival strategy.[36]

The Brazil/India connections do not end, however, in this similar epistemological substrate. In addition to the primacy of the force and political legitimacy of social mobilisations, *O Direito Achado na Rua* and the International Law *desde abajo* have another encounter, given that both identify gaps in Marxist propositions, despite their contribution to the understanding of the various mechanisms of social domination implemented by modernity. In Rajagopal's perception, what Marx's does not seem to capture are the most important social struggles that took place within the Third World; those dedicated to combating sensitive and profound issues in the countries of the Global South, such as, for example, massive environmental degradation, oppression against women and the expropriation of labor and goods from small farmers.[37]

Rajagopal also highlights the concrete advances in terms of equality, democratisation, and strategic litigation,[38] which took place through conceptual tools that allowed (i) the constitution of a discourse of alternative human rights, originating from social praxis; (ii) redefining civil society and democracy; (iii) the rupture of the nexus used to assess property rights, consequently rescuing local control over property resources; (iv) the criticism of the monolithic conception that globalisation

---

[34] Anghie (2007).

[35] As explains Rajagopal, "despite this encouraging pluralization of normative opportunities for contestation, the outcomes of social movements' engagements with the law are highly uncertain in terms of their impact either on law or on the movements themselves. Put differently, the pluralization of normative space and the ability to contest seem to offer neither a guarantee of success for social mobilization nor propel law in the direction that is most helpful to movement goals. The outcomes of the dialectic between law and social movements seem to depend on a number of scripts that are both internal and external to law, and seem to depend on particular local and national contexts. These scripts need to be unearthed and examined to properly appreciate the role of law in counter hegemonic globalization". See Rajagopal (2005a).

[36] Falk et al. (2006).

[37] Thus, Rajagopal argues that, in addition to being rigid and essentialist, the historical determinism established as a Marxist premise does not reach the real nature of many of the third-world social movements, which bring together the struggles for material aspects—of an economic nature—with the struggles for symbolic meanings—of a cultural nature, incidents on the construction of narratives, of the imaginary and of the normative orders that perpetuate them and that prevent them from actively participating in any institutional environment. See Rajagopal (2003).

[38] Falk et al. (2006).

inevitably leads to the marginalisation of the local due to the praise of transnationalism.[39] The emphasis of social movements is, then, as the author explains, on the importance of non-institutional forms for the success or failure of institutional forms themselves.[40]

Thinking about institutionality matters in this debate because it is the institutions that, in the modern logic, represent the concrete manifestations of normative aspirations of Law in the international system.[41] Notwithstanding this, Rajagopal warns that the institutional apparatus cares little or nothing about the inherent relevance of society's political action. On the contrary, it is observed that legalistic rationality sees this action as an aberration that needs to be annihilated, therefore denying its impact on normative structures and, still, hiding the Law/social movements dialectic.[42]

This reality is nothing more, in his perception, than one of the consequences of the internationalist premise of the (discourse of) development, inaugurated when the Third World tried to free itself from the imperial shackles, between the 1950s and 1970s, as a new (discursive) tool aimed at maintaining the *status quo* at the international level,[43] and of all the violence that it was able to naturalise under the mantle (or would it be better to say 'myth'?) of progress, as if it were a new 'cloak of legality', as Pahuja[44] puts it, to the persistently exclusionary international normative developments.

In other words, the premise of development served as a scope to justify the violations of rights filed under the pretext of the much-celebrated sovereignty, whether including or excluding States in the world capitalist logic. Sovereignty and State inviolability were assumed as organising principles in International Law. They established borders, international legal capacity, veto power, participation in international organisations, exploitation of natural resources, etc. In fact, it was also the 'shadow of sovereignty' that introduced another paradox to the international order, that is, the exercise of sovereign violence that characterises the State itself, and the obligation of maintaining peace and mutual respect.[45]

When considering centre-periphery relationships around the globe, such complexity intensifies. This is because, as the Indian author points out, the economic market and the neoliberal ideology prevailing in the international arena are responsible for generating a dynamic—called globalisation—that concentrates wealth on those who already have a large arsenal of power and goods, reifying massive poverty in the Global South.[46]

This reality highlights three discontents related to International Law, namely: (i) that the fissures of this legal field always fall on the periphery of this World-System;

[39] Rajagopal (2003).

[40] Rajagopal (2005b).

[41] Rajagopal (2000).

[42] Rajagopal (2003).

[43] Afonso (2019).

[44] Pahuja (2005).

[45] Rajagopal (1999).

[46] Falk et al. (2006).

(ii) that this periphery is a complex arena today, not only defined by its position of subaltern and/or victim on the globe, but also by the tension between hegemony and counter-hegemony within it; and (iii) that the increase in complexity and tension in the Global South is a symptom of a generalised crisis in the global economy and politics, that, in fact, extends throughout *modern* history in different guises.[47]

Hence, the need for a critical review of International Law and the consolidation of disruptive movements with the current order remains indisputable. According to Falk, Rajagopal, and Stevens, this critical review would be possible with the emergence of alternative global orders to the historically perpetuated shades of hegemony that surround the subjects, the international division of labour and epistemology, which would result from the combination of regionalism, global civil activism, and counter-hegemonic normative commitments in terms of human rights, ecological sustainability and global rules on the use of force.[48]

We observe, therefore, that International Law, as Rajagopal reinforces, is just one facet of the counter-hegemonic power that exists today. In the author's words, "*The future of the world—its ability to deal with problems of peace, war, survival, prosperity, planetary health and pluralism—depends on a range of factor, including the politics of the 'multitude'*".[49] Following this reasoning, we again see the importance assumed by a collective organisation and attentive to regional institutional and normative fissures in Rajagopal's thought, as well as in his proposal of *another* International Law—which also finds place, in a Brazilian perspective, in the formulations of the New Brazilian Legal School.

In view of the above, we realise that the centre of *O Direito Achado na Rua* and of International Law *desde abajo* are in the process of expanding historically subordinated voices in the Global South; those that are excluded from normative production and decision-making spaces although they face the consequences of legal doctrine and institutional decisions. Thus, if we can consider social movements the first step to think about the place of the Third World in International Law, we need to reflect, in the same way, as the claim platform of *O Direito Achado na Rua* manages (or not) to reach legal orders beyond the Brazilian borders and rescue collective actions placed in the rubble of legality and institutionality itself, as advocated by Rajagopal.

It is precisely in this scope that we propose to verify, from the perspective of indigenous peoples and especially with regard to the claim for their ancestral lands, if it would be possible to say that *O Direito Achado na Rua* reached the Inter-American Court of Human Rights in regard to the perception on communal property, thus, allowing us to consolidate an International Law *desde abajo*.

---

[47] Rajagopal (2012).

[48] Falk et al. (2006).

[49] Rajagopal (2008).

3 The Inter-American System for the Protection of Human Rights as a Liberating Environment? Reflections on the Right to Communal Property and the (Persistent) Struggle for an Emancipated Institutional Space

3.1 The Liberal Foundations of the Inter-American System and the Change in the Perception of the Right to Property Promoted Within the Inter-American Court

The Inter-American Court of Human Rights is a judicial institution that, together with the Inter-American Commission on Human Rights, makes up the Inter-American System for the Protection of Human Rights, structured, in the current form, through the American Convention on Human Rights, dated from 1969 and in force since 1978. It is the *locus* of human rights in the Americas, currently comprising 23 Member States.

Linked to the Organisation of American States—OAS, this System may be said to have its foundations in the nineteenth century,[50,51] more specifically from 1889 onwards, when some kind of institutional seed began to be harvested. Here we specifically refer to the eight International American Conferences[52] that culminated in the construction of the "Pan American Union and, finally, with the expansion of its functions, the General Secretariat of the OAS".[53]

Not without debate, of course, because "if, on the one hand, the United States focused on expanding its liberal culture of protection of individual rights, on the other hand, Latin America turned to social rights".[54] However, as it can be seen from the debates that took place during the meetings and from the reading of the Organisation's own basic documents today, "individual rights were [clearly] privileged [...], including the inviolability of property", making "liberal internationalist ideology" its "doctrinal and ideological basis"[55, 56].

---

[50] Scarfi (2020), 118, 128.

[51] Obregón (2016), 100.

[52] I Washington Conference (1889–1890); II Conference of Mexico City (1901–1902); III Rio de Janeiro Conference (1906); IV Buenos Aires Conference (1910); V Conference of Santiago (1923); VI Havana Conference (1928); VII Montevideo Conference (1933); VIII Conference of Lima (1938). See Hanashiro (2001).

[53] OEA (2022).

[54] Silva (2022), 74.

[55] Ibid, 76–77.

[56] In other words, "*the compelling power of Pan-Americanism*" (and its "*imperial aspiration of civilizing Latin America through the promotion of US legal values*") was advanced "*as an ideal and policy*", having "*a lasting impact on the creation and institutionalization of the Inter-American System*", as it can be seen of the rights inscribed there in the post-World War II period. See Scarfi (2017), 179–182.

In this case, when specifically verifying the American Declaration of the Rights and Duties of Man of 1948, the first intergovernmental document on the subject,[57] and the American Convention itself, which came to give an obligatory status to those rights years later, one can see the wide preference for individual rights. As it can be seen in this last document, economic, social, and cultural rights (ESCR) are grouped together in a single prescription, namely, Art. 26, which was not considered until a few years ago, an autonomously justiciable rule before the System.[58, 59]

A perfect example of an individual right is the right of property, set forth in Art. 21 of the American Convention. It prescribes the right of one to use and enjoy property, making it impossible to deprive him/her of it, except through just compensation for reasons of public utility or social interest. In theory, it is not a 'shared right', that is, with social and/or cultural, diffuse, and/or collective features; but for individual use and enjoyment only. However, from the debates around the defence of the rights of indigenous peoples, an expansion is seen with regard to the interpretation and use of this right in the Inter-American Court jurisprudence.

The first case to come across this issue was the *Mayagna Awas Tingni v. Nicaragua*. In this case, the leader of 142 families petitioned the IACHR to order Nicaragua to take effective measures to protect the Community's property rights to the land they were located on that was inappropriately granted to the company SOLCARSA for exploration purposes. And since the case was not preliminarily solved by the IACHR, it was submitted to the Court, which understood that Nicaragua needed to create mechanisms to (i) protect the rights of the natives to their ancestral lands, and that if it did not do so, it would be exposing the Community to a direct threat to their existence, values and customary way of life[60]; (ii) protect local diversity based on the identification and recognition of land ownership by the Awas Tingni Community; (iii) create procedural means for requests future demarcation and titling could be processed in the Nicaraguan legal system, insofar as the State already recognised the possibility of such a right.

Not less important, the Court established some very significant parameters regarding the interpretation of the right to property in a collective, economic, social, and cultural sense, deserving the following to be highlighted:

> Among the indigenous there is a community tradition about a communal form of collective ownership of land, in the sense that land ownership is not centered on an individual, but on the group and its community. Indigenous people, by virtue of their very existence, have the

---

[57] Ibid, 184.

[58] This view only changes with the *Lagos Del Campo vs. Peru* case, judged by the Inter-American Court of Human Rights in 2017. See Marques and Squeff (2018). For a critique, see Cerqueira (2018).

[59] It should be noted that the 1988 Protocol of San Salvador foresees limitations regarding the justiciability of ESCR provided for therein. Article 19(6) stipulates the possibility of only bringing before the System complaints regarding arts. 8(a) (union rights), and 13 (education). This fact even today makes it difficult to assume the full possibility of claiming, via the IACHR and Court, the effectiveness of some rights prescribed for in the Protocol vis-à-vis the States. IACtHR (2018a), para. 88.

[60] Squeff (2016), 58.

> right to live freely in their own territories; the close relationship that indigenous people have with the land must be recognized and understood as the fundamental basis of their cultures, their spiritual life, their integrity and their economic survival. For indigenous communities, the relationship with the land is not merely a matter of possession and production, but a material and spiritual element that they must fully enjoy, including to preserve their cultural legacy and pass it on to future generations[61]

In other words, the Court affirmed the need for the State to recognise the existence of *another* type of property—one different from the one prescribed in Art. 21 of the American Convention, based on an individual right. It should be a communal one; one that could encompass the territory that these peoples usually inhabited 300 years ago,[62] as a way of valuing the maintenance of culture and their own physical and psychological/identity existence, without any individualisation. This issue is taken up again in the case of the *Yakye Axa Indigenous Community v. Paraguay*, a jurisprudence, perhaps, even more paradigmatic regarding the disrespect for the right of indigenous communities to their ancestral lands.

This refers to a case presented by *Yakye Axa* representatives against Paraguay before the IACHR in 2000 for not guaranteeing the ancestral property right to the community, who have been claiming the demarcation of their lands since 1993. This situation arose from a continuous expulsion of the *Yakye Axa* from their lands, dating back to the nineteenth century, when several fractions of land were sold to entrepreneurs in the agricultural sector and even to missions of the Anglican Church, which kept the indigenous people working for themselves in deplorable living conditions, consequently forcing their displacement.[63]

However, its members wanted to return to their lands, starting a dispute in the domestic order that did not give rise to any satisfactory resolutions, despite Paraguay being constitutionally called a Pluricultural State that recognises "the indigenous component in its social structure", culminating, in this way, in the settlement of several indigenous families on the side of a road between *Pozo Colorado* and *Concepción*, in a situation of economic, food, medical and sanitary aggravated vulnerability in the community, putting at risk the survival of its members, in addition to their own integrity and existence, insofar as they not only do not receive any type of regular government assistance, but are also threatened by third parties for the territorial claims they were pleading for.[64]

The IACHR found the State responsible for that situation, recommending that the Paraguayan authorities guarantee the community the exercise of its activities in the ancestral territory, adopting measures to definitively revert to the narrated situation of vulnerability, in addition to protecting the claimed habitat until the communal title was finally granted, in view of the equally necessary domestic procedural changes to ensure such right. After four months without a response, the IACHR decided to present the case to the Court.

---

61 IACtHR (2001), para. 149.

62 Ibid, para. 19.

63 IACtHR (2005), 13, 15, 28.

64 Ibid, 10, 27, 49–52.

The latter, in turn, endorsed such conclusions, specifically pointing to Art. 21 that this provision could not be read in isolation, "deeming useful and appropriate to use other international treaties other than the American Convention, such as ILO Convention No. 169, to interpret its provisions in accordance with the evolution of the inter-American system", taking into account the development experienced in this matter in the International Law of Human Rights".[65, 66]

The Court thus understood that Art. 21 could not be interpreted otherwise than that pointed out by the victims' representatives, for whom the "concept of the right to land ownership [is] distinct from the general concept of the right to private property".[67] That is, the property, comprising the existing resources and other "intangible elements that come off of them", would be the place where tradition, economy, and health, in short, prosper, making the norm, in this way, to have at the same time social and diffuse characteristics, as it presents "an integral element of the cosmovision, religiosity and, thus, of [indigenous] cultural identity".[68]

With the recognition of such a collective cosmovision on the ancestral habitat that was advocated by the Yakye Axa community finally recognised, the improvement of the concept of property since this claim was made is demonstrated, which, in its community aspect, "must take into account that the land is closely related to oral traditions and expressions, customs and languages, arts and rituals, knowledge and uses related to nature, culinary arts, customary law, dress, philosophy and values" of the group.[69]

This issue was debated again in another case, this time against Brazil, of the *Xucuru Indigenous People and their members*, submitted to IACHR in 2002, due to the delay in the de-intrusion and demarcation of the ancestral lands of this community, pleaded in 1989. After a long process before the Commission, in 2015, it issued a report on the merits, concluding that the right to communal property had been violated, as well as the need to adopt legislative and/or administrative measures to proceed with the demarcation, without delay, from the ancestral habitat of the Xucurú Indigenous People "in accordance with their customary law, values, uses and customs".[70]

Due to the non-compliance with such recommendations, the case was taken in 2016 to the Court, which found the State responsible for the violation of Art. 2, read from its communal perspective. The Court highlighted that "the historical references to the Xucurú Indigenous People date back to the sixteenth century", that is, to the

---

65 Ibid, para. 127.

66 Thus, it pointed out that: [...] Convention No. 169 of the ILO contains several provisions that relate to the right to communal property of the indigenous communities being examined in this case, provisions that may illustrate the content and scope of Art. 21 of the American Convention. [...] [And] making use of the criteria indicated, this Court has emphasized that the close relationship that indigenous peoples have with the land must be recognized and understood as the fundamental basis of their culture, spiritual life, integrity, economic survival and preservation and transmission to future generations", as mentioned in IACtHR (2005), para. 130–131.

67 Ibid, para. 121.b.

68 Ibid, para. 135, 137.

69 Ibid, para. 154.

70 IACtHR (2018b), para. 2.a.

arrival of the Europeans in Brazil.[71] Furthermore, it pointed out that in addition to the 7.726 indigenous people who live in indigenous villages, there are still approximately 4.000 indigenous people who live in the city, denoting the 'integralist bias' that for years led to Brazilian indigenous policy.[72] Not only that, the repeated attempts to prevent the demarcation of their lands were narrated, even after the constitutional amendment promoted in 1988 through the new Constitution,[73] which culminated in several acts of violence and hostility against members of the community.[74]

In relation to Art. 21, the Court indirectly expressed the link between the right to property and the Protocol of San Salvador, renewing the broader understanding of this right, therefore, moving away from the traditional liberal perspective.[75] In this way, the State could not "refrain from performing acts that [might] lead agents of the State itself, or third parties who act with their acquiescence or tolerance, to affect the existence, value, use or enjoyment of its territory". It should also remove any non-indigenous people from the land, delimiting it and demarcating it for the benefit of the community, so that it could enjoy its ancestral habitat according to its traditions, and freely manage/use the natural resources found there.[76] Also, the Court made clear that this act was carried out for the purpose of guaranteeing legal certainty to the Xucurú People regarding the full and peaceful enjoyment of their lands, without interference.[77]

Finally, the Inter-American System also had the opportunity to debate this issue in the case of *Indígenas Miembros de la Asociación Lhaka Honhat v. Argentina*, considered to be paradigmatic jurisprudence insofar as, in addition to discussing the violation of Art. 21, it also addresses the direct violation of Art. 26 of the American Convention when referring to the violation of cultural identity derived from free movement and "the action of [non-indigenous] third parties when installing wiring, illegal logging and the use of [ancestral] space for cattle grazing".[78]

This case refers specifically to the claim made by the *Lhaka Honhat* Association on behalf of 132 indigenous communities who inhabit the same territory[79] in 1998. After a very slow process, the merits report was approved by the IACHR in 2012, which included Argentina's violation for not demarcating the ancestral lands, which dates back to the seventeenth century,[80] not providing an effective procedure for this (after all, 28 years have passed with no demarcation/titling[81]), and not consulting with the indigenous people regarding the construction of an international bridge that

[71] Ibid, para. 60.

[72] Squeff (2016), 45–49.

[73] IACtHR (2018b), para. 73.

[74] Ibid, para. 76, 87.

[75] Ibid, para. 115.

[76] Ibid, para. 117–118.

[77] Ibid, para. 120–121, 124.

[78] Squeff and Rosa (2020).

[79] IACtHR (2020), para. 28, 32, 50.

[80] Ibid, para. 49.

[81] Ibid, para. 148, 151.

passes through their territory, culminating in the violation of a series of rights, such as food, health and their cultural traditions.

After numerous extensions granted by the Commission to comply with the measures, in 2018, it decided to present the case before the Court.[82] This body, in turn, also found Argentina responsible in 2020. Regarding Art. 21, the Court took up the arguments raised in the previous cases,[83] but, as we have previously said, it innovated with regard to the debates carried out within the scope of Art. 26. Argentina, by not demarcating, and by allowing the incursion of non-indigenous people into the indigenous territory did not directly protect the right to cultural identity[84] and, consequently, the right to water and food (creating, thus, vulnerabilities), and the right to a healthy environment.[85]

On this, the Court recalled its Advisory Opinion of n. 23/17, in which it pronounced for the first time on the right to the environment as an *autonomous* right, highlighting the connection indigenous people have to the land itself—not considering it as property per se.[86] Thus, recalling the obligation of states to preserve such cosmovision by acting *ex ante* to any environmental damage[87] or the generation of vulnerabilities[88] that might endanger indigenous cultural identity,[89] which includes the demarcation and titling of ancestral lands.

This way, it is possible to verify the normative transformation that the Inter-American Court has provided in relation to what is understood by the property right provided for in Art. 21 of the American Convention, escaping its liberal ideology foundations. This change did not come from the Court itself, but from the provocation made by several indigenous communities to see their rights protected, demonstrating the relevance not only of the interpretation of *the streets*, but also from the claims coming *desde abajo*, as it will be pointed below.

3.2 Is the Inter-American System an Emancipated Environment Capable of Reproducing 'O Direito Achado Na Rua'?

Based on what has been exposed so far, especially in view of the interpretative evolution conferred on Art. 21 of the American Convention by the Court, apparently, it seems to us that the indigenous cosmovisions, sprouting within the indigenous villages (that is, on *the streets*), did indeed reach the international level, and, with that,

82 Squeff and Rosa (2020), 253–270.

83 IACtHR (2020), para. 92–98.

84 Ibid, para. 251.

85 Ibid, para. 209.

86 Ibid, para. 203.

87 Ibid, para. 207.

88 Ibid, para. 210–230.

89 Ibid, para. 231–242.

it was promoted—even if in a punctual way—the necessary and urgent recognition of the organisation of indigenous peoples as "an expression of the struggle of collective subjects of rights capable of thinking and elaborating meanings and practices to overcome realities of oppression both externally and internally to their groups".[90]

In a way, when we focus our analysis on this essay on one of the normative fields pointed out by Rajagopal as a favourable environment for the tensioning of the limits of Law, that is, the International Courts, we were also able to verify the emancipatory possibility that these institutions can generate, especially to marginalised groups, such as indigenous communities. After all, these are institutions whose legitimacy would be linked to their (in)capacity to incorporate the struggles and emerging demands of social movements.[91] However, it cannot be said that International Law would "be the 'regulator' of social life within the State, not only through Treaties, but mainly through decisions of International Courts",[92] since this same institutional space is still very rooted in the colonial/imperial dynamics of the international arena, which do not count on the real and concrete participation of all groups when it comes to the production of norms.[93] The Fourth World, as the studies on the prompt exclusion of indigenous peoples are called today, projects precisely this question.[94]

In the cases of the *Awas Tingni* and *Yakye Axa* communities analysed above, despite the advances regarding the recognition of the right to communal property, emphasising the right as a space of struggle and the possibility of consecration of *other* views on the rules (im)posed, allowing for the sedimentation of the indigenous cosmovision about what they understand by ownership of their lands, and, thus, having *O Direito Achado na Rua* consecrated, this occurred in part. This is because there is still a need to process the request through the existing institutions themselves, which were inaugurated without any type of consultation or even with the effective participation of those, representing a space, in itself, still colonised, above all, by the liberal western logic.

The deterritorialisation of power as a way of guaranteeing human rights is, in fact, an important measure, especially when it comes to countermajoritarian groups, which are also excluded from the domestic normative-State logic.[95] It cannot be denied that the organisation of indigenous communities around the territorial agenda, in not seeing their lands (and therefore culture and life) threatened, can also be read from the right of *the streets* and *desde abajo*, insofar as a social articulation for the claim of their rights is seen, to the detriment of a long wait for a positive action to be taken by the modern and still steeped in imperiality Nation-State, which, like Nicaragua and Paraguay, despite recognising the right to demarcation and titling in its legislation, nothing did to revert it.

---

[90] Sousa Júnior and Fonseca (2017).

[91] Rajagopal (2007).

[92] Squeff (2016), 16.

[93] Squeff (2021).

[94] Fukurai (2018).

[95] Squeff (2016), 16.

The Lhaka Honhat case, for example, despite being quite positive, also demonstrates some limitations in the very perception of the use of *O Direito Achado Na Rua*. This is because, in that judgment, the Court stated that any activity to be carried out within the indigenous territory (or even in the one to be demarcated), which is supported by the exceptions provided for in Art. 21 of the American Convention, it would be possible, provided that there was, in return, compensation in favour of those affected. In other words, the Court, when contrasting the types of property rights, understood the liberal view, even though in doing so it highlighted the need for the act to be preceded by concrete, effective, and prior consultation with the affected indigenous people, also providing for the need for the State to design a plan for the communities involved to perceive some type of benefit from the work.[96]

At one point, the Court even went so far as to state that "the Convention cannot be interpreted in such a way that it prevents the State from carrying out, by itself or through third parties, projects and works on the territory", although, afterwards, it affirmed that "their impact cannot under any circumstances deny the capacity of the members of indigenous [...] peoples for their own survival".[97] Dubious issues like this, in an emancipated environment, would not be sustained, especially in view of the important advance towards the dialogue between Art. 21 and 26, which in this case was indirectly promoted.

Thus, by way of conclusion, it cannot be said that the Inter-American System is a fully 'liberating' environment. Analysing the cases that ascended to its jurisdictional body in view of our proposal to verify whether *O Direito Achado na Rua* reaches the Inter-American Court and impacts its perception of communal property, the answer is positive, as it made it possible to the establishment of a new (cosmo)vision from the indigenous villages. Despite this, when we still question the possibilities of facing an advance that eventually consolidates International Law *desde abajo*, we can say that there is still a lot to improve in terms of *participation* in the handling of the institutional machine.

4 Conclusion

The present article had as its main objective the purpose of presenting *O Direito Achado na Rua* ('The Law Found on the Street') as a critical theory, which, in addition to coming from the margins of the World-System, is not very well known, despite having bases to effectively promote the inclusion of marginalised peoples in the production of norms that directly affect them. Thus, it was tried to demonstrate that the advance of the understanding of the property right beyond its strict, individual, and liberal sense, by the Inter-American Court, now understanding the possibility of having a communal property right, which belongs to the communities collectively by virtue of the relationship they have with their ancestral habitat, and which are

[96] IACtHR (2020), para. 174.

[97] Ibid, para. 175.

equally important for their own survival and existence, is an example of the use of *lyrian* philosophy. After all, it was possible to advance a claim by the *indigenous villages* that was not embraced by the majority logic, which ideologically supported the construction of the Inter-American System.

Nevertheless, the present text also aimed to build a bridge between *the streets* and the thought *desde abajo*, verifying if the legal transformations eventually advanced by marginalised groups also represent changes in the international institutional arena. Therefore, exploring Rajagopal's theory of how social movements can offer new ways to think about (International) Law, given that it is anchored in European, modern, colonial, and imperial bases, therefore, proposed by a small number of actors to organise all life in society, it was found that the evolution of the Inter-American Court comprehension on the property right highlight that the indigenous communities are not simply abstract holders of rights, but, above all, they must be considered active participants in the spheres of normative elaboration and decision-making that, despite its importance, have been marginalised from certain spaces.

When the Inter-American Court expands its vision about the property right, it is possible to conclude that this jurisdictional body can be used as a political space where the enunciative practices of rights are developed and where this new subject—indigenous community as a representation of *O Direito Achado na Rua*—shows itself as a collective subject of law, capable of designing a political project of social transformation. Hence, when the indigenous (cosmo)vision emerges from the margins and sensitises the Court to the need to rethink its own perception of property, and insofar as these views, to a certain extent, are incorporated into the decisions, we can establish new legal categories as a result of solidary and counter-hegemonic relationships.

We can say that the use of the Inter-American Court to advance the indigenous cosmovision on the territory is quite important, even though it is not yet sufficient to concretely include indigenous peoples in the international institutional map in participatory terms. Considering that the indigenous claim platform needs to go through a legal apparatus marked out by coloniality, it is important to emphasise the possibility of deconfiguration of their demands to fit in a vertical International Law—when not subsumed and consumed by modern colonial power.

So, if we want to project and consolidate an International Law from Below, we need, urgently, to recognise that *O Direito Achado na Rua* is not only a horizon to an emancipated world, but also a solid and palpable path when we break with the premises of the modern-colonial world-system. Regarding the right to property, the indigenous movements—or, in this work, *The Law Found in the Villages*—prove capable of putting pressure on the legal order to recognise their communal property, collaborating for a *derecho otro.*

References

Afonso, Henrique Weil. 2019. A questão desenvolvimentista na segunda metade do século XX: um olhar desde as TWAIL. *Revista Quaestio Iuris* 12(3): 101–124. https://doi.org/10.12957/rqi.2019.38776

Akal, Zibechi, Raúl. 2015. *Descolonizar el pensamiento crítico y las prácticas emancipatorias.* Bogota: Ediciones Desde Abajo;

Anghie, Anthony. 2007. The evolution of international law: Colonial and postcolonial realities. *Third World Quarterly* 27(1): 739–753. https://doi.org/10.1080/01436590600780011.

Borges, Rosa Maria Zaia and Santana, Jackeline Caixeta. 2021. O Direito Achado na(s) Rua(s) de Paraisópolis: pandemia, linguagem emancipatória e práxis decolonial. In *Decolonialidade a partir do Brasil*, eds. Paulo Henrique Rocha, José Luiz Quadros de Magalhães and Silvia Teixeira. São Paulo: Dialética.

Campilongo, Celso Fernandes, and José Eduardo Faria. 1991. *A Sociologia Jurídica no Brasil.* Porto Alegre: Sergio Antonio Fabris Editor.

Catusso, Joseane. 2007. Pluralismo Jurídico: Um novo paradigma para se pensar o fenômeno jurídico. *Revista Eletrônica Do CEJUR, Curitiba* 1(2): 119–147. https://doi.org/10.5380/cejur.v1i2.16749.

Cerqueira, Daniel. 2018. La justiciabilidad de los DESCA bajo la Convención Americana. *Blog de La Fundación para el Debido Proceso.* https://dplfblog.com/2018/05/29/la-justiciabilidad-de-los-desca-bajo-la-convencion-americana. Accessed 27 May 2022.

Costa, Alexandre Araújo, and Inocêncio Mártires Coelho. 2017. *Teoria Dialética do Direito: A filosofia jurídica de Roberto Lyra Filho.* Brasília: Faculdade de Direito da Universidade de Brasília.

Falk, Richard, Balakrishnan Rajagopal, and Jacqueline Stevens. 2006. Reshaping justice: International law and the third world: An introduction. *Third World Quarterly* 27(5): 711–712. https://doi.org/10.1080/01436590600779948.

Ferraz Júnior, Tercio. 2006. *Teoria da Norma Jurídica.* Rio de Janeiro: Forense.

Fukurai, Hiroshi. 2018. Fourth World Approaches to International Law (FWAIL) and Asia's indigenous struggles and quests for recognition under international law. *Asian Journal of Law and Society* 5 (1): 221–231. https://doi.org/10.1017/als.2018.10.

Hanashiro, Olaya Silvia. 2001. *O Sistema Interamericano de Proteção de Direitos Humanos.* São Paulo: Edusp.

Hegel, Georg. 2011. *Ciência da lógica: (excertos).* Seleção e tradução Marco Aurélio Werle. São Paulo: Barcarolla.

Hoekema, André. 2002. Hacia un pluralismo jurídico formal de tipo igualitário: Pluralismo jurídico y alternatividad judicial. *El Otro Derecho* 26 (27): 63–98.

IACtHR. 2005. *Comunidade Indígena Yakye Axa vs. Paraguai.* 17 June, Series C-125.

IACtHR. 2020. *Indígenas Miembros de la Asociación Lhaka Honhat vs. Argentina.* 6 February, Series C-400.

IACtHR. 2001. *Mayagna Awas Tingni vs. Nicaragua.* 31 August, Series C-359.

IACtHR. 2018a. *Cuscul Pivaral otros vs. Guatemala* .23 August. Series C-359.

IACtHR. 2018b. *Povo Indígena Xucuru e seus membros vs. Brasil.* 5 February, Series C-346.

Lander, Edgardo (Ed.). 2003. *La colonialidad del saber: eurocentrismo y ciencias sociales. Perspectivas latinoamericanas.* Buenos Aires: CLACSO.

López, Liliana E. 2014. El Pluralismo Jurídico: Una propuesta paradigmática para repensar el Derecho. *UMBRAL—Revista De Derecho Constitucional* 4 (1): 31–64.

Lyra Filho, Roberto. 1982. A Nova Escola Jurídica Brasileira. *Direito e Avesso: Boletim da Nova Escola Jurídica Brasileira* 1(1).

Marques, Claudia Lima, and Squeff, Tatiana Cardoso. 2018. Novas Contribuições do Sistema Interamericano para a Proteção dos Consumidores no Brasil. In *Coletânea de Direitos Humanos*, ed. Cristiane Feldmen Dutra, Dani Rudinicki, and Germano Schwartz, 3: 1–17, Rio de Janeiro: Lúmen Juris.

Obregón, Liliana. 2016. Regionalismo construído: Uma breve história do Direito Internacional. In *Direito global e suas alternativas metodológicas*, ed. Michelle Badin, Adriane Brito, and Deisy Ventura, 97–118, São Paulo: FGV Direito, 100.

OEA. 2022. *Nossa História*. https://www.oas.org/pt/sobre/nossa_historia.asp. Accessed 27 May 2022.

Pahuja, Sundhya. 2005. The postcoloniality of international law. *Harvard International Law Journal* 46 (2): 459–469.

Rajagopal, Balakrishnan. 1999. International Law and the Development Encounter: violence and resistance at the margins. *ASIL—The American Society of International Law*. Proceedings of the 93rd annual meeting. 93(1): 16–27. https://doi.org/10.1017/S0272503700066763.

Rajagopal, Balakrishnan. 2000. From resistance to renewal: The third world, social movements, and the expansion of international institutions. In *New critical writings in political sociology*, ed. Alan Scott and Anna Marie Smith, 530–578. London: Routledge.

Rajagopal, Balakrishnan. 2003. *International Law from below: Development, social movements, and third world resistance*. New York: Cambridge University Press.

Rajagopal, Balakrishnan. 2005a. Limits of law in counter-hegemonic globalization: the Indian Supreme Court and the Normada Valley struggle. In *Law and globalization from below: Towards a cosmopolitan legality*, ed. Boaventura de Sousa Santos, and César Rodríguez-Garavito. Cambridge: Cambridge University Press.

Rajagopal, Balakrishnan. 2005b. International Law and social movements: Challenges of theorizing resistance. *Columbia Journal of Transnational Law* 41 (2): 397–433.

Rajagopal, Balakrishnan. 2007. Pro-human rights but anti-poor? A critical evaluation of the indian supreme court from a social movement perspective. *Human Rights Review* 8(3): 157–186.

Rajagopal, Balakrishnan. 2008. Counter-hegemonic international law: Rethinking human rights and development as a third world strategy. *International Law and the Third World*. Routledge-Cavendish.

Rajagopal, Balakrishnan. 2012. International law and its discontents: Rethinking the global south. *Proceedings of the Annual Meeting—American Society of International Law* 6(1): 176–181. https://doi.org/10.5305/procannmeetasil.106.0176.

Ramos, Esdras Oliveira. 2012. Direito alternativo, direito vivo, direito achado na rua e pluralismo: uma conjugação para o ensino libertário. *Em tempo—Revista da área de Direito da UNIVEM*, 11:88–105. https://doi.org/10.26729/et.v11i1.335.

Santos, Boaventura de Souza, and Menezes, Maria Paula (Eds.). 2010. *Epistemologias do sul*. São Paulo: Cortez.

Sartre, Jean Paul. 1971. *Materialismo y revolución*. Buenos Aires: La Pléyade; Marx, Karl. 2004. *Miséria da filosofia*. São Paulo: Ícone.

Scarfi, Juan Pablo. 2017. *The hidden history of international law in the Americas: Empire and legal networks*. Oxford: Oxford University Press.

Scarfi, Juan Pablo. 2020. La intervención del derecho internacional (latino) americano: La hegemonía estadounidense y el debate sobre la intervención en los orígenes del sistema interamericano. *Estudios Sociales* 59(2): 113–135, 118, 128. https://doi.org/10.14409/es.v59i2.9508.

Silva, Bianca Guimarães. 2022. *América para os americanos ou para a humanidade?* Estudo crítico dos diálogos transjudiciais na jurisprudência da Corte Interamericana de Direitos Humanos sobre Migrações Internacionais. 256p. Dissertação (Mestrado em Direito)—Universidade de Brasília, Faculdade de Direito. Brasília: UnB.

Sousa Júnior, J.G., and L.G.D. Fonseca. 2017. O Constitucionalismo achado na rua—uma proposta de descolonização do Direito. *Revista Direito e Práxis* 8(4): 2882–2902. https://doi.org/10.1590/2179-8966/2017/31218.

Sousa Júnior, José Geraldo de. 1984. *Para uma crítica da eficácia do direito*. Porto Alegre: Sergio Antonio Fabris Editor.

Sousa Júnior, José Geraldo de. 1993. *Introdução crítica ao direito*. 4 ed. 144p. Universidade de Brasília, Brasília: UnB.

Sousa Júnior, José Geraldo de. 2008. *Direito como Liberdade:* o Direito Achado na Rua, experiências populares emancipatórias de criação do Direito. 338p. Tese (Doutorado em Direito)—Universidade de Brasília, Brasília: UnB
Sousa Júnior, José Geraldo de. 2017. Concepção e prática de O Direito Achado na Rua: plataforma para um Direito Emancipatório. *Cadernos Ibero-Americanos de Direito Sanitário* 6(1): 145–158. https://doi.org/10.17566/ciads.v6i2.389.
Sousa Júnior, José Geraldo de. 2019. O Direito Achado na Rua: condições sociais e fundamentos teóricos. *Revista Direito e Práxis* 10(4): 2776-2817. https://doi.org/10.1590/2179-8966/2019/45688
Squeff, Tatiana Cardoso, and Marina Rosa. 2020. Corte Interamericana de Direitos Humanos: Caso comunidades indígenas membros da Associação Lhaka Honhat. *Revista De Direito Ambiental* 100(1): 253–270.
Squeff, Tatiana Cardoso. 2016. *Estado Plurinacional*: a proteção do indígena em torno da construção da hidrelétrica de Belo Monte. Curitiba: Juruá.
Squeff, Tatiana Cardoso. 2021. Overcoming the 'Coloniality of Doing' in International Law: Soft Law as a Decolonial Tool. *Revista Direito GV* 17(1): 1–31.
Warat, Luis Alberto. 1981. À procura de uma semiologia do poder. *Sequência—Estudos Jurídicos e Políticos* 2(3): 79–83.
Wolkmer, Antonio Carlos. 1997. *Pluralismo Jurídico:* fundamentos para uma nova cultura do direito. São Paulo: Alfa Omega.
Wolkmer, Antonio Carlos. 2017. *Teoría crítica del derecho desde América Latina.* México.

The U.S. Recognition of Jerusalem as a Capital of Israel and the Movement of Its Embassy to Jerusalem: The Question of Jerusalem and Beyond

Hadeel S. Abu Hussein

Abstract This Chapter tracks the recent developments linked with the United States' recognition of Jerusalem as Israel's capital city and the movement of its embassy from Tel-Aviv to Jerusalem. It is an attempt to examine the legal impact of this action, provide a brief historical background of the Israeli-Palestinian conflict, and explore the status of Jerusalem. It gives an account of the law governing this subject and explores narratives, power, and the sovereignty question of this struggle through an international law lens. It shows the historical background of the current status to explore the profound impact of narratives on shaping the past, present, and future. This decision is controversial in many ways because Jerusalem is at the core of the ongoing Israeli-Palestinian conflict. Jerusalem's sensitive status has been the key and obstacle to peace negotiations for decades. I will start by providing a brief background of the Israeli-Palestinian conflict followed by highlighting the unique case of Jerusalem and briefly understanding international law focusing on the annexation question. I will then turn to the implications of the formal recognition of Jerusalem as the capital of Israel, all of which will affect the final peace resolution that will include Jerusalem.

Keywords Jerusalem · Israeli-Palestinian conflict · U.S. Middle East policy · International law · Annexation

H. S. Abu Hussein (✉)
The Faculty of Law, Economics and Governance, Utrecht University, Utrecht, Netherlands
e-mail: h.abuhussein@uu.nl

T. Venthan Ananthavinayagan and A. Viswanath Shenoy (eds.), *The Wretched of the Global South*, International Law and the Global South,
https://doi.org/10.1007/978-981-99-9275-1_11

1 Introduction

This chapter explores the legality of recognising Jerusalem as the capital of Israel and moving the U.S. embassy from Tel-Aviv to Jerusalem by President Trump in May 2018.[1] It is an attempt to unpack the legal implications of moving the U.S. embassy to Jerusalem and recognising it as the official capital of Israel. This chapter presents a chronological overview to understand the reality behind such a decision. It illustrates the steps which Israel conducted through the years to annex East Jerusalem as a starting point. Second, I look at how international law responded to Israel's annexation of Jerusalem, long viewed as void and invalid by the Palestinians. Third, I turn the focus to the U.S. position and policies before highlighting the development that recently occurred. The Israeli-Palestinian conflict is being waged through contradictory narratives competing for support from the United States, the United Nations and the international community. Therefore, it is essential to note that claims have arisen that this act undermines the role of the U.S. as a sponsor of any future peace process. The understanding of the importance of Jerusalem to both sides and to many others around the world should not be ignored, and question the failure of international law to provide practical solutions and maintain the legal order in crucial contemporary times instead of promoting global justice.

2 Historical Background and Post-War Development on the Status of Jerusalem

The Israeli-Palestinian conflict[2] has been referred to as a 'meta-conflict' because there is a conflict about the nature of the conflict itself, as well as an ongoing conflict between two peoples with competing historical narratives. The principal disagreements involve opinions about identity rights to territory and victimhood (Shalim 2004).

By the end of World War II, the British mandate over Palestine expired, leaving 1,269,000 Arabs and 608,000 Jews living within the borders of Mandate Palestine (Benin and Hajjar 2014). The British government approached the newly established United Nations (UN) to resolve the fate of Palestine. Subsequently, the UN appointed a committee to investigate the situation on the ground, despite disagreement among the committee members with regard to the political nature of the resolution. There was general agreement that the country would have to be divided between Palestinian Arabs and Jews. The vote on a partition plan for Palestine took place on November

---

[1] The press statement issued by U.S. Secretary of State Mike Pompeo on 14 May 2018. https://www.state.gov/secetary/remarks/2018/05/282066.htm (Accessed 10 October 2019).

[2] This began before the 1948 War, as in 1917 the Balfour Declaration, supported by the British government, stipulated the establishment of 'a Jewish national home in Palestine' as well as 'civil and political rights of existing non-Jewish communities'. Following this, Zionist institutions became extensive and the Jewish population grew. Violent uprisings erupted in 1929 and 1936 and later.

29th 1947, and was approved by the UN General Assembly in UN Resolution 181.[3] The UN General Assembly recommended a partition plan that proposed the partition of Mandate Palestine into two separate states, with 57% of the territory allocated to a Jewish state and 43% to a Palestinian state (see United Nations 1947, p. 131, 139).[4] Upon the partition plan resolution, the Jewish state owned only 7% of historic Palestine's land area (Khalidi 2005). The Zionist leadership of Israel agreed to the UN partition plan, but the Arab and Palestinian leadership rejected it,[5] viewing the resolution as unfair and harmful to Palestinians. They argued that the plan was not sufficient for the demographics of the population (Cattan 1976, p. 37; Jamal 2005)[6] and instead demanded the establishment of an Arab State in all parts of historical Palestine. On May 15th, 1948, British troops withdrew from Palestine and David Ben-Gurion[7] announced the establishment of the State of Israel. Following the adoption of the resolution, (Quigley 1990, pp. 47–53)[8] the British evacuated Palestine and fighting began between the Palestinian Arabs and the Jews.

On the one hand, according to the Palestinian narrative, what occurred in 1948 is described as 'Al-Nakba—The Catastrophe' (Sa'di 2006, pp. 57–79; Zureiq 1948; Kahlidi 1961, pp. 22–28). In the wake of the war, Palestinian scholars describe the situation as the loss of a homeland, the collapse of society, and the failure of a national project and dream (Sa'di 2006, pp. 57–79). Additionally, it meant living in exile or becoming citizens of the newly founded state over their motherland's remains. As a result of the 1948 war, Palestinians fled and became refugees in neighbouring countries. On the other hand, according to the dominant Israeli narrative, what happened in Palestine in 1948 was called 'the War of Independence', in Hebrew '*Milhemet haa'tzmaout*', and the liberation and creation of a national Jewish homeland (Shalim 2004).[9] The distance between the two narrative labels reveals two conflicting memories.

In 1949, the war between Israel and the Arab States was concluded with several armistice agreements, which marked the end of the 1948 Arab–Israeli war. The war ended with Israel controlling 78% of Mandate Palestine and other parts occupied by Jordan and Egypt (Kedar and Yiftachel 2006). Israel and neighbouring Egypt,

---

[3] United Nations General Assembly Resolution 181, UN GAOR. 1ST Sess., UN Doc. A/64 (1946), 29 November 1947.

[4] United Nations General Assembly Resolution 181, UN GAOR. 1ST Sess., UN Doc. A/64 (1946), 29 November 1947, 131, 139.

[5] With the exception of some leaders of the National Liberation League and the communists.

[6] Moreover, some Palestinian narrative scholars argue that Israel is a 'colonial product' imposed upon the Arabs, and as a result of the unfair partition plan proposal, they could not accept it; they blame Israel for the expulsion of the Palestinians who became refugees after the war.

[7] David Ben-Gurion was the primary founder of the state of Israel and Israel's first prime minister and defence minister in 1948–1953 and 1955–1963.

[8] It is important to highlight that the General Assembly had no power to grant territory. In addition, the resolution was a proposal conditional on approval by the two parties, which means that it could be implemented only if the two parties agreed to it.

[9] Facts about Israel, 1985, Jerusalem: Israel Information Centre.

Lebanon, Jordan, and Syria established armistice separation lines.[10] that divided the newly established Israel from other parts of Mandate Palestine. The Palestinian state proposed by the UN partition plan was never established and historical Palestine was divided into three parts, including separate political control for Israel. Following the 1948 war, Israel established itself over 77% of the territory. In the founding declaration of Israel, the Jews stated that they had legal sovereignty over the territory (see Declaration of the Establishment of the State of Israel 1948),[11] while the coastal plain around the Gaza Strip fell under Egyptian military administration. Furthermore, Jordan governed East Jerusalem and the hill country of central Palestine (Beinin and Hajjar 2014, p. 4).

Additionally, it is essential to highlight that Israel won a second territorial war in 1967, called the Six-Day War, in which it occupied Jerusalem and Golan Heights. As a result, Israel created massive demographic changes. As a consequence of the 1948 and 1967 wars, Jews became a majority rather than a minority in the territory, and controlled the majority of territory. From this point onward, the Palestinians were subject to Israeli rule that has been jurisdictionally divided into three areas, each of which has a distinct legal status: the first area is the sovereign territory of Israel following the 1948 war, located within the 1949 armistice line (often referred to as the 'Green Line').[12] People of those areas became citizens of Israel. The second area consists of those parts of the Occupied Territories that have been de facto annexed following the 1967 Six-Day War, where Palestinians are described as residents, such as people living in East Jerusalem. Both fall under the Israeli legal system and jurisdiction. Finally, there is the Israeli military administration that was initially established to govern Palestinians in the West Bank and Gaza. In August 2005, Israel 'withdrew' from the Gaza Strip, and since then the military legal administration (which includes military courts) only applies to citizens of the West Bank.

1948 marked the beginning of a long struggle between Palestinians and Israelis over land. Although there are, as noted earlier, various historical narratives that inform and sustain the conflict, what is perhaps less argued is that competing claims to land are at the core of the Israeli-Palestinian conflict. It is the unresolved and competing claims to territory that cause the prolonged nature of the conflict. The right to self-determination has been repeatedly upheld with respect to the Palestinian people by the UN General Assembly, UN Security Council, the UN Commission on Human Rights (now the UN Human Rights Council), and the International Court of Justice. In

---

[10] Referred to as the 'green line'; the Green Line is a term originally used to define Israel's borders with Jordan from the period following Israel's 1948 independence war until the Six Day War when Israel captured the West Bank and East Jerusalem.

[11] Declaration of the Establishment of the State of Israel, 1 *Laws of the State of Israel* (1948), at 3, 4, 5.; Cohen, Raymond, Deborah Weissman, S. J. James Bernauer, Eugene Korn, O. P. Ruth Lautt, Leonard Greenspoon, Ursula Rudnick, Dennis Hale, Peter Pettit, and Racelle Weiman. "The Declaration of the Establishment of the State of Israel: Reflections on its Sixtieth Anniversary." *Studies in Christian-Jewish Relations* 3, no. 1, 2008.

[12] Referred to as the 'green line'; the Green Line is a term originally used to define Israel's borders with Jordan from the period following Israel's 1948 independence war until the Six Day War when Israel captured the West Bank and East Jerusalem.

Resolution 2005/1 the Commission on Human Rights (see Human Rights Resolution 2005)[13] reaffirmed that the right to self-determination was not only jus cogens in international law but that its achievement by the Palestinian people was a basic condition for achieving just, lasting and comprehensive peace in the region of the Middle East. The same Resolution further described the right to self-determination of the Palestinian people as inalienable, permanent and unqualified, and includes the right to live in freedom, justice and dignity and to establish their independent state (Getachew 2019).

It is essential to shed light on the fact that the General Assembly consistently reaffirmed the right to self-determination for the people of Palestine. A series of resolutions passed in 1970 under the title of 'Importance of the universal realisation of the right of peoples to self-determination and the speedy granting of independence to colonial countries and peoples for the effective guarantee and observance of human rights'. This was seen as an affirmation of the legitimacy of the armed struggle of the liberation movement (see The Affirmation by the United Nations of the Right of Self Determination of the Palestinian People 1969).[14] Furthermore, in 1975, the recommendation of the Committee on the Exercise of Inalienable Rights of Palestinian People, established by the General Assembly, affirmed the right to self-determination for the Palestinian people without external interference, alongside the

[13] Situation in occupied Palestine/Right of the Palestinian people to self-determination—CHR—Resolution Situation in occupied Palestine, Human Rights Resolution 2005/1, *38th meeting 7 April 2005*, Adopted by a recorded vote of 49 to 1, with 2 abstention, https://www.un.org/unispal/document/auto-insert-178904/.

[14] The Affirmation by the United Nations of the Right of Self-Determination of the Palestinian People (pp. 33–37).

(1) United Nations	General Assembly resolution 2535 B (XXIV) of 10 December 1969
(2)	General Assembly resolution 2672 C (XXV) of 8 December 1970
(3)	General Assembly resolution 3210 (XXIX) of 14 October 1974
(4)	General Assembly resolution 3237 (XXIX) of 22 November 1974
(5)	General Assembly resolution 3376 (XXX) of 10 November 1975
(6)	General Assembly resolution 32/14 of 7 November 1977. The vote was 113 in favour, 3 against and 18 abstentions. The preceding resolutions in the series were: 2621 (XXV) of 12 October 1970 2787 (XXVI) of 6 December 1971 2955 (XXVII) of 12 December 1972 3070 (XXVIII) of 30 November 1973 3246 (XXIX) of 29 November 1974 3382 (XXX) of 10 November 1975 31/34 of 30 November 1976 Resolution 2955 (XXVII) did not specifically mention Palestine.
(7)	Document A/31/35

right to independence and sovereignty. Following that, the Security Council drafted a resolution in 1976 that stated:

> Affirms the inalienable rights of the Palestinian people to self-determination, including the right of return and the right to national independence and sovereignty in Palestine, under the Charter of the United Nations (see Security Council drafted resolution 1967).[15]

Due to the United States veto, the resolution failed. In 1977, the Security Council considered the Committee's report yet adjourned the discussion without taking action, and the issue remains on its agenda.

Even though the self-determination of the Palestinian people has been recognised in the Mandate, the Partition Plan, and various U.N. Resolutions (see General Assembly Resolution 1970),[16] the Palestinians remain the 'one case in which the rule restricting self-determination to colonial peoples has not been followed by the U.N' (Schoenberg 1989). Therefore, the Palestinian people's right to self-determination was denied and ignored for decades by the United Nations.

Over time, the independent state, self-determination, and inclusiveness were the main requests of the Palestinian national struggle (Strawson 2001; Getachew 2019). However, challenges and critical discussion arose from the meaning of Palestinian statehood, which forced Palestinians to explore alternatives in the broader contexts of decolonisation while thinking about the notions of citizenship, sovereignty, nationhood, justice and international legal mechanism. Therefore, the modern Palestinian self-determination entails new terms for the debates over the Palestinians' future beyond the partition. As Rashid Khalidi stated:

> At a juncture when independent Palestinian statehood seems unachievable, these astute reflections are particularly welcome. They offer innovative suggestions for providing renewed dynamism to the Palestinian struggle outside the confines of a two-state solution that Israel has systematically sabotaged for over fifty years.

As he comments, rethinking statehood sets the terms of debate for the future of Palestine beyond the partition:

> At a juncture when independent Palestinian statehood seems unachievable, these astute reflections are particularly welcome. They offer innovative suggestions for providing renewed dynamism to the Palestinian struggle, outside the confines of a two-state solution that has been systematically sabotaged by Israel for over fifty years (Khalidi 2020).

---

[15] Security Council drafted a resolution of 1976, Report of the Committee on the Exercise of the Inalienable Rights of the Palestinian People, General Assembly, Official Records: Thirty-First Session, Supplement No. 35 (A/31/35), United Nations, New York, 1976. Assembly, General. *Report of the Committee on the Exercise of the Inalienable Rights of the Palestinian People*. A/72/35, (September 5, 2017).

[16] G.A. Res. 2649, 25 U.N. GAOR, Supp. (No. 28) 73, U.N. Doc. A/8028 (1970); G.A. Res. 2672B, 25 U.N. GAOR, Supp. (No. 28) 35, U.N. Doc. A/8028 (1970); G.A. Res. 2787, 26 U.N. GAOR, Supp. (No. 29) 82, U.N. Doc. A/8429 (1971); G.A. Res. 2792 D, 26 U.N. GAOR, Supp. (No. 29) 47, U.N. Doc. A/8429 (1971); G.A. Res. 2963 C-E, 27 U.N. GAOR, Supp. (No. 30) 28, U.N. Doc. A/8730 (1972); G.A. Res. 3089D, 28 U.N. GAOR, Supp. (No. 30) 27, U.N. Doc. A/ 9030 (1973); G.A. Res. 3236, 29 U.N. GAOR, Supp. (No. 31) 4, U.N. Doc. A/9631.

To propose any future peace solution, the question concerning the legality of East Jerusalem annexation that occurred following the Six-Day War is one of the core issues of Israeli-Palestinian conflict. Hence, Jerusalem's status is a critical point. Moreover, the annexation is an obstacle because Palestine and Israel each consider Jerusalem their capital (Khalidi 2020; Kattan 2009; Beinin and Hajjar 2014).[17] Therefore, recognising United Jerusalem as the capital of Israel by the U.S. and relocating its embassy has crucial implications. This is an endeavour to explore how this decision could be contrary to international law examining the illegality of the annexation.

It is crucial to emphasise that the question is Jerusalem is not a mere geographical or territorial issue. It is beyond that, since East Jerusalem has religious significance, being the seat of various holy locations within the old city of Jerusalem for Christians, Muslims, and Jews (Dumper 2002; Glass and Khamaisi 2005).[18] The Palestinians as people living under occupation should be able to profess and practice their religion and language effectively and enjoy their culture according to the International Covenant on Economic, Social, and Cultural Rights.[19]

3 The Palestinian Approach

According to the Palestinian point of view, the unique character of Jerusalem stems from its spiritual, religious, and cultural dimensions. Therefore, the Palestinians express support for the international community to protect and preserve the city's special status.

The first attempt at protection can be located in Resolution 181 (II), Partition Plan (see General Assembly Resolution 181 1047).[20] 'Future Government of Palestine requiring independent Arab Jewish States and Special International Regime for the City of Jerusalem in Palestine'. It stipulated that 'the city of Jerusalem shall be established as a *corpus separatum* under a special international regime'.

It continues:

> The city of Jerusalem shall include the present municipality of Jerusalem plus surrounding villages and towns, the most eastern of which shall be Abu Dis; the most southern, Bethlehem; the most western, Ein Karim (including a built-up area of Motsa); and the most northern Shu'fat.

The Arab League rejected the Partition Plan (see General Assembly Resolution 181 1047),[21] but the Palestinians focused on the primary principles of this resolution,

---

[17] I avoid explicitly examination of the complexities of the conflict's Israeli and Palestinian narratives; these complexities have received attention elsewhere.

[18] Followers of each of these religions have controlled all or part of the city over the past few thousand years.

[19] Israel signed the International Covenant on Economic, Social and Cultural rights on 19 December 1966, and ratified it on 3 October 1991.

[20] UNGA Res.181, UN GAOR. 1ST Sess., UN Doc. A/64 (1946), 29 November 1947.

[21] Ibid.

highlighting the necessity to protect the distinctive character of the city and its unique status. Therefore, the principles underlying this resolution have continued to serve as a solid foundation for all following resolutions relating to Jerusalem. The UN continued to advocate the special status of Jerusalem despite the violation of Resolution 181 with Israel's occupation of West Jerusalem, followed by the Armistice Agreement of 3 April 1949 (see also Waage 2011),[22] which de facto led to a divided Jerusalem.

Next, the General Assembly adopted Resolution 303 (IV), 'Palestine, Question of an International Regime for the Jerusalem Area and the Protection of the Holy Places', which articulated:

> its intention that Jerusalem should be placed under a permanent international regime, which should envisage appropriate guarantees for the protection of the Holy Places, both within and outside Jerusalem, and to confirm specifically the following provisions of General Assembly resolution 181 (II). (1) The City of Jerusalem shall be established as a *corpus separatum* under a special international regime and shall be administered by the United Nations.

The Palestinian approach to Jerusalem was expressed *inter alia* in 1988 and 2002. In November 1988, the proclamation of the establishment of the State of Palestine (Kassim 1997)[23] by the Palestine Liberation Organisation declared that Jerusalem was the capital of the Palestinian State. In October 2002, the Palestinian Legislative Council adopted the Law on the Capital, which states that 'Jerusalem is the capital of the Palestinian State and the main seat of its three branches of government'.[24] Moreover, the State of Palestine is the sovereign over Jerusalem and its Holy Places.[25] Furthermore, any statute or agreement that diminishes the rights of the Palestinian State in Jerusalem is invalid.[26] Under Article 5, this decree can be amended only with the consent of two-thirds of the members of the Palestinian Legislative Council.[27]

4 Israeli Measures Gradually to Annex Jerusalem

After the 1948 war, in particular on 3 April 1949 once the hostilities had ceased and Israel and Jordan signed the Armistice Agreement, Israel gradually acquired legal title over Jerusalem. The western part of the city was under Israeli sovereignty and the eastern part was under Jordanian sovereignty. After the Six-Day War, on 28 June 1967, Israeli Parliament, the Knesset, announced that united Jerusalem was incorporated into the municipal and administrative sphere of the Israeli government

[22] The Rhodes Agreement. UN Doc S/1302/Rev.1, 3 April 1949, The Armistice Agreement between Jordan and Israel signed on 3 April 1949.

[23] In November 1988 the proclamation of the establishment of the State of Palestine.

[24] Article 1, Law on the Capital.

[25] Article 2, Law on the Capital.

[26] Article 4, Law on the Capital.

[27] Article 5, Law on the Capital.

(Wolfrum 2013).[28] Thus, East Jerusalem, which since 1948 had been part of the West Bank under the Jordanian administration, fell under Israeli governance based on two Ordinances passed after the Six-Day War (Imseis 1999, pp. 1039–1040).

First, Administrative Ordinance, Amendment No. 11,[29] approved by the Knesset, announced that all Israeli law, administration, and jurisdiction applies to any territory to which the government decided it applied, including areas formerly part of Mandatory Palestine. This was to include:

> any part of Palestine which the minister of defence has defined by proclamation as being held by the defence army of Israel.

An amendment to this ordinance on 27 June 1967 reads as follows:

> In the Law and Administration Ordinance, 1948, the following section shall be inserted after section IIA: IIB.
>
> The Law, Jurisdiction and Administration of the State shall apply in any area of Eretz Yisrael designated by the government by order.

This amendment changed the definition of the areas that the minister of defence could control, although Israeli law is not applicable in these areas. The Israeli army ordered that areas such as the West Bank and Gaza Strip, besides East Jerusalem, could now be controlled by government order, given that they are areas where Israeli law could be enforced.

The second ordinance passed under Amendment No. 11, which was adopted on 27 June 1967, was the Municipalities Corporations Ordinance (Amendment No. 6),[30] which entitled the interior minister with the following power:

> At the discretion and without holding any inquiry, to enlarge by proclamation the area designated by the order under section IIB of the Law and Administration Ordinance.

Hence, the Knesset authorised the extension of the municipal boundaries where Israel's jurisdiction had been applied following Amendment No. 11.[31] In effect, this ordinance expanded the boundaries of East Jerusalem by the annexation of 64 km^2 of territory in the West Bank, 6 km^2 in the east of the city and 38 km^2 in the west.

Meanwhile, the Israeli officers explained to the international community that this was not annexation. For instance, the Israeli minister of foreign affairs described the issue to the Secretary-General of the United Nations as follows: 'The term 'annexation' is out of place'. He added:

> The measures adopted relate to the integration of Jerusalem in the administrative and municipal spheres, and furnish legal basis for protection of the Holy Places.[32] Accordingly, the

[28] Law and Administration Order [ni.1], 5727–1967. On the legal status of Jerusalem.

[29] Law and Administration Ordinance, published in the official gazette on 22 September 1948.

[30] Adopted on 27 June 1967; Knesset passed the Municipalities Corporations Ordinance (Amendment No. 6), volumes 1–2: 1947–1974.

[31] The Israeli government issued an appropriate order to apply Israeli law to East Jerusalem, which was under the jurisdiction of the municipality of Jerusalem.

[32] UN Doc.S/8052, 10 July 1967.

> purpose of the administrative measure is solely to equalise the municipal services to all the residents of the municipal area besides the protection of the Holy Places.[33]

Various Israeli courts upheld the administrative incorporation of Jerusalem into Israel in the following years.[34] In fact, Israel completed full annexation when the Knesset enacted the Basic Law: Jerusalem the Capital of Israel in 1980. Israel declared an undivided Jerusalem as the united capital of Israel. Article 1 asserted that 'Jerusalem, complete and united, is the capital of Israel'.[35] Article 2 of the law states that it is 'The seat of the President of the State, the Knesset, the Government, and the Supreme Court'.[36]

In addition, it is crucial to highlight that Israel did not identify the borders of Jerusalem nor reference Israel's exclusivity in controlling the area. The term annexation is also absent, conceivably to allow the establishment of new settlements in the surrounding area.[37] Therefore, in 1993, the ambiguity in the Israeli laws that concern the internal boundaries of Jerusalem or its municipality, as for the demarcation lines in the area, with no definition, the exact border or the area of Jerusalem enabled the expansion of more Jewish settlement referred to as greater Jerusalem.[38] This enabled references to the status of Jerusalem as one of the issues that needed to be further negotiated between the Israeli government and the Palestinians.[39] Nonetheless, in 2000 the Knesset proposed a new amendment to the Basic Law: Jerusalem Capital of Israel 1980,[40] explicitly stating the boundaries of the city as determined by order of the Israeli government on 28 June 1967 and that Israeli control is exclusive.[41] Furthermore, the amendment stipulates that any change in the area of Jerusalem and any transfer of powers require the consent of an absolute majority of the Knesset members.[42] Initially, the Supreme Court of Israel's approach was to stop short of interpreting the government's order as effecting annexation, and it stated that 'the mere

[33] Note that the controversies linked to the contemporary status quo of the holy religious places relate to matters beyond the scope of this article and exceed the intention of this chapter.

[34] The Basic Law: Jerusalem 1980, published in Sefer Ha-Chokkim No. 980, page 186; Hanzails' Case, a judgment delivered on 10 March 1969 by the Supreme Court of Israel in the Hanzalis' case [Hebrew]. See also the comments by Shaki, Id page 356–357, 284 the human dimension of war.

[35] Article 1, passed on 30 July 1980, published in Sefer Ha-Chokkim No. 980, page 186; page 205.

[36] Article 3 of the Basic Law: Jerusalem stipulated that the Holy Places will be protected. Furthermore, Article 4 of this law states that the government and other authorities have to provide for the development and prosperity of Jerusalem.

[37] Published in Sefer Ha-Chukkim No. 980 of the 23rd Av, 5740 (5 August 1980): 186; the Bill and an Explanatory Note were published in Hatza'ot Chok No. 1464 of 5740: 287.

[38] Greater Jerusalem consists of region around 500 km, including, Maale Adumim, Givat Zeev.

[39] In Israeli/Palestinian Declaration of Principles of 1993.

[40] In 2000 an amendment of the Basic Law: Jerusalem Capital of Israel 1980, was passed.

[41] Articles 5 and 6, passed on 7 December 2000, and published in Sefer Ha-Chukim No. 1760, page 28.

[42] In order to change or amend this Basic Law would have to pass through the enactment of another Basic Law approved by more than half of the Knesset members.

application of the Israeli norm to an area situated outside Israel does not necessarily make that area a part of Israel' (see HCJ 205/82).[43]

Nonetheless, this approach changed following the passing of the Basic Law in 1980. Since then, the Court has considered effectively that the 'annexation' of East Jerusalem is lawful and legitimate (see HCJ 282/88).[44] This implies the denial of the Palestinian quest for statehood and its right to self-determination (Getachew 2019). The next section will focus on the issues relating to Jerusalem and international law.

5 Overview of the Legal Issues Relating to Jerusalem and International Law

In the wake of the Six-Day War in 1967, Israel applied the Israeli common civil administration in Jerusalem in an attempt to extend its jurisdiction over the city.[45] In response, the General Assembly held a fifth emergency Special Session on 4 July 1967, in which it adopted Resolution 2253 (ES-V), 'Measures Taken by Israel to Change the Status of the City of Jerusalem'. The resolution articulated deep concern about the situation (see General Assembly Resolution 1967).[46] Consequently, common civil administration was internationally viewed as maintaining annexation and accordingly was criticised by the UN Security Council as null and void (see General Assembly Resolution 1981).[47] The General Assembly even added that this was an 'act of aggression' (General Assembly Resolution 1981).[48] Furthermore, it considered these measures 'invalid' and requested Israel 'rescind all measures already taken and desist forthwith from taking any action which would alter the status of Jerusalem' (see General Assembly Resolution 1967).[49] Accordingly, the General Assembly, and later the Security Council acting under Chapter VI, affirmed that Israel's occupation of East Jerusalem, the Gaza Strip, the West Bank

---

[43] Justice Cohen's opinion in HCJ 283/96 Ruweidi v. Military Court in the Hebron District, 24(2) PD 419, 423 (1970), approved in HCJ 205/82 Kanj Abu Salakh v. Minister of Interior, 37 (2) PD 718 (1983), But of Justice Kahan's opinion in Ruweidi, holding the 1967 declaration as effecting annexation.

[44] HCJ 282/88 Awad v. Prime Minister et al. 42(2) PD 424, 429 (per Justice Barak).

[45] Israel initially wanted to utilize local legislation to change the legal status of the entire area of Jerusalem.

[46] The situation prevailing in Jerusalem as a result of the measures taken by Israel to change the status of the City; UNGA Res. 2253 (ES-V) 4 July 1967.

[47] UNSC Res. 497 (1981).

[48] UNGA Res. 36/226A (1981); UNGA Res 39/146A (1984).

[49] UNGA Res. 2253(ES-V), 4 July 1967; UNGA Res 2254(ES-V), 14 July 1967. For Israel's view that this action did not alter the status of Jerusalem (and thus did not amount to annexation), see A/ 6753-S/8052, 10 July 1967.

and the Golan Heights should be categorised as belligerent occupation under international humanitarian law.[50] Moreover, it regularly reaffirmed the inadmissibility of the acquisition of territory by use of force (see General Assembly Resolution 1967)[51] and the overriding necessity of Israel's withdrawal of armed forces from occupied territories.[52] It opposed the measures taken to change the status of Jerusalem. Hence, it contrasted Israel's legal declarations on East Jerusalem[53] and its evident de facto annexation of other occupied territories.[54] On 21 May 1968, the Security Council adopted Resolution 252 that stipulated,

> All legislative and administrative measures and actions taken by Israel, including expropriation of land and properties thereon which tend to change the legal status of Jerusalem, are invalid and cannot change that status (see The Security Council Resolution 252 and 267 1969).[55]

In the wake of the 1980 Basic Law concerning Jerusalem, the Security Council adopted two significant resolutions. 'Concerning the Status of Jerusalem', Resolution 476 (1980):

> *Reconfirms* that all legislative and administrative measures and actions taken by Israel, the occupying Power, which purports to alter the character and status of the Holy City of Jerusalem have no legal validity and constitute a flagrant violation of the Fourth Geneva Convention relative to the Protection of Civilian Persons in Time of War and also constitute a serious obstruction to achieving a comprehensive, just and lasting peace in the Middle East;
>
> *Reiterates* that all such measures which have altered the geographic, demographic and historical character and status of the Holy City of Jerusalem are null and void and must be rescinded in compliance with the relevant resolutions of the Security Council:
>
> *Urgently calls* on Israel, the occupying Power, to abide by this and previous Security Council resolutions and to desist forthwith from persisting in the policy and measures affecting the character and status of the Holy City of Jerusalem.

Following this, the Security Council condemned Israel. Noting that Israel had not complied with Resolution 467 (1980), the Security Council decided "not to recognise the 'Basic Law' and such other actions by Israel that as a result of this law, seek to alter the character and status of Jerusalem". In addition:

(a) All Member States accept this decision.

---

[50] Israel's Belligerent Occupation of the Palestinian Territory, including Jerusalem and International Humanitarian Law, 15th July 1999 Geneva, Conference of the High Contracting Parties to the Fourth Geneva, Convention on Measures to Enforce the Convention in the Occupied Palestinian Territory, including Jerusalem.

[51] UNSC Res. 24 (1967), 252 (1968), 267 (1969), 298 (1971), 476 (180), UNSC Res. 478(1980), 20 August 1980), and 2334 (2016); UNGA Res. 2628 (XXV), 2799 (XXVA), and 2949 (XXVII).

[52] See, SC Resolution 242(1967), 476 (180), GA Resolutions 2628 (XXV), 37/86 and 41/162.

[53] Basic Law: Jerusalem, Capital of Israel, 5740–1980 (31 July 1980), Article 1 of the Basic Law provides that Jerusalem, complete and united, is the capital of Israel.

[54] Particularly through establishing Israeli civilian settlements.

[55] The Security Council maintained its position and reaffirmed Resolution 252 in Resolutions 267 of July 1969, 271 of 15 September 1969 and 298 of 25 September 1971.

(b) Those States that have established a diplomatic mission at Jerusalem to withdraw such mission from the Holy City.

Therefore, the Security Council condemned Israel's legal claim to East Jerusalem as 'null and void' and called upon states not to recognise it, in particular by moving established diplomatic missions from the city (see General Assembly Resolution 476 1980)[56] and relocating them elsewhere in compliance with Security Council Resolution 476 (1980) (see Questions relating to the Middle East 1980).[57] Additionally, the General Assembly adopted the same approach on numerous occasions (see General Assembly Resolution 36/120E 1981).[58]

To summarise, the General Assembly considered the 1967 act 'invalid' (see General Assembly Resolution 252 1967).[59] The Security Council condemned the Basic Law 1980 as a violation of international law, in addition to its being 'null and void', and therefore decided not to recognise it. It also continued to criticise Israel as an occupant of the area (see General Assembly Resolution 478 1980).[60] The dominant international community opinion, as expressed in the UN, is that East Jerusalem has been an occupied territory since 1967 and is subject to the Geneva Convention IV 1949 (see the Geneva Convention (IV) 1949).[61] Moreover, international law prohibits annexation and the acquisition of territory by force, according to the *jus ad bellum* in the Charter of the United Nations (see UN Charter 1945).[62] Furthermore, The Hague Regulations of 1907 (see Hague Convention (IV) 1907)[63] did not admit the right of annexation, even following a war of self-defence, unless

[56] UNSC Res. 476(1980), 30 June 1980; UNSC Res. 478(1980), 20 August 1980.

[57] Questions relating to the Middle East, *Yearbook of the United Nations* 1, Section 1, Chapter 12; 405, 1980. Chile Ecuador and Venezuela moved their diplomatic mission from Jerusalem, later Bolivia, Colombia, Costa Rica, the Dominican Republic, El Salvador, Guatemala, Haiti, the Netherlands, Panama, and Uruguay also withdrew their embassies from Jerusalem (between 22 August and 9 September 1980).

[58] UNGA Res. 36/120E, 10 December 1981; UNGA Res. 37/123C, 16 December 1982; UNGA Res. 39/146C, 14 December 1984.

[59] UNSC Res. 252 (1967); 267 (1969); 298 (1971); 446 (1979); 445 (1980); UNGA Res.2253 (ES-V0 (1967); 2254(ES-V) (1967); 31/106A;33/113 (1978).

[60] UNSC Res. 478(1980), 20 August 1980. See also, UNGA Res. 36/120E (1980); 37/123C (1982); 39/146C (1984).

[61] The Geneva Convention (IV) relative to the Protection of Civilian Persons in Time of War. Geneva, (12 August 1949) https://www.icrc.org/applic/ihl/ihl.nsf/Article.xsp?action=openDocument&documentId=77068F12B8857C4DC12563CD0051BDB0 (Accessed 10 October 2019).

[62] UN Charter, 'Charter of the United Nations' (1945), 26 June, 59.

[63] International Conferences (The Hague), Hague, Hague Convention (IV) Respecting the Laws and Customs of War on Land Its Annex: Regulations Concerning the Laws and Customs of War on Land, 18 October 1907. Israel has not signed or ratified the 1907 Hague Regulations, but the Israeli High Court has found that the 1907 Hague Regulations are part of customary international law, and thus binding on all states, including those not party to the treaty but the Israeli supreme Court has applies 1907 Hague Regulations as being part of customary international law, which automaticity part of Israel's law but not treaty law, which needs to be specifically ratified and incorporated into Israeli law by the Israeli parliament, the Knesset.

the annexation was part of a peaceful resolution. Article 46 of The Hague Convention (see Hague Convention (IV) 1907)[64] particularly places a prohibition on land confiscation in occupied territory. In addition, Article 49, Paragraph 6 of the Geneva Convention (see the Geneva Convention (IV) 1949)[65] also specifies that 'the occupying power shall not deport or transfer parts of its own civilian population into the territory it occupies' (see the Geneva Convention (IV) 1949).[66] Furthermore, in the Wall Advisory Opinion of the International Court of Justice, in 2004 (see International Court of Justice Advisory Opinion 2004),[67] the ICJ addresses East Jerusalem as an 'Occupied Palestinian Territory' (The Palestine Yearbook of International Law 2004; see also International Court of justice Advisory Opinion 2004),[68] which the Palestinians also agreed with. Believing that 'the status of Jerusalem… should be decided not unilaterally/individually but in consultation with all the concerned' (see General Assembly Resolution 1967),[69] the UN Security Council condemned the adoption of the Basic Law: Jerusalem, Capital of Israel[70] in Resolution 478 (Tomeh et al. 1975; see also General Assembly Resolution 478 1980).[71] In Paragraph 2 it states that the law is 'a violation of international law'. Furthermore, it invited member states with embassies located in Jerusalem to move them from the city. Following

---

[64] Hague Convention (IV) 'Respecting The Laws and Customs of War on Land and its Annex: Regulations Concerning the Laws and Customs of War on Land. The Hague' (18 October 1907) <http://www.icrc.org/applic/ihl/ihl.nsf/Article.xsp?action=openDocument&documentId=E719FBF0283E98E3C12563CD005168BD> accessed 18 June 2016.

[65] Ibid. Israel ratified the Geneva Conventions on July 6, 1951, but it is important to highlight that while Israel signed the Geneva Conventions, the Israeli Parliament, the Knesset, did not ratify them, therefore they never became part of the Israeli domestic law.

[66] Ibid.

[67] International Court of Justice (hereafter, ICJ), Legal Consequences of the Construction of a Wall in the Occupied Palestine Territory, Advisory Opinion, ICJ Reports 2004, 200 (paragraph 159). In the Wall advisory opinion, the ICJ held that all states were 'under an obligation to recognize the illegal situation resulting from the construction of the wall in the Occupied Palestinian Territory, including in and around East Jerusalem' (page 200, paragraph 159). Nonetheless, the court did not elaborate on the content of the obligation of non-recognition, leaving the matter to be determined by the political organs of the UN acting within their respective spheres of competence. The court stipulated that 'the United Nations, and especially the General Assembly and the Security Council should consider what further actions are required to bring to an end the illegal situation resulting from the construction of the wall and the associated regime, taking due account of the present Advisory Opinion' (page 200, paragraph 160). Hence, the ICJ's decision not to elaborate on the content of the obligation in the Wall case left the states with a particular uncertainty as to what duty entails, if anything, in circumstances which do not necessarily result in legal claims.

[68] The Wall Advisory Opinion of the International Court of Justice, ICJ Reports, 2004 ICJ Rep 136, paragraph 78.

[69] UN GA Official Records, 5th Emergency Session, 1554th Plenary Meetings, United Nations Document No. 1 A/PV.1554 (1967), 14 July 14 1967, 10.

[70] Basic Law: Jerusalem, Capital of Israel, Published in Sefer Ha-Chukkim No. 980 of the 23rd Av, 5740 (5 August 1980): 186; the Bill and an Explanatory Note were published in Hatza'ot Chok No. 1464 of 5740: 287.

[71] UNSC Res. 478 (1980), 20 August 1980.

the resolution, 13 embassies departed the city.[72] In 1980, the European community[73] adopted the Venice Declaration on the Middle East (see Venice Declaration on the Middle East 1980)[74] that addresses the Jerusalem issue. In Paragraph 8 it stipulates that:

> The Nine [Members of the European Community] recognise the special importance of the role played by the question of Jerusalem for all parties concerned. The Nine stressed that they would not accept any unilateral initiative designed to change the *status of Jerusalem* and that the agreement on the city's status should guarantee freedom of access for everyone to the Holy places.[75]

Consequently, in 1999, the president of the European Union, who was the German ambassador in Israel, affirmed that the European Union supported the idea that Jerusalem is still subject to the *corpus separatum* status, and he wrote in a diplomatic note that[76] 'The European Union reaffirms its known position concerning the specific status of Jerusalem as *corpus separatum* (Cassese 1986, pp. 13–39)'. On 23 December 2016, in Resolution 2334, the Security Council *inter alia* had confirmed its previous resolutions linked with Jerusalem, including Resolution 478 (1980). Both the General Assembly and the Security Council have consistently affirmed that actions or decisions intending to change Jerusalem's character, status, or demographic composition will be deprived of legal consequences and be null and void under international law.

6 U.S. Law Policy and Practice Concerning Jerusalem

Following the 1948 war and the establishment of the state of Israel, President Truman recognised the state of Israel in a signed statement of recognition (see Statement of President Truman 1964).[77] Yet, this statement did not recognise Israeli sovereignty over Jerusalem. Over the last 60 years, neither President Truman nor any of the U.S. presidents since then have issued an official statement or declaration regarding any country's sovereignty over Jerusalem.[78] The executive branch of U.S. government consistently highlighted the need for Jerusalem to be given an international regime, demonstrating that the U.S. did not plan to recognise any sovereignty over Jerusalem.

[72] The Costa Rican Embassy returned to West Jerusalem, as did El Salvador. However, in 2006, they were also withdrawn.

[73] The European Community only comprised nine members in the summer of 1980. EEC Bulletin, 1980, no. 6, paragraph 1.1.6 sub-paragraph 8.

[74] Venice Declaration on the Middle East (1980) 13/6 BullCE 10.

[75] EEC Bulletin, 1980, no. 6, paragraph 1.1.6 sub-paragraph 8.

[76] Diplomatic note.

[77] Statement by President Truman Announcing Recognition of State of Israel, Public Papers of the Presidents, May 14, 1948, page 258 (1964).

[78] Although that various Actros have sought to assert full or partial sovereignty over Jerusalem, that will include, Israel, Jordan and the Palestinians.

It maintained that the 'status of Jerusalem…should be decided not unilaterally but [through] consultation with all concerned' (see UNGA Official Records 1967).[79] For instance, the American Embassy's response to a proposal to move the Israeli Foreign Ministry from Tel-Aviv to Jerusalem, on 22 July 1952, states:

> The government of the United States has adhered to and continues to adhere to the policy that there should be a special international regime for Jerusalem which will not only provide protection for the holy places but which will be acceptable to Israel and Jordan as well as the world community.

Since the question of Jerusalem was internationally important, the U.S. Government believed that the UN should be able to devise a status for Jerusalem which would sufficiently preserve the interests of the world community and the directly concerned states. Consequently, the U.S. Government did not view the transfer of the Foreign Office of Israel to Jerusalem favourably (Whiteman 1963). In a dispatch to the Secretary of State, the American Consul General at Jerusalem, on 30 December 1958, affirmed the above approach:

> The majority of the UN member nations, including the United States and the Soviet Union, have continued to respect the United Nations resolutions despite the *de facto* occupancy of the city of Jerusalem, part by Israel and part by Jordan. As a result, an anomalous situation exists today embodied, in the case of the United States, by a Consulate General whose district is the 'international city' and certain adjacent areas on the Jordanian side. Other nations which maintain similar establishments are the United Kingdom, Turkey, Italy, Spain, Greece, and Belgium. Many other countries mark their respect for the internationalisation resolutions by establishing embassies in Tel-Aviv, thus avoiding recognition of Jerusalem as the capital of Israel and, by implication, as Israel's *de facto* sovereign territory (Whiteman 1963, p. 594).

A similar approach was repeated on 5 April 1960, when the U.S. Ambassador in Amman highlighted, *inter alia*, in a dispatch to the Secretary of State:

> The Government of the United States of America has adhered to and continues to adhere to a policy which respects the interest of the United Nations in the status of Jerusalem. The United States Government, therefore, cannot recognise or associate itself in any way with actions to confer upon Jerusalem the attributes of a seat of government of a sovereign State and are thus inconsistent with this United Nations interest in the status of that city (Whiteman 1963, p. 594).

Additionally, on 28 June 1967, the U.S. approach was restated: 'The U.S. has never recognised such unilateral actions by any of the States in the areas as governing the

[79] UNGA Official Records, 5th Emergency Sess., 1554th Plenary Meetings, United Nations Doc. No. 1 A/PV.1554, page 10 (July 14, 1967); see, e.g., Remarks by President Obama in Address to the United Nations General Assembly (Sep. 21, 2011), 2011 Daily Comp. of Pres. Doc. No. 00661, page 4 ('Ultimately, it is Israelis and Palestinians, not us, who must reach agreement on the issues that divide them', including 'Jerusalem'). In a letter to Congress, then-Secretary of State Warren Christopher expressed the executive's concern that '[t]here is no issue related to the Arab–Israeli negotiations that are more sensitive than Jerusalem'. See 141 Congress Record 28967 (1995) (letter to Robert Dole, Majority Leader (June 20, 1995)). He further noted the Executive's opinion that 'any effort… to bring it forefront' could be 'very damaging to the success of the peace process' (letter to Robert Dole, Majority Leader (June 20, 1995)).

international status of Jerusalem'.[80] On 25 September 1971, the U.S. representative to the U.N. Security Council stated:

> In our view, the ultimate status of Jerusalem should be determined through negotiation and agreement between the Government of Israel and Jordan in the context of an overall peace settlement, taking into account the interests of its inhabitants, of the international religious communities who hold it sacred, and other countries in the area.[81]

However, in 1948, the U.S. Congress, passed H.Con.Res. 352 stating that the U.S. embassy should be moved from Tel Aviv to Jerusalem. Over the years, the Congress generally has supported Israeli claims to sovereignty over the city and has opposed the policy of avoiding actions that might prejudice negotiations. Clyde Mark points out further that:

> Congress passed S.Con.Res. 106 and H.Con.Res. 290 in 1990, stating that Jerusalem is the capital of Israel and that the city should remain undivided. A similar resolution, S.Con.Res. 113, passed both houses in 1992. In 1993, the House and Senate passed H. R. 3474 stating that the United States should veto any United Nations resolutions that called Jerusalem 'occupied territory', but the section was deleted in the conference.

Finally, the U.S. Congress adopted the Jerusalem Embassy Act in 1995,[82] which became law on November 8, 1995, without the President's signature. Section 3(a) states categorically that it is the policy of the United States: that Jerusalem should be Undivided; that it should be recognised as Israel's capital; and that the U.S. embassy should be moved to Jerusalem by 31 May 1999. However, the Congress gave the President the authority to waive, if necessary, Section 3(b) for 6 months. if, according to his/her opinion, it 'Is necessary for national security interests of the United States'.[83]

Notably, former presidents officially avoided fulfilling the Jerusalem Embassy Act.[84] American presidential candidates from both Democratic and Republican parties have promised to move the US Embassy in Israel to Jerusalem. Bill Clinton as presidential candidate in 1992, stated, 'Jerusalem is still the capital of Israel and must remain an undivided city accessible to all'. In 2000, George W. Bush while running for presidency pledged to 'begin the process of moving' the US embassy to Jerusalem as soon as assumed the office. Furthermore, In 2008 Barack Obama took an even more strong stand supporting Israel than his predecessors. In 2008, Obama emphasised, 'Jerusalem is the capital of Israel and must remain undivided'. Once elected, they refrained from implementing the Act.

On 6 December 2017, U.S. President Donald Trump decided to fulfil the Act, which recognised Jerusalem as the capital of Israel and called for Jerusalem to remain an undivided city, and he decided to relocate the U.S. embassy from Tel-Aviv to Jerusalem. Following this decree on 14 May 2018, on the same day as the 70th

[80] Department State Bull (July 17, 1967), 60.

[81] Department State Bull (1971), 469.

[82] Jerusalem Embassy Act (1959), Public Law 104–54, adopted by the U.S. Congress in 1995.

[83] Section 7(a)(1), Jerusalem Embassy Act (1959), Public Law 104–54.

[84] Section 7(a)(1), Jerusalem Embassy Act (1959), Public Law 104–54.

anniversary celebrations of the establishment of the State of Israel, the new embassy of the United States was introduced.

This being said, it is important to highlight that President Trump's decision was unambiguously a culmination of 30 years of the US legislative branch of the government maintaining a position on Jerusalem as the capital of Israel since the immediate aftermath of Oslo. Trump was simply executing the Jerusalem Embassy Act passed by Congress in 1995 but had been continuously postponed by his predecessors, Trump went beyond rhetoric and delivered the decision (Erakat 2019).

7 A Sneak Peek into U.S. Legal Practices and Supreme Court Decisions: Prior to Trump's Decision

One example that can reflect the U.S. official standing point prior to the official moving of the embassy to Jerusalem is worth mentioning here is the case of *Zivotofsky v. Kerry (see Zivotofsky v. Kerry 2015)*,[85] which examined the question of sovereignty over Jerusalem. The case dealt with Zivotofsky's parents, whose son was an American citizen born in the city of Jerusalem and who requested to have their son's birthplace recorded as 'Jerusalem, Israel', or 'Israel'. According to the Foreign Relations Authorization Act,[86] citizens or a legal guardian of a U.S. citizen born in the city of Jerusalem are eligible to request that their recorded place of birth be Israel. The parents' demand was denied. A U.S. embassy official mentioned the executive branch's constant policy to deny recognition of any national sovereignty claim over Jerusalem, and the U.S. Supreme Court indicated that the case raised a delicate query within subjects linked with Jerusalem (*see Zivotofsky v. Kerry 2015*).[87] In accordance with the U.S. Supreme Court, similar matters are committed to the legislature and the executive, not to the judiciary (*see Zivotofsky v. Kerry 2015*).[88]

The Supreme Court addressed the substance of international debate and the conflicts concerning the Jerusalem statute. The Court emphasised that this critical issue was for Congress and the president to decide upon in order to shape the nation's foreign policies, in addition to the legal consequences of formally recognising Jerusalem (*see Zivotofsky v. Kerry 2015*).[89] The Court mainly explored two questions to decide in the case. Firstly, does the president have exclusive power to grant recognition to a foreign sovereign? Secondly, if the president has that power, then the court must determine whether Congress can command the president and

[85] *Zivotofsky ex rel. Zivotofsky v. Kerry*, 135 S. Ct. 2076, 576 U.S., 192 L. Ed. 2d 83 (2015).

[86] Forging Relations Authorization Act, Fiscal Year 2003, 11 Stat. 1350, 30, September 2002 (United States).

[87] *Zivotofsky ex rel. Zivotofsky v. Kerry*, 135 S. Ct. 2076, 576 U.S., 192 L. Ed. 2d 83 (2015), paragraph 3.

[88] *Zivotofsky ex rel. Zivotofsky v. Kerry*, 135 S. Ct. 2076, 576 U.S., 192 L. Ed. 2d 83 (2015).

[89] *Zivotofsky ex rel. Zivotofsky v. Kerry*, 135 S. Ct. 2076, 576 U.S., 192 L. Ed. 2d 83 (2015), paragraph 18.

his or her secretary of state to issue a formal statement to contradict the earlier recognition. The court held that the president has the exclusive power to recognise (or not recognise) foreign nations (*see Zivotofsky v. Kerry 2015*)[90]; therefore, Congress cannot require the State Department to indicate in passports that Jerusalem is part of Israel. The Court also held that precedent and history support the view that formal recognition power belongs exclusively to the president. Because the executive branch has maintained a neutral position by not recognising any nation's sovereignty over Jerusalem, the federal statute in question unconstitutionally infringes on the president's recognition power.[91]

That means the former American presidents were aware of the importance of formal recognition of the sovereignty of Israel over United Jerusalem, and therefore they postponed it as it is not a symbolic shift, unlike Trump.[92] The Supreme Court decision reflects the fact that there is embedded significant power of recognition of the sovereignty of Israel over United Jerusalem that is challenging the international community's view of East Jerusalem's status. It has an impact on the ground, under some circumstances, it might lead to an outbreak of war but also brings certain privileges to the country's legal system. The Supreme Court until *Zivotofsky ex rel. Zivotofsky v. Kerry (see Zivotofsky v. Kerry 2015)*,[93] had never been called upon to determine whether the president alone, the Congress or the president and the Congress concurrently possessed the power of the recognition the Israeli sovereignty over United Jerusalem (Reinstein 2013),[94] through stipulating the place of birth section in the U.S passport[95] which indicated to add the place of the birth as Israel.[96] Thus, this provision contrasts the executive branch's long-held position not to recognise any nations possessing formal sovereignty over Jerusalem (*see Zivotofsky v. Kerry 2015*).[97] Therefore, the Supreme Court refrained from using such a powerful move by rejecting the approval of the registration (*see Zivotofsky v. Kerry 2015*).[98]

---

[90] According to the 1787 constitution (United States), paragraphs 27 and 56, neither Israel nor any other country was acknowledged as having sovereignty over Jerusalem. 57, *Zivotofsky ex rel. Zivotofsky v. Kerry*, 135 S. Ct. 2076, 576 U.S., 192 L. Ed. 2d 83 (2015).

[91] At 8 June 2015, thus before Trump decision.

[92] Jerusalem Embassy (1995), Public Law 104–54. Former presidents officially avoided fulfilling the Jerusalem Embassy Act. American presidential candidates from both Democratic and republican parties have promised to move the US Embassy in Israel to Jerusalem. Bill Clinton a presidential candidate in 1992, stated, 'Jerusalem is still the capital of Israel and must remain an undivided city accessible to all'. In 2000, George W. Bush while running for the presidency pledged to 'begin the process of moving' the US embassy to Jerusalem as soon as assumed the office. Furthermore, In 2008 Barack Obama took an even stronger stand in supporting Israel than his predecessors. In 2008, Obama emphasized, 'Jerusalem is the capital of Israel and must remain undivided'. However, once elected, they refrained from implementing the idea.

[93] *Zivotofsky ex rel. Zivotofsky v. Kerry*, 135 S. Ct. 2076, 576 U.S., 192 L. Ed. 2d 83 (2015).

[94] Reinstein, Robert J. "Is the President's Recognition Power Exclusive." *Temp. L. Rev.* 86 (2013): 4.

[95] Section 214(d) of the Foreign Relations Authorization Act (2003).

[96] 135 S. Ct 2076 (2015).

[97] *Zivotofsky ex rel. Zivotofsky v. Kerry*, 135 S. Ct. 2076, 576 U.S., 192 L. Ed. 2d 83 (2015).

[98] *Zivotofsky ex rel. Zivotofsky v. Kerry*, 135 S. Ct. 2076, 576 U.S., 192 L. Ed. 2d 83 (2015).

l consequences on the formal recognition of Jerusalem as part of the sovereign territory of Israel. Therefore, this will raise questions touching upon the history and holiness of Jerusalem and its present legal and international status, which are among the most problematic and controversial issues in international affairs.

The international community, through the UN Security Council, challenged the U.S. proposal. On 18 December 2017, when they listened to a report on the issue by Special Coordinator for the Middle East Peace Process and Personal Representative of the Secretary-General Nickolay Mladenov (See UN Doc S/PV.8128),[99] at Egypt's initiative, a draft resolution was tabled before the Security Council. Although 14 members approved and voted in favour, as a result of the U.S. delegation's veto, the resolution failed to be adopted. Turkey and Yemen also drafted a text along the same lines, which was then introduced before the General Assembly, convened in the resumed tenth emergency session on 21 December 2017. The following text was adopted by the General Assembly as resolution ES-10/19, by 129 votes in favour and nine against,[100] with 35 abstentions.[101] The resolution ES-10/19 stipulates that the General Assembly:

> 1. Affirms that any decisions and actions which purport to have altered the character, status or demographic composition of the Holy City of Jerusalem have no legal effect, are null and void and must be rescinded in compliance with relevant resolutions of the Security Council, and in this regard calls upon all States to refrain from the establishment of diplomatic missions in the Holy City of Jerusalem, pursuant to Council resolution 478 (1980);
>
> 2. Demands that all States comply with Security Council resolutions regarding the Holy City of Jerusalem, and not recognise any actions or measures contrary to those resolutions (see the meeting record of the Security Council 2017).[102]

In the Security Council and General Assembly meeting regarding the U.S. initiative to move the embassy to Jerusalem as contradicting international law, The United Nations failed to fulfil its responsibility to maintain international peace and security by not maintaining the status quo and stopping actions contrary to the resolutions, for instance, not preventing land expropriation, houses demolition that allowed the establishment of Jewish settlements in East Jerusalem, as the Israeli government establishing 'facts on the ground' strategy is through repudiation of international law to make it right, through the imposition of unilateral coercive measures violated

[99] See UN Doc S/PV.8128 (8 December 2017).

[100] Members states that voted against the resolution: Guatemala, Honduras, Israel, Marshall Islands, Micronesia, Nauru, Palau, United States.

[101] Member states that abstained: Antigua-Barbuda, Argentina, Australia, Bahamas, Benin, Bhutan, Bosnia-Herzegovina, Cameroon, Canada, Colombia, Croatia, Czech Republic, Dominican Republic, Equatorial Guinea, Fiji, Haiti, Hungary, Jamaica, Kiribati, Latvia, Lesotho, Malawi, Mexico, Panama, Paraguay, Philippines, Poland, Romania, Rwanda, Solomon Islands, South Sudan, Trinidad-Tobago, Tuvalu, Uganda, Vanuatu.

[102] The meeting record of the Security Council meeting held on 18 December 2017, The Situation in the Middle East, including the Palestinian Question (S/PV. 8139) and the press release issued the same day (UNSC/13125). During the meeting, the United States vetoed Draft Resolution S/ 2017/1060. There were no abstentions during the vote, and 14 other states composing the Security Council voted in favour of adoption.

international human rights.[103] This resulted in the General Assembly holding an emergency special session, during which it adopted Resolution ES-10/19, where it confirmed:

> That any decisions and actions which purport to have altered the character, status or demographic composition of the Holy City of Jerusalem have no legal effect, are null and void and must be rescinded in compliance with relevant resolutions of the Security Council.

Additionally, it called upon:

> all States to refrain from the establishment of diplomatic missions in the Holy City of Jerusalem, pursuant to Council resolution 478 (1980).[104]

Moreover, based on its resolutions on the status of the holy city, the General Assembly condemned the U.S. decision as having no legal effect and as being null and void. Notwithstanding all of the attempts to prevent the U.S. embassy from moving to Jerusalem, the U.S. inaugurated its embassy in Jerusalem on 14 May 2018.[105] To summarise, this is a critical matter because recognising United Jerusalem as the capital of Israel and relocating the U.S. embassy to Jerusalem might reflect the legitimacy of Israel's annexation. Also, this case includes violations of fundamental rules in international law, such as the prohibition of territorial acquisitions through the use of force. Furthermore, the outcome—that the Security Council did not act or provide any assistance—may help in consolidating the illegal situation.

8 The Palestinian Endeavour to Access the International Justice System

The Vienna Convention on Diplomatic Relations can be used as a tool to request that the U.S. embassy withdraw from Jerusalem. Under Article 2 of the Vienna Convention on Diplomatic Relations, to reflect a state's sovereignty, the right of legation[106]—the establishment of diplomatic relations between states and of permanent diplomatic missions—must take place by mutual consent and is an essential step. The general practice is for missions to be established in the seat of government of the receiving state and for the government to be followed if it moves, either permanently or to a summer residence (Denza 2016). This was a substance of convenience, reflecting the need for a mission to conduct business with the government. Yet, neither international nor customary law requires missions to be sent to the receiving state's capital or seat of government (Denza 2016). This might explain why most diplomatic missions to

[103] Mechanism established by the United Nations General Assembly Resolution 377 (V), Uniting peace. Adopted on 3 November 1950.

[104] UNSC Res. ES-10/19, 2334 (2016).

[105] The press statement issued by the Secretary of State of the United States Mike Pompeo on 14 May 2018, available at https://www.state.gov/secetary/remarks/2018/05/282066.htm (Accessed on 10 October 2019).

[106] Ius legationis.

Israel remained in Tel-Aviv, given that moving missions to Jerusalem implies the acceptance of Israel's sovereignty and establishment of its seat of government (see Article 12 Vienna Convention on Diplomatic Relations 1961).[107]

Therefore, the government of the State of Palestine submitted an application to the ICJ instituting proceedings against the U.S.[108] The Palestinians requested that the Court settle the dispute over moving the embassy to Jerusalem based on the Vienna Convention on Diplomatic Relations.[109] This step was followed by the government initially addressing the U.S. through a *note verbale* expressing that relocating the embassy comprised a violation of the court's request to settle the dispute over the embassy moving to Jerusalem, based on the Vienna Convention on Diplomatic Relations,[110] alongside the related UN Security Council resolutions on the alteration of the status of Jerusalem, particularly resolution 478 (1980).[111] According to the submission, the U.S. embassy's relocation to Jerusalem breached the Vienna Convention on Diplomatic Relations (see Vienna Convention on Diplomatic Relations 1961).[112] the Palestinian government considered the convention as an implementation of international relations resolutions.[113] According to Article 1 of the Vienna Convention on Diplomatic Relations, the main purpose of diplomatic missions is 'representing

[107] Article 12, Offices away from the seat of the mission; diplomatic law, Vienna Convention on Diplomatic Relations, 18 April 1961.

[108] On July 2018, according to the UNSC Res. (9) (1946) Article 35 (2) of the Statute of the Court, a 'Declaration recognizing the Competence of the International Court of Justice' for the settlement of all disputes that may arise or that have already arisen covered under Articles I and II of the Optional Protocol.; The State of Palestine institutes proceedings against the United States of America, On 28 September 2018. The State of Palestine instituted proceedings in the Hague, against the United States of America before the International Court of Justice (ICJ), the principal judicial organ of the United Nations, with respect to a dispute concerning alleged violations of the Vienna Convention on Diplomatic Relations of 18April 1961. Available: https://www.icj-cij.org/public/files/case-related/176/176-20180928-PRE-01-00-EN.pdf [last visited march 2022].

[109] Article I of the Optional Protocol concerning the Compulsory Settlement of disputes provides that disputes arising out of the interpretation or application of the International Court of Justice may accordingly be brought before the Court by an application made by any party to the dispute being party to the present protocol. This provision covers any dispute related to the interpretation or application of the Convention on Diplomatic Relations, to which Palestine and the United States are contracting parties.

[110] Dated 14 May 2018.

[111] Adopted 20 August 1980.

[112] Vienna Convention on Diplomatic Relations, 18 April 1961.

[113] The Preamble of the Vienna Convention on Diplomatic Relations, stipulated:

> Having in mind the purposes and principles of the Charter of the United Nations concerning the sovereign equality of States, the maintenance of international peace and security and promotion of friendly relations among nations. Furthermore: Believing that an international convention on diplomatic intercourse, privileges and immunities would contribute to the development of friendly relations among nations, irrespective of their differing constitutional and social systems.

the sending State in the receiving State'.[114] This clearly states that the representational function of any diplomatic mission should be performed on the territory of the receiving state, which raised the sovereignty question about Jerusalem. Furthermore, Article 3(b) states that the interests of the sending state and its nationals are protected in the receiving state, within limits permitted by international law.[115] Additionally, section d of Article 3 discusses 'Ascertaining by lawful means conditions and development in the receiving State, and reporting thereon to the Government of sending State'.[116] The significance of this provision is that the sending state must establish its diplomatic mission on the territory of the receiving state, 'within limits permitted by international law' (see 12 Vienna Convention on Diplomatic Relations 1961).[117] This contradicts both the general approach to approval of Jerusalem's annexation and the Palestinian opinion both considering the annexation of East Jerusalem as illegal which raised the sovereignty question about Jerusalem. According to Palestine state argued that the diplomatic mission of a sending State must be established on the territory of the receiving State which means that the mission must be established in the receiving state. Jerusalem is not Israeli territory, and therefore moving the embassy there meant that it was not established in the receiving state. Therefore the relocation of the United States Embassy in Israel to Jerusalem constitutes a breach of the Vienna Convention (see ICL No. 2018/47 2018).[118] Furthermore, Article 21, paragraph 1 of the Vienna Convention on Diplomatic Relations specifies that 'The receiving State shall either facilitate the acquisition on its territory in accordance with the laws, by the sending State of premises necessary for its mission or assist the latter in obtaining accommodation in some other way'.[119] The Vienna Convention on Diplomatic Relations states a framework for the actions and purposes of diplomatic missions and proposes general limitations:

> The premises of the mission must not be used in any manner incompatible with functions of the mission as laid down in the present Convention or by other rules of general international law or by any special agreement in force between the sending and receiving State (see article 41, paragraph 3, Vienna Convention on Diplomatic Relations 1961).[120]

Therefore, the abovementioned provisions of the Vienna Convention on Diplomatic Relations illustrate that the sending state can expect to establish a diplomatic mission in the receiving state and should emphasise that the diplomatic mission must accomplish its tasks while respecting the rule of law in general and international law in particular. Therefore, the relocation of the U.S. embassy to Jerusalem violates

[114] Article 3, paragraph 1(a), Vienna Convention on Diplomatic Relations, 18 April 1961.

[115] Article 3, paragraph 1(b), Vienna Convention on Diplomatic Relations, 18 April 1961.

[116] Article 3, paragraph 1(d), Vienna Convention on Diplomatic Relations, 18 April 1961.

[117] 'In the receiving state' is presented in 12 provisions of the Vienna Convention on Diplomatic Relations, (18 April 1961) not just in article 3.

[118] ICL No. 2018/47 28 September 2018 The State of Palestine institutes proceedings against the United States of America.

[119] Article 21, Vienna Convention on Diplomatic Relations, 18 April 1961.

[120] Article 41, paragraph 3, Vienna Convention on Diplomatic Relations, 18 April 1961.

the Vienna Convention on Diplomatic Relations and other rules of general international law (see Vienna Convention on Diplomatic Relations 1961).[121] The Palestinian government filing its application was a positive action, as it seeks to investigate new strategies and paths with which to advance Palestinians' desire for freedom and just peace.

This step can be viewed as Third World moment, similar to the Nicaragua case (see The Republic of Nicaragua V. The United States of America, 1986),[122] where the ICJ held that the U.S. had violated international law by supporting the Contras in their rebellion against the Sandinistas and by mining Nicaragua's harbours. The U.S. was responsible for illegal military and parliamentary activities against Nicaragua. Although the question of jurisdiction and admissibility are primarily based on the principle the ICJ has only as much power as that agreed to by the parties, these can be complicated. The 1946 declaration of the U.S. and the 1929 declaration of Nicaragua were the main focus of these declarations and pointed out the respective parties' intent as it related to the ICJ jurisdiction (see The Republic of Nicaragua V. The United States of America, 1986).[123] In both instances, it is a Third World country challenging the U.S. in the ICJ. Yet, the challenges and the limitations should

[121] The objects and purposes that Vienna Convention on Diplomatic Relations refers; see also: The Wall Advisory Opinion of the International Court of Justice, ICJ Reports, 2004 ICJ Rep 136, paragraph 78, 4 July 2014.

[122] The Republic of Nicaragua V. The United States of America, 1986 I.C.J.14., ICJ, Nicaragua v. United States of America, Military and Paramilitary Activities, Judgments of 27 June 1986, Merits, online: http://www.icj-cij.org. the case concerning military and Paramilitary Activities in and against Nicaragua. This decision in the *Nicaragua* case is important judgments delivered by the International Court. It deals in detail with the multilateral treaty reservation of the United States (the "Vandenberg amendment"). It contains provocative reasoning about the genesis and maintenance of rules of customary international law, separate from treaties such as the United Nations Charter. It contains seminal findings on the use of force and the exercise of the inherent right of self-defense under Article 51 of the Charter. It presents fresh and doubtless controversial interpretations of the principle of nonintervention. It prescribes limits to "collective counter-measures" in response to conduct not deemed to amount to "armed attacks." It has broken new ground for the application of Article 53 of the Statute.

[123] The Republic of Nicaragua V. The United States of America, 1986 I.C.J.14, ICJ, Nicaragua v. United States of America, Military and Paramilitary Activities, Judgments of 27 June 1986, Merits, online: http://www.icj-cij.org. the case concerning military and Paramilitary Activities in and against Nicaragua. This decision in the *Nicaragua* case is important judgments delivered by the International Court. It deals in detail with the multilateral treaty reservation of the United States (the "Vandenberg amendment"). It contains provocative reasoning about the genesis and maintenance of rules of customary international law, separate from treaties such as the United Nations Charter. It contains seminal findings on the use of force and the exercise of the inherent right of self-defense under Article 51 of the Charter. It presents fresh and doubtless controversial interpretations of the principle of nonintervention. It prescribes limits to "collective counter-measures" in response to conduct not deemed to amount to "armed attacks." It has broken new ground for the application of Article 53 of the Statute.

be acknowledged for Palestine. Despite the fact that Palestine was granted non-member observer State status[124] and acceded to the Vienna Convention on Diplomatic Relations (see Vienna Convention on Diplomatic Relations 1961),[125] to reflect a state's sovereignty, the right of legation in 2014 and its Optional Protocol in 2018 (State of Palestine: Accession 2014),[126] this was over U.S. opposition.[127] The U.S. has stated that it does not recognise responsibilities under the the Vienna Convention on Diplomatic Relations (see Vienna Convention on Diplomatic Relations 1961),[128] vis-a-vis the Palestinian people.[129] In response to the ICJ suit, in 2018 the U.S. announced its withdrawal from the Optional Protocol (Galbraith 2019). Yet, it is unclear whether the withdrawal will have any effect on the case as it occurred after the Palestinian people initiated proceedings at the ICJ (Loureen 2018). Thus, the ICJ is undertaking jurisdictional and admissibility inquiries into the case which go to the heart of the dispute Therefore this time ICJ may not exercise its jurisdiction over the legal interests of a state absent (see Monetary Gold Removed from Rome 1943),[130] as If the case is successful it might contribute to decolonisation of the system in contrast with the ICJ Advisory Opinion on Construction of a Wall in the Occupied Palestinian Territory (see ICJ Rep 19, 32 1054).[131] as the judgment of the ICJ would be legally binding for both parties as stated in article 94 of the UN Charter (see UN Charter).[132] As a result, the ICJ judgment will give guidance on disputes on statehood and *erga omnes* obligations like the right of the Palestinian people to self-determination. This reflects the importance of this ICJ case.

9 Conclusion

As a result of the relocation of the U.S. embassy to Jerusalem, several countries followed suit and relocated their embassies to Jerusalem, such as Guatemala and Paraguay (Al-Haq 2018). However, while Paraguay decided to move its embassy,

[124] "General Assembly grants Palestine non-member observer State status at UN," UN News (November 29, 2012) *available at* https://news.un.org/en/story/2012/11/427052-general-assembly-grants-palestine-non-member-observer-state-status-un.

[125] Vienna Convention on Diplomatic Relations, 18 April 1961.

[126] State of Palestine: Accession (April 9, 2014) *available at* https://treaties.un.org/doc/Publication/CN/2014/CN.176.2014-Eng.pdf.

[127] United States of America: Communication (May 1, 2018) *available at* https://treaties.un.org/doc/Publication/CN/2018/CN.228.2018-Eng.pdf.

[128] Vienna Convention on Diplomatic Relations, 18 April 1961.

[129] United States of America: Communication (May 1, 2018) *available at* https://treaties.un.org/doc/Publication/CN/2018/CN.228.2018-Eng.pdf.

[130] *Monetary Gold Removed from Rome in 1943* (Italy v France, UK and US) (Preliminary Question) [1954] ICJ Rep 19, 32.

[131] ICJ Advisory Opinion on Construction of a Wall in the Occupied Palestinian Territory, Int'l Ct Justice July 9, 2004), 43 ILM 1009 (2004).

[132] UN Charter, https://treaties.un.org/doc/publication/ctc/uncharter.pdf.

on 5 September 2018, it cancelled its decision and moved its embassy back to Tel-Aviv. The Republic of Paraguay explained that the decision was made in line with its constitutional commitments to respect international law. The Czech Republic, Slovakia, Romania, Panama and Honduras, United Kingdom (Wintour 2022)[133] have all expressed their intention for future relocation.

The decision to recognise Jerusalem as the capital of Israel and to move the U.S. embassy to the city is part of what has been characterised as an 'outside-in' method to the Israeli-Palestinian conflict, with the U.S. client states in the region progressively normalising relationships with Israel and consenting with Israeli views while simultaneously forcing the Palestinians to make further concessions to Israel (Khalidi 2018). Without dismissing the profound shifts in U.S. public opinion in particular and the new international environment in general, a future Israeli-Palestinian peace agreement on Jerusalem appears challenging. Against this backdrop, the follow-up question would be whether international law has any role to play in this complicated and politically loaded subject, or if its role will be merely peripheral to any political settlement. Although international law has repeatedly failed to provide answers and may not offer magical solutions, yet, relying on rules of international law might help to avoid political obstacles if all countries do not follow the U.S. recognition.[134]

Palestine should pursue all possible legal avenues to exercise pressure on Israel and on the U.S., while expressing intention as a law-enduring state willing to rely on international law against powerful Israel and U.S. who are unwilling to submit themselves to binding dispute resolution. In other words, this is an attempt to construct and further a Palestinian narrative linked with Jerusalem's status.

There is no question that self-determination is the absolute aspiration and right of all Palestinians and that the Palestinians are facing a continuing risk of violating their rights under international law—international human rights law and international humanitarian law. Nonetheless, it is pragmatic and essential to explore avenues to protect the Palestinian overlap between human rights and their cultural and religious practices. The annexation of East Jerusalem prevents the Palestinians from exercising the freedom to practice their cultural-religious practices, lifestyle, accessibility to reach the holy places and therefore, the annexation impact can lead to the degradation of their cultural practices and lifestyle in accordance with the International Covenant on Economic, Social and Cultural Rights.

The remaining question is if there is still faith that international law and the international community—including the majority that opposes the recognition of Jerusalem as the capital of Israel and considers the initiative null and void— still works for the Third World in this instance. International community should support searching for and providing suggestions for peace in this region. This means that under international law, a definitive settlement linked with Jerusalem can only be

[133] Liz Truss in the *UN general assembly meeting in New York*, 9.22.

[134] The decision is contrary to the well-established rule of international law which articulate that states must not recognize the fruits of conquest. Role can be played by General Assembly, ICJ proceeding against the U.S. Israel one legal position. Palestinians/ others have opposing that legal position against the recognition act to request sanctions or other coercive.

achieved by agreement between the concerned parties, subject to the consent of the UN. International law requires a negotiation process that involves the two parties of the area, the legitimate representatives of the Palestinian people and other members of the world community. Moreover, this process will necessarily require several mutual adjustments and compromises by the concerned parties and by global politics. Additionally, without forgetting the cruciality of Jerusalem's holiness to monotheistic religion, the process should also account for the international community's keen interest in safeguarding the city's holy places and making good on its promise of furthering global justice. It seems that only on these conditions can a peace resolution acceptable to the world community be achieved, rather than by approving an illegal annexation by a powerful state. Therefore, it is essential for Palestinians to improve and develop new mechanisms with which to reach freedom and a just peace.

The main part of the task ahead is political, not legal. However, while the law will not dictate any particular outcome, it can draw baselines for parties, set limits and help to advance negotiations by providing a common language for discussion. Ultimately, the question is about whose burden it is to break political stalemates when peace negotiations fail. It is suggested that the current U.S. administration, President Biden's administration refuses to contribute to efforts to reach a peaceful solution for the Israeli-Palestinian conflict. By recognising Jerusalem as the capital of Israel, the US should be internationally condemned because it supports the illegal annexation. Moreover, Israel has the duty, according to international law, to conduct negotiations in good faith for a peaceful solution. It would seem that Israel, with the support of the U.S., has proposed unreasonable conditions or otherwise obstructed peace negotiations to maintain control over Jerusalem, which could be considered violations of international law. The act of moving the embassy to Jerusalem is one example of the ultimate endorsement that the U.S. provided to Israel policy to ensure the hegemony over Jerusalem. Even post-Trump's administration, Biden's administration failed to meet his pledge to reopen a consulate for Palestinians in Jerusalem.[135] According to Biden's campaign, while addressing the Arab-American communities:

> As President, Biden will take immediate steps to restore economic and humanitarian assistance to the Palestinian people, consistent with U.S. law, including assistance to refugees, work to address the ongoing humanitarian crisis in Gaza, reopen the U.S. consulate in East Jerusalem, and work to reopen the PLO mission in Washington.[136]

By officially shuttering the consulate in Jerusalem in 2019, the U.S. downgraded the status of its primary diplomatic mission in Palestine by folding it into the U.S. Embassy to Israel. The claims that this will achieve significant efficiencies and increase effectiveness. Although portraying this act as merely a bureaucratic management move, de facto, this downgrading of the consulate has a powerful symbolic resonance that suggests indirect American recognition of the Israeli control over East Jerusalem. Secretary of State Mike Pompeo announced merging the consulate into

---

[135] American consulate in Jerusalem used to provide services to Palestinians in East Jerusalem, the West Bank, and Gaza since 1967, During Trump's administration the American consulate closed its doors.

[136] The Biden campaign's platform for Arab-American communities.

the embassy For decades, the consulate functioned as a de facto embassy to the Palestinians.[137] Now, that outreach will be handled by a Palestinian affairs unit under the command of the embassy.[138] Consequently, providing annual aid and military assistance packages enabled Israeli intransigence in its policies to expand Jerusalem's colonization and Jewish settlements expansion and encouraged Israel's policy to ensure hegemony over all of Jerusalem. Trump's administration's recognition of Jerusalem made it evident that the U.S. was never a neutral mediator in the Israeli-Palestinian conflict challenging the decades long U.S. position that indicated that the status of Jerusalem should be determined in negotiations and such a shift complicated future peace (Erakat 2019).

Furthermore, state support might be considered a disadvantage, as a peaceful settlement of the conflict should be driven by the sensible interests of both parties. This suggests that any measure aimed at creating new hurdles to the negotiations by shifting the status quo in Jerusalem will also be contaminated with illegality (Hussein 2021; Erakat 2021). The correct solution can only be found by weighing the damage that such steps would cause to the future peace solution and the various interests involved.

References

Al-Haq. 2018. *Guatemala and Paraguay Embassy Relocation to Jerusalem Blatantly Disregards Jerusalem Internationally Protected Status and Violates United Nations Resolutions*. 23. May. www.alhaq.org/advocacy/6200.html.

Beinin, Joel, and Lisa Hajjar. 2014. Palestine, Israel and the Arab-Israeli Conflict. *Middle East: The Middle East Research and Information Project*, 4.

Cassese, Antonio. 1986. Legal considerations on the International Status of Jerusalem. *The Palestine Yearbook of International Law Online* 3(1): 13–39.

Cattan, Henry. 1976. *Palestine and International Law: The Legal Aspects of the Arab-Israeli Conflict*. Longman Publishing Group, 37.

Dumper, Michael. 2002. *The politics of sacred space: The Old City of Jerusalem in the middle east conflict*. Lynne Rienner Publishers.

Denza, Eileen. 2016. *Diplomatic law: Commentary on the Vienna convention on diplomatic relations*. Oxford University Press; Hardy, Michael James Langley. *Modern diplomatic law*, vol. 9. Manchester University Press, 1968.

Erakat, Noura. 2019. Justice for some. In *Justice for some*. Stanford University Press.

Erakat, Noura. 2021. Justice for some: Law and the question of Palestine (2019). *The Palestine Yearbook of International Law Online* 22(1): 201–216.

Getachew, Adom. 2019. Worldmaking after Empire. In *Worldmaking after Empire*. Princeton University Press.

[137] Press Statement Michael R. Pompeo Secretary of State Washington, DC, October 18, 2018. Previously, the consul general running the Jerusalem consulate had his/her own chief of mission authority. The closest comparable case to the Jerusalem situation is the U.S. consulate in Hong Kong, which also has its own chief of mission who does not report to the U.S. ambassador in Beijing.

[138] Press Statement Michael R. Pompeo Secretary of State Washington, DC, October 18, 2018.

Glass, Joseph B., and Rassem Khamaisi. 2005. Report on the socio-economic conditions in the Old City of Jerusalem. *The Jerusalem Project, Munk Centre for International Studies, University of Toronto.*

Galbraith, Jean. 2019. Palestine brings a case against the United States in the international court of justice at a fraught time for US-Palestine Relations. *American Journal of International Law* 113: 143, 145.

Hussein, Hadeel S. Abu. 2021. *The struggle for land under Israeli law: An architecture of exclusion.* Routledge.

Imseis, Ardi. 1999. Facts on the ground: An examination of Israeli municipal policy in East Jerusalem. *American University International Law Review* 15: 1039–1040.

Jamal, A. 2005. *The citizenship glossary for the Arab students in Israel.* Jerusalem: Hebrew University [Arabic].

Jerusalem Embassy Act. 1959. Public Law 104-54, adopted by the U.S. Congress in 1995.

Kassim, Anis F., ed. 1997. *The Palestine Yearbook of International Law, 1995.* Martinus Nijhoff Publishers.

Kattan, V. 2009. 'From coexistence to conquest: international law and the origins of the Arab-Israeli conflict' Pluto Pr: 1891–1949.

Kedar, Alexander Sandy, and Oren Yiftachel. 2006. Land regime and social relations in Israel. *Swiss Human Rights Book* 1: 127, 130.

Khalidi, Walid. 2005. Why did the Palestinians leave, revisited. *Journal of Palestine Studies* 34(2): 42–54. With the exception of some leaders of the National Liberation League and the communists.

Khalidi, Walid. 1961. Plan Dalet: Master plan for the conquest of Palestine. *Middle East Forum* 37 (9): 22–28.

Khalidi, Rashid. 2020. *The Hundred Years' war on Palestine: A history of settler colonialism and resistance, 1917–2017.* Metropolitan Books.

Khalidi, Rashid I. 2018. And now what? The trump administration and the question of Jerusalem. *Journal of Palestine Studies* 47(3): 93–102.

Loureen Sayej. 2018. State of Palestine takes United States to International Court of Justice over Jerusalem Embassy,Oxford Human Rights Hub (Nov. 8). https://ohrh.law.ox.ac.uk/state-of-palestine-takes-unitedstates-to-international-court-of-justice-over-jerusalem-embassy/.

Quigley, John. 1990. *Palestine and Israel: A challenge to justice*, 47–53. Duke University Press.

Reinstein, Robert J. 2013. Is the President's recognition power exclusive. *Temp. L. Rev.* 86: 4.

Sa'di Ahmad. 2006. Memory and identity. In "Towards a Historical Narrative of the Nakba" *Mada-al-Carmel*, The Arab Centre for Applied Social Research, Haifa, 57–79 [Arabic].

Schoenberg, Harris O. 1989. Limits of self-determination. In *Israel Yearbook on Human Rights, Volume 6 (1976)*, 91–103.97, Brill Nijhoff.

Shlaim, Avi. 2004. The war between Israeli Historians. *Annales. Histoire, Sciences Sociales* 59(1): 161–169. Editions de l'EHESS.

Strawson, John. 2001. Reflections on Edward Said and the legal narratives of Palestine: Israeli settlements and Palestinian self-determination. *Penn State International Review* 20: 363.

The Palestine Yearbook of International Law, E. 2004.Written statement submitted by palestine to the international court of justice with respect to the request for an advisory opinion regarding legal consequences of the construction of a wall in the occupied palestinian territory. *The Palestine Yearbook of International Law Online* 13(1): 133–399. https://doi.org/10.1163/221161405X00071.

Tomeh, G. J., Regina Sherif, and Michael Simpson, eds. 1975. *United Nations Resolutions on Palestine and the Arab-Israeli Conflict: 1947–1974*, vol. 1. Institute for Palestine Studies.

Waage, H.H. 2011. The winner takes all: The 1949 Island of Rhodes armistice negotiations revisited. *Middle East Journal* 65 (2): 279–304.

Whiteman, Marjorie Millace. 1963. *Digest of international law*, vol. 15. US Department of State.

Wintour, P. 2022 Arab diplomats urge Liz Truss not to move British embassy to Jerusalem. *The Guardian*, 30 September. https://www.theguardian.com/politics/2022/sep/30/arab-diplomats-urge-liz-truss-not-move-british-embassy-jerusalem.

Wolfrum, Rudiger, ed. 2013. *The Max Planck Encyclopedia of Public International Law: Index and Tables*, vol. 11. Oxford University Press.

Zureiq, Constantin. 1948. "The Meaning of Disaster"—'Maa'na Al-Nakba', Beirut:11 [Arabic].

The Struggles for Corporate Accountability in the UN: A Global South Perspective

Flávia do Amaral Vieira

Abstract This chapter investigates the civil society experience of struggling for the adoption of a binding instrument for holding transnational corporations accountable for human rights violations. Since the historical adoption of the 2014 UN Resolution 26/9, that initiated the negotiations of a treaty on business and human rights, every year, civil society groups attend and participate in the negotiation sessions. The chapter engages in participatory observation research in two of these sessions. Describing them and exploring the power asymmetries that characterise global civil society, it questions the representations of international institutions and how human rights are created in this context. It relies on the insistence of the third world approach to international law (TWAIL) that issues of distribution and power imbalances affect the way international law is produced and understood. Observations indicate that these sessions offer more than opportunities for activism and contestation. For civil society, they are also spaces for knowledge production and learning, for acquiring and applying expertise, an integral part of how people learn to be human rights experts, sharing experiences and striving to influence the setting of international standards.

1 Introduction

On December 4, 1972, Salvador Allende, then president of Chile (1970–1973), delivered a historic speech at the 27th General Assembly of the United Nations (UN). "International law does not have to be identified with the interests of large capitalist companies", Allende (1972) stated, expressing his frustration over embedded forms of imperialism posing threats to Chile. It was the first time that the role of foreign transnational companies in the construction of instabilities in democratically elected governments was mentioned in that space. Just when decolonisation processes were on the rise in different parts of the world, that was followed with frustration over the

F. do Amaral Vieira (✉)
Federal University of Santa Catarina, Florianópolis, Brazil
e-mail: ei_flavia@hotmail.com

T. Venthan Ananthavinayagan and A. Viswanath Shenoy (eds.), *The Wretched of the Global South*, International Law and the Global South,
https://doi.org/10.1007/978-981-99-9275-1_12

lack of change in global economic systems and standards of living in post-colonial states (Hammouri 2020).

Indeed, the *coup d'état* in Chile, which took place shortly after Allende's speech marks the beginning of the rise of neoliberalism, which first hegemonised Chile, and subsequently much of Latin America. Allende's speech galvanised the proliferation of solidarity movements across the Global South and at the UN where it culminated in the New International Economic Order. One important theme of these movements was the integration of corporate accountability into human rights framework. Since then, two perspectives on the subject have emerged: one advocating for an international treaty that imposes legally binding human rights obligations on transnational corporations; and another that favours their regulation through soft law instruments (Deva 2013; Rodrigues-Garavito and Evans 2018).

Unsurprisingly, the business community presented a united front against the creation of any human rights standard that could affect its structure and operation. That has resulted in their successful efforts to stop attempts since the 1970s at the UN for adopting a binding instrument, such as the UN Code for Transnational Corporations and the Draft Norms on the Responsibilities of Transnational Corporations and Other Business Enterprises with regard to Human Rights. Instead, several soft law instruments were adopted, such as the 1976 OECD Guidelines for Multinational Enterprises, and the 1999 Global Compact.

In 2011, the Human Rights Council adopted the UN Guiding Principles for Business and Human Rights (UNGP), recognised as the most prominent instrument within this agenda. The UNGP was the result of the work of John Ruggie as UN Special Representative of the Secretary-General on the issue of human rights and transnational corporations and other business enterprises (RESG). In its 2008 report, he formulated the conceptual framework "Protect, Respect and Remedy: A Framework on Business and Human Rights", offering global parameters to prevent and address negative human rights impacts related to business activities (UNHRC 2008).

Even so, critics of the UNGP and other soft law instruments highlight that they are not capable to effectively challenge the control that corporations, especially transnationals (TNCs), exercise over their own accountability process (Aragão and Roland 2017). In this sense, despite the opening of new forums, they are instruments very similar to those of Corporate Social Responsibility (CSR). Peña Guterrez (2012) defines CSR as an internal code of conduct for the company that includes a set of rules and principles concerning ethical values and responsible actions aimed at workers, company managers, and other interested parties. It is basically characterised by voluntariness, unilaterality—it is the company itself that defines the content of the code and its control mechanisms-, self-regulation—controls are usually carried out by independent external audits, which are often paid by the companies themselves—and not legally binding. Today, CSR involves a complex market of companies, consultancies agencies, and NGOs, made up of several instruments of private regulation. Good corporate practices exist when they are translated into shareholder returns, and that is why CSR mobilises an industry created to identify business vulnerabilities, acquiring greater ability to neutralise conflicts, to prevent any social action capable of negatively affecting the corporate reputation and the expected income (Acserald 2019).

Taking this into account, it is remarkable that in 2014, with the support of States as Equator and South Africa, a new path was opened, with the historical adoption of Resolution 26/9, now known as the 'treaty resolution'. The resolution created the Open-ended Intergovernmental Working Group on Transnational Corporations and Other Business Enterprises with respect to Human Rights (OEIGWG) to negotiate a binding instrument on business and human rights. Since then, every year, civil society groups have attended and participated in the negotiation sessions.

In this chapter, I offer a Global South perspective to shed light on their experiences in the struggle for the adoption of a binding instrument for holding transnational corporations accountable for human rights violations. Assuming that it is important to understand human rights activism as a set of practices, forms of social action, that engage in a 'labour of transformation', in the struggle for justice and reparation, through different institutional spaces and even divergent ideological orientations (Baxi 2007), I explore the specific set of activism and resistance of the treaty movement for corporate accountability, particularly interested on the possibilities of the creation of human rights in this context.

In 2016 and 2019, I followed the sessions of the OEIGWG at one of the UN main buildings, in Geneva. By describing how these sessions operated and through interviews I conducted with women from social movements and NGOs who actively participate in the sessions,[1] I question the representations of international institutions that focus only on the content of their documents and public statements. I show how the OEIGWG sessions are not only a space of activism and contestation but also a meeting point, a place for knowledge production and learning, for acquiring and applying expertise. They are an integral part of how people learn to be UN and human rights experts, by sharing experiences and striving to influence the creation of international standards and reforms.

Dealing with the idea of immersing ourselves in the daily life of international law, we can challenge the traditional ways and forms in which international law is represented: as the law of exceptional actions and relations centred on the State and its position as normatively superior and foreign (Eslava and Pahuja 2011). For that, I engage with Third World Approaches to International Law (TWAIL), in search of tuning the operation of international law to those sites and subjects that have traditionally been positioned as the 'others of international law', emphasising that issues of distribution and power imbalances affect the way legal thought is produced and understood. Here, TWAIL works as a lens to understand international law and human rights, sharing this method of sensitivity to the South, this replacement of the Global South as a legitimate place of knowledge production, reading the lines of history of the political order as facts and as myths, from the post-colonial experience.

In the following, I explain primary issues on global civil society and its asymmetries of power, to present the background of the debate on the binding treaty. I

---

[1] All participants in this research were informed of its objectives and agreed to participate freely, authorizing the publication in anonymity.

then explore documents, interviews, and memoirs from the sessions of the Working Group that negotiate the approval of the UN binding instrument, critically reflecting on the limits and potential scope of this document. Finally, I consider the challenges and potentialities related to the role of civil society there and how this affects the possibility of a treaty, considering that Global South people cannot be mere observers in this process.

2 On Global Civil Society and Human Rights

In general, civil society is understood as the non-state sphere, which involves private dimensions and components outside the State (in its restricted perspective) (Gramsci 1999) and beyond the State. Global civil society is the historically constructed space where different political projects face each other in the international arena, based on the ideological struggle to reproduce their common sense; a result of globalisation (Farias Junior 2015). Considering that the production of knowledge is not neutral and devoid of ideological potential (Grosfoguel 2011), we can understand this concept, in which human rights activism can be identified.

Nowadays, human rights activism has directed a large part of its activities towards the normative production of legal norms at all levels (local, regional, national, supranational, and transnational/global) and to the practices of preservation, protection, promotion and updating of them, what has been called as advocacy, in addition to the involvement in strategic litigation for human rights. This normative production focuses on politics 'of' and 'for' human rights, in other words, they reinforce and reinvent the practices of the 'politics of production' of human rights norms and the 'production of politics' (Baxi 2007).

Sassen (2007) highlights that at the same time that the transnationalised capitalist mode of production has favoured some, it also gave rise to a class of underprivileged, of hyper exploited workers, and traditional communities that have lost their territories and/or are being deprived of their way of life, subaltern groups denied their rights, victims of environmental disasters; united by the condition of being affected by the systematic violation of their human rights, especially in the Global South. It is in this scenario that human rights movements that discuss anti-corporate globalisation emerge, named by Baxi (2007) as the 'movement of movements', given its broad and comprehensive character in relation to possible demands.

Many of the contemporary human rights practices[2] take the associative form of non-governmental organisations (NGOs). This does not exclude the existence of

[2] It is worth highlighting past histories of human rights activist practices: "the assemblages of the practices of resistance and struggle stand named as the 'old' social movements—which did not have access to the contemporary languages of human rights but, rather, paved ways for their emergence. The 'old' social movements include at least five specific forms: the movement for the abolition of chattel slavery, the movement for international humanitarian law, the suffragist movement, decolonization movements, and the working class movements. To name all these together is to invite attention to their disparate origins, development, and futures" (Baxi 2007, pp. 68–69).

other forms, such as social movements, collectives, political parties with that kind of agenda, etc., which according to Baxi (2007) are the main actors that constitute the human rights movement. This activism is affected by global structural inequality, on issues such as funding. The flow of South-South resources for the promotion and protection of human rights is much lower than the flow within Global North and North–South resources. So, funding remains one of the main challenges for NGOs in the Global South, as non-governmental economic actors and agencies that fund human rights NGOs remain largely embedded in the cultural traditions of philanthropy, socially reproduced more readily in the North than in the Global South (Baxi 2007).

These issues highlight the coloniality of power in these relations. This phenomenon is understood as the continuity of the forms of domination produced by colonial cultures and capitalist structures, based on the political, cultural and scientific construction of the idea of race, which perpetuates racism in contemporary times (Quijano 2005). This issue is aggravated when the neoliberal logic, with its pillars of privatisation, flexibilisation of labour rights, low regulation, etc., also produces effects within organisations. They must compete for funding and visibility, which requires great bureaucratisation, high demand for resources to support advocacy on international organisations, the possibility of using publicity on human suffering to obtain funding, and precarious work, in some cases overloaded and with low wages. In this sense, it is fundamental to highlight that the production—that is, the creation and implementation—of human rights consume a lot of resources and costs that include capital, labour and information.

Cost considerations also justify the varied constructions of human rights production and implementation hierarchies: some human rights regimes remain historically better established compared to others; for example, 'good governance' oriented human rights production[3] thrives faster than those that seek to implement human rights of refugees or indigenous peoples (Baxi 2007). Furthermore, at the UN and in most of the large NGOs, internships are unpaid, which affects the formation of an elite labour market, a workforce made up mostly of white people from the Global North. In addition, historically, there is a dialogical interaction between organisations; and UN expert advisors often emerge from the NGO communities. In short, human rights activism could also be identified as an actor of the logic of reproduction of the coloniality of power. However, there is also resistance and, in some cases, affected peoples and communities in struggle have a crucial role in the creation of human rights norms and standards.

Rajagopal (2005) points out that international law was crucially shaped during the twentieth century by the form and nature of the Global South's resistance to development. This is largely due to the realisation, among social movements, indigenous peoples, peasants and civil society, that it is not the lack of development that

---

[3] The Business and Human Rights Forum, organized by the UN Working Group on Business and Human Rights, is a case in point. The event, which took place annually before the pandemic, gathered more than two thousand people. Focused on the Guiding Principles, it had a strong presence of business consultants and advocacies of their good practices.

causes poverty and violence and destroys the natural environment and their ways of living. Instead, they are caused by the very process of exploring development. That is, predatory economic growth that is not accompanied by policies of access to the distribution of resources. Therefore, the State and global financial structure's reforms are vital parts of the agenda of human rights movements. The main purpose is to make economic power increasingly responsible, governance progressively fair and State conduct increasingly ethical (Baxi 2007). This duality of engagement—of resistance and reform—is a characteristic of TWAIL approaches (Eslava and Pahuja 2011).

This was the context for the emergence of the business and human rights agenda at the UN. To some civil society groups, the Guiding Principles on Business and Human Rights are not enough to break with the logic of corporate impunity as they are not able to establish a different level of corporate responsibility. This is evidenced in the milestone of ten years of its publication, in 2021. They continue to demand a legally binding instrument.

3 The Struggle for a Binding Treaty on Business and Human Rights

Among the actors involved, materialising this alliance of NGOs, collectives, and social movements that guide the advocacy for a treaty, the Treaty Alliance stands out. It is an alliance of more than 600 non-governmental organisations, movements, and social collectives from around the world—mostly from the Global North. The other main actor is the Global Campaign for the Dismantling of Corporate Power and for the Sovereignty of Peoples, (henceforth Global Campaign or Campaign), also made up of a broad spectrum of collectives, NGOs and social movements, which differs from the first by having broader claims, which would not end with the publication of a binding instrument on corporate accountability. As an agenda capable of bringing together all these movements and unifying them around a single struggle, there is the fight against global capital and the predatory development model, largely carried out by transnational companies around the world. Thus, global civil society turns out to be the political, ethical and ideological space of dispute and struggle of this alliance against a transnational capitalist development model (Farias Junior 2015).

The alliance has its roots on previous experiences of mobilisations and protests facing corporate power, as within Permanent People's Tribunal (PPT)[4] sessions.

[4] The PPT is a court independent of any state authority, composed of recognized persons appointed by the Board of the Lelio Basso International Foundation for the Rights and Liberation of Peoples. Lelio Basso was an Italian senator who took the initiative to organize an Opinion Court to judge the crimes committed by Latin American dictatorships of the 60's/70's, especially the dictatorships of Brazil and Chile. In the 1960s, given the authoritarian character of government that reverberated in different parts of the world in the Cold War, a movement for popular opinion courts had emerged, in spaces where there was greater democratic freedom. The PPT followed the work of the Russel Tribunal (1966–1967) that investigated and evaluated American foreign policy and military

PPT is a court of opinion whose purpose is to give visibility and characterise, from a legal point of view, cases of human rights violations that have not been dealt with by national and international institutional bodies. On two occasions, the court held specific sessions on corporate abuses, such as the session for European TNCs in Latin America (2006–2010) and the one on TNCs on mining and land grabbing in the South African region (2016–2018).[5] For Brennan and Berron (2020), the TPP judgments were a watershed in the movement towards a binding treaty. These trials, especially the first one, made it possible a learning process and exchange of experiences that greatly influenced the strategies of civil society at the OEIGWG.

Thus, it was in parallel to this experience that in 2012, a group of human rights organisations, groups of the affected communities, social movements, and intellectuals, among others, founded the Campaign, following an extensive consultation on how to develop a strategy against corporate impunity, targeting the mega-institutions of corporate power and neoliberal globalisation (Brennan and Berrón 2020). The Campaign has two pillars of action: the legal one, which is connected to the elaboration of proposals for the binding treaty, and that of activism for democracy and sovereignty of peoples.

As already mentioned, the treaty project is not new, and has strengthened over the decades by the advocacy of civil society, social movements and communities affected by transnational corporations. This demand surfaced in September 2013, when Ecuador and South Africa—supported by at least 85 States—sent a joint statement to the 24th Regular Session of the Human Rights Council indicating their intention to reopen the agenda of a legally binding regulatory framework for transnational enterprises,[6] immediately supported by the Campaign in a statement.[7] Soon after, their members launched the Treaty Alliance, with several other human rights networks and organisations to establish a broad coalition towards a binding Treaty in Geneva.

So, on September 26, 2014, during the 26th session of the UN Human Rights Council, two resolutions were approved on the same topic. The first guaranteed the

intervention in Vietnam. To see more, check the Fondazione Lelio e Lisli Basso Issoco website. Available at: <http://permanentpeoplestribunal.org/>. Access on 11 May 2020.

[5] The judgment on The European Union And Transnational Corporations In Latin America analysed 46 cases and the one on Mining and Land Grabbing in the Southern Africa 16 cases, whose verdicts can be found at: www.enlazandoalternativas.org/IMG/pdf/TPP-verdict.pdf and: http://aidc.org.za/download/ppt_2018/List-of-Cases-presented-in-previous-PPT-Hearings.pdf. Assessed on 3 September 2021.

[6] Learn more at: Joint Statement on behalf of a Group of Countries at the 24th Session of the Human Rights Council (African Group, the Arab Group, Pakistan, Sri Lanka, Kyrgyzstan, Cuba, Nicaragua, Bolivia, Venezuela, Peru and Ecuador), 2013. Available at: https://media.business-humanrights.org/media/documents/files/media/documents/statement-unhrc-legally-binding.pdf. Assessed on 3 September 2021.

[7] Learn more at: Global Campaign, Statement to the Human Rights Council in support of the initiative of a group of States for a legally binding instrument on transnational corporations. September 13, 2013. Available at: https://www.stopcorporateimpunity.org/statement-to-the-human-rights-council-in-support-of-the-initiative-of-a-group-of-states-for-a-legally-binding-instrument-on-transnational-corporations/. Assessed on 3 September 2021.

continuity of the UNGP process, seeking to deepen its implementation, while the other, in a historic vote, established the creation of a Working Group in charge of preparing a project for a binding instrument on Human Rights and Business, the OEIGWG. Indeed, the two resolutions approved simultaneously, even though with the same objective, have a different perspective and orientation.

The approval of resolution 26/9, the 'treaty resolution', was made by a small majority in the Council—supported by the governments of the Global South and opposed by each EU member, as well as by the states in which the main transnational companies are based—such as Japan and the United States. In general, it can be said that the States that are the headquarters of the main transnational corporations and the international and national business associations were those that rejected the opening of an international negotiation of a treaty. Together with them, there are Global South States that, due to ideological affinity, political pressure, or convenience (such as to avoid blocking potential investments), prefer to support the process of the Guiding Principles than the treaty. After all, one of the main obstacles to acting against the illegal actions of transnational corporations is the concrete threat that companies will move their facilities to another country with fewer restrictions, putting jobs and corporate tax revenues at risk. In this sense, the vote was a historic moment in which a narrow majority made the geopolitical fault lines on the issue visible.

At that moment, human rights organisations played a fundamental role. They monitored the negotiation process and emphasised the importance of centralising the debate on victims to break the cycle of impunity, voluntarism, and procedural imbalance (Ladino 2014). This group which had held seven meetings (2015–2021) by the time that work on this chapter was concluded, proposed recognising transnational corporations as subjects of responsibilities under international law, subject, therefore, to accountability for human rights violations (Homa 2015).

The process of the treaty negotiation has advanced significantly since the approval of Res. 26/9. The first two sessions discussed the content and scope of the treaty. In the third session, in 2017, the so-called 'Elements' were presented by the OEIGWG, an initial document that would serve as a starting point for the discussion of the future treaty. It must be mentioned that Resolution 26/9 did not provide in its clauses the obligation to prepare a draft of the text. However, at the end of the third session, it was decided they would present it (UNHRC 2018). The effective draft of the treaty was presented in August 2018, followed by a revised draft in 2019, the second draft in 2020 and the third in 2021.

For Brennan and Berron (2020), the negotiation of the binding instrument has been contested at every step of the way, revealing the often conflicting but sometimes coincident interests between the three main actors involved: the states, corporations and the group that involves affected communities, social movements, and civil society organisations (CSOs). For the latter group, the role played there is that of persistent resistance and advocacy.

As it is an ongoing process, the considerations made in this chapter suffer a series of limitations; after all, it is not possible to outline a prognosis about the future of the treaty. In this process, we can only delineate a few of the many possible paths. In this way, my analysis will be limited to the sessions that have already taken place in the working group between 2014 and 2020, critically reflecting on the advances and the limits of this process that is the result of the mobilisation of a civil society historically connected to the struggles for the accountability of transnational companies for human rights violations in the international arena.

4 Negotiation Process of the Binding Treaty: Engaging with a Global South Perspective

As mentioned in the previous section, the OEIGWG has already held seven sessions. The annual sessions last five days in Room XX of the Palais de Nations in Geneva, where delegates from member states of the Human Rights Council, Working Group members, civil society organisations, and observers meet. Despite budgetary limitations and the obstacles posed by the UN institutional framework, it is remarkable that, thanks to the effort of support networks, the participation of representatives of groups directly affected[8] by business activity during the sessions, especially from the Global South, remained constant through this period. The program of work consists of an official schedule, organized by OEIGWG members and side events that are commonly organised by CSOs.

In two of these sessions, in 2016 and 2019, I was able to follow them as an observer, and as a member of civil society. This participation was built from my job position as Business and Human Right's Fellow at the Human Rights Clinic of Amazon (CIDHA-UFPA),[9] a research hub at the Federal University of Pará. It should be mentioned that this field of legal research in Brazil was still very incipient when the research began in 2016. Over the years, the area has expanded more and more, with the creation of research groups, academic journals and the organisation of seminars. That can be understood as a natural result of the development of the two United Nations Working Groups on the subject, and also of the successive occurrence of events of serious proportions in terms of human rights violations related to business activity in the southeast of the country,[10] such as the disruption of the Fundão mining

[8] Considering that social categories are historically generated, some social movements, such as the Movement of People Affected by Dams—"MAB", have advocated using the nomenclature of "affected" for a broader definition than that of "victims", usually used in the legal field. By affected, it is understood a sphere beyond the heritage, considering intangible capital—the way of life, cultural dimensions, the network of sociability, community life, the loss of the landscape in which they were socialized and involved—which are not recoverable, nor capable of being reconstructed in the same way (Renk and Winckler 2017).

[9] Learn more at: https://www.cidh.ufpa.br/index.php/pt/. Accessed on 12 July 2022.

[10] This is not to say that there are no other events of serious proportions of human rights violations related to transnational corporations in other regions of the country, but it only emphasizes the influence that the Southeast exerts on the rest of the country, as it is the region with the greatest concentration of wealth and where the main media are based.

tailings dam, in the Rio Doce basin region in 2016, and the Brumadinho dam in 2019, both owned by the transnational company Vale.[11]

Thus, the first time I followed the sessions of the OEIGWG, in 2016, I was researching the subject due to my activities at CIDHA-UFPA, who funded this mission. In 2019, at the second opportunity, I was there as a PhD student working on my thesis. In this sense, my writing and experience, to be narrated below, is identified between academic and militant practice, as a researcher and activist. These variables guide my gaze, more directed towards Brazil and the struggles for human rights of the peoples of the Amazon, and my privileged position, as I had the social conditions necessary for this undertaking, from knowing how to speak in English to how to access funding from a public university, which enabled the extremely costly trips. Positionality is vital because it forces us to recognise our own power, privilege and prejudices, at the same time as we denounce the power structures that surround our objects. Also, I was one of the few women from the Amazon, from the north of Brazil, directly from the Global South, present in these initial negotiations.

When I first arrived in Geneva, as a first-time observer there, I had no idea what the routine of a week-long session of a UN Working Group was like, what the agenda of events would be, what they would be like and who could participate. My encounter with that 'Palace of Hope', a term coined by Niezen and Sapignoli (2017) about global organizations, was initially like being in postcard, a tourist spot. Indeed, Geneva meets the expectations of anyone with an interest in 'human rights tourism'. After all, the city is also known as the 'Capital of Peace', as it was the place where the Convention that inaugurates humanitarian law was signed, the Geneva Convention of 1864, a document that stipulates the set of laws and customs of war, in addition to of also being the cradle of humanitarian NGOs. In Place des Nations, a big square situated in front of the UN building, there is also the monument of the Broken Chair, 12 m in height chair created in honour of the victims of landmines. The Place is commonly used for protests, and during the 2016 session, it was where the Global Campaign organised their activities, within a tent being set up to serve as a space for the 'Week of Mobilisations', an event that took place parallel to the sessions.

To actively participate in a UN conference, that is to be able to speak there, it is essential to have ECOSOC credentials, which is the special consultative status of the UN Economic and Social Council (ECOSOC). Consultative status provides NGOs with access to not only ECOSOC, but also to its many subsidiary bodies, the various

[11] In 2015, two iron ore tailing dams operated by Samarco Mineração SA, a joint venture of Brazilian transnational mining company Vale SA and the Anglo-Australian BHP Billiton (now BHP), collapsed in Brazil. The dam rupture poured roughly 40 million cubic meters of mining waste into communities, the Rio Doce valley and the Atlantic Ocean, across 650 km. It is considered to be an industrial disaster that has caused the greatest environmental impact in Brazilian history and the largest in the world involving tailing dams. Nine months before Samarco's licence was granted, another disaster affected the state of Minas Gerais, the mining industry and Brazilian socio-environmental conditions—the Brumadinho disaster, in Paraoapeba river, in which over 200 people died in another dam rupture owned by Vale SA. These two great mining related tragedies marked the 2010s in Brazil.

human rights mechanisms of the UN, ad-hoc processes on small arms, as well as special events organised by the President of the General Assembly.

Taking any UN division as an object of research requires the approbation of the length of stay and of the focus of research, and the negotiation of boundaries and identities (Niezen and Sapignoli 2017). To meet these requirements, my identities there alternated either as 'researcher', 'civil society member/Campaign/Treaty Alliance', 'visitor', etc. Despite the possible difficulties of accreditation and the high cost of travel, the number of civil society organisations that participated in the OEIGWG's annual meetings remained constant and significant over time. Global Campaign and Treaty Alliance member organisations that have ECOSOC seek to organise the participation of others that do not, through prior contact at preparatory meetings. I obtained my ECOSOC badge to access the Palace of Nations in 2016 and 2019 thanks to their support. It is the ECOSOC status that allows you to issue written and oral statements, and organise side events and essential activities on the agenda of the sessions. Without ECOSOC, it is possible to be an observer, by pre-registering, via email, on the associated website.

In 2016, the weekend before the OEIGWG session, I had the opportunity to participate in the Treaty Alliance preparatory meeting. It is the last step in months of prior work, when all documentation must be collected and uploaded online, reservations are made for the side events, people must be registered, and so on. In a meeting room of a Swiss association, the members of the movement gathered to organise at that time, in just one day, practically all the spots for speeches available to civil society during the week, who would speak, on behalf of whom, on what topics. The deliverance of statements is the main activity by which official communication takes place in plenary, in addition to the presentation of special reports made by members of the Special Rapporteurs or UN agencies. Thus, the main session is the place where all these interventions are heard, a place of exchange, where, ideally, knowledge and information about the topic becomes public.

Civil society usually speaks in the last half hour of each block of the OEIGWG session, in interventions that should last up to three minutes. Of course, this is only for organisations with ECOSOC, that allows comments on the terms just outlined. Those wishing to actively participate must communicate with the registration desk, where the Secretariat includes their names and the name of the organisation with which they registered. In 2016, we were at least fifteen Brazilians, and were given specific time slots for our group to speak during the sessions. I was invited to speak about my research on development and human rights, and I promptly accepted. At this point, I should highlight the prestige that Brazilian civil society has within these spaces, which denotes both recognition of an active trajectory, and the geopolitical weight in international relations, which ensures, with certain frequency, opportunities and spaces for domestic issues to be heard at the UN plenary.

Thus, in 2016, I participated on Panel VI on "Lessons learned and challenges to access to remedy (selected cases from different sectors and regions)", of the 2nd Session of the Treaty WG, in Room XX of the Human Rights Council. There, I spoke about a procedural incident that is widely used in Brazil to guarantee the construction of mega-projects, such as hydroelectric dams, even if there are irregularities in the licencing process.[12] The purpose of this statement was to help ensure that, in the future treaty, human rights issues take precedence over economic policies. I spoke in Spanish, as Portuguese, my mother tongue, is not one of the official UN languages.

In this sense, each day, people, documents, and data that enter and leave the Council's meeting rooms constitute a vast network of advocacy, interests and experience. It certainly can be imagined as a central hub, with many formal and informal spaces for interaction and knowledge production that extend from it, especially considering the side events. The fact of sharing the same accreditation processes, meetings, coffee breaks, and cafeterias with activists and other NGO delegates, involved me as another collaborator in the activities and, in the process, I also learned about human rights from their perspectives. For example, sitting in the Serpentine coffee area, at the Palais des Nations, in 2019, I listened to a Brazilian indigenous activist, talking about the campaign for the Treaty:

> [...] they are all aligned; I believe that we suffer from the same problems. For example, people in Guatemala, or in China, elsewhere, we all suffer from the same problems, human rights violations. Our territory is under pressure from international investments, transnational corporations. They violate our right to prior consultation, which is guarantee by the UN, by the ILO. They violate the Charter of the United Nations. And we face our lands destruction, we suffer the consequences... This is because these companies install themselves in our territory, they capture our natural resources, our water, and leave devastation, deforestation, disease, disunity among the people, they destroy our sacred soil, our social organization and culture. So, we have the same problems, we are just in different places. Then, everyone is aligned here, we have a refined argumentation. It is our priority to advance the discussions to negotiate a better proposal, so that we can make a good treaty that can cover everyone who suffers the same problem, whether anywhere

This comment illustrates well what allows the construction of what I previously called global civil society. At those spaces, concepts and agreements are signed, from the understanding that the struggle is collective, that there is identity and unity between these different groups and requests. For that, the work of translators is fundamental, the persons who facilitate and enable communication between everyone, the information's flows from local to global and vice versa. That is what makes human rights movements inherently interactive, converting cases of human rights violations to human rights action, at local, regional, national, supranational and global levels.

---

[12] The procedural instrument questioned was the suspension of the preliminary injunction and interlocutory relief—SLAT, commonly known as "*suspensão de segurança*", an instrument of Brazilian law widely criticized as a law of exception and as a violation of human rights in concrete cases, mainly because it is frequently used by the State when judicializing the construction of a hydroelectric mega-project. SLAT allows the president of a court to suspend the execution of sentences and injunctions signed by lower court judges to avoid "serious harm to public order, health, safety and economy" (Law No. 8.437/1992, article 4). Through the interpretation given to the expressions "injury to public order" and "injury to the public economy" it is created a justification to not be required to respect the rules of environmental licensing, given the supposed need for expansion of the electricity sector. By cancelling the decisions of lower courts and taking advantage of the delay in the judgment of the cases by the collegiate bodies, the construction of the discussed project is completed, as well as the foreseen violations of law.

5 Challenges and Potentialities

Since its beginning, the process has revealed the conflicts of interests of the three main actors: States, TNCs, and civil society. My field notes register the political challenges of this construction process and, notably, the issue of broad civil society participation, a characteristic that marks the entire process, is one of the most sensitive issues.

From 2015 to 2020, all ambassadors who coordinated the OEIGWG sessions as Chair-Rapporteurs were representatives of the State of Ecuador: María Fernanda Espinosa (2015 and 2016), Guillaume Long (2017), Luis Gallegos (2018), Emilio Rafael Izquierdo Miño (2019, 2020 and 2021), so it can certainly be said that the Ecuadorian delegation played a very important role in promoting the treaty's agenda. From the approval of Res. 26/09 to the conduction of work in subsequent sessions, Ecuador's mission at the UN played a progressive leadership role and opened dialogue with civil society. For example, many of the members of the Global Campaign and the Treaty Alliance were invited to join the working tables in the first sessions, being able to present contributions to the discussions on the scope and content of the international instrument.

On the other hand, this condition indicates the degree of dependence between the success of an undertaking of this level, a treaty of international law and matters of domestic policy of a leading authority. The leading role of the Ecuadorian delegation has been repeatedly threatened by the political changes that Ecuador has been going through in the last decade, with the alternation of power in its government. If in 2014, international geopolitics still favoured progressive left blocs, this reality is completely different in 2021, in a post-Trump scenario.

Corporations also participate in the sessions, through their associations, and as 'civil society' organisations with ECOSOC status, where they are represented through the International Chamber of Commerce (ICC), the international trade organisation and the International Organisation of Employers- IOE, the largest private sector network in the world.[13] Both organisations presented their perspectives on the OEIGWG panels, and took the floor during the sessions, presenting written positions in the formal process, in which they have consistently stated that the proposed treaty will have a negative impact on investment in developing countries (Brennan and Berrón 2020). While the TNCS allies with governments, mainly from those States that host the largest transnational corporations; social movements are allied with some supportive governments from the Global South, while urging governments from the Global North to participate in the process actively and constructively.

[13] There is a long debate about why the ICC and IOE are classified as civil society organizations with ECOSOC status. In contrast, the WHO Framework Convention on Tobacco Control excludes tobacco corporations from bodies that implement the Convention as a result of campaigns that have already denounced corporate funding in so-called "independent research" on the plant.

At the end of the session, the OEIGWG writes a final report.[14] The principle of consensus should govern decisions about the drafting process, but in the discussion, not everyone participates in the same way. As Sapignoli (2017, 96) points out, people with extensive experience at the UN, in international law and with a better command of the official UN languages—and especially of English—have a central role in deciding which recommendations to adopt and how to formulate them.

In 2020, the session took place during the coronavirus pandemic. There were several changes resulting from the restrictions imposed by the global health crisis: experts could not be present, each delegation could send only one representative to attend the event in Geneva, and several participations occurred remotely, with pre-recorded videos or with interventions to the alive. HOMA (2020) highlighted that participation decreased significantly throughout the week, an effect that can be attributed to the pandemic. From the Elements (2017) to the drafts presented, there have already been significant advances and setbacks in the text of the treaty. With the beginning of the negotiation phase, the OEIGWG sessions started to address each article of the drafts in their work programs, in a dynamic that has already heard substantive contributions from more than 30 states, in addition to parliamentarians, experts, affected communities, and civil society.

The current draft Treaty has 24 articles, including a core set of structural provisions—several with the potential to facilitate access to justice. It establishes in its preamble that business enterprises, regardless of their size, sector, location, operational context, ownership, and structure have the obligation to respect internationally recognised human rights, including by avoiding causing or helping human rights abuses through their own activities and addressing such abuses when they occur, as well as by preventing or mitigating human rights abuses that are directly linked to their operations, products or services by their business relationships (UNHRC 2021a, b).

The current project pays significant attention to access to justice and remedies, but it has been criticised for being configuring itself as a victims-oriented and State-oriented treaty. For Guamán (2018), the project deviates from the purpose foreseen in the text of Res. 26.9, that is, "to elaborate an international legally binding instrument to regulate, in international human rights law, the activities of transnational corporations and other business enterprises" (UNHRC 2014). There is no longer any reference to the primacy of human rights over investment treaties, a prescription that was included in the Elements (2017) and is understood as crucial in this debate. I will not dive into the successive drafts of the treaty, proposals, or drafts, which propose a re-empowerment of the State in confronting human rights violations by transnational corporations and other businesses. However, I must emphasise that the proposals do not necessarily consider international geopolitics and the historical relations of imperialism and coloniality between the States of the North and the Global South.

[14] Lear more on the final reports at: https://undocs.org/Home/Mobile?FinalSymbol=A%2FHRC%2F49%2F65&Language=E&DeviceType=Desktop&LangRequested=False. access at 16/07/2022.

The current state of UN procedures could be improved if some form of monetary assistance was provided to allow broad participation from scholars and activists from the Global South. My main argument is that, in a world under corporate governance (Dardot and Laval 2013), where we have no difficulty finding cases of human rights violations related to corporations, civil society acts as an important counterpart against *corporate capture*, understood as the power connecting States (especially those from the Global North) and transnational corporations (TNCs) (Vieira 2022).

Indeed, in nearly 50 years of international attempts to regulate the activity of transnational corporations, this is the first time that affected people and civil society are actively engaged in an official process, and in significant numbers. As mentioned, since 2015, the CSOs presented dozens of proposals and written opinions during the sessions and made several interventions from the plenary proposing specific changes to the official texts and relating specific situations to the need for a binding instrument. Also noteworthy is the hard dedication to the work of bringing together representatives of all government missions in the UNCHR in side events. Recently, a group of delegates and interested organisations from the Global Campaign have started a series of informal 'political dialogues', mainly with parliamentarians, to explore common positions and strategies. This could influence the proposals of national or supranational regulations too, as the Directive of the European Parliament and of the Council on Corporate Sustainability Due Diligence and amending Directive,[15] presented in 2022.

Even though the treaty negotiation is an ongoing process, my observations recorded part of this story. From the inside of civil society groups, often at the end of the day, people shared concerns about the future of the treaty, the pain of facing with realism what happened in the daily sessions, the search for the best strategies for the next day, the doubts about the meanings of human rights. In short, it is an experience of international solidarity. With all the contradictions inherent to human rights politics, these practices carry a performative weight of accumulated experiences and knowledge, which certainly is not static. There are voices, documents, and records, that are moving towards the creation and construction of alternatives claimed by people and communities affected by human rights violations by corporations. I recall an excerpt from another interview with a member of Brazilian social movements, from 2019:

> I think that any process of change and building resistance today has three levels. It has the local level; it has the national level, and it necessarily must have the international level. For the affected communities, this dispute at the national level it is already very difficult. In a country like ours, which is such a big country, so difficult to mobilize, to move... A country where post-truth is dominating the scene, so it's been very difficult to have more critical discourses, but at the international level it's even more difficult, there are language barriers, financial barriers, infinite barriers of political understanding for these spaces... But it necessarily must be, what I believe is that we need to have strong organizations. Organizations at the local level are hardly strong if they do not have a policy of alliances at the national level, but we are also understanding that we cannot just stay in the national movement. We are full of

[15] Learn more on this proposal at: https://ec.europa.eu/info/sites/default/files/1_1_183885_prop_dir_susta_en.pdf. Access at 16/07/2022.

> solidarity, but more than that, we are building an international movement, you need to build a strategy, and solidarity sometimes does not move towards a common strategy.

Certainly, this testimony illustrates the challenges of building this international movement, facing the impossibility of creating a unique strategy of translating communication from local to international demands. However, recalling to Baxi (2007), the potential of human rights is met only when theory and practice develop the narrative potential of pluralising the meta-narratives that creates human rights, beyond the time space of the European imagination. Such an endeavour must rest on the premise that all nations come as strangers to the task of protection and promotion of human rights. This does not deny that the Euro-American discourse made a head start, from the XVII onwards, in elaborating the modern conceptions of human rights, but reminds us that these conceptions coincided with the catastrophic practices of cruelty towards the non-Euro-American Other. Here, reflecting from and with the South, accompanied by the testimonies of my fellow militants, I examined a contemporary process that, on some fronts, seeks to break with this traditional trajectory, through mobilisations, advocacy, and the participation of subaltern peoples in the process of creating international law.

Scholars like Grietjee Baars (2020) elucidate another side of this debate. Baars has developed a scathing critique of corporate accountability mechanisms, understanding that they end up absorbing both criticisms of capitalism and popular anti-capitalist resistance. That is, it reduces the inherent violence of capitalism to 'corporate irregularities', which carry the illusion that, once accountability mechanisms exist, the corporation and thus capitalism can be 'fixed'. What Baars (2020) points out is that, despite the best efforts of activists, all these strategies share the gap of not challenging the corporate structure of irresponsibility itself, that is, the broader system of corporate capitalism. Furthermore, these strategies also work within the inherent dynamics of capitalism that unevenly distribute violence along lines of gender, race, and class at the global level, as I also mentioned in this chapter.

Nonetheless, it cannot be denied that the efforts to achieve corporate accountability for human rights violations—from CSR to the process of negotiating the binding instrument, to national laws[16] and through corporate accountability cause lawyering—had many positive effects. Litigation often forces companies to disclose details of their operations that were not previously in the public domain. Corporate responsibility campaigns stimulate public debates that educate the public as well as policy makers. In addition, collaboration between communities and progressive lawyers during the time it may take to prepare a case or campaign can be empowering, as is the case with the Treaty on Business and Human Rights movement.

[16] As examples: United Kingdom has the 2015 Modern Slavery Act; California, at the United States, has the Transparency in Supply Chains Act of 2010; the European Union has Directive 2014/95 which came into force in 2017; in France there is the Corporate Duty of Vigilance Law; and in Australia, the 2018 Modern Slavery Act, all of which impose public disclosure obligations on large companies regarding the human rights impacts of their supply chain operations. Switzerland, Germany and the Netherlands are some of the countries discussing legislative proposals on mandatory rules on due diligence in the production chains of their transnational corporations.

In addition, people and communities affected by corporations do not resort to human rights because they want to. They fall back on this as a last resort, the only one possible to redress and access to justice in these contexts. Thus, it is not possible to omit the importance that the language of human rights has today, especially for those affected, and the potential this discourse represents in specific cases. In this register, human rights compete with the broader language of CSR as ideal rhetoric. Yet, states are invariably vulnerable to corporate influences and/or decisions. Also considering colonialism and imperialism inherent of capitalism, and civil society's capacity for resistance, the struggle of having effective regulations and institutions to enforce them seems quite reasonable. According to Costas Douzinas (2000), Law, the principle of polis, prescribes what constitutes a reasonable order accepting and validating some parts of collective life, while prohibiting, excluding others, making them invisible. In capitalist society, law and rights link language with things or beings; they name what exists and condemn the rest to invisibility and marginality. The attempt to establish legally binding obligations for TNCs through an international treaty rests on an understanding centred on law and normativity, as well as on the moral imperative to recognise and remedy human rights violations.

The future of human rights may not lie in its creation, but in its potential to 'recreate' the actual social conditions that exist (Baxi 2007). It is the possibility of recreating that gives human rights languages the subject, the potentiality of thought that marks the possibility of a revolutionary beginning. In the same line, Pires (2017) highlights that the more we name the categories, the more we name structural racism, sexism and other social markers, we break with the myth of universality and neutrality constituted and reinforced by hegemonic Eurocentric thinking, and the greater are the possibilities of to produce a political agenda of transformation anchored in the experience of social movements. Maybe, as Anghie (2014) pointed out, international law can be transformed into a mean by which the marginalised may be empowered. In this record, it should be mentioned that it is thanks to a series of human rights achievements that today State sovereignty cannot be fully articulated outside its discourse, as to restore the legitimacy of the colonial enslavement of peoples or apartheid formations.

In this sense, there is an endless learning process that results from the realignments of power and opportunities in the human rights system. Sometimes States come to the Council, year after year, with consistent and conservative positions on the main issues, but occasionally they come with major policy projects, such as the case of the movement that gave rise to the Treaty Resolution.

6 Conclusions

Certainly, what I described here may have been specific to the two OEIGWG sessions I followed and may not apply to prospective sessions. In 2021, the United States decided to participate in the treaty negotiation process for the first time, as a (proclaimed) part of the US' return to multilateral venues. There, instead of focusing on the current and carefully drafted proposals, the US delegate, in its opening statement, expressed its openness to exploring alternatives to the 3rd Revised Draft, including specifically "a legally binding framework agreement" that would build on the UNGPs.[17] In that, putting forward the idea that the OEIGWG should explore an alternative approach which more stakeholders—including the business community—could support. According to a statement of part of the civil society groups engaged in the previous sessions, the participation of the U.S. delegates was only to delay or obstruct this process.[18] Putting this in perspective, the global rise of authoritarianism and the setback of democratic processes will likely continue to produce negative consequences to the treaty process, which should continue to face challenges.

In this chapter, my main objective was to investigate the experience of struggling for the adoption of a binding instrument for holding transnational corporations accountable for human rights violations from a Global South perspective. I described the routine of the OEIGWG sessions, questioning the monolithic representations of international institutions, focusing on the power asymmetries and civil society participation. When confronting—or adapting to—the capitalist mode of production, this debate becomes a key point of this historical time, in which we live in a pandemic, given the announcement of climate changes considered irreversible connected to human impact—let us say mainly from large industries—and with the deepening of extreme poverty on the planet. This context is also undergoing dramatic transformations regarding its forms of political-legal regulation and market governance. The consequences of the privatisation and deregulation policy of the late 1970s, and the involvement of Western nations in the formation of emerging economies in the East and the South still are the main topics for public debate.

On expertise and knowledge production in and through the Global South related to the movement for the binding treaty, it is worth mentioning that, despite the efforts of most of its members, it still faces the challenge of transforming its agenda into an intersectional work—that is, with greater integration of diverse political groups. The movement articulates its agendas according to different interests, often not aligned with the decolonial paradigm, or with a perspective towards the Global South. However, in many countries, such as Brazil, these groups have spearheaded strong proposals for domestic laws on business and human rights,[19] boosting the strengthening of a national debate on the topic.

Also, in decades of international attempts to regulate the activity of transnational corporations, this is the first time that civil society groups from six continents are

---

[17] Learn more at: US Statement at the seventh session of the OEIGWG, 2021, available at: https://owncloud.unog.ch/s/uimBIlpxsyirMpm?path=%2F01.%20General%20statements%2F1.%20States#pdfviewer. Access at 27/07/2022.

[18] Learn more at: Civil society organizations Statement on the US proposal (2021). Available at: https://docs.google.com/document/d/1MCc6Px1pqLvC16VTSWyXPUyxiU2YZMmBH31BlxDM7M0/edit#heading=h.pzgr25g8tayg. Access at 27/07/2022.

[19] Learn more of this Project (in Portuguese) at: https://www.camara.leg.br/noticias/861969-projeto-cria-marco-nacional-sobre-direitos-humanos-e-empresas/. Accessed 16 October 2022.

actively engaged in an international proposal of a human rights framework. Furthermore, considering the lack of reparations related to imperialism and colonialism, the work of the OEIGWG led by a Third World nation marks a singular moral advance.

To succeed, any version of a treaty should strive to ensure prevention, protection and remediation of business-related human rights abuses. For the moment, business profits remain concentrated in large corporations and for the benefit of their shareholders, while the damages and risks associated keep being unevenly distributed in society, especially in the Global South. To recover the ability to think about the role of the State, as a guarantor of collective interests, is a path of analysis. This rescue is even more necessary when one realises that, in the past, in part, the discourse of human rights as a utopian project exerted influence on the depoliticisation of social demands. However, new ways of resisting are emerging and old ways of fighting corporate capitalism are making a comeback. In this scenario, all imagination, creativity, and courage are needed, as international law has always been implicated in the process of world-making.

Acknowledgements I would like to thank the editors for their invaluable comments and suggestions to improve this piece. The field-work component for this chapter was possible thanks to the support of the CIDHA-UFPA and CAPES Foundation. I am also grateful for the encouragement of Antonio Moreira Maués and Manoela Roland in this research, for Alicia Pastor careful reading of this chapter and for Tchenna Maso and Vandria Borari insights on alternative uses to human rights.

References

Acserald, H. 2019. Prefácio. In Conflitos ambientais, corporações e as políticas do risco, ed. R.G. Pinto. Rio de Janeiro, RJ: Garamond.

Allende, S. 1972. Speech at the UN General Assembly on December 4, 1972. https://undocs.org/en/A/PV.2096. Accessed 1 Sept 2021.

Anghie, A. 2014. *Imperialism, sovereignty and the making of international law*. Cambridge: Cambridge University Press.

Aragão, D.M., M.C. Roland. 2017. The need for a treaty: Expectations on counter hegemony and the role of civil society. In *Building a treaty on human rights: Context and contours*, ed. S. Deva, D. Bilchitz. Cambridge University Press.

Baxi, U. 2007. *The future of human rights*, 2nd edn. Delhi: Oxford University Press.

Baars, G B. 2020. The limits of law: Why 'corporate accountability' will not change the corporation. The Corporation – State of Power, Transnational Instititute. https://www.tni.org/en/publication/the-limits-of-law#note5 .

Brennan, B., and G. Berron. 2020. Touching the nerve: How a people's campaign at the United Nations is challenging the corporate rule. In *The corporation—State of power*. Transnational Institute. https://longreads.tni.org/touching-a-nerve/. Accessed 03 Sept 2021.

Dardot, P., and C. Laval. 2013. *The new way of the world: On neoliberal society*. London: Verso Books.

Deva, S. 2013. Treating human rights lightly: A critique of the consensus rhetoric and the language employed by the guiding principles. In *Human rights obligations of business*, ed. D. Bilchitz, S. Deva. Cambridge: Cambridge University Press.

Douzinas, C. 2000. *The end of human rights: critical legal through at the fin-de-siecle*. London, UK: Hart Publishing. ISBN 9781841130002.

Eslava, L., and S. Pahuja. 2011. Between resistance and reform: TWAIL and the universality of international law. *Trade, Law and Development* 3(1): 103–130. ISSN 0976-2329.

Farias Junior, L.C. 2015. A Batalha de Davi Contra Golias: Uma Análise Neogramsciana da Agenda das Nações Unidas em Direitos Humanos e Empresas. Dissertation, Programa de Pós-Graduação Stricto Sensu em Direito e Inovação da Universidade Federal de Juiz de Fora.

Guamán, A. 2018. El Draft 0 del Binding Treaty: análisis crítico del contenido del texto y su adecuación con el objetivo de la Resolución 26/9. Cadernos de Pesquisa Homa 1(6). http://homacdhe.com/wp-content/uploads/2018/09/Artigo-Analisys-Draft-Zero.pdf. Accessed 3 Sept 2021.

Gramsci, A. 1999. Cuadernos de La Cárcel, Tomo V. Edición Crítica Del Instituto Gramsci a cargo de Valentino Gerratana. 2. Ed. Puebla: Ediciones Era/Benemérita Universidad Autónoma de Puebla.

Grosfoguel, R. 2011. Decolonizing post-colonial studies and paradigms of political-economy: Transmodernity, decolonial thinking, and global coloniality. *TRANSMODERNITY: Journal of Peripheral Cultural Production of the Luso-Hispanic World* 1(1). https://doi.org/10.5070/T411000004. https://escholarship.org/uc/item/21k6t3fq.

Hammouri, S. 2020. Revisiting Allende's 1972 speech at the United Nations General Assembly: Histories repeated with a twist. TWAILR: Reflections #20/2020. https://twailr.com/revisiting-allendes-1972-speech-at-the-united-nations-general-assembly-histories-repeated-with-a-twist/. Accessed 03 Sept 2021.

Homa. 2015. Tratado sobre Direitos Humanos e Empresas: duas questões principais. http://homacdhe.com/wp-content/uploads/2015/11/Artigo-Tratado-sobre-Direitos-Humanos-e-Empresas-Duas-Quest%C3%B5es-Principais.pdf Accessed 03 Sept 2021.

Ladino, J. 2014. El camino hacia una convención sobre empresas y derechos humanos. RIDH. http://ridh.org/news-and-events/news-articles/el-camino-hacia-una-convencion-sobre-empresas-y-derechos-humanos/. Accessed 03 Sept 2021.

Niezen, R., and M. Sapignoli. 2017. Introduction. In *Palaces of Hope—the anthropology of global organizations*, ed. R. Niezen and M. Sapignoli, 1–30. Cambridge: Cambridge University Press.

Peña Gutiérrez, D. 2012. Responsabilidad Social Corporativa. In Diccionario Critico de las empresas transnacionales. OMAL, Observatorio de Multinacionales en la America Latina. 2012. http://omal.info/spip.php?page=article_diccionario&id_article=4816. Accessed 28 July 2022.

Pires, T. 2017. O que significa renunciar a uma categoria?. Empório do Direito [sítio eletrônico]. http://emporiododireito.com.br/leitura/o-que-significa-renunciar-a-uma-categoria-1508244312. Accessed 28 July 2022.

Quijano, A. 2005. Colonialidade do poder, eurocentrismo e América Latina. In *A colonialidade do saber: eurocentrismo e ciências sociais. Perspectivas latino-americanas*, Edgardo Lander (org). Colección Sur Sur, CLACSO, 227–278. Ciudad Autónoma de Buenos Aires, Argentina.

Rajagopal, B. 2005. El derecho internacional desde abajo: el desarrollo, los movimientos sociales y la resistencia del Tercer Mundo. Colección En clave de Sur. 1ed. ILSA, Bogotá, DC, Colombia.

Renk, A., and S.T. Wincker. 2017. De atingidos a vítimas do desenvolvimento: um estudo junto à população afetada direta ou indiretamente pela UHE Foz do Chapecó na região Oeste de Santa Catarina. *Revista Direito Ambiental e Sociedade* 7 (2): 187–211.

Rodriguez-Garavito, C., and P. Evans. 2018. Introduction: Building and sustaining the ecosystem of transnational advocacy. In *Transnational advocacy networks twenty years of evolving theory and practice*, ed. C.R. Garavito, P. Evans (org.). Dejusticia Series, Bogotá, Colombia.

Sapignoli, M. 2017. A Kaleidoscopic institutional form: Expertise and transformation in the UN permanent forum on indigenous issues. In *Palaces of Hope - the anthropology of global organizations*, ed. R. Niezen and M. Sapignoli, 78–105. Cambridge: Cambridge University Press.

Sassen, S. 2007. *A sociology of globalization*. New York, W.W: Norton.

UNHRC. 2021. Open-ended intergovernmental working group on transnational corporations and other business enterprises with respect to human rights, https://www.ohchr.org/EN/HRBodies/HRC/WGTransCorp/Pages/IGWGOnTNC.aspx. Accessed 03 Sept 2021.

UNHRC. 2021. OEIGWG chairmanship third revised draft—Legally binding instrument to regulate. In *International Human Rights Law, The Activities of Transnational Corporations and other business enterprises*. https://www.ohchr.org/Documents/HRBodies/HRCouncil/WGTransCorp/Session6/LBI3rdDRAFT.pdf. Accessed 03 Sept 2021.
UNHRC. 2014. Resolution adopted by the Human Rights Council 26/9 Elaboration of an international legally binding instrument on transnational corporations and other business enterprises with respect to human rights. https://documents-dds-ny.un.org/doc/UNDOC/GEN/G14/082/52/PDF/G1408252.pdf?OpenElement. Accessed 03 Sept 2021.
UNHRC. 2018. Report on the third session of the open-ended intergovernmental working group on transnational corporations and other business enterprises with respect to human rights, A/HRC/37/67. https://undocs.org/en/A/HRC/37/67. Assessed 3 Sept 2021.
UNHRC. 2008. Report of the Special Representative of the Secretary-General on the issue of human rights and transnational corporations and other business enterprises, John Ruggie. https://view.officeapps.live.com/op/view.aspx?src=https%3A%2F%2Fwww2.ohchr.org%2Fenglish%2Fbodies%2Fhrcouncil%2Fdocs%2F8session%2FA-HRC-8-5.doc&wdOrigin=BROWSELINK. Accessed 16 Oct 2022.
Vieira, F.A. 2022. Resisting corporate capture: A Plaidoyer for a binding treaty from a civil society perspective. *Völkerrechtsblog*. https://doi.org/10.17176/20220623-153022-0.

Using Law to Prevent Further Unequal Access to Food in North Korea

Yi Seul Kim

Abstract This chapter aims to incorporate critical legal thinking in the right to food, and discuss how the current North Korean food legal framework is structured to solidify inequality and persist unequal access to food. It also specifically aims to question and answer how policies should be re-directed to ensure people in the country have sufficient access to food, regardless of where he or she lives. Today, a person's access to food is determined by the location of his or her residence, and deeply rooted power structure determines the latter. In essence, geopolitical predicaments compromise the general legal food order and access to food in the country. This work requires revisiting existing regulations and proposing revisions to the laws and policies in the country. There are currently very few studies done on North Korea's food regime, and a careful review of existing laws and policies will assist in understanding the country's systematic deprivation of human rights more deeply. Various factors determine how much food a person has in North Korea—it is not merely about income levels or education backgrounds as in many other modern societies.

1 Introduction

If one, as a lawyer and scholar, were to judge the achievements and failures in building the right to food in general, it would be difficult to do so merely based on the recent legal reformations and developments that took place in large economies. Instead, one needs to take a macroscopic view of a pan-Asian food legal order, in which one cannot exclude even the most politically secluded countries such as North Korea. This is because human rights are universal and access to food remains an interconnected issue particularly when humanity faces a global pandemic, despite

The author is grateful to the editors, anonymous reviewers, Ray, and Colby.

Y. S. Kim (✉)
The University of Hong Kong, Hong Kong, China
e-mail: yiseul87@gmail.com

T. Venthan Ananthavinayagan and A. Viswanath Shenoy (eds.), *The Wretched of the Global South*, International Law and the Global South,
https://doi.org/10.1007/978-981-99-9275-1_13

the lack of an 'internationally coordinated action' (Fakhri 2021). One could possibly even argue that studying politically secluded countries like North Korea is of utmost importance as it allows us to come to a genuine understanding of how far we have come in the study of food law and look into how we can address states' failure in guaranteeing land tenure along this line (Fakhri 2021).

In understanding North Korea's food legal order, it is first important to understand that it is not *the* law per se that we need to study, but that we need to apply a broader lens because "the norms of the legal order are created by individuals who are empowered by [...]the legal order to do so." It is a study that requires a broader understanding of what an 'order' may be (Kelsen 1982). In other words, the most powerful individuals play an absolute role in both the creation and application of food laws, policies, and norms. This may be what differentiates this study from many others. In this country, it is more than mere 'social stratification' based on gender, social inequality, and discrimination that prevents access to food (Kong 2009).

In North Korea, there is almost no separation of powers in the food legal regime. Norms are simply that powerful in their existence because they can be utilised to expand the authority of individuals who made them. This also supports the idea that contours of the right to food in North Korean Law may be different from those we see elsewhere—based on the *juche* ideology, the political leader is more than a political figure and a symbol. He is often described as a god who can read people's minds (Withnall 2014). In addition, anyone who does not have the power to make the norms becomes mere political tools and only have laws imposed on them. To better identify this North Korean food legal order, it is meaningful to look into the different national laws, policies, and norms altogether. Only by doing so can we understand the solid unequal access to food due to geopolitical predicaments.

2 Geopolitical Predicaments Compromising the Legal Food Order

In North Korea, geopolitical predicaments rigidly compromise the legal food order, and geographical scope of the analysis centres on Pyongyang. Starting from the city square in Pyongyang known as the Kim Il-Sung Square, discrimination based on structural hierarchy extends nationwide. With the Kim Il-Sung Square being marked as the 'kilometer zero' (Talmadge 2017) when every road distance in the country is measured, the Square acts as a symbol of overarching power and control. The close monitoring and control over how Pyongyang ensures the government's simultaneous supervision over the unique capital city and the rest of the country. Simply put, the closer an individual resides from Pyongyang's Kim Il-Sung Square, the more affluent, politically powerful, and socially privileged he or she is (Em and Ward 2021) Proximity to the Square is a consideration that extends nationwide and a dream for people around the whole country due to the strict control over who can enter the city. It is more than a mere capital city in another country but rather a geographical centre where discrimination stems from. The Kim Il-Sung Square is a symbolic establishment located at the core of the capital city along with Juche Tower. On noting the significance of these establishes, one architect writes that the Kim Il-Sung Square and the Tower "create a major axis of symbolic spaces" together (Yim 2017). Given the symbolic value of these architectures, placing the politically powerful and the economically affluent in Pyongyang was no coincidence. It was carefully planned this way based on the state's core value and policy: juche. Loosely translated as 'self-reliance' (Kim 2017), the juche ideology aims to build public consolidation around a single godly leader to make the country independent from foreign influence (Park 2021). It is more than an ordinary policy or national directive seen in other countries; it is a metaphysical belief that people practice. And it is so fundamental that it is also very well embedded in the formation of the most basic infrastructure of the country: urban policy and planning. This is where unequal food access begins.

To an outsider, it seems bewildering that the state can manage to so deeply and systematically embed *juche* values from the core as they justify discrimination and human injustice when it becomes entangled with food. Right to food is seen as an international human right in the modern era (Narula 2006). Nevertheless, a careful reading of the national laws shows indications of patterns and languages of discrimination, which in effect perpetuate the justification behind the state-led discrimination. *Juche* values and laws written to maintain them together support the coalition of the politically powerful and the economically rich in Pyongyang. These privileged people in Pyongyang face much fewer food availability issues and are in general given the most access to the safest food products in the country (Kim 2020). The rest of the people are mere agents who serve the power hierarchy at the cost of an efficient food legal order. They are subject to constant discrimination on a daily basis when it comes to having access to food.

a. Centrally Planned but Locally Administered Food Production

Food production is centrally planned and administered, but it appears rather fragmented in its execution. To begin with, the food industry is a sector administered by the Light Industry Department in the central government (Ministry of Unification 'Food Industry' 2021a) and is planned according to state norms and policies largely derived from *juche* ideology. However, in the capital city, the 'Central Enterprise of Pyongyang' produces food and beverages according to a production plan prepared by the National Planning Committee that is overseen by the Ministry of Food and Beverage Industry. This plan is rather detailed and includes information such as the amount of planned production of food by quarter, month, and index. Most other local enterprises throughout the country prepare a draft plan and submit it to the relevant Local People's Committee, which then formulates the final production plan and submits it to the Central Enterprise for further approval. There is no other official channel of food imports, ensuring that all food channels are centrally monitored with minimal external influence and prods (Korea Development Bank 2015).

For food ingredients used during food production, the Central Enterprise of Pyongyang procures the best quality raw ingredients from around the nation, whereas local enterprises are limited to using local products and produce only (Ministry of Unification 'Management and Operation of Food Industries' 2021b). This results in not only dissimilar qualities of food but also different amounts of food available to various regions in the country.

Policy-wise, North Korea's food industry system is divided into two major categories: 'large-scale central industry', and 'regional medium-and small-scale local industry'. Sizeable factories in major cities such as Pyongyang make up the first category with corn processing, crop, flour processing, and general food factories. Smaller factories fall under the second category of 'regional medium-and small-scale local industry'. There is one local factory allocated in each city or county for each product or produce (Ministry of Unification 'Food Industry' 2021a). With most of North Korea's food factories having been built in the 1970's, most of these factories in the second category run on outdated facilities and scarce raw materials (Korea Development Bank 2015).

b. Historical Roots of Unequal Food Production in the State

Disintegrated and fragmented food production is deeply rooted and such practices trace date back to 1954 when the country introduced its first Three-Year Plan (Kuark 1963). Around this time, still, many arrangements in the country were products from Soviet-Marxism and the state was "hostile to the notion of human rights in capitalist societ[ies]" (Song 2011). It also made sense to carefully monitor the usage of land so that it would not be subject to 'individual acts of violence' (Marx 1990) Accordingly, following the division of the Korean Peninsula and from the rubbles of the Korean War, the central government placed focus on rebuilding much of its food production facilities from Pyongyang first. The country aimed to double the production of food factories soon after the planning of the Three-Year Plan, and factories were newly built and renovated in the city. The Pyongyang Crop factory was a representative example of this state-led initiative, along with the establishment of a meat processing factory in the Yongseong area in Pyongyang and the fish can factory in Shinpo. By 1958, there was raised confidence in the general food production and the Central government announced its plans to strengthen the food processing industry and to quadruple its production rate. In practice, such development plans were geographically restricted and while there were some efforts made to develop local facilities such as the Wonsan oil factory, most of the focus was placed on Pyongyang and cities directly bordering it (Ministry of Unification 'Food Industry' 2021a). Around this time, still many arrangements and their fundamental bases in the country were products from Soviet-Marxism. This was even so when the Koreans were slowly building their own viewpoints that rejected Soviet's influence in the midst of the Soviet Union and China's disagreements on Marxism-Leninism (Stock 2019). Discussion of human rights was a political tool to stigmatise and criticise other ideologies with the *juche* ideology in the country (Song 2011). This has dominated the perception of the right to food until today.

By the 1970s, there was a national policy designed to develop food processing of both staple crops and supplementary food. This policy was instigated under the slogan that 'women were to be freed from housework' (Korea Development Bank

2015). It became important to improve the state storage capacity of frozen food to 120,000 tons. At the same time, crop factories were built around the country for more equitable growth in Pukchang, Hweryung, Kangkye, Uiju, Hamheung, Wonsan, Sariwon, and Hyeju, with the existing Pyongyang crop factory undergoing expansion work. Jade rice factories were also built in four different locations throughout the country. Nevertheless, there were still many more resources spent on developing the food production industry in Pyongyang and the nearby cities. For example, a Comprehensive Processing Flour Factory that allowed up to 100,000 tons of flour per annum was built in the capital city only. This was in addition to the building and expansion of the Children's Food Factory, and kimchi factories were planned for further construction in Pyongyang. Differences in plans were still very much acceptable under the state's perception of human rights. In what coincided with Marx's theory of historical materialism, the *Dictionary of the Works of Great Leader Kim Il Sung (1982)* wrote that "concepts of human rights are different from one society to another, depending on the class characteristics of a society and the state's socioeconomic structure" (Song 2011). Like what we see today, there were continued justifications in the food production and supply gap then as well. When the production of starch, starch syrup, and glucose began to decrease due to the shortage of corn a decade later, residents living outside of Pyongyang were most affected. And in the 1990s, when the country was suffering from a shortage of raw materials and electricity (Korea Development Bank 2015), people outside of Pyongyang suffered from hunger even more.

In the 2000s, the country sought to promote basic food production base and undertake nationwide growth. In the year 2000 alone, 12 basic food factories were newly built around the country to serve as supplementary food supply bases for each provincial region (Republic of Korea Ministry of Unification 'Food Industry' 2021a). As a result, today, each province has one crop factory. However, unresolved disparities continue to exist with differences in production capacities of these factories being significant. For example, the Pyongyang Crop Factory is reported to have a production capacity of 30,000 tons and 50,000 tons of starch and corn syrup, respectively. Likewise, the Bukchang Crop Factory located nearby produces 35,000 tons and 50,000 tons of these goods. Yet, production levels for the same products are substantially lower in other factories around the country, such as in Uiju, Haeju, Sariwon, Hamheung, Kangkye, Wonsan, and Hyeryung, at a range between 5000 tons and 1.7 tons. Similarly, while the Pyongyang Flour Comprehensive Processing Factory produces 100,000 tons of flour, Nampo Milling Factory 150,000 tons, and Hyeju Milling Factory 20,000 tons of flour, these only supply to major cities. Otherwise, noodles made from these flours are only supplied to the residents of the local regions where noodles are made, or as meals for state workers such as miners working on coal mining sites (Ministry of Unification 'Food Industry' 2021a).

(i) Pyongyang

One of the quickest ways to improve food security is to increase food production (FAO 2021). As an administrative matter, food supply is closely monitored as an endeavour to make ends meet and stabilise the capital city. It is stipulated in law that

Pyongyang Municipal People's Committee and the relevant agencies calculate the supply and demand conditions of food (Pyongyang Management Law, Article 38). As such, food production is carefully planned and designed so that the privileged group of people in Pyongyang can continue to show support for the *juche* and the state willingly (Cho 1983). The national planning agency, relevant agencies, and organisations together plan the amount of food and fuel to be supplied to Pyongyang City (Pyongyang Management Law, Article 38). With what appears as a political move, agricultural and livestock production bases have been additionally built inside Pyongyang as part of the effort to vamp necessary production to further sustain the food supply (Pyongyang Management Law, Article 12).

The Socialist Commercial Law provides insight into the societal and political significance of sustaining food security. It reads "Product supply is an important business for securing and supplying goods to meet the growing material and cultural demands of the people ... guaranteeing a more affluent and civilised life for the people" (Socialist Commercial Law, Article 8). Yet, while this body of law stipulates that the central commercial guidance organ and local government organs should take control of the goods uniformly and supply the necessary goods to the people in an evenly order, this is mostly applied and enforced in Pyongyang only (Socialist Commercial Law, Article 8).

Large-scale factories in Pyongyang are equipped with modern facilities and are thus able to produce and process crops, flour, kimchi, bread, beer, refreshments, meat, and cigarettes (Korea Development Bank 2015). While there is not much information available on the production lines of their food products, some of the well-known factories include Daedonggang Foodstuff Factory (2009) Pyongyang Ryongseong Food Factory (2009), Pyongyang Basic Food Factory (2013), and Pyongyang Children's Food Factory that exclusively to serve the local population in the capital city.

Pyongyang City additionally carries out several management projects that do not exist elsewhere. Noting the importance of water quality (World Bank 2020), Pyongyang's urban management institutions further run modern water supply facilities and adopt advanced water disinfection and refining technologies to ensure adequate quality of potable water for their residents (Pyongyang Management Law, Article 21). This is seen as an integral component of one of the main ingredients of food. Factors such as population concentration is also closely watched by setting major water supply management standards such as the population limit, population density, industrial population ratio, industrial interview ratio, and green area per capita in Pyongyang city (see Pyongyang Management Law).

In what is viewed as a symbolic political gesture, the Kim family places heavy emphasis on food production by visiting production facilities in Pyongyang. As one example, it was reported that both Kim Il-Sung and Kim Jong Il visited the Pyongyang Goksan Factory that produces corn syrup and candies was frequented by, 15 and 7 times, respectively. Kim Jong Un also has been reported to visit other food production facilities in the capital city, such as the February 20th factory of the Korean People's Army, which has since then become a model factory for North Korean food factories.

Kim Jong Un was even known to have personally reviewed the results of the one-year factory modernisation project of the 534th Army Unit of the Korean People's Army and scientists and engineers (Chosun News 2014). In fact, Kim Jong Un is known to have emphasised to the people the automated production processes used in the production of food such as pickled meat, soybean paste, soy sauce, and butter (Noh 2013). Strengthened food quality has also been advertised for factories such as Daedonggang Foodstuff Factory, for its Pyongyang soju. Pyongyang's Taedonggang Foods Factory was also reported to have produced Pyongyang *Mejujang* that met the import standards of the state's neighbouring countries (Chosun News 2008).

For other products such as milk, processed dairy products are rarely placed on the market even in Pyongyang. Still, while individuals raise goats to make their own milk or sell them on the market in other parts of the country, there is a factory that produces yogurt in Pyongyang with a production capacity of 1,500 tons of yogurt. Meanwhile, fruit processing is mainly carried out in the fruit districts of Pyongyang and Hwanghae Province, and Bukcheong County in South Hamgyong Province. The Pungcheon Fruit Processing Plant of the Fruit District has a production capacity of about 17,000 tons, and the Hwangju Fruit Processing Plant has a production capacity of 1,500 tons. It is known that the processing of vegetables is carried out at the Sinpo Canning Factory and the Yongseong Meat Processing Factory, but the majority of North Korean defectors have never tried processed vegetables. In fact, even in Pyongyang where it has been supplied to the residents, production and supply have often been disrupted due to a lack of vegetable availability (Breen 2004).

(ii) Second Tier cities

In North Korea, satellite cities around Pyongyang assist in controlling the capital's population concentration while sharing some of its economic and social service responsibilities. The Cabinet, the national planning agency, and the relevant agency determine the order in which satellite cities as determined and constructed (Pyongyang Management Act, Article 11).

Generally speaking, the farther away from either the state border or Pyongyang, the more food-related problems a person faces. Living by the state border facing China allows people to engage in small scales of trading with Chinese food traders (Zwirko 2021). Imported food sometimes reaches the people here illegally via unofficial channels such as marketplaces (Breen 2004). In the more affluent cities such as Cheongjin and Shineuiju provinces, there are also refreshment, meat, and cigarette production facilities. Residents of these second-tier cities do not have to rely on self-prepared cigarette and meat, unlike those in the rural regions given such facilities available locally (Ministry of Unification 'Food Industry' 2021a).

Local government agencies, commodity production institutions, enterprises, and organisations are mandated to set up raw material bases and produce various food-stuffs from the raw material sources they produce locally (Socialist Commercial Law, Articles 13, 14). This, however, only occurs after first supplying the best local ingredients and produce to Pyongyang as aforementioned. State-owned enterprises are to take over fishery products from fisheries institutions, enterprises, and organisations to supply them evenly to the local residents (Socialist Commercial Law Article 13,

14). Yet, such supply of food very often is insufficient to meet the demand level. For example, while the national fish product processing capacity was estimated to be about 410,000 tons per year in the 1990s, fish product today is only sent to the capital city and other few major cities. Supply of raw materials for aquatic products has dropped and failure to modernise facilities such as processing technology and refrigeration storage have made it more challenging to see an increase in fish product processing.

Furthermore, while there are meat processing factories in North Korea, most of the processed meat products are supplied exclusively to soldiers and government officers. If not, they are reported to be provided to embassies and hotels (Dunlop 2017) rather than to citizens. Ordinary citizens are rationed merely about one kilogram of pork from the country per year, and there is no other known supply of processed products. While the right to food, should be applied as part of everyone's right to demand responsibility from the state (Dumas 2010), inequality is exacerbated by the severe rarity of seafood and meat processed food in general.

(iii) Third-Tier Rural Areas

In the rest of the country, there are additional small-to-medium sized factories for corn processing, sauce, oil, alcohol, and sweets for local residents. Particularly in some regions where crops are grown, the central government builds factories in order to minimise production costs. For example, flour factories are constructed near ports such as Nampo Flour Factory. Fruit processing factories are centred around Gwail province, Hwangju province, Bongsan-province, Hamnam province, and Bukchung-province. Likewise, seafood processing factories are located around Sinpo, Gimchaek, and Wonsan (Ministry of Unification 'Food Industry' 2021a). Such is the case for processing factories in larger cities, food products from factories such as these are first sent to Pyongyang, and then to major cities.

There is not much information available on mass food production facilities or channels in third-tier, rural areas. Particularly after the 1980s, ordinary residents in rural areas are frequently forced to depend on their own food production, rather than on state rations. These foods are produced at homes privately and are even sold on illegal markets. It is known that with the growing private market after the July 1, 2002 measures, the amount of general foodstuffs produced by individuals at home outweighed that of the state-produced foodstuff (Ministry of Unification 'Food Industry' 2021a).

3 Access to Food as a Critical Human Rights Concern

It is important to reflect on how such unequal access to food can be seen as a critical human rights concern, especially when a person's political status and family history determine where he or she will reside. In North Korea, the national construction supervisory authority and the relevant supervisory and control authority together oversee the formulation of urban planning projects. Supervision and control over the housing sector project are carried out by the relevant city management guidance agency and supervisory control agency. The city management guidance institution and the relevant supervisory and control institutions ordinarily supervise and control the construction, transfer, acquisition, registration, allocation, use, and management of the housing house (Living House Act, Article 59). All of these state organs, in practice, exercise power in determining how much food a person has access to on an ordinary day.

a. Pyongyang Residents as the Privileged Few

With the three-year construction plan that ran from 1954 to 1956, North Korea designed Pyongyang applying socialist values, to eliminate disparities between the capital city and other rural areas and to maximise labour production. A unit district system was developed to systematically combine industrial and residential areas, and further allow Pyongyang residents to easily consume their local products. For the same purpose, leisure parks were placed nearby historical sites (Yim 2017).

At the most basic level, North Korea has a framework built on *juche* sentiments that encourage exclusiveness with Pyongyang as the pivot. Urban and rural planning not only serve the functional purpose of 'development of open land' and revitalising existing land usage (Fainstein 2021), but it has had a material effect of dominating the human psyche. It constructs a systematic power hierarchy and continues to reinforce it by politicising science and carefully selecting who can live in the special city as opposed to those who have an inferior political background. This isolates the rest of the country from the city of Pyongyang and seemingly justifies a treatment different from those applied to other parts of the nation.

Pyongyang Management Law validates the effort of singling out Pyongyang for special treatment. Article 2 reads that Pyongyang was *magnificently* and *splendidly* built under the state's well-crafted capital construction policy, patriotic enthusiasm, and creativity of the people (Pyongyang Management Law, Article 2). Management of Pyongyang is separately written as 'an honorable duty for citizens', (Pyongyang Management Law, Article 3) and the state strengthens socialist patriotism education so that people may actively participate in the Pyongyang city management project. In other words, there is a strong correlation between patriotism and city management drawn by the state; showing the willingness to take care of the city demonstrates the level of obedience to the People's Working Party, the Kim family, and the country as a whole.

As an administrative centre, Pyongyang city is divided into two regions: the central area and the peripheral area. In the central area, there is a designated area centred on Mansudae, and in the surrounding area, there are protected areas, satellite cities, and rural areas (Pyongyang Management Law, Article 7). Even within Pyongyang, the closer you are to the central square area and the state-protected areas, the tighter the management gets. For example, this central urban area is designated for special management of residents as written into law (Pyongyang Management Law, Article 9), ranging from how they must behave to how they can dress. As an administrative management matter, the Cabinet is responsible for determining the boundaries of the central area, the width of the state-protected area, and the satellite city. The Cabinet must align the boundaries of the central area with the boundaries of the administrative divisions so that the central area and protected areas are well organised (Pyongyang Management Law, Article 9). The Pyongyang City People's Committee and the City Management Municipal area in charge of renovating and repairing people's living quarters to improve the appearance of the capital (Pyongyang Management Law, Article 40).

Living in Pyongyang city is considered a social privilege for these selected few (Daily NK 2021). Those aspiring to reside in Pyongyang must register for residency, which is then reviewed by the Cabinet itself (Pyongyang Management Law, Article 3). To prove this privileged status, citizens over the age of 17 living in Pyongyang City are awarded a Pyongyang Citizenship Card. They are required to carry their citizenship card, possess a *noble* spirit and moral character, and strictly observe the law and order of the country. It is also stipulated in law that they should set an example in protecting their honour as a citizen of the capital. If a Pyongyang citizen seriously violates the laws and orders of the state, the Pyongyang Citizenship Card is then revoked (Pyongyang Management Law, Article 32), and any violation of law results in administrative or criminal liability for Pyongyang residents (Pyongyang Management Law, Article 53).

b. State-Initiated Unequal socio-political treatment

A textual reading of the Social Security Act appears to suggest that North Korea built its nationwide social security system to protect public health and to guarantee stable living environments and conditions on a nationwide basis (Social Security Act, Article 3), but reality proves otherwise. In practice, this has not meant that everyone receives fair and equal treatment. To start with, the state endorses a divided population dependent on political ranking: the core class, the wavering class, and the hostile class. The core class is known to account up to 25–30% of the nation's population. Most, if not all, are based in Pyongyang. These are people who are considered elite government officials, members of the Communist Party (Cho 2013), and those who have made significant contributions to the state (Koryo Tour 2021). The wavering class consists of people who entered North Korea from South Korea during the Korean War, teachers, former merchants, farmers, and others (Cho 2013). They are seen as inferior to the former population class, and it becomes more difficult for them to reside in Pyongyang. This class takes up roughly half of the nation's population. The last, hostile class takes up the remaining 25 percent of the population, and are those who are politically tainted. They are members of the society who are seen as 'hostile' as those who attempted to flee the country, their relatives, and family members of those who fled to South Korea during the Korean War (Cho 2013). These people live farther away from the capital city.

Such classification of people by social rankings perpetuates organized injustice instigated by the state. While in principle, construction for residential housing is carried out to meet the increasing demand for housing (Social Security Act, Article 4), the government actively and exclusively scrutinises people's given character in the allocation of households and monitors household management (Social Security

Act, Article 6). A person's unique character, his or her family's political status and history become a means to judge a household, in order to give preferential treatment to revolutionary fighters, families of revolutionary martyrs, families of patriots, heroes, war veterans, and soldiers (Social Security Act, Article 4), while disproportionately discriminating others. In fact, social security is also granted to citizens based on several factors: name and age, job title, reason for applying, experience, and meritocratic relationship of those who wish to receive social security (Social Security Act, Article 11). As such, not all applicants are eligible for social security, and the central labour administrative guidance organ and the relevant People's Committee make a decision to approve or reject it upon receipt of the application for social security (Social Security Act, Article 12). Thus, the state maintains and applauds a hierarchy rigidly based on people's political status.

State-run social security institutions are required by law to provide sufficient conditions and environment for workers to live without any inconvenience (Social Security Act, Article 31). The state runs social security institutions, which must have modern welfare facilities such as study rooms, bedrooms, restaurants, clinics, rebalance rooms, and laundry facilities, and guarantee the necessities of life necessary for social security workers (Social Security Act, Article 31). However, another layer of problem exists in that one cannot receive social security benefits without national merit (Lee and Hankuk 2021). Most residents do not receive the benefits of the social security system, except for those with national recommendations such as by Central Party cadres, military generals or the Order of Kim Il-sung, Kim Jong-il Citation, Hero Title, People's and Meritorious Title, and the Order of the National Flag, etc. (Lee and Hankuk 2021). They are all residents of Pyongyang.

4 Reconceptualising Right to Food within the North Korean Context

Discussions surrounding human rights to food still have a long way to go (Kong 2009). While some may argue that its contours live in the Universal Declaration of Human Rights, the International Covenant on Economic, Cultural and Social Rights (ICESCR), and the Universal Declaration of World Hunger and Malnutrition (1974) provided a foundation to the notion (Alston and Tomaševski 1984, Kent 2005) when the Food and Agricultural Organisation was silent on the right to food at its foundation. ICESCR article 11(2) prescribes both the right to adequate food and the fundamental right to be free from hunger. While what is considered adequate in terms of the ICESRC is undetermined, according to General Comment 12, the Committee's interpretation of the right to food shows that food must meet the needs of consumers and be available to everyone in the society, even to the future generation (ECOSOC 1999; Dumas 2010). According to Dumas, this interpretation only accentuates the state's duty to prevent the deprivation of access to food for the people (Dumas 2010). In looking at the relationship between the right to adequate food and the right to be free from hunger, Philip Alston argues that the latter is a narrower concept than the right to food, and that it relates to meeting the minimum needs of the people. In this sense, realising the right to adequate food is the stepping stone to further realising the broader interest of being free from hunger (Alston 1985; Kong 2009).

Sometimes, scholars see problems related to food availability and hunger often having their answers in science (Milà-Villarroel et al. 2016). While this may have changed recently with several developments, especially on the international level, there is much more to be done in looking into ways that would increase access to food uniformly across countries like North Korea given the unique socio-political situation. In fact, there is an increasing call to implement modern considerations of social, political, and economic rights of the citizens around the world (Burgess 2010).

Particularly after the 2007 food crisis, studies on the right to food took on multiple aspects (Kong 2009), including analysing the relationship between the right to food and climate change (Dumas 2010), conducting comparative reviews of constitutional protections of the right to food (Burgess 2010), taking interdisciplinary approaches to the subject from the perspectives of access to other resources such as natural resources (Cotula et al. 2008), land (Tura 2017), water (McCaffrey 1992), gender equality (Bettinger-Lopez et al. 2022), and children's rights (Duramy 2018).

At the most fundamental level, one needs to return to mainstream scholarship that supports the idea that human rights are universal values that regulate the interaction between states and individuals (Cole 2012). It is intrinsic to defining what a government's duties are to the people. Thus, people should be able to make claims against the government, big or small, when human rights are not abided. This is because "[b]inding expectations … [is] the glue that holds normative systems together" (Cole 2012). This is even more important in the food dialogue because access to food is different from other economic, social, or cultural human rights: without food, people simply cannot survive. It is undoubtable that recognition of the right to food on national levels is sparse. (McDermott 2012)

Therefore, building compatibility among *juche*, meritocracy, and people's improved right to food is a task at hand. Doing so will allow further legal remedy and well matured sets of policies and directives for the country (Cohen et al. 2005) in the long run. This can and should be done by revisiting concepts of both *juche* and meritocracy, while reconstructing urban planning and local food production. Understanding that the right to food is more than a civil-political philosophy, but a right per se is an essential part of improving the society as a whole. Today, the geopolitical structure ensures that the Party continues to govern the people. It is carried out by appropriation of land and by mystification of the capital city, Pyongyang. In short, it is the destruction of human dignity built into the most fundamental infrastructure of the country.

To make ends meet, alternative designs in the country's legal framework are necessary to prevent further solidification of inequality and unequal access to food. This would require more than the country reconceptualising Pyongyang from being the special city for the 'selected people' to that where anyone with economic means and will move to as a policy matter. The practice of ranking people based on political backgrounds should also be eliminated as a whole.

(a) Reconceptualising Urban Planning by Viewing Everyone as Equals and Fixing the Law Accordingly

One of the first steps to eliminating the notion of seeing the Pyongyang residents as the selected special population that deserves better treatment is to understand the historical context of such practice. North Korea's state-led endorsement of ancestral lineage can be traced to the Neo-Confucian ideology during Chosun Dynasty (1392–1910) and in the Kyongguk Taejon [Great Code of Governance] of 1471 (Goedde 2004). If one were to evaluate this from the sole perspective of the right to food, this would be a classic example of how the national government is unwilling to take measures to realise the basic right to food (Dumas 2010).

Following the separation of the two Koreas, the Korean Workers' Party continued to use family names as the defining factor in categorising its people. In a way, it was perhaps the most efficient method to monitor and control the population. Today, such political status carries over to the next two generations and everyone regardless of their political status are subject to surveillance alike (Goedde 2004). Further, in order to strengthen the Kim family's lineage, the state combines the *juche* ideology and lineage. According to the 1972 Constitution, the *juche* ideology is a "creative application" (*changjeoguro jeogyong*) of Marxist-Leninist revolutionary ideology in which socialist ideas were re-written in a national form to suit North Korea's socio-political reality.[34] In order to maintain the purest form of a socialist state, the state needed "not a legal system exercising ex-post functions against breaching actions" but rather, "preliminary instruction and campaigns guiding people on socialist norms and rules" (Nam 2004). According to this view, people need to internalise and become independent from external influences that may waver the power of Kim family.

However, it is essential to understand that dividing its population into hierarchical social classes at birth produces undesirable outcomes of meritocracy. There are much less guarantees of individual human rights (Tan et al. 2010), while Kim Jong-Il and Kim Il-Sung are seen as divine figures. Anyone acting outside Kim family's guidance is subject to criminal persecution such as torture, forced labour, and even death. Combined with *juche*, people themselves even form a socio-political organism: people become tools and objects of surveillance that in return also monitor others in the same class. Unlike in other states where urban planning is concerned with the interest of the community (Bettman 1923), similar plannings in North Korea are strictly based on the Party's need to categorise and monitor people. Furthermore, people continue to monitor each other at will to ensure compliance with Kim guidance and *juche* ideology. Urban planning was not devised to satisfy residents' needs or minimise tax burdens. Nor were the health and welfare of the residents a consideration (Dunham 1958). Instead, it has constantly been to maximise internalisation and ensure continued monitoring of the people.

The UN Committee on Economic, Social and Cultural Rights (CESCR) in its interpretive General Comment no. 12 on the right to adequate food (1999) wrote that this is correlated to "full and equal access to economic resources [...] including the right to inheritance and the ownership of land and other property." In other words, access to food is based on the availability of multiple factors, including righteous access and ownership of land and property (Martignoni 2018). This allows us to reconsider the current inaccessibility of Pyongyang to the majority of the state's population and how the city is safeguarded for the political power. Everyone should be guaranteed dignity and self-determination regardless of their place of residency. This can be done by employing a rights-based approach in reconceptualising access to Pyongyang and other major cities. Law may become a starting point (See ICESCR, Article 2(1)).

One, people should be granted more freedom in actively choosing where they reside, even if it means for a limited amount of time and applying for licenses (See Kam et al. 2009, Chan and Zhang 2009). Such freedom should be written into bodies of law such as the Pyongyang Management Law. More specifically, it should no longer be the case that caring for Pyongyang *alone* is a form of patriotic expression (Pyongyang Management Law, Article 2). Similar bodies of law should be designed in approaching provinces and regions, to reconceptualise the relationship and the dynamics of existing communities. Two, cities around the country should be developed in a way that supports everyone's equal access to food, freedom from oppression, and a 'right to dignified life' (Allison et al. 2012). While this may propose equal development plans throughout the country, the country may implant the concept into related bodies of law such as the Social Security Act. People should no longer be privileged for their family's political background, particularly in the textual reading of the law.

It is of no doubt that there is a long way to go. North Korea is a socialist rule-by-law country built on totalitarianism under the name of *juche* without a civil society as in a democratic nation. Law can even be a mere political tool advocated by autocrats (Goedde 2004). In fact, the way the country is designed largely defies the general understanding of city planning. In Europe and North America, city planning has been done with wide public interest (Nelson 1916). Such systems have allowed more input from the people involved in residing it. And residents of small towns and villages receive necessary information and the study of plans, rather than have these plans unilaterally imposed upon them. In North Korea, however, the socio-political environment is drastically different (Nelson 1916), and city planners are merely state agents. People living in them are only tools to maximise state interests that align with the political will of the Kim family. It is important to understand that fundamentally humans are all born equal, and when food is at the core of survival, access to food should be equal as well. With this, a practical and a modest starting point would be to consider where the law can be fixed to reconceptualise the dynamics among cities and how social security is defined.

(b) Re-channeling Food Distribution

In addition, food distribution mechanisms need to be re-channeled. Given that even Kim Jong Un recently made a nationwide warning of a 'tense' food supply due to natural disasters, COVID-19, and sanctions (Choe 2021), it would be high time to consider taking national measures that are more controllable. First, private markets should be allowed while minimising state power to control grain production and demand. In fact, it should not be that the Korean Workers' Party and the state concentrate on farming exclusively as stated by Kim at the Central Committee of his ruling Workers' Party. Rather, the food regime must be managed by the people and the market where and when demand exists (Choe 2021). The current food distribution channels are heavily anchored to the existing city planning schemes, and serve as a means to celebrate the *juche* ideology of the country. As an example, individuals are strictly restricted from selling food products and markets are known to have been banned altogether until recently (Pearson 2015). The state is not the most ideal agency in determining the optimal supply and demand of food. Like we see today, the administration of the national food regime is extremely fragmented with unclear boundaries of involved agency jurisdictions (Ministry of Unification 'Power Structure' 2021c). While the country has recently and slowly allowed private marketplaces to run in limited places, there is a need to further expand and speed up this authorisation. Today, illegally run and unofficial market trading systems known as *jangmadang* (White et al. 2021) are in operation to feed a small proportion of the population, but this should be expanded and become widely available on a systematic level. It would become an important source of income where people in rural areas can feed themselves and their family from.

Furthermore, food ingredients should not only be used by the local residents. The government should build protection for its people and ensure that they are not deprived of their access to food (Kong 2009).

Currently, the way markets are operated and regulated has become a classic example of a rule of man system that fails to justify its purpose. People, particularly those in the more rural areas, face two critical food problems: lack of food in the local community and fluctuating food prices (Son and Park 2021). In fact, this has become such a prevalent issue that it has also started to affect those in Pyongyang with the closing down of state borders following the COVID-19 outbreak (Son et al. 2021). Food ingredients should be sent to markets and people all over the country, rather than being sent to Pyongyang and the local population. It is, simply put, a very inefficient way of handling food ingredients. Human rights are interdependent in that realisation of the human rights of those in the most rural areas promote and protect the human rights of those even in Pyongyang. Taking a rights-based approach, it is important that the state accept access to food as a right, not only a need. Only by doing so will food insecurity be solved, and eradicate state-led discrimination (Godrich et al. 2021).

5 Conclusion

In studying the creation of a North Korean food legal order, it is possible to conclude that the ruling Kim family alone determines the norms and the frameworks. Governance is, in essence, a way to extend the power and control of the family. Naturally, food security norms are developed by a few individuals and are a feature of political ruling. This is what separates North Korea's experience as a politically secluded country from the rest of the world's. Many face the 'risk of oversimplification' in understanding food security (Sen 1982) without fully comprehending the socio-political factors, and it would be tempting to do so, especially when there is much lack of scholarship on North Korea's food governance. In a way, there is almost an absence of legal discussion over North Korea's food studies from a domestic perspective. Yet, it is possible to learn that from the city square in Pyongyang to the most impoverished rural areas, inequality in access to food persists in various forms. Various regulations are put in place to ensure that the powerful continue to rule, and that the rest of the general population are tools for their power stability. Unequal access to food is consciously built into the most basic infrastructure of the country and is also systematically embedded in the *juche* values that people practice on a daily basis. It has its historical roots, and further work should be done in reconceptualising the right to food within the North Korean context. Access to food should be rightfully understood and mechanically perceived as an inherent, interdependent right that is shared by everyone in the country (International Covenant on Economics, Cultural and Social Rights, Article 11). While the current North Korean food legal framework is built to solidify inequality, people in the country should gain sufficient access to safe food, regardless of where he or she lives. A theoretical question that we should continue to explore is whether and how unequal access to food within the North Korean context can fit in the dialogue of food sovereignty. Food sovereignty movements would propel further self-reliance under the juche ideology, and this perhaps sheds light on how meticulously food sovereignty movements are to be designed as both a theoretical and a practical matter. Academic research on food sovereignty movements should better review self-reliance on a dynamic spectrum and understand North Korea's experience as a case study exemplifying what not to do.

References

Allison, Edward H., Blake D. Ratner, Bjo¨rn A°sga°rd, Rolf Willmann, Robert Pomeroy, and John Kurien. 2012. Rights-based fisheries governance: from fishing rights to human rights, fish and fisheries, 13, 14–29, at 19.

Alston, P., and K. Tomaševski. 1984. *The Right to Food*. 228. The Hague: Martinus Nijhoff Publishers.

Alston, Philip. 1984. International Law and the Human Right to Food. In The right to food, 9, 32. Springer.

Bellows, Anne C., Flavio L.S. Valente, Stefanie Lemke, and María Daniela Núñez Burbano de Lara. Gender, Nutrition, and the Human Right to Adequate Food: Toward an Inclusive Framework, 4 (Routledge).

Bettinger-Lopez, C., Córdova Montes, R. Denisse, and Maxwell Zoberman. 2022. The duty to protect survivors of gender-based violence in the age of covid-19: An expanded human rights framework. *University of Miami International and Comparative Law Review* 29:235.

Bettman, A. 1923. The Law of City Planning and Zoning by Frank Backus Williams. New York: The Macmillan Co. pp. Xvii, 738, 36 Harv. L. Rev. 772. 1923

Breen, Michael. 2004. *Kim Jong-Il: North Korea's Dear Leader, 156*. New Jersey: Wiley.
Burgess, Jesse. 2010. Let them eat cake: Constitutional rights to food. *Willamette Journal of International Law and Dispute Resolution* 18: 261.
Cho, In Su. 1983. Rays of Juche All Over the World. *In Kim Jong-Il The People's Leader*, 341. Pyongyang: Foreign Languages Publishing House for North Korea's Official Interpretation of the Effect of Juche Ideology.
Cho, J. Jeanyoung. 2013. Systemizing the fate of the stateless North Korean migrant: A legal guide to preventing the automatic repatriation of North Korean migrants in China. *Fordham International Law Journal* 37 (175): 187–188.
Choe, Sang-Hun. 2021. North Korea is facing a 'tense' food shortage. The New York Times, June 16.
Chosun News. 2008. North Korea "Neighboring countries are requesting collaboration on Pyongyang Bean Paste." July 14. http://nk.chosun.com/news/articleView.html?idxno=107621
Chosun News. 2014. North Korea's Kim Jong Un inspects food factory for the military … "we revolutionize for this reason", Nov 15. 【北김정은, 군납식표품공장 시찰…"이런 멋에 혁명한다"】 https://www.chosun.com/site/data/html_dir/2014/11/15/2014111501011.html
Cohen, Marc J.J., Mary Brown, and Mary Ashby. 2005. Access to Justice and the Right to Adequate Food, *Sustainable Development Law & Policy* 6: 54, 55.
Cole, Wade M. 2012. Human rights as myth and ceremony? Reevaluating the effectiveness of human rights treaties, 1981–2007. *American Journal of Sociology* 117: 1131–1171.
Cotula, Lorenzo, Moussa Djiré, and Ringo W. Tenga. 2008. The Right to Food and Access to Natural Resources: Using Human Rights Arguments and Mechanisms to improve resource access for the rural poor, Food and Agriculture Organization of the United Nations.
Daily NK. 2021. North Korea begins selecting new residents for Pyongyang's 10,000 new homes, 13 July. https://www.dailynk.com/english/north-korea-begins-selecting-new-residents-pyongyang-10000-new-homes/. Last visited Nov 7, 2021.
Democratic People's Republic of Korea Living House Act 2014.
Democratic People's Republic of Korea Pyongyang Management Law 2010.
Democratic People's Republic of Korea Social Security Act 2012.
Democratic People's Republic of Korea Socialist Commercial Law 2021.
Dumas, Graham Frederick. 2010. A greener revolution: Using the right to food as a political weapon against climate change. *New York University Journal of International Law & Politics* 43.
Dunham, A. 1958. A legal and economic basis for city planning making room for Robert Moses, ed. William Zeckendorf, A City Planner in the Same Community, 58 Colum. L. Rev. 650, 656.
Dunlop, Fuchsia. 2017. Eating in North Korea: 'We were being fed a story.' Financial Times, September 21.
Duramy, Benedetta Faedi. 2018. Childhood obesity and positive obligations: A child rights-based approach. *Seattle University Law Review* 42: 87.
Em, Pavel P., Peter Ward. 2021. City profile: Is Pyongyang a Post-Socialist City? *Cities* 108. https://doi.org/10.1016/j.cities.2020.102950
Fainstein, Susan S. 2023. Britannica, Urban Planning. https://www.britannica.com/topic/urban-planning
Fakhri, Michael. 2021. Right to Food [A/HRC/46/33] Report of the Special Rapporteur on the right to food, Human Rights Council Forty-sixth session, Promotion and protection of all human rights, civil, political, economic, social and cultural rights, including the right to development. https://reliefweb.int/sites/reliefweb.int/files/resources/A_HRC_46_33_E.pdf.
Food and Agriculture Organization of the United Nations. 2002. Production and food security.
Godrich, Stephanie L., Liza Barbour, and Rebecca Lindberg. 2021. Problems, policy and politics—perspectives of public health leaders on food insecurity and human rights in Australia. *BMC Public Health* 21: 1132.
Goedde, Patricia. 2004. Law "of our own style": The evolution and challenges of the North Korean legal system. *Fordham International Law Journal* 27(1265): 1274.

Food and Agriculture Organization of the United Nations, Production and Food Security. 2021.http://www.fao.org/3/y3918e/y3918e04.htm
International Covenant on Economic, Cultural and Social Rights. 1976.
Kam, Wing Chan and Li Zhang. 2009. The Hukou System and Rural-Urban Migration in China: Processes and Changes, 160 China Quarterly, 818 (12 February)
Kelsen, Hans. 1982. The concept of legal order. *The American Journal of Jurisprudence* 27: 73.
Kent, George. 2005. *Freedom from want: The human right to adequate food.* Washington D.C.: Georgetown University Press.
Kim, Sung Kyung. 2017. Juche (Self-Reliance) in North Korea. *The Wiley-Blackwell Encyclopedia of Social Theory*. https://onlinelibrary.wiley.com/doi/abs/10.1002/9781118430873.est0820.
Kim, Yi Seul. 2020. The case of anticipating changes in the North Korean food safety regime. *Journal of Environmental Law and Litigation* 35: 299
Kong, Karen. 2009. The right to food for all: A right-based approach to hunger and social inequality. *Suffolk Transnational Law Review* 32(525): 529.
Korea Development Bank. 2015. North Korea tends to rely on its own domestic food production. 북한의 산업 The North Korea's Industry, 851.
Koryo Tour. Mirae street. 2021.https://koryogroup.com/travel-guide/mirae-street-pyongyang-north-korea-travel-guide.
Kuark, Yoon T. 1963. North Korea's industrial development during the post-war period. *The China Quarterly* 14: 51–64.
Lee, Jung, and Tongil Hankuk. 2014. Click! Education on Unification: North Korea, I'm curious 32; How is the social security system? http://unikorea21.com/?p=4302.
Lewis, P. Nelson. 1916. *The planning of the modern city: A review of the principles governing city planning*. Michigan: University of Michigan Library.
Martignoni, Joanna Bourke. 2018. Engendering the right to food? International human rights law, food security and the rural woman, 9 Transnational Legal Theory 400: 406–407.
Marx, K. 1990. 'So-Called Primitive Accumulation': Capital: A Critique of Political Economy, Vol. I, 885
McCaffrey, Stephen C. 1992. A human right to water: Domestic and international implications. *Georgetown International Environmental Law Review* 5: 1.
McDermott, Michael J. 2012. Constitutionalizing an enforceable right to food: A new tool for combating hunger. *Boston College International and Comparative Law Review* 35(543): 548.
Milà-Villarroel, R., C. Homs, J. Ngo, J. Martín, M. Vidal, and L. Serra-Majem. 2016. Famine, hunger, and undernourishment. In *Encyclopedia of food and health*, ed. Benjamin Caballero, Paul M. Finglas, and Fidel Toldrá, 581–588. Cambridge: Academic Press.
Nam, Sangmin. 2004. The legal development of the environmental policy in the Democratic People's Republic of Korea. *Fordham International Law Journal* 27 (1322): 1327.
Narula, Smita. 2006. The Right to Food: Holding Global Actors Accountable Under International Law, 44 Columbia Journal of Transnational Law 691, 705. "The right to food has been part of the international human rights regime since its inception."
Noh, Jaehyun. 2013. North Korea's Kim Jong Un inspects the seafood base and the food factory for the military. Newsis, May 26. https://www.yna.co.kr/view/AKR20130526010400014.
Park, Jeong Yon. 2021. North Korea preaches self-reliance to struggling citizens. Radio Free Asia, June 11.
Pearson, James. 2015. North Korea's black market becoming the new normal. Reuters, Oct. 29.
Republic of Korea Ministry of Unification. 2021a. Food industry (식료품 공업). https://nkinfo.unikorea.go.kr/nkp/overview/nkOverview.do.
Republic of Korea Ministry of Unification. 2021b. Management and Operation of Food Industries. (식료공업의 관리운영체계) https://nkinfo.unikorea.go.kr/nkp/overview/nkOverview.do.
Republic of Korea Ministry of Unification. 2021c. Power Structure. https://nkinfo.unikorea.go.kr/nkp/theme/getPowerStructureDang.do.
Sen, Amartya K. 1982. The food problem: Theory and policy. *Third World Quarterly* 4: 447.

Son, Hyemin, and Jeong Yon Park. 2021. Citizens anxious as food prices fluctuate in North Korea. Radio Free Asia, June 14.

Song, Jiyoung. 2011. The Marxist rights thinking of the DPRK. In *Human rights discourse in North Korea*, ed. Jiyoung Song, 94.

Stock, Thomas. 2019. North Korea's Marxism-Leninism: Fraternal Criticisms and the Development of North Korean Ideology in the 1960s. *Journal of Korean Studies* 24: 127, 128.

Talmadge, Eric. 2017. Lonely highways: On the road in Kim Jong Un's North Korea, AP News, November 20.

Tan, Morse H. 2010. A State of Rightlessness: The Egregious Case of North Korea, 80 Miss. L.J. 681, 692, citing Sung-Chul Choi, *Human Rights in North Korea in the Light of International Covenants, in* International Community and Human Rights In North Korea 53, 56 (Sung-Chul Choi ed., 1996) (quoting a statement by Nam-Joon Paek in 1993 at the World Conference on Human Rights in Vienna).

Tura, Husen Ahmed. 2017. Linking land rights and the right to adequate food in Ethiopia: Normative and implementation gaps. *Nordic Journal of Human Rights* 35: 85.

United Nations Economic and Social Council (ECOSOC) Committee on Economic, Social & Cultural Rights, Substantive Issues Arising in the Implementation of the International Covenant on Economic, Social and Cultural Rights: General Comment No. 12, The Right to Adequate Food, 14 U.N. Doc. E/C.12/1999/5 (May 12, 1999).

White, Edward, and Buseong Kang. 2021. North Korea pummelled by swings in currency and food prices. Financial Times, June 25.

Withnall, Adam. 2014. North Korean defector says she believe Kim Jong-il was a god who could read her mind. Independent April 10.

World Bank. 2020. *Water in agriculture*. https://www.worldbank.org/en/topic/water-in-agriculture.

Yim, Dongwoo. 2017. A brief urban history of Pyongyang, North Korea—and how it might develop under capitalism, The Architect's Newspaper, August 24.

Zwirko, Colin. 2021. North Korea praises new food factories, but construction often dragged for years. NK Pro. December 21.

Correction to: Nomads and Forest Rights, Is It a Myth? An Indian Perspective on the Forest-Dependent Pastoral Communities and Their Practices in Protected Areas

Kumarjeeb Pegu

Correction to:
Chapter 7 in: T. Venthan Ananthavinayagan and A. Viswanath Shenoy (eds.), *The Wretched of the Global South*, International Law and the Global South, https://doi.org/10.1007/978-981-99-9275-1_7

The original version of Chapter "Nomads and Forest Rights, Is It a Myth? An Indian Perspective on the Forest-Dependent Pastoral Communities and Their Practices in Protected Areas" was published with some inaccuracies which have been corrected as follows:

a. On Page 132, the year of Act was incorrectly mentioned as 1947. This has been corrected as 1847.

b. On Page 136, the acronym CFR was incorrectly mentioned as CRF. This has been corrected.

c. On Pages 137, 141, 142, and 143, the acronym CWH was incorrectly mentioned as CWLH. These instances have been corrected.

d. On Page 142, the provision of law incorrectly cited as "Rule 4(1)(e)" has been corrected as "Section 4(2)(e)".

The chapter has been updated with the changes.

The updated version of this chapter can be found at
https://doi.org/10.1007/978-981-99-9275-1_7

T. Venthan Ananthavinayagan and A. Viswanath Shenoy (eds.), *The Wretched of the Global South*, International Law and the Global South,
https://doi.org/10.1007/978-981-99-9275-1_14

Editor's Conclusion

This book is concluding now. And it was a breathtaking journey from Brazil to Palestine, from India to North Korea. The journey was filled with narratives, hopes, and visions for a more just world. We have learnt about the critical human rights approaches rooted by the Global South, of the Global South, by the Global South. This book borrows its title from the seminal book of the thinker Frantz Fanon—and as Edmund Burke wrote already in 1976, "*The book is thus a spiritual guide for an unspiritual age on how to achieve revolutionary beatitude.*"[1]

Our book, our common effort is an attempt towards decolonisation, an attempt for a different direction. Fanon himself wrote: "*Let us decide not to imitate Europe and let us tense our muscles and our brains in a new direction. Let us endeavour to invent a man in full, something which Europe has been incapable of achieving*".[2]

In the chapters which you read, Fanon is echoed. For Fanon, modern colonialism is the foundation of the most pervasive conceptions of humanity in the modern/colonial world, not a minor aberration or issue brought about by Western nations in their march towards an ever-widening notion of freedom and equality. Any new decolonial understanding of humanity must first be liberated from the power, knowledge, and being structures of modern colonialism.[3]

To this end, the colonial is still present, despite the new directions we want to take, as Hadeel Abu Hussein has demonstrated in her chapter and the legacies of colonialism in Palestine. Oreva Okap's article furthered the thoughts on the contemporary nature of the effects of colonialism with case-mapping the Mubi, while Yiseul Kim explained how internal colonialism by the elite is disenfranchising its own peoples.

[1] Edmund Burke, Frantz Fanon's "The Wretched of the Earth", Daedalus Vol. 105, No. 1, In Praise of Books (Winter, 1976), pp. 127–135.

[2] Fanon, Frantz (2004), *The Wretched of the Earth*. New York: Grove Press. Translated by Richard Philcox, p. 236).

[3] Nelson Maldonado-Torres, "On the Coloniality of Human Rights", *Revista Crítica de Ciências Sociais*, 114 | 2017, 117–136.

T. Venthan Ananthavinayagan and A. Viswanath Shenoy (eds.), *The Wretched of the Global South*, International Law and the Global South,
https://doi.org/10.1007/978-981-99-9275-1

Flavia do Amaral Vieira, at this juncture, explains how it is the civil society which needs to be included in the making at building international from the below. And it is this interesting, interrelated nature of the various chapters. We have read how Selbi Durdiyeya, Alejandra Ramírez Bermeo, and Moara Assis Crivelente demonstrated in their respective chapters that decoloniality and subaltern eptisomologies need to be promoted and expanded upon to lead to emancipation for the sake of the most vulnerable.

Punsara Amarasinghe, Kumarjeeb Pegu, Thang Nguyen Toan, Yen Nguyen Thi Hong, and Trang La Minh highlighted in each of their chapters the plight of forgotten and neglected communities at the margins in contexts of Vietnam, India and Sri Lanka. And following on this thread of thought, we have read in the chapter Tatiana Cardoso Squeff and Jackeline Caixeta Santana about the institutional response by the Inter-American Court of Human Rights to address the grievances of indigenous communities in Brazil.

All these chapters are united in their mission: to emphasise, to highlight, and to further the causes of the forgotten of the Third World. It is for that reason why the title of the book is "The Wretched of the Global South". The book aims to give not only space, but especially it gives: visibility. And it is visibility which gives access, opportunity, and ability. And eventually, it empowers.[4] The Wretched of the Global South will turn into the actors of change.

We would like to, at this point, thank our colleagues Prof. Robert McCorquodale, Dr. Matt Windsor, Dr. Julia Dehm, Prof. Michael Fakhri, Dr. Jens Theilen, Prof. Leila Choukroune, Dr. Mohsen al-Attar, Prof. Ramani Garimella, Dr. Sué González Hauck and Dr. Lys Kulamadayil. Your help and enduring support was important for us to produce this edited book of highest quality.

Finally, our gratitude goes to our outstanding research assistants, Jeevan Justin and Omkar Hemanth. What we hold in our hands is the product of the tireless work behind the scenes, coordination, proof-reading, communication with the contributors/ colleagues and countless zoom calls across various time zones. Their work is the building block of this book, not more, not less. Thank you. We also, finally, want to thank Springer Publishers and Nupoor Singh for her patience, dedication and interest to bring the cause of human rights back home: the values of the Global South found their safe haven here.

Thank you.

[4] David Theo Goldberg, In/Visibility and Super/Vision Fanon on Race, Veils, and Discourses of Resistance, p. 179, Fanon: A Crticiual Rader, Lewis, R Gordon, T. Denean Sharpley Whiting and Renée T. White, Blackwell, 1996.

MIX
Papier aus verantwortungsvollen Quellen
Paper from responsible sources
FSC® C105338

FSC
www.fsc.org

If you have any concerns about our products,
you can contact us on
ProductSafety@springernature.com

In case Publisher is established outside the EU,
the EU authorized representative is:
Springer Nature Customer Service Center GmbH
Europaplatz 3, 69115 Heidelberg, Germany

Printed by Libri Plureos GmbH
in Hamburg, Germany